The Ultimate Book
of Bible Trivia

THE
Ultimate
Book of
Bible Trivia

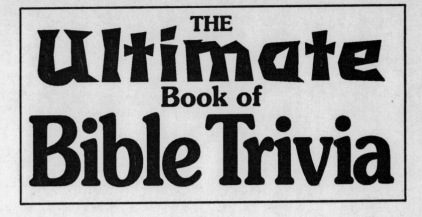

J. STEPHEN LANG

Tyndale House Publishers, Inc.

WHEATON, ILLINOIS

CEDAR RAPIDS, IOWA

Originally published as *The Whimsical Quizzical Bible
Trivia Book*

Scripture quotations are taken from the *Holy Bible,* King
James Version. In many instances the author has
paraphrased the KJV by modernizing certain archaic
pronouns.

Library of Congress Cataloging-in-Publication Data

Lang, J. Stephen.
   The ultimate book of Bible trivia / J. Stephen Lang.
     p. cm.
   ISBN 0-8423-7949-5 (pbk.)
   1. Bible—Miscellanea.   I. Title
BS612.L2626 1997   97-8874
220—dc21

Printed in the United States of America

03 02 01 00 99 98
7   6   5   4   3   2

To my grandmother Pauline Morris

CONTENTS

INTRODUCTION

Can we speak of *the Bible* and *trivia* in the same breath? I raised that question in my introduction to *The Complete Book of Bible Trivia,* first published in 1988. After numerous reprintings of that successful volume, I have concluded that, yes, people do indeed like the Bible—and trivia—and Bible trivia. They also seem to like the format of having the questions on the right-hand pages with the answers on the back of each page. More important, they seem to like the feeling of having a *fun* book.

In this book, I followed the topical approach. The topics vary: "Fat of the Land" (for our weight-conscious era), "Po' Folks," "Tempting Situations," "Pharaoh Land: Egypt," "Words, Words: Our Bible-Saturated Language," and so on. I hope the choice of topics will itself provide some chuckles. The category "What's Wrong with This Question?" is just for laughs, and so are some questions I've sneaked into almost every category. As a departure from the question-and-answer format, I've also included "Familiar Verse, Peculiar Order"—jumbled word puzzles that involve unscrambling a set of words to form a familiar Bible verse. There are also pre- and post-tests for you to see how much you know and how much you've learned.

I've included (particularly in parts 1, 3, 4, and 5) questions not only about the Bible text itself, but about its presence and influence in human life—in songs, in books, in vocabulary, in naming people and places. These questions raise the larger question, How much of human life—past and present—shows the influence of the Bible? You may be surprised at how deep an impression the Scriptures made (and make) on humankind.

The topics are arranged under twelve sections. However, despite the loose attempt at organization, the book is for browsing. It was made to fill up your time commuting on the train, the hour you spend waiting at the dentist's office, the few minutes before dinner is on the table, the hours on the freeway when you and the other two people in the car pool are in the mood for a game of Quiz Me. In other words, the book is designed to be read randomly, anywhere, and with no preparation of any kind. It is designed to entertain any person who unashamedly likes to be entertained—and challenged.

Happy reading! I hope you enjoy getting better acquainted with the divine—and very human—Book of books.

TEST YOUR BIBLE IQ SCALE

At the beginning of each part of this book there is a ten-question quiz titled Test Your Bible IQ After you've taken each quiz, turn back here to see how you rate.

10 correct Excellent: *You should be teaching at a seminary.*
8–9 correct Very Good: *You should be teaching Sunday school.*
6–7 correct Average: *You've read most of the Bible.*
5 correct Below Average: *You've probably read parts of the Bible.*
0–4 correct For shame: *Did you know Bibles open up?*

DO YOU REMEMBER? SCALE

At the end of each part of this book there is a ten-question post-test to see how much trivia you remember. After you've taken each quiz, turn back here to see how you rate.

10 correct Excellent: *You may want to write a trivia book of your own.*
8–9 correct Very Good: *You are obviously a student of the Bible.*
6–7 correct Average: *You'd hold your own in a Bible trivia challenge at church.*
5 correct Below Average: *You could keep score for a Bible trivia challenge at church.*
0–4 correct For shame: *Fortunately, God is a God of grace.*

PART 1

The Bible Turned Loose on the World

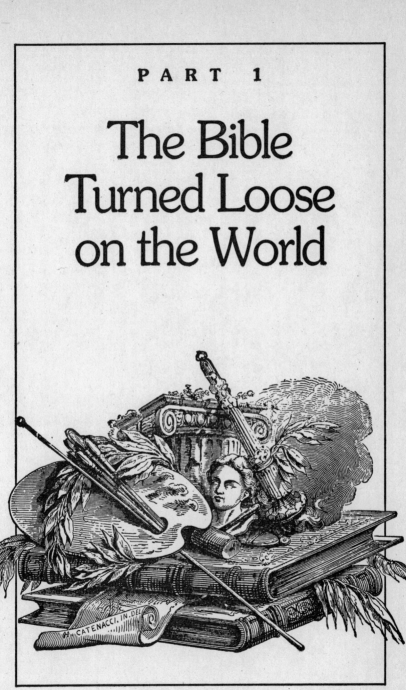

Test Your Bible IQ

☞ This quiz contains questions covering the topics in part 1, "The Bible Turned Loose on the World." Do your best, then turn the page to see how you did. If you are brave enough to see how your Bible IQ rates, turn to page xii for our scale.

1. What do we call a person who goes out of his way to help someone?
2. What organization, founded in 1898, is famous for placing Bibles in hotel rooms?
3. John Steinbeck's novel *To a God Unknown* takes its title from a passage in which New Testament book?
4. There are many paintings with the Latin title *Ecce Homo,* which means "Behold the man." They show Jesus with a certain Roman official. Who?
5. Thornton Wilder's play *The Trumpet Shall Sound* takes its title from a description of Christians' resurrection. In which New Testament epistle does this appear?
6. David Garrett's novel *Two by Two* concerns which Old Testament man?
7. How many church buildings are mentioned in the Bible?
8. Who said this: "The Scripture is like an open town in time of war, which serves the occasions of both parties"? (Hint: the author of *Gulliver's Travels*)
9. Scotland is home to a town that is supposedly the birthplace of the game of golf. What apostle is the town named for?
10. A place that gives protection and safety from disaster is sometimes called what?

Test Your Bible IQ (answers)

1. A Samaritan, or a Good Samaritan, so named for Jesus' parable of the Samaritan who helped the beaten traveler while the religious people passed by and gave no aid (Luke 10)
2. The Gideons
3. Acts; when Paul preached to the Athenians, he refers to seeing a monument inscribed "To the Unknown God" (Acts 17:23).
4. Pontius Pilate; he publicly displayed Jesus wearing his crown of thorns. After Pilate uttered the fateful words "Behold the man," the Jews then began to shout "Crucify him!" (John 19:4-6). The subject is one of the most emotional ever painted.
5. 1 Corinthians; 15:52 says, "The trumpet shall sound, and the dead shall be raised incorruptible, and we shall be changed."
6. Noah, of course; the title refers to the pairs of animals entering the ark.
7. None; the first generation of Christians did not have (or even want) special buildings for worship. They met in homes, or wherever they could gather a group of believers together.
8. Jonathan Swift (1667-1745); Swift was a clergyman as well as an author.
9. Andrew; he is considered the patron saint of Scotland. The town is St. Andrews (and no, the Scots don't put an apostrophe in Andrews—for some strange reason).
10. An ark, after the boat that saved Noah and his family from the Flood

Words, Words:
Our Bible-Saturated Language

☛ Is our culture becoming biblically illiterate? Perhaps. But it would take the English language a long, long time to get rid of all words and names that are rooted in the Bible. Bible names and words crop up in the strangest places—houses, gardens, wine cellars, and in ordinary conversation. Test your awareness of how the Bible has pervaded everyday life and speech.

1. What wicked Old Testament queen's name now means "an evil and shameless woman"?
2. What jumbo-sized wine bottle is named for a king of Israel?
3. What Philistine giant's name is often applied to any oversized person or thing?
4. What part of the human body is named for a man in Genesis?
5. What New Testament book's name has come to mean "the end of the world," especially if occurring with great violence and destruction?
6. What Old Testament prophet (and book) has come to be a common nickname for a Quaker?
7. What group of people, often criticized by Jesus, had a name that now means "legalistic hypocrites, especially the religious kind"?
8. What pagan people, mentioned often in the Old Testament, had a name that has come to mean "crude, uncultured folk"?
9. What sinful city in Genesis has given its name to sexual sins in general, and one sexual sin in particular?
10. Which disciple of Jesus has lent his name to tiny seabirds that flutter just above the surface of the ocean waters?
11. What horrible hill, notable in Jesus' life, now means "place or experience of intense suffering"?
12. What do we call a comforter who is more prone to criticize than to provide real comfort?
13. What do we call a cab driver, particularly one who provides a wild, furious ride?
14. What Old Testament city lends its name to a vegetable that is called an artichoke but isn't?
15. What Old Testament conqueror's name now means "hunter," particularly an overbearing one?

Words, Words: Our Bible-Saturated Language (answers)

1. Jezebel (1 and 2 Kings), the pagan wife of Israel's King Ahab
2. Jeroboam; no one is sure why the bottle was named for the king.
3. Goliath, the giant slain by the shepherd boy (and later king) David
4. The Adam's apple, of course; the bulge in the neck is, according to legend, the piece of the forbidden fruit that stuck forever in the throat of the sinning Adam.
5. Revelation, which in the original Greek is *Apokalypsis* (and is Apocalypse in Catholic Bibles); the name is appropriate, since Revelation deals with wars, plagues, and the end of life as we know it.
6. Obadiah; no one knows exactly why.
7. The Pharisees, whom Jesus criticized not only for their hypocrisy, but for their obsessive attention to unimportant details
8. Philistines; not that they were particularly uncultured, but for some reason the English author Matthew Arnold (writing in the 1800s) used the name Philistine and gave it this new meaning
9. Sodom, with *sodomy* being a word applied to homosexuality, based on the attempted male rape of Lot's guests in Genesis
10. Peter; the birds are called *petrels,* since Peter tried to walk on the sea as Jesus did (but, unlike the birds, he sank).
11. Calvary, the name of the hill on which Jesus was crucified (The hill is also called Golgotha.)
12. A Job's comforter, named for Job's three so-called friends who, as Job himself said, were "miserable comforters"
13. A Jehu, named for the king who exterminated the idol-worshiping royal dynasty of King Ahab; in his plan to overthrow the royal family, Jehu (who had been anointed by God's prophet Elisha) had to do some fast maneuvering, and he was mentioned in the Bible as one who "driveth furiously" (2 Kings 9:20).
14. Jerusalem; the Jerusalem artichoke is actually a type of sunflower, but its edible roots are mistakenly called artichokes.
15. Nimrod, who was "a mighty hunter before the Lord" (Genesis 10:9)

16. The name of what son of Abraham has come to mean "outcast"?
17. What purple-flowered vine, common wild and in gardens, is named for an event in Jesus' life?
18 What long-lived Old Testament man's name is given to a wine bottle holding about six liters?
19. What New Testament woman's name occurs in a word that now means "sickeningly sentimental"?
20. What do we call a person who goes out of his way to help someone?
21. What city visited by Paul lends its name to a wild, pleasure-loving person?
22. What do we call a scheming, beautiful, seductive woman, particularly one that leads a man to ruin?
23. What do we call the final battle at the end of time?
24. What pagan empire's name now means a place devoted to sensuous pleasure and materialism?
25. What biblical feast day now lends its name to Christians who emphasize spiritual gifts such as speaking in tongues and healing?
26. What Old Testament town's name has come to mean a small church or chapel of a small denomination?
27. What biblical name is given to the summer cypress plant?
28. What do we call a person believed to bring bad luck?
29. The name of what beloved friend of David has come to mean a New Englander?
30. What do we call grave robbers?

16. Ishmael, Abraham's son by his maid Hagar; Genesis 16:12 describes him as "a wild man; his hand will be against every man, and every man's hand against him." (The narrator in the novel *Moby Dick* is a social outcast and named, appropriately, Ishmael.)

17. The passionflower, so called because the flower's center reminds many people of a body on a cross; Jesus' crucifixion is often referred to as his *passion*—that is, intense suffering.

18. Methuselah; according to Genesis 5, he lived 969 years. As with the name Jeroboam, no one knows why the bottle has the name.

19. Mary Magdalene; the word is *maudlin,* an old shortened form of Magdalene. The word is based on the fact that many old paintings of Mary Magdalene show her as a weeping and repentant woman.

20. A Samaritan, or a Good Samaritan, so named for Jesus' parable of the Samaritan who helped the beaten traveler while the religious people passed by and gave no aid (Luke 10)

21. Corinth; a Corinthian (then and now) was one with high living and low morals. In fact, the word goes back even further than Paul's day, for Corinth had a long pre-Paul reputation as sin city.

22. A Delilah, named for the Philistine mistress of Samson; she wormed out of him the secret of his strength, resulting in his capture and blinding by the Philistines (Judges 16).

23. Armageddon, from the book of Revelation's description of the battle on the great day of God Almighty (Revelation 16:16ff.); many people use the word to refer to a possible showdown of high-tech weaponry.

24. Babylon, noted in the Old Testament for its luxury and idolatry

25. Pentecost, the Jewish feast day that, in Acts 2, is the day on which the Holy Spirit manifested itself by people speaking in tongues

26. Bethel; much more common in England than the U.S., Bethel was often the name of a chapel of a Nonconformist church—that is, any denomination not part of the state-supported Church of England

27. Burning bush; it is named for the bush Moses saw, which burned but was not consumed. The summer cypress has bright red foliage in the fall.

28. A Jonah, after the poor prophet who disobeyed the Lord's command to go to Nineveh; when he set sail for other parts, a storm struck the ship, and Jonah admitted that it was his fault (Jonah 1). He solved the problem by asking to be thrown overboard (and you know the rest of this fishy story, of course).

29. Jonathan; no one is sure why, although Old Testament names were very popular in the earliest days of New England

30. Resurrectionists; grave robbing is no longer practiced, but in times past, the so-called resurrection men would dig up graves, either to supply bodies to scientists or to rob the corpses of any jewels they were buried with. They were called resurrectionists because, as in the case of Jesus, there was an empty tomb.

31. What plant is named after a kinsman of Jesus?
32. What do we call the practice of buying or selling a church office?
33. What plant is named for a painful plant in Jesus' life?
34. What Old Testament food's name now means "a sudden and unexpected source of gratification"?
35. What name is given to a hospital for people with contagious diseases, particularly leprosy?
36. Which disciple of Jesus has a tree named for him?
37. What do we call a long, eloquent lament?
38. What New Testament garden's name now means "a place of intense mental or spiritual suffering"?
39. What disciple's name can mean "a peephole"?
40. The name of what king of Israel is used for a mammoth-size drinking vessel?
41. What Old Testament time of liberation has come to mean simply "party time"?
42. What burial ground for paupers is named for the place purchased by Judas's betrayal money?
43. What yucca tree of the southwest U.S. is named for an Old Testament military leader?
44. What word means "showing great wisdom under trying circumstances" and is named for a wise king of Israel?
45. What Australian bird, noted for building mud nests, is named for Jesus' followers?
46. What cooking herb is also known as "Bible leaf"?

31. St. John's bread, named for John the Baptist; more commonly called the carob plant, St. John's bread yields sweet-tasting pods that, according to legend, were the food that John the Baptist lived on. Some scholars think that the "locusts" the Gospels say John ate might have been carob pods.

32. Simony, named for Simon the magician, who wanted to buy spiritual power from Peter (Acts 8); simony was widely practiced years ago when the church was state-supported and high-ranking church leaders were well paid.

33. The Christ's-thorn plant, a name given to several prickly plants growing in the Middle East; the name, of course, comes from the crown of thorns put on the head of Jesus when he was being mocked by the Roman soldiers (Matthew 27:29).

34. Manna, the name of the food miraculously supplied to the Israelites after they fled from Egypt (Exodus 16)

35. Lazaretto, a name derived from Lazarus, the name of the leprous beggar in Jesus' parable of the rich man and the beggar (Luke 16)

36. The *worst* disciple, Judas; the Judas tree is cultivated for its showy red flowers. The name stems from the belief that Judas hung himself on a tree of this kind and the flowers, once white, turned red. The redbud tree of the eastern U.S. is often called a Judas tree.

37. A jeremiad, named for the prophet Jeremiah, who lamented over the fate of fallen Jerusalem in the book of Lamentations

38. Gethsemane, the garden where Jesus agonized over his fate on the night he was betrayed (Matthew 26:36)

39. Judas; a peephole is sometimes called a Judas, a Judas hole, or a Judas window. The name obviously refers to Judas's treachery and deceit.

40. Joram (in some translations, Jehoram), though the cup's name is usually spelled *jorum;* as with other wine container terms, no one knows what the connection is.

41. Jubilee, the year of emancipation every fifty years; slaves were liberated, and lands were restored to their former owners. Gradually the word came to mean a fiftieth anniversary, then, eventually, any time of celebration. (See Leviticus 25.)

42. It's called a potter's field (Matthew 27:7). At that time it was intended to be a place for burying foreigners, but later the term was extended to include burial for paupers and criminals and anyone else outside mainstream society.

43. The Joshua tree (which was also the name of an album by the rock group U2)

44. Solomonic, for wise King Solomon

45. The apostle bird

46. Costmary, a name that itself means (in Greek) "fragrant root of Mary"

47. What "optical" phrase, found three times in the Bible, is a common phrase meaning "something dear and precious"?

48. What biblical type of ladder would you find on a ship or pier?

49. What seedy Asian grass is named for a very unfortunate Old Testament man?

50. What woman's garment is named for an Old Testament man with a famous garment?

51. The flowering yucca plant, common in gardens, also goes by what biblical name?

52. A leave of absence for education or training is called a what?

53. An adjective meaning "possessing incredible strength or size" is rooted in the name of an Old Testament hero. What is the word?

54. What flower is named for a son of King David?

55. The modern-day political movement to give Jews a homeland in Palestine goes by what name?

56. What yellow garden flower is named for a New Testament kinsman of Jesus?

57. A word meaning "bosom friend" comes from a passage in one of Paul's epistles. What is the word?

58. A lovely spot of unspoiled beauty is called a what?

59. What thorny tree of the tropics takes its name from the crown of thorns that was placed on Jesus' head?

60. What tall, flowering garden plant is named for a biblical flower?

61. A tyrant is often called what (after a famous king in the Old Testament)?

62. What houseplant with red berries is named for a biblical city?

63. What peculiar plant is named for a Canaanite city captured by Joshua?

64. What name was given to an annual contribution given by Roman Catholics to the pope?

65. A place that gives protection and safety from disaster is sometimes called what?

66. What is "Bible paper"?

67. On what food fish would you find "St. Peter's thumb mark"?

68. What place name, mentioned often in the Gospels, is given to the porch at the entrance to a church?

69. What place name, the name of a biblical city, is given to a church or chapel for seamen?

47. "Apple of the eye" (Deuteronomy 32:10; Psalm 17:8; Proverbs 7:2); it literally refers to the eye's pupil. In these three verses, the contexts indicate that the pupil is precious and protected.
48. A Jacob's ladder, which is the common name for a rope or chain ladder with wooden or metal rungs; the reference is to Jacob's dream of the ladder to heaven (Genesis 28).
49. Job's tears, a plant whose seeds are thought to resemble tears
50. A Joseph; this term was once used to refer to a long coat for women. The name comes from the "coat of many colors" that Jacob gave to his favorite son, Joseph (which aroused the jealousy of his eleven brothers, of course).
51. Adam's needle
52. A sabbatical, taking its name from *sabbath,* of course, the biblical day of rest
53. Samsonian, rooted in the name *Samson,* the mighty judge of Israel
54. Solomon's seal
55. Zionism, named for the biblical Mount Zion, one of the hills of Jerusalem
56. The very lovely St. John's wort, named for John the Baptist
57. Yokefellow, which in fact is a translation of the Greek name Syzygus (Philippians 4:3); Bible scholars still argue over whether Syzygus is an actual person's name, or if Paul was perhaps referring to a friend as his "yokefellow."
58. An Eden, of course, after the Garden of Eden in Genesis
59. The Jerusalem thorn
60. The rose of Sharon (*Hibiscus* family); however, it definitely is not the same plant referred to in Song of Solomon 2:1. Sharon, by the way, was the name of the Mediterranean coastal plain west of Israel.
61. A pharaoh, based on the oppressive Pharaoh in Exodus
62. The Jerusalem cherry, which is not actually a cherry at all
63. The rose of Jericho, which rolls up when dry and expands when it is wet
64. Peter's pence, named for the tradition that the first pope was the apostle Peter
65. An ark, after the boat that saved Noah and his family from the Flood
66. The very thin, very durable paper used in many Bibles, dictionaries, and other books that will (supposedly) be used frequently
67. The haddock; the "thumb mark" is the blotch behind the gill. No one is quite sure how Peter's name became attached to the fish, although Peter was (as the New Testament says) a fisherman.
68. Galilee; the name is commonly used in English churches, not quite so common in America.
69. Bethel; no one knows why, exactly.

Familiar Verse, Peculiar Order

☞ Placed in their proper order, the words are a familiar verse from Luke.

against for is he is not us us that

The Bible in America

☞ Is a America a Christian nation? That question can prompt a pleasant discussion—or a knock-down-drag-out. Whether it was—or still is—a Christian nation, the U.S.A. has historic ties to the Scriptures—morally, legally, and culturally. Part 3 of this book concentrates on the Bible's obvious influence on the naming of American geography. The questions here focus on the Bible's role in the great republic's history.

1. What version of the Bible did the Pilgrims bring with them to America in the 1620s?
2. What dictionary entrepreneur published a "corrected" King James Version in which he pointed out words that had changed in meaning since the first publication of the KJV?
3. What American president produced his own version of the Gospels, in which he cut out all references to miracles?
4. What organization, founded in 1898, is famous for placing Bibles in hotel rooms?
5. In what language was the first American Bible?
6. What noted American Indian leader devised an alphabet that was the basis of the Cherokee Indian Bible?
7. When Richard Nixon took his oath of office as president, who held the Bible for him?
8. What perennially popular Bible paraphrase was first published in 1970?
9. What religious group, famous for their door-to-door evangelism, publishes the New World version of the Bible?
10. What name is often applied to areas of the U.S.—particularly in the South—that take the Bible more or less literally?
11. What future president of the 1800s got over a broken engagement by reading the Bible?

Familiar Verse, Peculiar Order (answer)

He that is not against us is for us. (Luke 9:50)

The Bible in America (answers)

1. The Geneva Bible, a translation made in 1560; though the King James Version was published in 1611, it was not yet popular when the Pilgrims came to America.
2. Noah Webster, who published his "corrected" Bible in 1833
3. Thomas Jefferson, who admired Jesus as a moral teacher but (apparently) did not believe Jesus worked miracles—or was raised from the dead
4. The Gideons
5. Algonquin Indian—*not* English; until the American Revolution, all English Bibles came from England. The Algonquin Bible was published in 1661.
6. Sequoyah, a Tennessee teacher whose Cherokee alphabet was devised from a combination of Greek and Latin letters; through the aid of his alphabet, thousands of his people were taught to read and write. The Cherokee Bible was published by the American Bible Society in 1831.
7. His wife, Pat Nixon; this was a departure from the tradition of the chief justice of the Supreme Court holding the Bible.
8. *The Living Bible,* paraphrased by Ken Taylor (published by Tyndale House, who also published the book you are now holding)
9. The Jehovah's Witnesses
10. "Bible Belt"
11. Abraham Lincoln, who said the Bible was "the best cure for the blues"

12. What famous dispensational Bible version was first published in 1909?

13. What notable feature of the King James Version was left out of the Americans' King James Version?

14. What evangelical magazine editor authored the 1976 book *The Battle for the Bible?*

15. What name was given to the modernized King James Version first published in 1982?

16. In what year did the Supreme Court rule that laws requiring Bible reading in public schools are unconstitutional?

17. What atheist activist was involved in the Supreme Court case mentioned in question 16?

18. What denomination probably has the longest name of any Christian group in the U.S.?

19. Which Bible version do the Mormons use?

20. Which religion uses both the Bible and a book titled *Science and Health, with Key to the Scriptures?*

21. What Nobel prizewinning American author wrote *The Story Bible?*

22. What was the first book printed in America? (No, it wasn't the Bible, but you're on the right track.)

23. In what year was the first English Bible published in America?

24. What famous American movie director enjoyed making lush epics about subjects from the Bible?

25. What pop singing duo (now divorced) appeared in pro-Bible ads produced by the American Bible Society?

26. What popular TV game show regularly features questions about the Bible?

27. Who were the "Bible communists"?

28. What Bible passage was ordered removed from Kentucky public school classrooms after the 1980 Supreme Court decision *Stone v. Graham?*

29. What leader of a Christian sect deduced (wrongly) from the Bible that the second coming of Jesus would occur on March 21, 1844?

30. Which state was intended by its founders to be a "Bible commonwealth"?

31. Which original Supreme Court justice helped support the American Bible Society in its early days?

12. *The Scofield Reference Bible*
13. The dedication to King James (who had been dead for more than 150 years); in the era of the American Revolution, and afterward, Americans felt a certain bitterness toward England and its monarchy. However, American versions of the KJV eventually did (and still do) contain the dedication to King James.
14. Former *Christianity Today* editor Harold Lindsell
15. The New King James Version (surprise!)
16. 1963
17. Madalyn Murray O'Hair
18. Bible Way Church of Our Lord Jesus Christ World Wide, founded in 1957, with headquarters in D.C.
19. The King James Version, in addition to their *Book of Mormon* and *Doctrine and Covenants*
20. Christian Science, founded in America by Mary Baker Eddy
21. Pearl Buck, noted for her novels about China, particularly *The Good Earth*
22. *The Bay Psalm Book,* published in Massachusetts in the 1600s; it consisted of rhyming paraphrases of the Psalms.
23. 1777—significantly, the year after the Declaration of Independence was signed
24. Cecil B. DeMille, who directed *The Ten Commandments* and *Samson and Delilah*
25. Sonny and Cher (believe it or not)
26. "Jeopardy"
27. They are better known as the Oneida Community, founded in 1848 in Oneida, New York, by John Humphrey Noyes. The commune's practices were highly questionable (to put it mildly), as they practiced communal marriage and various other practices that put them outside the mainstream of Christianity.
28. The Ten Commandments; the 1980 decision was that the state of Kentucky (and, thus, any state) could not mandate the posting of the Ten Commandments in public schools
29. William Miller, founder of the Seventh-day Adventists
30. Massachusetts; the original Puritan settlers in the 1600s wanted the colony to order itself according to biblical principles.
31. John Jay, who is also famous as one of the authors of *The Federalist Papers*

32. Which great American statesman defended the Bible's authority in the famous Scopes evolution trial in 1925?

33. In the years before the Civil War, what Bible passages did the abolitionists use to prove that slavery was unchristian?

34. What is the claim to fame (biblically speaking) of New York Commissioner of Education James Edward Allen, Jr.?

35. What 1984 law gave public school students the right to hold religious meetings and study the Bible in schools—*after* class hours?

36. What well-known religious sect owns the Watch Tower Bible and Tract Society?

37. What world-renowned American evangelist (and former shoe salesman) founded a famous Bible college in Chicago?

38. Biola University is a well-known Christian university in California. Biola is actually an acronym for what?

39. What American reference Bible, used by millions around the world, is based on the system known as *dispensationalism?*

40. What is the distinction of the American woman Julia E. Smith?

41. What organization, famous for distributing free or inexpensive Bibles, was founded in 1816?

42. In 1881 the Hare family of Philadelphia published the *Christian Spiritual Bible.* What strange teaching, popular today, was behind this version?

43. What religious denomination published a Bible that left out most of the New Testament and much of the Old?

44. What Bible passage was behind the Salem, Massachusetts, witch trials in the 1600s?

45. What do we call the practice of opening a Bible and reading a passage at random?

46. What was the distinction of *The New England Primer,* the first children's spelling book published in America?

47. The first Bible version in America in a European language was not in English. What language was it in?

48. In what century was the first children's Bible published in America?

49. Hiram Bingham, a missionary from Vermont, translated the Bible for what island (which later became a state)?

50. What organization, with its headquarters in Yankee territory, supplied Bibles for Confederate soldiers?

32. William Jennings Bryan, who had served as secretary of state under Woodrow Wilson
33. None; the Bible does not directly condemn slavery—a fact that slave-holding Christians in the South were much aware of.
34. Allen (who died in 1971) ordered the removal of the Ten Commandments from New York schools.
35. The Equal Access Law
36. The Jehovah's Witnesses
37. Dwight L. Moody, founder of the Moody Bible Institute
38. Bible Institute of Los Angeles; The school is not in Los Angeles now, but in nearby La Mirada.
39. *The Scofield Reference Bible,* first published in 1909; it has been published in numerous editions and still sells well.
40. She has been the only woman to translate the entire Bible by herself. She published her translation in Connecticut in 1876.
41. The American Bible Society
42. Reincarnation; people living at that time often referred to it as the "Reincarnation Bible."
43. The Swedenborgians; this small group based their teachings on the many writings of Swedish author Emanuel Swedenborg. The American Swedenborg Bible, published in Boston in 1837, leaves out Acts and the Epistles from the New Testament and leaves out Ruth, 1 and 2 Chronicles, Ezra, Nehemiah, Esther, Job, Proverbs, Ecclesiastes, and the Song of Solomon from the Old.
44. Exodus 22:18: "Thou shalt not suffer a witch to live." This is not, by the way, the only Bible passage to condemn sorcery and the occult.
45. Bibliomancy; through the centuries many people have done this, apparently expecting that God will aid the person to open the Bible to just the right verse.
46. It taught the letters of the alphabet by linking each letter to a biblical person or idea; for example, the entry for A reads "In Adam's fall / We sinned all." The Z entry reads "Zacchaeus he / Did climb the tree / Our Lord to see." (Quite a difference from "A is for Apple, B is for Boy, C is for. . . .")
47. German, published in Pennsylvania in 1740, when all English-language Bibles were still required to be printed in England
48. The twentieth; the first one, called (appropriately) *The Children's Bible,* was published in 1902.
49. Hawaii; he published the Hawaiian translation in 1839.
50. The American Bible Society, headquartered in New York; there was also, in the Civil War years, a Confederate Bible Society.

51. The verse "Eye hath not seen, nor ear heard, . . . the things which God hath prepared for them that love him" was significantly *mis*quoted at a major political gathering of 1992. What two political figures quoted the verse?

52. In 1993, the publisher Simon & Schuster published *The Bible, Arranged and Edited,* an edition that eliminated chapters and verses and also eliminated large chunks of the Old Testament Law. Which translation was used in this edition?

53. What was the old-fashioned way of getting rid of a worn-out Bible?

54. When Christopher Columbus landed in 1492, what biblical name did he give to the place where he first touched ground?

55. What Old Testament book influenced Abraham Lincoln to issue the Emancipation Proclamation, freeing all slaves in America?

56. What great Revolutionary War hero wrote a book denying that the Bible is the Word of God?

57. What small denomination broke away from the Methodist Church in 1940, accusing the Methodists of denying the inspiration of the Bible?

Familiar Verse, Peculiar Order

☛ Placed in their proper order, the words are a familiar verse from one of Paul's letters.

death your is O is O sting where victory grave where your

51. Bill Clinton and Al Gore, at the 1992 Democratic Convention; the verse (found in 1 Corinthians 2:9, quoting Isaiah 64:4) was given a humanistic spin by the Democrats, who politely removed any reference to God.
52. The King James Version (first published in 1611); this is amazing, since the publisher wanted an edition of the Bible that would appeal to modern readers.
53. Burying it; this was (and still is) intended as an act of reverence and respect. There are still many people who cannot bring themselves to burn a Bible or to throw it in the garbage.
54. He named it *San Salvador*—the Spanish name for "Holy Savior." (It was probably one of the Bahama Islands, by the way.)
55. Exodus, with its story of the Hebrew slaves being freed from Egypt; Lincoln claimed to be especially influenced by Exodus 6:5: "I [God] have also heard the groaning of the children of Israel, whom the Egyptians keep in bondage; and I have remembered my covenant."
56. Ethan Allen; he was the leader of the famous Green Mountain Boys of Vermont. Allen wrote a tract, published in 1784, titled *Reason the Only Oracle of Man*. In it he discussed his religious beliefs, among which was his belief that human reason made a divinely revealed Bible unnecessary.
57. The Bible Protestant Church, which still has about two thousand members in the eastern U.S.

Familiar Verse, Peculiar Order (answer)

O death, where is your sting, O grave, where is your victory? (1 Corinthians 15:55)

Back to the Books:
The Bible and Literature

☛ The Bible has had an enormous effect on the world's literature, not only in its morality, but also in lending plots and titles to innumerable novels, stories, and poems. Test your knowledge of the Bible and its presence in the world's great books.

1. What noted twentieth-century science fiction author also wrote (surprisingly enough) a *Guide to the Bible?*
2. American novelist Joseph Heller wrote the humorous 1984 novel *God Knows.* Which Old Testament character is its main character?
3. What noted American author wrote the novel *East of Eden* (which takes its title from the Bible)?
4. Modern Greek author Nikos Kazantzakis wrote a controversial book about Jesus that was made into an even more controversial film. What was the title?
5. What American humorist (famous for his tales set along the Mississippi River) wrote *The Diary of Adam and Eve?*
6. *Lord of the Flies,* a much-read 1955 novel by Nobel prizewinner William Golding, takes its title from what pagan god mentioned in the Bible?
7. Ernest Hemingway wrote a novel titled *The Sun Also Rises.* From what Old Testament book did he take his title?
8. The narrator in the novel *Moby Dick* has what biblical name?
9. *Christus,* a long poem about Christ, was the favorite poem of a great American author better known for *Paul Revere's Ride* and *The Song of Hiawatha.* Who was he?
10. A scandalous French author penned a book titled *One Hundred and Twenty Days of Sodom.* Who was he?
11. Russian author Fyodor Dostoyevsky's novel *The Possessed* is a story of political terrorists, but he took its name from a character in the Gospels. Which character?
12. Russian novelist Leo Tolstoy, famous for *War and Peace,* wrote a novel with a biblical title. What was it?
13. English poet Matthew Arnold, writing in the 1800s, borrowed the name of an Old Testament nation and used it to refer to people who are uncultured and crude. What were these people called?

Back to the Books: The Bible and Literature (answers)

1. Isaac Asimov
2. David
3. John Steinbeck, also famous for his *Grapes of Wrath;* "East of Eden" refers to the land where Cain lived after he murdered Abel.
4. *The Last Temptation of Christ*
5. Mark Twain, more famous for *Tom Sawyer* and *Huckleberry Finn*
6. Beelzebub (see 2 Kings 1:2 and Matthew 12:24); the name Beelzebub literally translates as "lord of the flies."
7. Ecclesiastes (1:5—"The sun also rises, and the sun goes down")
8. Ishmael; the novel begins with the words "Call me Ishmael."
9. Henry Wadsworth Longfellow
10. The Marquis de Sade, who lent his name to the practice of *sadism*
11. The demoniac who was healed by Jesus; the demoniac was possessed by a "Legion" of demons. Dostoyevsky believed the political agitators were similarly possessed.
12. *Resurrection*
13. The Philistines; the term is still often used as Arnold used it.

14. English poet Lord Byron, who led a scandalous life, wrote a famous poem about the Lord destroying an Assyrian king's army. What king?

15. English novelist George Eliot wrote a long narrative poem about a little-known Old Testament character connected with the invention of music. Who was he?

16. Lloyd Douglas, a Lutheran pastor, wrote a novel titled *The Big Fisherman*. Which apostle is the main character?

17. Mississippi novelist William Faulkner's novel *Absalom, Absalom* is named for the wayward son of what king of Israel?

18. English poet John Masefield wrote a long poetic drama titled *A King's Daughter*. What notorious Old Testament woman is the main character?

19. English poet John Milton's great 1671 poem *Paradise Regained* is based on what key event in Jesus' life?

20. On which Gospel did Milton base his poem?

21. Ben Ames Williams wrote a 1947 Civil War novel titled *A House Divided*. What person in the Bible used the phrase "A house divided against itself cannot stand"?

22. American poet Robert Frost wrote a long humorous poem titled *The Masque of Mercy*, which is concerned with an unfortunate Old Testament prophet. Which one?

23. Christopher Smart, the English poet of the 1700s who lived in an insane asylum, wrote a long poetic masterpiece dedicated to an Old Testament king. Who?

24. One of the best-selling books in colonial America was *The Day of Doom*, a long poem by Michael Wigglesworth. What biblical event is it concerned with?

25. The great English poet John Milton wrote a masterpiece about what Old Testament strongman?

26. Contemporary American novelist Howard Fast wrote a novel titled *Prince of Egypt*. What Old Testament character is the lead character?

27. Offbeat American poet Ezra Pound wrote a strange poem titled *The Ballad of the Goodly Fere*, concerned with Jesus' resurrection. What lesser-known apostle is its narrator?

28. American novelist Robert Nathan wrote the novel *The Son of Amittai*. What Old Testament prophet is its main character?

14. Sennacherib; the poem is titled *The Destruction of Sennacherib* and is based on 2 Kings 19.
15. Jubal; the poem, published in 1874, was *The Legend of Jubal.* (See Genesis 4:21.)
16. Peter
17. David; the title comes from David's lament for the dead Absalom (2 Samuel 18:33).
18. Jezebel, Ahab's wife
19. His temptation by Satan
20. Luke's
21. Jesus; he was referring to accusations that he could cast out demons because he himself was the prince of demons (Matthew 12:25).
22. Jonah
23. David; the title is *Song to David.*
24. Judgment Day (of course)
25. Samson; Milton's poem, published in 1672, is *Samson Agonistes,* and it deals with Samson's imprisonment by the Philistines.
26. Moses
27. Simon the Zealot
28. Jonah, who is called the son of Amittai

29. The great American poet Louis Untermeyer wrote a novel about which Old Testament liberator?

30. English Romantic poet John Keats wrote a beautiful poem about a biblical king's strange dream. Which king?

31. English poet Robert Browning titled several of his poetry collections *Bells and Pomegranates*. Believe it or not, he took the title from the Old Testament. What do "bells and pomegranates" refer to?

32. Modern American poet T. S. Eliot wrote a long dramatic poem titled *The Rock*. What does the "rock" refer to?

33. American novelist Edith Wharton wrote a novel titled *The Valley of Decision*. From what Old Testament book of prophecy did she take the title?

34. What great English poet wrote the masterpiece *Paradise Lost*, based on the first few chapters of Genesis?

35. American poet Robert Frost's 1945 poem *A Masque of Reason* is a dialogue between God and which pitiful Old Testament man?

36. American novelist Elmer Davis's 1928 novel *Giant Killer* is about which Old Testament character?

37. Older literature sometimes refers to the "Nine Worthies," nine famous and noble soldiers. Three of them are Bible characters. Can you name them?

38. What great English novelist, famous for *Silas Marner*, wrote the poem *The Death of Moses?*

39. *The Four Horsemen of the Apocalypse* by modern Spanish novelist Vicente Blasco Ibanez takes its name from which New Testament book?

40. American novelist Winston Churchill wrote *The Inside of the Cup*, which takes its title from Jesus' attacks on which group of people?

41. American novelist Lloyd Douglas's novel *The Robe* is the story of whose robe?

42. *The Quest of the Historical Jesus* was written by a famous German organist, missionary, and doctor. Who was he?

43. John Steinbeck's novel *To a God Unknown* takes its title from which New Testament book?

29. *Moses,* the novel's title
30. Nebuchadnezzar; the poem is *Nebuchadnezzar's Dream* (1817) and is based on the book of Daniel.
31. The decorations on the fringe of Israel's high priest's clothing (Exodus 28:33); no one knows what Browning meant by his title.
32. The church; Eliot apparently was thinking of Jesus' words to Peter: "Upon this rock I will build my church" (Matthew 16:18).
33. Joel (3:14—"The day of the Lord is near in the valley of decision")
34. John Milton; the poem was published in 1674 and has been a classic ever since.
35. Job
36. David, of course
37. Joshua, David, and Judas Maccabeus (Judas being from the Apocrypha, not the Old Testament or the New)
38. George Eliot
39. Revelation, which is sometimes called the Apocalypse; the title refers to the symbolic horses in Revelation 6, symbolizing war, conquest, famine, and death.
40. The Pharisees; Jesus said, "Woe to you, scribes and Pharisees, hypocrites! For you cleanse the outside of the cup . . . , but inside they are full of extortion and self-indulgence. Blind Pharisee, first cleanse the inside of the cup" (Matthew 23:25-26). (By the way, this Winston Churchill is *not* the same as the British prime minister.)
41. Jesus'
42. Albert Schweitzer
43. Acts; when Paul preached to the Athenians, he refers to having seen a monument inscribed "To the Unknown God" (Acts 17:23).

44. American novelist Albion Tourgee wrote many novels about the Reconstruction era in the South. One of the novels, *Bricks without Straw,* takes its title from which Old Testament book?

45. The first book printed in America was a rhyming version of what Old Testament book?

46. *The Legacy of Cain* is a novel by Austrian author Leopold van Sacher-Masoch. What sexual abnormality is named after the author?

47. The demented ship captain who is the chief character in *Moby Dick* has what biblical name?

48. What French poet, a friend of Reformation leader John Calvin, made a notable translation of the Psalms into French?

49. John Bunyan's famous allegorical story *The Pilgrim's Progress* has a New Testament demon as a character. Who was he?

50. D. H. Lawrence, the English author of several controversial and sensuous novels, also wrote *The Man Who Died.* What New Testament character is it concerned with?

51. The famous American short story "The Gift of the Magi" takes its title (but not its plot) from Matthew's story of the wise men and their gifts to the baby Jesus. Who wrote this famous story?

52. *Moses and Monotheism* was the last publication of a famous psychiatrist who was very critical of religion. Who was he?

53. Germany's Nobel prizewinning author Thomas Mann wrote four long novels dealing with a noted character from Genesis. Who?

54. Scandalous English poet Lord Byron wrote a long poem about which violent character from the book of Genesis?

55. American novelist Taylor Caldwell's book *Great Lion of God* (1970) tells the story of which apostle?

56. American poet Timothy Dwight wrote a long poem, published in 1785, titled *The Conquest of Canaan.* It is considered the first epic poem written in America. Who is its main character?

57. Modern French novelist Marcel Proust published the novel titled (in English) *Cities of the Plain.* What two immoral Old Testament cities does the title refer to?

44. Exodus; it refers to the Hebrews being forced by the Egyptians to make bricks without straw (Exodus 5).
45. Psalms; the book is known as *The Bay Psalm Book,* published in 1640.
46. Masochism
47. Ahab
48. Clement Marot; this was considered radical at the time (the 1500s), since church services had always been in Latin.
49. Apollyon, mentioned in Revelation 9:11
50. Jesus
51. O. Henry
52. Sigmund Freud
53. Joseph; Mann's work, finished in 1943, was collectively titled *Joseph and His Brothers.*
54. *Cain,* the title of the poem
55. Paul
56. Joshua
57. Sodom and Gomorrah; in fact, the original French title is *Sodome et Gomorrhe.* The novel, true to its title, deals with the theme of homosexuality.

58. What contemporary English novelist, famous for such violent, sensuous books as *A Clockwork Orange,* also wrote *Man of Nazareth?*
59. English novelist George Moore's 1916 novel *The Brook Kerith* concerns a meeting of the risen Jesus with which apostle?
60. In John Milton's great epic *Paradise Lost,* what biblical name does he give to the bottomless pit?

Familiar Verse, Peculiar Order

☞ Placed in their proper order, the words are a familiar verse from Matthew.

eye a an tooth an and eye for a for tooth

Canvas and Gallery: The Bible in Art

☞ A visit to any art museum will convince you that the Bible has inspired painters and sculptors for ages, producing some of the greatest masterpieces of civilization. You don't have to be an art expert to answer the questions here—just remember your Bible, and the answers won't be too hard to guess.

1. *Madonna* is the name usually given in artwork to what New Testament woman?
2. According to legend, which New Testament writer is supposed to have painted an actual picture of Mary, Jesus' mother?
3. There are many types of paintings and sculptures of Christ hanging on the cross. What is the *Christus triumphans* type?
4. What do we call the paintings—so popular in Eastern Orthodox churches, especially Russian—of Bible saints and Christ?
5. A nativity portrays what event found in the Gospels?
6. What do we call the circle of light (or gold) surrounding the head of Christ or a saint in a picture?

58. Anthony Burgess
59. Paul; Moore's novel, which departs significantly from the Gospels, has Jesus claiming that Paul has distorted the original gospel message.
60. Abaddon, taken from Revelation 9:11

Familiar Verse, Peculiar Order (answer)

An eye for an eye, and a tooth for a tooth. (Matthew 5:38, quoting Exodus 21:24; Leviticus 24:20; or Deuteronomy 19:21)

Canvas and Gallery: The Bible in Art (answers)

1. Mary, the mother of Jesus, of course; *Madonna* literally means "my lady."
2. Luke; this legend probably stems from the attention he gives in his Gospel to Mary. Several art academies in Europe were named "Academy of St. Luke" in observance of this legend.
3. This is the "triumphant Christ"—eyes open, arms outstretched, standing on (rather than hanging from) the cross.
4. Icons, which means "images"
5. The birth of Jesus, of course
6. A halo; the Christians borrowed this device from the way that some emperors were represented in art.

7. In artwork, which disciple is often pictured with a rooster?
8. What portrait painters are mentioned in the Bible?
9. In art, what prominent New Testament man is often shown holding a lamb and wearing very rough clothing?
10. In paintings that show an elderly, bald man being crucified upside down, who is being portrayed?
11. What great Italian artist painted the glorious (and terrifying) *Last Judgment* pictures in the Vatican in Rome?
12. In artwork, the apostle Paul is usually shown with a sword. Why?
13. Many paintings that show King David also show a naked woman in the picture. Who is she?
14. In an artwork called a pietà, the dead Christ is being held by what person?
15. In paintings of the Last Supper, which disciple is usually shown holding a bag in his hand?
16. In paintings of the Last Supper, which disciple is usually the only one who doesn't have a beard?
17. What do we call the chubby little naked angels in pictures?
18. A picture called a *sacra conversazione* shows what people from the Bible?
19. In artwork, what saintly New Testament man is shown being pelted with stones?
20. When you see a painting showing a beautiful woman looking at a decapitated head on a platter, what New Testament scene is being illustrated?
21. In artwork, the four authors of the Gospels are often represented by symbols. Which Gospel and author are represented by a lion?
22. Which Gospel is represented by an eagle?

7. Peter, calling to mind his denying Christ three times before the rooster crowed (Matthew 26:34)

8 None are; because the second commandment prohibits "graven images," the Jews were not willing to carve or paint the human figure (Exodus 20:4). They were also reluctant to portray animals, since the pagan nations had the habit of making idols in the shapes of animals or humans, or sometimes a mixture of the two.

9. John the Baptist; his clothing is referred to in the Bible. The lamb appears because John referred to Jesus as the "lamb of God."

10. Peter; legend says that he asked to be crucified upside down because he did not deserve to be crucified in the same manner as Christ.

11. Michelangelo

12. According to tradition (not the Bible itself), Paul was beheaded with a sword. Also, one of his epistles mentions "the sword of the Spirit, which is the word of God" (Ephesians 6:17).

13. Bathsheba; artists have always enjoyed showing the incident of David seeing the bathing Bathsheba on her rooftop (2 Samuel 11). It is not one of the most "inspiring" stories in the Bible, but it did give artists an excuse to paint an attractive naked woman.

14. Mary, his mother; there are many pietàs, the most famous being the one in stone by Michelangelo, sculpted around 1500.

15. Judas Iscariot; the bag contains, naturally, the thirty pieces of silver he had accepted to betray Jesus.

16. John; no one knows why, exactly, and certainly there is nothing in the Bible to indicate that John would have been the only beardless disciple—especially since beards were almost universal among Jewish men at that time.

17. *Putti,* plural for *putto*; they are sometimes called, incorrectly, cherubs. In fact, it is questionable whether the putti are angels or just mythological figures. They certainly do not seem anything like the fully adult, awe-inspiring angels in the Bible.

18. The baby Jesus, his mother Mary, and saints—which may be saints from the New Testament, or later saints; *Sacra conversazione* means "holy conversation."

19. Stephen, the first Christian martyr, who was stoned to death (Acts 7)

20. John the Baptist's head being presented to Herodias's daughter, as she had requested (Mark 6); this grisly subject appears in many works of art.

21. Mark; no one knows why the lion is associated with this Gospel, though it might be because the Gospel begins with Jesus being led into the wilderness where he was "with the wild beasts" (Mark 1:13).

22. John; again, no one knows exactly why, although it may be because the eagle symbolized "flying high," and John's Gospel is often said to present the most divine view of Jesus.

23. Which Gospels are represented by an ox and by a winged man?

24. Which New Testament follower of Jesus is shown in art meditating before a cross and a skull?

25. In artwork, which notable angel of the Bible is pictured as an armored man carrying a sword and a shield?

26. When you see a painting of a man lying on his back, his eyes closed, a strange light shining into his face, who is being shown?

27. Which apostle is shown in artwork holding two very large keys?

28. In many medieval works of art, there is an *imago pietatis.* Who is this?

29. Many paintings have the title *Flight into Egypt.* What New Testament characters are being portrayed?

30. In a picture titled *Annunciation,* an angel is shown appearing to a certain woman. Who?

31. In many works of art, an old man is shown on a desert island, writing in a book. Which of Jesus' apostles is he?

32. In an artwork called *Man of Sorrows,* Jesus is shown in what condition?

33. Many pictures are titled *Presentation in the Temple.* Just who is being presented in the temple?

34. In paintings of Jesus' baptism by John, he is not immersed, but is baptized by the pouring of water from a peculiar object. What is it?

35. Who painted the most famous *Last Supper* in the world?

36. In paintings of the Last Supper, which disciple is usually shown resting his head on Jesus' chest?

37. Many biblical paintings show a fattened calf being led into a house while a man embraces a younger man. Which of Jesus' parables does this portray?

38. In paintings of the child Jesus and his mother, what other child is often included in the picture?

39. When you see a painting of a swordsman about to cut a child in half, what scene from the Old Testament is being portrayed?

40. When you see a picture showing Jesus' disciples with flames above their heads, what biblical scene is being portrayed?

23. Luke (the ox) and Matthew (the winged man, or angel); an ox may be Luke's symbol because the Gospel opens with Zacharias in the temple, which was associated with sacrificing oxen and other animals. Matthew may be represented by an angel because of the role the angel plays in the birth of Jesus.

24. Mary Magdalene; she is shown this way probably because she felt sorrow over her past sinful life.

25. Michael; the armor is there because Revelation 12:7 speaks of Michael leading the angels in warfare against the dragon (Satan) and the evil angels.

26. The apostle Paul; artists are fond of showing his experience with the blinding light and his conversion on the road to Damascus (Acts 9).

27. Peter; Matthew 16:19 has Jesus saying to Peter, "I will give to you the keys of the kingdom of heaven."

28. Christ, standing upright in his tomb; *Imago pietatis* means "image of devotion." (If you knew this answer, give yourself an A in art.)

29. Joseph, Mary, and the baby Jesus; the pictures are based on the story of the family fleeing to Egypt to escape Herod (Matthew 2:13-15).

30. Mary; the angel Gabriel announced that she would bear the child Jesus (Luke 1:26-38). It is one of the most popular Bible stories in art.

31. John, who wrote Revelation while he was exiled on the island of Patmos (Revelation 1:9)

32. Wearing his crown of thorns, scourged and bleeding

33. The infant Jesus; usually the other characters present are Joseph and Mary, plus the aged Simeon and Anna, who blessed the child (Luke 2:22-38).

34. Usually a shell; no one knows why. During the Middle Ages and Renaissance, most people (usually infants) were baptized not by immersion but by pouring.

35. Leonardo da Vinci; his famous picture is painted on a wall in the church of Santa Maria delle Grazie in Milan, Italy. It is in terrible condition (and was so even before the artist died), but its image is known throughout the world.

36. John; John 13:23 says, "Now there was leaning on Jesus' bosom one of his disciples, whom Jesus loved." The Gospel does not name the disciple, but traditionally it is assumed to be John.

37. The Prodigal Son; Luke 15:23 has the happy father saying, "Bring the fatted calf here, and kill it, and let us eat and be merry."

38. John the Baptist, the child of Mary's relative Elizabeth; John, according to Luke's Gospel, would have been born shortly before Jesus, so conceivably the two children could have been "cribmates."

39. Solomon's judgment on the two prostitutes who were arguing about a child they both claimed was theirs; Solomon's judgment was to divide the child, knowing that the real mother would give up the child rather than allow this to happen (1 Kings 3:16-28).

40. Pentecost; Acts 2:3 claims that "tongues of fire" rested on each of the apostles.

41. In paintings titled *Adoration,* Jesus is being worshiped by whom?

42. Some paintings show certain Christians who have stigmata on their bodies. What are these?

43. In paintings of Jesus' baptism, what is usually shown above his head?

44. In a Christian painting, what is a bambino?

45. German artist Albrecht Dürer produced a familiar picture titled *Hands of an Apostle.* By what name do we usually call this picture?

46. Michelangelo's famous nude statue of David has an "error" in it. What is it?

47. Many paintings have been done of a richly dressed woman finding a baby in a basket by a riverside. What Old Testament incident is being portrayed?

48. Many artists have enjoyed painting a sumptuous banquet where a disembodied hand writes Hebrew letters on a wall. What is the subject of these pictures?

49. A praying Jesus, an angel, and three sleeping disciples were a popular subject for pictures. What incident from the Gospels is this?

50. Many paintings feature the cup used by Jesus at the Last Supper. By what name is the cup called?

51. What type of crucifix is the *Christus patiens?*

52. A *Maesta* picture shows what New Testament figures?

53. The prophet Jonah was a popular figure in the earliest Christian art. Why?

54. Who is portrayed in a *Majestas Domini?*

55. Which of Jesus' disciples is represented in art by an X-shaped cross?

56. What New Testament man is usually depicted with carpenter's tools?

57. What biblical character is often portrayed standing on—or fighting with—a dragon?

41. The shepherds or the wise men; unlike most of our modern nativity scenes, most older paintings showed either the shepherds or the wise men, but not both—possibly because one Gospel (Luke's) tells of the shepherds, while Matthew's speaks of the wise men.
42. Bleeding wounds on the hands and feet, the same places where Christ was wounded on being crucified
43. A dove, representing the Holy Spirit; Matthew 3:16 says that Jesus saw the Spirit descending like a dove and lighting on him, and Mark and Luke say the same.
44. The baby Jesus—*bambino* being the Italian word for "baby"
45. Praying Hands
46. His David is uncircumcised; this would not have been the case for the David of the Bible, since as a Hebrew he certainly would have been circumcised. Michelangelo, a brilliant man, would have known this, so no one knows exactly why he sculpted the statue in this way.
47. The finding of Moses by Pharaoh's daughter (Exodus 2:5-10); artists throughout the centuries have chosen to dress the characters in whatever rich people of their own period were wearing, not what the actual Pharaoh's daughter would have worn.
48. Belshazzar's feast; Daniel 5 tells the story of the feast of the Babylonian ruler Belshazzar, at which the ghostly hand wrote words predicting Belshazzar's downfall. The story makes a great subject for a picture, and probably the most famous is *Belshazzar's Feast* painted by Rembrandt in the 1600s.
49. Jesus' agony in the Garden of Gethsemane; it has been painted hundreds of times, most notably by the Spanish artist El Greco.
50. The Holy Grail
51. One that shows Jesus hanging dead (or dying) on the cross; *Christus patiens* means "suffering Christ."
52. Mary and the child Jesus in heaven, surrounded by angels; it was a popular art subject in the Middle Ages. The word *Maesta* means "majesty."
53. Christians liked to compare Jonah's time in the fish's belly to Jesus' time in the tomb—followed by his resurrection. Jesus himself made the comparison: "For as Jonah was three days and three nights in the belly of the great fish, so will the Son of Man be three days and three nights in the heart of the earth" (Matthew 12:40).
54. Christ as ruler of the universe, usually holding the Book of Life in one hand and often surrounded by four figures representing the four Gospels
55. Andrew; according to old tradition, he was crucified in Greece on an X-shaped cross.
56. Joseph, the husband of Mary, who was himself a carpenter (Matthew 13:55)
57. The archangel Michael; as the leader of heaven's armies of angels, he is supposed to triumph over the armies of the dragon, Satan (Revelation 12:7).

58. What Old Testament prophet is often depicted with ravens?
59. Hundreds of paintings have been done showing the Assumption of the Virgin—Mary being taken bodily into heaven. What Bible passage is the basis for these paintings?
60. What Dutch painter, who did many biblical pictures, was noted for taking street people and using them as models for Bible characters?
61. In pictures showing Jesus' disciples, which disciple usually appears to be the oldest?
62. What Babylonian king is often portrayed with long hair, a long scraggly beard, long fingernails, and a wild look on his face?
63. Who is probably the most famous illustrator of the Bible?
64. What do we call the hand-drawn Bibles from the Middle Ages that were full of beautiful and colorful illustrations?
65. The Transfiguration of Jesus was a popular subject for artists. In such pictures, Jesus is shown with two Old Testament figures. Who are they?
66. In many pictures of Mary and the baby Jesus, the baby has an adult face. Why is that?
67. In what well-known U.S. cemetery would you find the largest biblical painting in the world?
68. In what conservative Southern university would you find a well-stocked sacred art gallery with many masterpieces of biblical art?
69. What sculptor, noted for the presidents' faces on Mount Rushmore, also did the beautiful Twelve Apostles sculptures in New York's Cathedral of St. John?
70. The German artist famous for his Praying Hands pictures also produced some striking pictures illustrating the book of Revelation. Who was he?
71. What biblical characters gave artists the opportunity to draw nudes?
72. What twentieth-century Jewish artist from Russia produced colorful illustrations of Bible stories?
73. English artist Ford Madox Brown painted a picture of a famous medieval Bible translator. Who was he?

58. Elijah, since the Lord sent ravens to feed him in the wilderness (1 Kings 17:6)
59. None is; the Assumption is not mentioned in the Bible, but it has been a favorite subject for Roman Catholic artists.
60. Rembrandt (1606–1669); aside from the fact that such models worked cheaply (!), Rembrandt liked the idea of poor and ordinary people serving as models for the heroes of the Bible.
61. Peter; this is either because he appears to be the leader of the group or because Jesus referred to him as "the rock" on which the church would be built. There is actually no statement in the Bible that he was older than the others.
62. Nebuchadnezzar; Daniel had predicted that the king would cease to rule, and the king "was driven from men and ate grass like oxen; his body was wet with the dew of heaven till his hair had grown like eagles' feathers and his nails like birds' claws" (Daniel 4:33). Artists liked to paint Nebuchadnezzar, since his bizarre appearance let their imaginations run rampant.
63. Probably the French artist Gustave Doré, who lived in the 1800s; he produced black-and-white drawings that could be engraved on wood and printed in book form. He illustrated many books, including the Bible, and the *Doré Bible* is still a delight to the eye.
64. Illuminated manuscripts; before the printing press was invented in the 1400s, Bibles were slowly copied by hand by monks, who chose to beautify the text with ornate illustrations, especially at the beginning of chapters.
65. Moses and Elijah; the Transfiguration is told in Matthew 17 and Luke 9.
66. The artists may have been thinking that Jesus was older than Mary—since the Christ, or Logos, existed with God from all eternity (John 1:1, for example). Many pictures of "Madonna and child" *do* in fact show Jesus as a normal human baby.
67. Forest Lawn, in California; the cemetery's *Crucifixion* is indeed the largest religious painting in the world.
68. Bob Jones University in Greenville, South Carolina
69. Gutzon Borglum
70. Albrecht Dürer, who produced his Revelation woodcuts in 1498
71. Adam and Eve, of course; during periods when the painting of nudes was frowned on, artists could always get away with portraying our first parents in the nude.
72. Marc Chagall (1887–1985), famous for his brightly colored pictures of village life and also noted for painting the ceiling of the Paris Opera House
73. John Wycliffe (1329–1384); he dared to translate the Bible into his native English in an age when translations were officially forbidden by the Catholic church. The beautiful painting's title is *Wycliffe Reading His Translation of the Bible to John of Gaunt.* (John of Gaunt was an English knight and Wycliffe's patron.)

74. Practically every art museum has at least one painting of the world's most famous Bible translator, usually portrayed with a lion nearby. Who was the translator?
75. One of the great English poets of the 1700s was also an artist who illustrated his own poems. He also produced some dazzling illustrations of the book of Job. Who was he?
76. A German artist brotherhood in the 1800s had a name based on Jesus' hometown. What was the group called?
77. There are many paintings with the Latin title *Ecce Homo,* which means "Behold the man." They show Jesus with a certain Roman official. Who?

Familiar Verse, Peculiar Order

☞ Placed in their proper order, the words are a familiar verse from Matthew.

as be come done earth heaven in is it kingdom on thy thy will

Footlights:
The Bible on Stage

1. What ever-popular musical play bills itself as being "based on the Gospel according to St. Matthew"?
2. What controversial rock opera ends with Jesus' crucifixion, not his resurrection?
3. *It Should Happen to a Dog* is the title of Wolf Mankowitz's play about which Old Testament prophet?
4. You'd never guess it from the title, but *The Flowering Peach,* by American playwright Clifford Odets concerns a notable man from Genesis. Which one? (Hint: rainy days)
5. What rock opera, popular on Broadway in the 1980s, deals with Jacob and his twelve sons?
6. What fishy Old Testament prophet is the subject of Gordon Bennett's play *Why Does That Weirdo Prophet Keep Watching the Water?*
7. In the Middle Ages, what were the plays that presented Bible stories in the town squares?

74. Jerome; he lived in the 300s and produced the famous Latin Bible known as the Vulgate. For some reason Jerome became a favorite subject of artists, who portray him as a bearded, sometimes half-naked older man, absorbed in his writing. (Why he came to be associated with a lion is anybody's guess.)
75. William Blake (1757–1827); he is famous for his *Songs of Innocence and Experience,* which includes his most famous poem, "Tiger, tiger, burning bright." Blake's personal religion was an odd mixture of Christian elements and what we would today call New Age thought.
76. The Nazarenes; Jesus, who grew up in Nazareth, was known as a Nazarene. The Nazarene artists in Germany produced *The Bible in Pictures* and other works.
77. Pontius Pilate, who publicly displayed Jesus wearing his crown of thorns; after Pilate uttered the famous words "Behold the man," the Jews then began to shout "Crucify him!" (John 19:4-6). The subject is one of the most emotional ever painted.

Familiar Verse, Peculiar Order (answer)

Thy kingdom come. Thy will be done on earth, as it is in heaven. (Matthew 6:10)

Footlights: The Bible on Stage (answers)

1. *Godspell,* which, in fact, includes material from Luke's Gospel as well as Matthew's
2. *Jesus Christ Superstar,* by Andrew Lloyd Webber and Tim Rice
3. Jonah; Mankowitz's play is an amazingly comical view of poor Jonah.
4. Noah
5. *Joseph and the Amazing Technicolor Dreamcoat*
6. Jonah, of course
7. Mystery plays

8. What play from the 1960s concerns an insane English nobleman who believes he is Jesus (and who hangs on a cross on his drawing room wall)?

9. American prize-winning poet Archibald MacLeish wrote the 1926 play *Nobodaddy*. What noted characters from Genesis are the subjects of this unusual play?

10. Oscar Wilde was noted for his witty comedies, but his one tragic play concerns the imprisonment and death of John the Baptist. What is the play's title?

11. Twentieth-century English author Christopher Fry's play *The Firstborn* deals with what prominent Old Testament character? (Hint: no, it isn't Adam.)

12. Norman Nicholson's 1946 play *The Old Man of the Mountains* deals with a fiery prophet and a wicked king from the Old Testament. Who are they?

13. *The Man Born to Be King* was a twelve-part play series written by a famous English mystery writer (and friend of C. S. Lewis). Who was she?

14. American playwright Eugene O'Neill wrote a peculiar play dealing with a New Testament character who meets a Roman emperor. Who was this character?

15. The Lillian Hellman play *The Little Foxes,* about a conniving Southern family, takes its title from the Bible. What book of the Bible?

16. The great French author Jean Racine wrote a tragedy about what villainous Old Testament queen?

17. American poet Archibald MacLeish wrote an unusual stage play in 1958, *J. B.* What Old Testament character is this based on? (Hint: the character's name sounds a lot like J. B.)

18. In all of Shakespeare's plays, what one role is the only character mentioned in the Bible?

19. In English plays of the 1600s, the character of a maid often had the name of what Old Testament character?

20. *Auto sacramentals* had nothing to do with cars. They were short biblical plays presented in the Middle Ages in what European country?

21. Legendary English writer George Bernard Shaw wrote a peculiar play containing the name of what long-lived Old Testament man?

8. *The Ruling Class* by Peter Barnes; it was made into a film starring Peter O'Toole.
9. Adam, Eve, Cain, and Abel
10. *Salome,* named for the daughter of Herodias who asked for John's head on a platter
11. Moses
12. Elijah and Ahab
13. Dorothy Sayers
14. Lazarus; the play is *Lazarus Laughed.*
15. The Song of Solomon: "The little foxes, that spoil the vines" (2:15)
16. Athaliah; Racine wrote the play (*Athalie* in French) in 1691.
17. Job
18. Octavius in *Julius Caesar;* Octavius is better known as Augustus Caesar, who is mentioned in Luke's Gospel.
19. Abigail
20. Spain
21. Methuselah; the 1921 play's title was *Back to Methuselah.*

22. One of Shakespeare's plays refers to the treachery of the New Testament king Herod by using the phrase "It out-Herods Herod." What play contains that line?

23. Sidney Howard, noted for writing the script for *Gone with the Wind*, wrote a play with a biblical title—*The Silver Cord*. What book of the Old Testament does this mysterious title come from?

24. German author Hermann Sudermann wrote a play titled *The Fires of St. John*. Who is the central character of the play?

25. American playwright Thornton Wilder wrote a popular comedy titled *The Skin of Our Teeth*. Which book of the Bible did he borrow the title from?

26. The French atheist author Andre Obey wrote a colorful play about which Old Testament character?

27. English comic author Jerome K. Jerome wrote *The Passing of the Third Floor Back*, about a New Testament character living in a modern boarding house. What character?

28. American playwright John Van Druten wrote the curiously titled play *The Voice of the Turtle*. From what Old Testament book does the play take its name?

29. Spearfish, South Dakota, is home to what renowned biblical play, staged outdoors?

30. American poet Robinson Jeffers wrote a play that tries to enhance the reputation of a particular disciple of Jesus. Which disciple?

31. What play presents Old Testament stories as presented by black plantation slaves?

32. Which apostle is the subject of Thornton Wilder's play *Now the Servant's Name Was Malchus*?

33. The Pulitzer prizewinning play *There Shall Be No Night* takes its title from which New Testament book?

34. American author Don Marquis is noted for creating the comic characters Archy and Mehitabel, a cockroach and a cat. More seriously, he wrote *The Dark Hours*, a play about the last days of what person?

35. Paddy Chayevsky, noted screenwriter and playwright, wrote an offbeat play about one of Israel's judges. Which one?

36. The poet Howard Nemerov, at one time poet laureate of the U.S., wrote the play *Endor*. What pitiable Old Testament king is its subject?

22. *Hamlet* (Act III, scene ii, if you care to look it up)
23. Ecclesiastes 12:6: "Remember your Creator before the silver cord is loosed, or the golden bowl is broken."
24. John the Baptist (not John the apostle); the play (1897) is concerned with John's imprisonment and execution by Herod.
25. Job: "I am escaped with the skin of my teeth" (19:20).
26. *Noah,* the title of the play
27. Christ
28. The Song of Solomon (2:12); the "turtle" is actually referring to the turtledove.
29. The Black Hills Passion Play, presented every summer since 1939; with its cast of more than two hundred, the production moves in winter to Florida.
30. Judas; the play is *Dear Judas.*
31. *The Green Pastures* by Marc Connelly (1930)
32. Peter; the title refers to the incident in Gethsemane in which Peter cut off the ear of the high priest's servant, named Malchus (John 18:10).
33. Revelation; the words are a description of the New Jerusalem.
34. Jesus; unfortunately, Marquis's serious works have never been as popular as Archy and Mehitabel.
35. *Gideon;* the play modernizes Gideon and makes him even more doubtful of miracles than he is in Judges.
36. Saul; the title refers to the witch of Endor, whom Saul ordered to summon up the ghost of Samuel.

37. French playwright Edmond Rostand, author of the popular *Cyrano de Bergerac*, also wrote a play about a woman whose life was deeply changed by meeting Jesus. Who was she?

38. Laurence Housman wrote a play titled *The Kingmaker,* which concerns an Old Testament prophet and his dealings with two important kings. Who was he?

39. What small Arkansas town is home to America's largest and best-known Passion play, depicting the last days of Jesus?

40. What famous George Gershwin play contains the song "It Ain't Necessarily So," questioning the reality of such Bible stories as Jonah in the fish?

41. Thornton Wilder's play *The Angel That Troubled the Waters* takes its title from an incident in the Gospel of John. What incident?

42. Maxwell Anderson's play *Journey to Jerusalem* recounts the boyhood of what New Testament character?

43. Philip Barry is best known for his sophisticated high-society comedies, but he also wrote the play *John*. Which New Testament John is its subject?

44. Thornton Wilder's play *The Trumpet Shall Sound* takes its title from a description of Christians' resurrection. Which New Testament epistle does this appear in?

45. One of Shakespeare's contemporaries wrote a play about King David's involvement with a voluptuous woman. Who was she?

46. In what Southern state could you see the outdoor production of *Damascus Road,* the story of the apostle Paul?

47. What German town is associated with the world-famous Passion play depicting the last days of Jesus?

48. Laurence Housman's play *The Burden of Nineveh* concerns which Old Testament prophet?

49. The biblical play *The Divine Tragedy* was written by the American poet better known for *Hiawatha* and *Paul Revere's Ride*. Who was he?

50. The musical *Two by Two,* which opened on Broadway in 1970 with Danny Kaye as the lead, concerns which man from Genesis?

37. *The Woman of Samaria,* also known as the woman at the well; the play gives her name as Photine, and it opens with the ghosts of Abraham, Isaac, and Jacob present at the well where Photine later meets Jesus.

38. Samuel; the play concerns his relations with Saul and David, and it takes a very critical view of Samuel, portraying him as vain and devious.

39. Eureka Springs; the Great Passion Play has a cast of more than two hundred, performing in a forty-four-hundred-seat amphitheater.

40. *Porgy and Bess*

41. Jesus' healing of the man at the pool of Bethesda in Jerusalem (John 5:1-15); verse 4 says that an angel occasionally stirred up ("troubled") the pool's waters, and whoever entered the water first would be healed of his sickness.

42. Jesus

43. John the Baptist

44. 1 Corinthians 15:52 says, "The trumpet shall sound, and the dead shall be raised incorruptible, and we shall be changed."

45. Bathsheba; the play is *David and Bathsheba,* by George Peele, written in 1598. Curiously, Bible characters were seldom presented on stage in those days.

46. Tennessee, near the town of Townsend in the Smoky Mountains

47. Oberammergau; the play has been staged there for hundreds of years and attracts visitors from around the world.

48. Jonah; Housman takes a critical view of the subject. Notice that Jonah has been a subject of some interest to playwrights.

49. Henry Wadsworth Longfellow

50. Noah; "Two by two" refers to the pairs of animals entering the ark, of course.

Familiar Verse, Peculiar Order

☞ Placed in their proper order, the words are a familiar verse from Luke.

and God has my in Lord magnifies my rejoiced
Savior soul spirit the my

Back to the Books:
The Bible and Literature (Part II)

1. What biblical novel (also famous as a motion picture with Charlton Heston) was written by a Civil War general?
2. American novelist Taylor Caldwell's novel *Dear and Glorious Physician* (published in 1959) centers around which New Testament man?
3. *Quo Vadis,* the great novel about the persecution of Christians under Emperor Nero, features which two apostles as key characters?
4. Gore Vidal's controversial 1992 novel *Live from Golgotha* centers around a perverse relationship between the apostle Paul and which of his followers?
5. Par Lagerkvist, a Nobel prizewinning Swedish novelist, wrote a great novel about which criminal character in the life of Jesus?
6. In the great medieval poem *The Divine Comedy* by Dante, what evil character is in the lowest region of hell?
7. Which of Jesus' disciples is there with him?
8. In Russian author Fyodor Dostoyevsky's masterpiece, *The Brothers Karamazov,* which Bible character is examined and condemned by the Grand Inquisitor?
9. Louis Bromfield's 1924 novel *The Green Bay Tree* takes its title from the Psalms' description of a certain type of man. What type?
10. In John Milton's poem about Eden, *Paradise Lost,* Satan is the leader of the fallen angels. What biblical demon is his second-in-command?
11. Gloomy American poet Robinson Jeffers published a book of poems named for a scandalous Old Testament woman. Who?

Familiar Verse, Peculiar Order (answer)

> My soul magnifies the Lord. and my spirit has rejoiced in God my Savior. (Luke 1:46-47)

Back to the Books: The Bible and Literature (Part II) (answers)

1. *Ben-Hur,* which is subtitled *A Tale of the Christ;* its author was former Union General Lew Wallace. Despite its subtitle, Christ is not a major character in the book.
2. Luke, whom Paul referred to as "the beloved physician" (Colossians 4:14)
3. Paul and Peter
4. Timothy
5. *Barabbas;* the novel was made into a movie starring Anthony Quinn.
6. Satan, of course
7. Judas Iscariot
8. Jesus
9. The wicked: "I have seen the wicked in great power, and spreading himself like a green bay tree" (Psalm 37:35).
10. Beelzebub, whom the Pharisees mention as the "prince of the devils" (Matthew 12:24)
11. Tamar, the daughter-in-law of Judah; the book of poems is *Tamar and Other Poems.*

12. Samuel Sewall, an author in colonial America, wrote an antislavery tract in 1700 titled *The Selling of* _____. What Old Testament character, sold into slavery, is named in the title?

13. American novelist Winston Churchill's 1915 novel *A Far Country* takes its title from which famous parable of Jesus?

14. *The Wanderings of Cain* is by an English poet, famous for *Kubla Khan* and *The Rime of the Ancient Mariner*—and also famous for being an opium addict. Who was he?

15. Modern American poet T. S. Eliot wrote a poem about which character associated with the baby Jesus' presentation in the temple?

16. English poet Robert Browning wrote a humorous poem titled *Solomon and Belkis*. By what biblical name is Belkis better known?

17. English master poet John Milton wrote a poem in which a newborn baby is shown frightening away the various pagan gods. Which baby is this?

18. Irish poet W. B. Yeats wrote a mysterious poem about the modern world, containing the famous line "Things fall apart, the center cannot hold." What biblical title did he give to this poem?

19. *Go Down, Moses* takes its title (but not its plot) from the Bible. What famous Southern author wrote this novel?

20. American novelist Zora Neal Hurston's 1934 novel is named _____'s *Gourd Vine*. Which Old Testament prophet's name fills in the blank?

21. English philosopher Thomas Hobbes wrote a pessimistic book of political philosophy named (curiously) for a mythical beast in the book of Job. What was the beast?

22. *The Pearl* is an anonymous medieval poem describing what noted city?

23. English pastor and poet George Herbert's touching poem *The Sacrifice* is about what event in Jesus' life?

24. What two biblical characters are the only humans in John Milton's epic poem *Paradise Lost?*

25. French author Andre Gide's novel *Strait Is the Gate* takes its title from Jesus' words about a narrow gate. What does the narrow gate lead to?

12. Joseph, who was sold by his brothers to be a slave in Egypt
13. The Prodigal Son; Jesus says, "The younger son gathered all together, and took his journey into a far country, and there wasted his substance with riotous living" (Luke 15:13). By the way, this novelist is *not* the same man as British prime minister Winston Churchill.
14. Samuel Taylor Coleridge
15. Simeon; the poem is *A Song for Simeon.*
16. The queen of Sheba; the Bible does not actually tell her name, but in legends she is usually referred to as Belkis.
17. Baby Jesus, of course; the poem is *On the Morning of Christ's Nativity* (1632).
18. *The Second Coming*
19. William Faulkner
20. Jonah; the vine, described in Jonah 4, is the one that sheltered Jonah from the sun while he sulked over the salvation of Nineveh.
21. *Leviathan;* God says to Job of the leviathan, "Any hope of overcoming him is false" (Job 41:9). Hobbes's book does not refer to this mythical beast, but to the almighty power of a government.
22. The New Jerusalem
23. The Crucifixion
24. Adam and Eve
25. To life, while the wide gate leads to destruction: "Strait is the gate . . . which leadeth unto life, and few there be that find it" (Matthew 7:14). "Strait" means "narrow," not "straight."

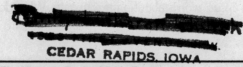

CEDAR RAPIDS, IOWA

26. English poet William Blake's strange poem *Jerusalem* is based on the idea that Jesus paid a visit to what country?

27. The novelist Carlo Maria Franzero wrote a novel about a famous Roman in Jesus' life. The novel is *The Autobiography of* _____. What man is named in the title?

28. German poet Friedrich Klopstock wrote a biblical epic poem with the same title as a famous choral work performed at Christmas. What was it?

29. English poet John Dryden wrote a long humorous poem about a famous rebellion in the Old Testament. The rebellion was against King David, but the poem is named for the two instigators. Who were they?

30. Polish-American author Sholem Asch's biblical novel *The Apostle* deals with *which* apostle?

31. In John Milton's *Paradise Lost,* which biblical angels are characters?

32. What American poet, famous for his *Leaves of Grass,* also wrote *Children of Adam?*

33. English poets Nahum Tate and Nicholas Brady produced a singable version of what Old Testament book?

34. In Henry van Dyke's famous Christmas story, how many wise men are there?

35. In the great American novel *Moby Dick,* what is the name of the character who tries to warn Ishmael, the novel's narrator, not to sail on Captain Ahab's ship?

36. Lord Byron's poem *The Harp the Monarch Minstrel Swept* concerns which famous Old Testament musician?

37. Archibald MacLeish wrote *Songs for* _____, glorifying the sin of a certain Old Testament woman. What woman?

38. A modern novel by Leon Uris concerns the settlement of Jews in Palestine. It has the same title as a book of the Old Testament. Which one?

39. Upton Sinclair wrote a modern novel titled *They Call Me Carpenter.* It contains such characters as Mr. Carpenter, Judge Ponty, and Mary Magna. What Bible character is it based on?

40. American novelist Winston Churchill wrote *The Dwelling Place of Light.* What Old Testament book is this title from?

41. David Garrett's novel *Two by Two* concerns which Old Testament man?

26. England; Blake's poem, by the way, is sung by a choir in the movie *Chariots of Fire.*
27. Pilate; the book's full title is *The Autobiography of G. Pontius Pilate.*
28. *Messiah;* the poem was written in 1773, about thirty years after Handel's oratorio *Messiah* was first performed.
29. *Absalom and Achitophel;* the poem (1681) was meant to compare Absalom's rebellion against David with the recent rebellion of England's Duke of Monmouth against his father, King Charles II.
30. Paul
31. Michael and Gabriel; many other angels are in the poem, but Michael and Gabriel are the only ones actually named in the Bible.
32. Walt Whitman
33. Psalms; their "New Version," published in 1696, was the basis for many hymns in the churches of England. Most modern hymnals contain a few of their versified psalms.
34. Four, but one of them is unable to go see the newborn Jesus. The 1902 story is titled *The Other Wise Man.* The fourth wise man finally meets Jesus—on Good Friday.
35. Elijah
36. David, who, as well as being king, was noted as a harpist—a "monarch minstrel"
37. Eve; MacLeish's collection is *Songs for Eve.*
38. Exodus
39. Jesus, who is the "Carpenter" of the title
40. Job; in 38:19, God asks Job, "Where is the way to the dwelling of light?"
41. Noah, of course; the title refers to the pairs of animals entering the ark.

42. French novelist Anatole France wrote a novel titled *The Procurator of Judea*. Which man from the Gospels is its main character?
43. English poet Robert Browning has a poem in which David speaks, but the poem is named for another king of Israel. Who?

Familiar Verse, Peculiar Order

☛ Placed in their proper order, the words are a familiar verse from Matthew.

art be father hallowed heaven in name our thy who

The Bible in Worship

1. Many pastors start their worship service with the words "This is the day that the Lord has made, let us rejoice and be glad in it." Where would you find that in the Bible?
2. "Holy, holy, holy" is a familiar phrase said (or sung) in many churches. Where does that phrase occur in the Bible?
3. What do you call a fixed set of Bible passages that are to be read in worship on particular days?
4. Some churches still practice "the holy kiss" in the worship service. Which New Testament books mention this practice?
5. "Peace be with you" is a part of many worship services. Where is that in the Bible?
6. Charismatic churches often "lift up hands to the Lord." What worshipful book of the Bible mentions this practice?
7. "Glory to God in the highest" is a common worship phrase. In the Gospels, who used these words?
8. "Father, Son, and Holy Spirit" are mentioned often in worship, but they are mentioned together in only one New Testament book. Which one?
9. Footwashing is still practiced in some churches. Which is the only Gospel to tell the story of Jesus washing the disciples' feet?
10. The Lord's Prayer is found in both Matthew's and Luke's Gospels. Which form is ordinarily used in Christian worship?

42. Pontius Pilate; in the novel, Pilate, years after Jesus' crucifixion, is unable to remember the event at all.
43. Saul

Familiar Verse, Peculiar Order (answer)

Our Father who art in heaven, hallowed be thy name. (Matthew 6:9)

The Bible in Worship (answers)

1. Psalms (118:24)
2. Isaiah (6:3); the words were said by the angels Isaiah saw in the temple.
3. Lectionaries; they are used in Catholic, Orthodox, Episcopal, and other churches.
4. Romans (16:16), 1 Corinthians (16:20), 2 Corinthians (13:12), 1 Thessalonians (5:26); 1 Peter (5:14); it apparently was common practice in New Testament times.
5. 1 Peter 5:14
6. Psalms (134:2); 1 Timothy 2:8 also mentions "lifting up holy hands."
7. The angels who announced Jesus' birth (Luke 2:14)
8. Matthew (28:19), Jesus' great commission, in which he tells the disciples to baptize in the name of the Father, of the Son, and of the Spirit
9. John (13)
10. Matthew's

11. What New Testament passage refers to infant baptism?
12. Which New Testament books mention speaking in tongues?
13. The Letter to the Ephesians refers to "making melody in your heart." Which denominations interpret this to mean that worship services should not have instrumental music?
14. Which apostle laid down the rule that women were not to be pastors?
15. The New Testament word *episkopos* is translated "bishop" in the King James Version, "superintendent" or "overseer" in some newer translations. Which New Testament books discuss the necessary qualifications for a bishop?
16. In what city was the first church building constructed?
17. In the early church, how often was the Lord's Supper celebrated?
18. Which New Testament letters are called the Pastoral Letters because they contain advice to deacons and pastors?
19. Which New Testament letter contains the most advice on conducting Christian worship?
20. What musical instruments are mentioned in connection with Christian worship?
21. What Old Testament book was used as a "hymnal" by the early church?
22. Which book of the Bible refers to a Christian marriage service?
23. In the Roman Catholic Mass, what familiar praise word is said (or sung) after the reading from the New Testament?
24. When songs or prayers from the Bible are sung in worship, what are they called?
25. What type of contemporary churches are noted for singing Bible passages set to music?
26. In the liturgical churches (Roman Catholic, Episcopalian, and some other denominations), what words are said after a person finishes a Scripture reading?
27. And what does the congregation say immediately afterward?
28. If you are in a church with a large Bible resting on a stand shaped like an eagle, what denomination is the church?
29. Which book of the Old Testament is reprinted in the Episcopalians' worship book, *The Book of Common Prayer?*
30. What books of the Bible are read in Roman Catholic churches but not in Protestant churches?

11. None; so far as we know, infants were not baptized in the early church.
12. Acts (2:4 and 19:6) and especially 1 Corinthians (12–14)
13. The Churches of Christ and some other "noninstrumental" churches
14. Paul, notably in 1 Timothy 2:12, which states that women are not to have authority over men
15. 1 Timothy and Titus
16. No one knows, since church buildings are not mentioned in the New Testament. In the early church, all churches were "house churches," meeting in private homes.
17. Apparently at every worship service (see 1 Corinthians 11)
18. 1 Timothy, 2 Timothy, Titus
19. Probably 1 Corinthians, which addresses such issues as the Lord's Supper, speaking in tongues, spiritual gifts, and order in worship
20. None are, which is why some denominations do not use instruments in worship.
21. Psalms
22. Not one; the New Testament gives the impression that Christians had been married either in a Jewish service or in a Roman civil ceremony.
23. Alleluia
24. Canticles; this word usually refers not to psalms, but to other Bible passages that are poetic and are often sung or chanted.
25. The "praise churches," that is, charismatic churches
26. "The Word of the Lord."
27. "Thanks be to God."
28. Probably Episcopalian
29. Psalms
30. The books of the Apocrypha, that is, the books between the Old and New Testaments; most Protestant churches do not believe that the Apocrypha is inspired—at least, not in the same way as the Old and New Testaments.

31. The church season known as Epiphany celebrates which two key events in the life of Jesus?

32. The famous "love passage" in the Bible, so often read at church weddings, is from what New Testament book?

33. In baptism, people are baptized "in the name of the Father, the Son, and the Holy Spirit." Which New Testament book indicates that this is the proper form for baptism?

34. The passage beginning "I know that my Redeemer liveth" is read in many Christian funerals. What Old Testament book is it from? (No, not Psalms.)

35. The word *Hallelujah* (or *Alleluia*) occurs frequently in worship. What is the only book of the Bible that actually contains the word?

36. Some denominations celebrate the Feast of Holy Innocents on December 28. What event in the Gospels is commemorated on this day?

37. What biblical event is commemorated every Sunday?

38. Many Christian burial services quote the words "I am the resurrection and the life." Who said this, and what book are the words recorded in?

39. In the liturgical denominations, what three divisions of the Bible are always read from in each worship service?

40. In what book of the Bible would you find the Apostles' Creed?

41. How many church buildings are mentioned in the Bible?

Familiar Verse, Peculiar Order

☛ Placed in their proper order, the words are a familiar verse from Matthew.

born he is Jews king of that the is where

31. The visit of the wise men, and also the baptism in the Jordan
32. 1 Corinthians 13: "Love is patient, love is kind. . . ."
33. Matthew's Gospel, in which Jesus commands the apostles to "go and make disciples" and baptize them with this formula Matthew 28:19)
34. Job (19:25)
35. Revelation (19:1, 3-4, 6); *but* in the original Hebrew Old Testament, the Hebrew words *Hallelujah* occur many times—and in our English translations, it almost always appears as "Praise the Lord" (which is what it means, of course).
36. King Herod's slaughter of the infant boys of Bethlehem when Jesus was born (Matthew 2:16)
37. The resurrection of Jesus, who was raised on the first day of the week
38. Jesus, of course, spoken before he raised Lazarus from the dead (John 11)
39. Old Testament, Gospel, Epistle. (Also, a Psalm is usually said—or sung—or chanted.)
40. It isn't in the Bible.
41. None; the first generation of Christians did not have (or even want) special buildings for worship. They met in homes, or wherever they could gather a group of believers together.

Familiar Verse, Peculiar Order (answer)

Where is he that is born King of the Jews? (Matthew 2:2)

Quote, Unquote:
What Did They Say about the Bible?

☛ Being the Book of books, the Bible has naturally provoked comments from famous (and infamous) people throughout history. See if you can guess who made the comments below. (We've provided some hints to make the guessing less painful.)

1. "I have spent a lot of time searching through the Bible for loopholes." (a hard-drinking American movie comic of the 1930s and 1940s)
2. "The Number One book of the ages was written by a committee, and it was called the Bible." (a powerful American movie producer, noted for his advocacy of wholesome values in movies)
3. "I know the Bible is inspired because it inspires me." (a widely traveled American evangelist, who has a school named after him)
4. "No sciences are better attested than the religion of the Bible." (an English scientist, associated with the fall of an apple)
5. "Within that awful volume lies,/The mystery of mysteries!" (the renowned Scottish author of *Ivanhoe* and many other historical novels)
6. "Most people are bothered by those Scripture passages which they cannot understand. But for me, the passages in Scripture which trouble me most are those which I *do* understand." (American humorist, creator of *Tom Sawyer*)
7. "Tell your prince that this book is the secret of England's greatness." (a queen of England in the 1800s)
8. "If we would destroy Christianity, we must first of all destroy man's belief in the Bible." (a French skeptic of the 1700s)
9. "I am a Bible-bigot. I follow it in all things, both great and small." (the founder of Methodism)
10. "O Bible, what follies and barbarities are defended in thy name." (one of the best-known American poets, famous for his *Leaves of Grass*)
11. "So great is my veneration for the Bible that the earlier my children begin to read it, the more confident am I that they will prove useful citizens to their country." (one of the first U.S. presidents)

Quote, Unquote: What Did They Say about the Bible? (answers)

1. W. C. Fields, who died in 1946; supposedly he made this comment during his final illness.
2. Louis B. Mayer (as in "Metro-Goldwyn-Mayer," MGM); Mayer made this comment to some movie scriptwriters who objected to changes made in their scripts.
3. Dwight L. Moody (1837–1899)
4. Isaac Newton (1642–1727)
5. Sir Walter Scott (1771–1832)
6. Mark Twain (1835–1910)
7. Queen Victoria (1819–1901); she addressed these words to an African chieftain when she presented him with a Bible.
8. Voltaire (1694–1778)
9. John Wesley (1703–1791)
10. Walt Whitman (1819–1892)
11. John Quincy Adams (1767–1848)

12. "On its pages are written the assurances of the present and our hopes for the future." (a great American statesman of this century)
13. "Good and holy men, the wisest and best of mankind, have declared it to be beyond compare the most perfect instrument of humanity." (an English poet of the 1800s)
14. "The New Testament is the best book the world has ever known or ever will know." (the English author of *David Copperfield* and other classics)
15. "The greatest source of material for motion pictures is the Bible, and almost any chapter would serve as a basic idea for a motion picture." (an American film director)
16. "The Bible grows more beautiful as we grow in our understanding of it." (Germany's most famous author, who wrote *Faust*)
17. "Hold fast to the Bible as the anchor of your liberties. To the influence of this book we are indebted for all the progress made in true civilization." (a Civil War general and, later, a U.S. president)
18. "There is a Book worth all other books which were ever printed." (a great American orator in the colonial era)
19. "England has two books, the Bible and Shakespeare. England made Shakespeare, but the Bible made England." (the great French author of *Les Miserables* and *The Hunchback of Notre Dame*)
20. "What you bring away from the Bible depends to some extent on what you carry to it." (an American humorist author)
21. "All that I am I owe to Jesus Christ, revealed to me in His divine Book." (the most famous missionary to Africa)
22. "Christ is the Master; the Scriptures are only the servant." (a great German Protestant leader)
23. "The Bible is a book in comparison with which all others in my eyes are of minor importance." (a Confederate general)
24. "The Bible is the greatest benefit which the human race has ever experienced." (a skeptical German philosopher of the 1700s)
25. "This great book is the best gift God has given to man. But for it, we could not know right from wrong." (a U.S. president of the 1800s)

12. William Jennings Bryan (1860–1925)
13. Samuel Taylor Coleridge (1772–1834)
14. Charles Dickens (1812–1870)
15. Cecil B. DeMille (1881–1959), who directed *The Ten Commandments* and many other classics
16. Johann Wolfgang von Goethe (1749–1832)
17. Ulysses S. Grant (1822–1885)
18. Patrick Henry (1736–1799), famous for his "Give me liberty or give me death" speech
19. Victor Hugo (1802–1885)
20. Oliver Wendell Holmes (1809–1894)
21. David Livingstone (1813–1873), famous as the Livingstone of "Dr. Livingstone, I presume?"
22. Martin Luther (1483–1546)
23. Robert E. Lee (1807–1870)
24. Immanuel Kant (1724–1804)
25. Abraham Lincoln (1809–1865)

26. "Throughout the history of the Western world, the Scriptures have been the greatest instigators of revolt against the worst forms of tyranny." (an agnostic British scientist)

27. "This is the people's book of revelation, revelation of themselves not alone, but revelation of life and of peace." (a U.S. president of this century)

28. "Love the Bible and wisdom will love you." (one of the earliest translators of the Bible)

29. "The Bible is for the government of the people, by the people, and for the people." (a medieval English translator of the Bible)

30. "Scripture is the school of the Holy Spirit." (a French leader during the Reformation)

31. "I believe that the intention of the Scripture was to persuade men of the truths necessary to salvation. Science could not render this, but only the Holy Spirit." (the most famous Italian scientist in history)

32. "The devil can cite Scripture for his purpose." (England's greatest poet)

33. "As society is now constituted, literal adherence to the precepts of the Gospels would mean sudden death." (an English mathematician-philosopher of this century)

34. "Had the Bible been in clear straightforward language, it would almost certainly have been a work of lesser influence." (a contemporary American economist)

35. "Prosperity is the blessing of the Old Testament. Adversity is the blessing of the New." (an English essayist and scientist of the 1600s)

36. "Sunrise and sunset, promise and fulfillment, birth and death, the whole human drama, everything is in this Book." (one of Germany's most famous poets)

37. "Scripture does not aim at imparting scientific knowledge, and therefore it demands from men nothing but obedience." (a skeptical Jewish philosopher)

38. "We ought to listen to the Scriptures with the greatest caution, for as far as our understanding of them goes, we are like little children." (the greatest theologian in the Roman Empire)

39. "You can learn more about human nature by reading the Bible than by living in New York." (a twentieth-century American literary critic)

26. Thomas H. Huxley (1825–1895)
27. Woodrow Wilson (1856–1924)
28. St. Jerome (350–420), who translated the Bible from Hebrew and Greek into the famous Latin translation known as the Vulgate
29. John Wycliffe (1330–1384)
30. John Calvin (1509–1564)
31. Galileo (1564–1642)
32. William Shakespeare (1564–1616), of course; the quotation is not Shakespeare himself speaking; it is a line in his play *The Merchant of Venice.*
33. Alfred North Whitehead (1861–1947)
34. John Kenneth Galbraith (1908–)
35. Francis Bacon (1561–1626)
36. Heinrich Heine (1797–1856)
37. Baruch Spinoza (1632–1677)
38. St. Augustine (354–430)
39. William Lyon Phelps (1865–1943)

40. "The Bible is a book of faith, and a book of doctrine, and a book of morals, and a book of special revelation from God." (an American statesman and orator of the 1800s)

41. "We are not at liberty to pick and choose out of its contents, but must receive it all as we find it." (an English Catholic leader of the 1800s)

42. "I always say that the studious perusal of the Sacred Volume will make better citizens, better fathers, and better husbands." (one of the first U.S. presidents)

43. "When you start a Bible movement, it means revolution—a quiet revolution against darkness and crime." (a twentieth-century Christian leader in Japan)

44. "No book has been subject to a greater variety of interpretations, many of them mutually incompatible." (a contemporary American philosopher and former Communist activist)

45. "My way of learning a language is always to begin with the Bible, which I can read without a dictionary." (an English historian of the 1800s)

46. "The vice of our theology is seen in the claim that the Bible is a closed book and that the age of inspiration is past." (American essayist and Unitarian minister)

47. "It is impossible to mentally or socially enslave a Bible-reading people." (American journalist and political leader of the 1800s)

48. "Of all commentaries upon the Bible, good examples are the best and the liveliest." (English poet and preacher of the 1600s)

49. "The blessed God, the God of the Bible, is the God of peace, but for now we ask his blessing upon our battle." (a very devout Confederate general)

50. "The word of God tends to make large-minded, noble-hearted men." (a noted American preacher of the 1800s)

51. "To the Bible men will return, and why? They cannot do without it." (English poet and critic of the 1800s)

52. "Fresh light shall yet break out from God's Word." (a leader of the Pilgrims who settled in Massachusetts)

53. "If the Bible had been the invention of men, the inventors would be greater than the greatest heroes." (a skeptical French philosopher of the 1700s)

40. Daniel Webster (1782–1852); the quote is from Webster's speech at the dedication of the Bunker Hill monument in 1843.
41. John Henry Newman (1801–1890)
42. Thomas Jefferson (1743–1826), who, by the way, was very skeptical about the miracles recorded in the Bible
43. Toyohiko Kagawa (1888–1960), who was an active evangelist and worker with the poor
44. Sidney Hook (b. 1902)
45. Thomas Macaulay (1800–1859)
46. Ralph Waldo Emerson (1803–1882)
47. Horace Greeley (1811–1872), famous for his advice "Go west, young man."
48. John Donne (1572–1631)
49. Thomas "Stonewall" Jackson (1824–1863)
50. Henry Ward Beecher (1813–1887), famous for tackling the subject of evolution; he is also noted for being the brother of author Harriet Beecher Stowe, who wrote *Uncle Tom's Cabin.*
51. Matthew Arnold (1822–1888)
52. John Robinson (1575–1625); he organized the Mayflower expedition but never actually came to America.
53. Jean-Jacques Rousseau (1712–1778)

54. "Nobody ever outgrows Scripture; the Book widens and deepens with our years." (the most noted English preacher of the 1800s)

55. "The Scripture is like an open town in time of war, which serves the occasions of both parties." (the author of *Gulliver's Travels*)

56. "That book is the rock on which our republic rests." (an early U.S. president)

57. "It is Christ Himself, not the Bible, who is the true word of God. The Bible, read in the right spirit and with the guidance of good teachers, will bring us to Him." (one of the most widely read Christian authors of this century)

58. "This is the great fountain of music, and every musician should play to the glory of its Author." (one of the greatest German composers)

59. "No one ever did himself harm from reading the Book." (a colonial American statesmen, scientist, and author, famous for his *Autobiography*)

60. "We have never truly breathed air nor seen light until we have breathed in the God-inspired Bible and seen the world by the Bible's light." (a Russian novelist, author of *Crime and Punishment* and other classics)

Familiar Verse, Peculiar Order

☞ Placed in their proper order, the words are a familiar verse from Matthew.

curse love enemies who you bless your those

World Atlas, Biblical Names

☞ Wherever there are Christians, there are places named from the Bible. Test your knowledge of some famous (and some not-so-famous) world sites named for people and places in the Scriptures.

1. Great Britain's royal court is officially known as the Court of St. _____. Which of Jesus' twelve disciples is the court named for?

54. Charles Haddon Spurgeon (1834–1892)
55. Jonathan Swift (1667–1745); Swift was a clergyman as well as an author.
56. Andrew Jackson (1767–1845)
57. C. S. Lewis (1898–1963), famous for *The Screwtape Letters, Mere Christianity, Miracles,* and many other books
58. Johann Sebastian Bach (1685–1750)
59. Benjamin Franklin (1706–1790)
60. Fyodor Dostoyevsky (1821–1881)

Familiar Verse, Peculiar Order (answer)

Love your enemies, bless those who curse you. (Matthew 5:44)

World Atlas, Biblical Names (answers)

1. James; any ambassador to Great Britain is referred to (officially) as "Ambassador to the Court of St. James." The name stems from St. James Palace, a royal dwelling place until Buckingham Palace became the chief residence.

2. Notre Dame cathedral in Paris is named for which New Testament woman?
3. A famous mountain in India is named for the disciple of Jesus who (according to legend) evangelized India. Which one? (Hint: doubt)
4. The stunningly beautiful cathedral of Cologne, Germany, is dedicated to a famous group of men in the New Testament. Who?
5. The site of the royal wedding of Prince Charles and Princess Diana was London's most famous cathedral. What New Testament figure is the cathedral named for?
6. Dublin, one of the most Catholic cities in the world, does not possess a Roman Catholic cathedral. It does contain a procathedral, which is named, appropriately, for one of the Catholic church's favorite saints. Who is she?
7. The grand church of the Vatican in Rome is named for the apostle who was (according to tradition) the first pope. Who was he?
8. France possesses two small islands off the eastern coast of Canada. One is Miquelon, and the other is named for one of Jesus' disciples. Which one?
9. Brazil's coast has some small rock islands named for an apostle who was shipwrecked. Which apostle?
10. Canada has both a major river (450 miles) and a major city named for an apostle and a New Testament author. Who?
11. Brazil's largest city (more than 7 million) is named for an active New Testament man. Who?
12. The nation of El Salvador in Central America is named for a title given to Jesus. What is it?
13. The old town of Santiago in Spain was probably one of the first "vacation hot spots" in Europe—mostly because it was supposed to be the resting place of one of Jesus' disciples. Which one?
14. The famous church Westminster Abbey in London is formally named for one of the most prominent apostles. Who was he?
15. The capital of the South American nation of Paraguay is named for a key event in the life of Jesus. What?
16. A famous church in London is the burial place of the famous John Smith, saved by Pocahontas. The church is named for a famous burial place in the New Testament. What place?

2. Mary, Jesus' mother; she is called (in French) *Notre Dame* (Our Lady). All the many Notre Dames across the globe are named for the Virgin Mary.
3. Thomas; the mountain is St. Thomas Mount. In fact, a very ancient Christian community exists in India, named the Mar Thoma (Sir Thomas) church.
4. The wise men; the city's coat of arms contains three crowns of the wise men (who, according to tradition, were three in number and were also kings—remember "We Three Kings"?).
5. St. Paul; it is one of London's most famous landmarks, noted for its high dome. It survived several German bombings during World War II.
6. St. Mary (that is, Jesus' mother); a procathedral is a church that substitutes for a cathedral. Dublin does have two regular cathedrals—both of them Protestant.
7. Peter; St. Peter's Basilica is one of the most visited churches in the world. It is also one of the largest, having a capacity of fifty thousand people.
8. Peter; the island is Saint Pierre—French for St. Peter.
9. Paul; the islands are known as St. Paul's Rocks.
10. St. John, the name of a river flowing into the Bay of Fundy and also a large city in the province of New Brunswick
11. Paul; the city is Sao Paulo (St. Paul).
12. Savior; *El Salvador* is Spanish for "the Savior."
13. James; *Santiago* is Spanish for "St. James." In the Middle Ages, thousands of Christians traveled across Europe to visit the (alleged) cathedral of the buried saint. (Since James's martyrdom in Jerusalem is recorded in the book of Acts, only legend can account for how his body came to rest in a town in Spain.)
14. Peter; the church's official name is the Collegiate Church of St. Peter. It is noted as the burial place of many of England's most famous people and is the usual site for coronations.
15. His ascension into heaven; *Asunción* is Spanish for "ascension."
16. The sepulchre (tomb) of Jesus; the name of the church is St. Sepulchre (Holy Tomb).

17. The most famous park in Dublin, Ireland, is a lovely green space named for a New Testament martyr. Who?
18. Heidelberg, Germany, has a stunning Gothic church named (in German) Heilig-Geist-Kirche. What person of the Bible is this named for?
19. Venice, Italy, has a cathedral and a plaza named for the city's patron saint, an author of a Gospel. Who was he?
20. Galway, Ireland, has a noted church named for one of the seven deacons in the book of Acts, and famous because Christopher Columbus supposedly prayed there before sailing for America. What is the name of the church?
21. The oldest church in London (built in 1123) was named for one of Jesus' lesser-known apostles. Who?
22. One Caribbean island tops them all for its surplus of New Testament names—parishes (that is, counties) named for James, Peter, Joseph, John, Philip, Thomas, Andrew, and Christ himself. What is the island?
23. The island of San Salvador in the Bahamas may be the first place Christopher Columbus landed. Who is the island named for?
24. Cuba, though officially Communist (and atheist), still has a city named Sancti Spiritus after a biblical figure. Who?
25. The great cathedral in Vienna, Austria, is probably one of the country's most photographed sights. What martyr is it named for?
26. The Caribbean island of Antigua has its capital and main harbor named for an apostle and Gospel author. Who?
27. Moscow's burial place of the czars is a cathedral named for whom?
28. In Budapest, Hungary, the city's grandest church is named for the "replacement" apostle who took the place of Judas Iscariot. Who?
29. The chief church in Geneva, Switzerland, is famous for being the church of Protestant leader John Calvin, who preached in it several times weekly. What apostle is it named for?
30. The great university in Oxford, England, has a college named for which famous female follower of Jesus?
31. Russia's large city once known as Leningrad has returned to its former name, named for an apostle. Who?
32. A beautiful church in London's Covent Garden area is known as "the Actors' Church," but named for an apostle. Which one?

17. Stephen; the park is St. Stephen's Green.
18. The Holy Spirit, or Holy Ghost, which in German is *Heilig-Geist*
19. Mark—San Marco in Italian
20. St. Nicholas; Nicholas is mentioned only once, in Acts 6:5 (and, no, he has no real connection with Santa Claus or Christmas).
21. Bartholomew; the church is named St. Bartholomew the Great.
22. Barbados
23. Jesus, the Savior; *San Salvador* is Spanish for "holy Savior."
24. The Holy Spirit; *Sancti Spiritus* is Latin (no, not Spanish) for "Holy Spirit."
25. Stephen; it is St. Stephen's Cathedral, or, in the native tongue, Stephansdom.
26. St. John
27. Not really a *who* but a *what*—an archangel; it is Archangel Cathedral, resting place of Czar Ivan the Terrible and some other Russian czars.
28. Matthias; the Matthias Church was the site of several coronations of Hungary's kings.
29. Peter; it is known as the Cathedral of St. Pierre.
30. Mary Magdalene; the college is known as Magdalen College (but it's pronounced *maudlin*, strangely enough).
31. Peter; the city is St. Petersburg
32. St. Paul (who probably wouldn't be too thrilled at being associated with the theatrical profession)

33. Both the city square and the cathedral in Munich, Germany, are named for the city's patron saint, a woman. Who was she?

34. Florence, Italy, is famous for its gorgeous baptism building (the Battistero) named for a Gospel writer. Who?

35. Of the many colleges at England's Cambridge University, the oldest has a curious name that includes an apostle's name. What is it?

36. The Vatican in Rome contains Nero's Circus. According to tradition, which apostle was executed there by order of Emperor Nero?

37. The cathedral of Frankfurt, Germany, is noted as the coronation site of the Holy Roman emperors. Which of Jesus' lesser-known apostles is it named for?

38. The most impressive church of France is probably the one off the coast of Normandy, almost an island, and named for an angel. What is it called?

39. Leipzig, Germany, has an old church famous for having composer Johann Sebastian Bach as its music director. Which doubting apostle was it named for?

40. Genoa, Italy, has a lovely church notable for being where Christopher Columbus was baptized. What martyr is it named for?

41. Autun, France, has a cathedral named for someone raised from the dead. Who?

42. What Caribbean island is named for Father, Son, and Holy Spirit?

43. The cathedral of Amalfi, Italy, is unique in being Arabic in design. Which apostle (a fisherman) of Jesus is it named for?

44. A small island republic of Africa is named for the apostle Thomas. What is the full name of the country?

45. The Canadian river connecting Lake Superior with Lake Huron is named for what New Testament woman?

46. What capital city of Central America is named for Joseph, the husband of Mary?

47. Teddy Roosevelt and his Rough Riders charged up a famous hill in Cuba, named for a New Testament man. Who?

48. What capital of a South American country is named for an apostle?

49. What Pacific island nation has a large city named Christchurch?

33. Mary; the square is Marienplatz (Mary's Square).
34. John; the building is the Battistero de San Giovanni (the baptistery of St. John). For years the building has been used for baptizing all infants born in Florence.
35. Peterhouse College, named for the apostle Peter, of course
36. Peter
37. Bartholomew
38. Mont-Saint-Michel—that is, St. Michael's Mount, named for the angel Michael
39. Thomas; in German, it is the Thomaskirche (St. Thomas Church).
40. Stephen; in Italian, *San Stefano*
41. Lazarus; it is known as the cathedral of St. Lazare.
42. Trinidad, which is Spanish for "Trinity"
43. Andrew; it is on the coast, and, traditionally, Andrew is the patron saint of sailors.
44. Sao Tome and Principe; the country was formerly a Portuguese colony, and *Sao Tome* is Portuguese for "St. Thomas." (Principe is one island, Sao Tome is another.)
45. Mary; the river is the Saint Mary's.
46. San José (Spanish for St. Joseph), the capital of Costa Rica
47. John; the hill was San Juan Hill.
48. Santiago, Chile; *Santiago* is Spanish for "St. James."
49. New Zealand

50. The South American nation Colombia has a Caribbean coastal city named for a New Testament woman. Who? (No, this one isn't named for Mary.)

51. What Pacific island chain bears the name of a wise Old Testament king?

52. Belem, the name of a city in Brazil, is the Portuguese form of a famous New Testament town. Which one?

53. What large German city has an infamous red-light district named after the apostle Paul?

54. Panama has a city named for one of Israel's greatest heroes. Who?

55. Scotland is home to a town that is supposedly the birthplace of the game of golf. What apostle is the town named for?

56. Ile Jesus (French for Jesus Island) lies near what metropolis in the Canadian province of Quebec?

57. A famous London landmark fortress has the Chapel of St. Peter ad Vincula (Chapel of Peter in Chains, referring to Peter's imprisonment, Acts 12). What is the fortress called?

58. A portion of London's Westminster Abbey is notable for being the meeting place of the men who produced the King James Bible. What biblical name is given to the room?

59. What famous university of England has both a Christ's College and a Jesus College?

60. What Caribbean island with a French heritage is named for one of Jesus' disciples?

61. Which enormous Roman church, named for an apostle, is known as "the church of the pope"?

62. In what sprawling city would you find St. Andrews Hill, St. Barnabas Street, St. James Square, St. John's Gardens, St. Luke's Road, St. Mark Street, St. Mary's Terrace, St. Paul's Churchyard, St. Stephen's Gardens, St. Peter's Terrace, and St. Thomas' Way?

Familiar Verse, Peculiar Order

☛ Placed in their proper order, the words are a familiar verse from the New Testament.

the of armor God on put whole

50. Martha, sister of Mary and Lazarus; the city's name (which is Spanish) is Santa Marta.
51. The Solomon Islands
52. Bethlehem
53. Hamburg, with its notorious St. Pauli district
54. David
55. Andrew; he is considered the patron saint of Scotland. The town is St. Andrews (and, no, the Scots don't put an apostrophe in Andrews—for some strange reason).
56. Montreal
57. The Tower of London, famous for its many celebrity prisoners over the centuries
58. The Jerusalem Chamber; it is also notable because England's King Henry IV supposedly died in the room, fulfilling an old prophecy that he would "die in Jerusalem."
59. Cambridge
60. St. Barthelemy, which is French for St. Bartholomew
61. The Church of St. John Lateran ("Lateran" being the name of the Roman hill on which the church stands)
62. London, England; note that these are *not* all the London streets named for people in the Bible.

Familiar Verse, Peculiar Order (answer)
Put on the whole armor of God. (Ephesians 6:13)

Do You Remember?

☞ Would you like to see how much Bible trivia you can remember? Answer the questions (which you should have answered already in this section), and then see how well you rate on the scale on page xii.

1. What group of people, often criticized by Jesus, had a name that now means "legalistic hypocrites, especially the religious kind"?
2. What world-renowned American evangelist (and former shoe salesman) founded a famous Bible college in Chicago?
3. English poet Matthew Arnold, writing in the 1800s, borrowed the name of an Old Testament nation and used it to refer to people who are uncultured and crude. What were these people called?
4. In many works of art, an old man is shown on a desert island, writing in a book. Which of Jesus' apostles is he?
5. One of Shakespeare's plays refers to the treachery of the New Testament king Herod by using the phrase "It out-Herods Herod." What play contains that line?
6. English master poet John Milton wrote a poem in which a newborn baby is shown frightening away the various pagan gods. Which baby is this?
7. Footwashing is still practiced in some churches. Which is the only Gospel to tell the story of Jesus washing the disciples' feet?
8. Who said this: "Most people are bothered by those Scripture passages which they cannot understand. But for me, the passages in Scripture which trouble me most are those which I *do* understand." (American humorist, creator of *Tom Sawyer*)
9. Notre Dame cathedral in Paris is named for which New Testament woman?
10. The modern-day political movement to give Jews a homeland in Palestine goes by what name?

Do You Remember? (answers)

1. The Pharisees, whom Jesus criticized not only for their hypocrisy, but for their obsessive attention to unimportant details
2. Dwight L. Moody, founder of the Moody Bible Institute
3. The Philistines; the term is still often used as Arnold used it.
4. John, who wrote Revelation while he was exiled on the island of Patmos (Revelation 1:9)
5. *Hamlet* (Act III, scene ii, if you care to look it up)
6. Baby Jesus, of course; the poem is *On the Morning of Christ's Nativity* (1632).
7. John (13)
8. Mark Twain (1835–1910)
9. Mary, Jesus' mother; she is called (in French) *Notre Dame* (Our Lady). All the many Notre Dames across the globe are named for the Virgin Mary.
10. Zionism, named for the biblical Mount Zion, one of the hills of Jerusalem

Word Play— And Why Not?

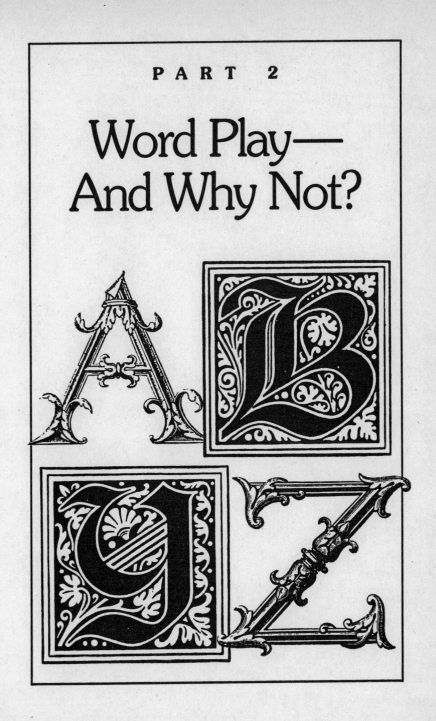

Test Your Bible IQ

☛ This quiz contains questions covering the topics in part 2, "Word Play—And Why Not?" Do your best, then turn the page to see how you did. If you are brave enough to see how your Bible IQ rates, turn to page xii for our scale.

1. Where did Jesus perform his first miracle, turning water into wine?
2. Guess this Bible book's name by this basic description: The triviality of most human pursuits.
3. Who named the animals God created?
4. What two men saw a chariot of fire drawn by horses of fire?
5. Guess this Bible person's real name by this nickname: Stoned Martyr
6. Guess the name of this Bible book by its abbreviation: Jon.
7. What jealous king threw a javelin at David?
8. Which Bible translation does this abbreviation refer to: TLB?
9. Guess this Bible person's real name by this nickname: Dry Bones Man.
10. Guess the English title for this Bible book's original Greek title: *Kata Loukan* (Hint: the third of four).

Test Your Bible IQ (answers)

1. Cana (John 2:1)
2. Ecclesiastes
3. Adam (Genesis 2:19)
4. Elijah and Elisha (2 Kings 2:11)
5. Stephen, the first man to die for the faith, stoned to death (Acts 7)
6. Jonah (no, not *John*)
7. Saul (1 Samuel 18:11)
8. *The Living Bible*
9. Ezekiel, the prophet who had a vision of a valley of dry bones being brought to life by God (see Ezekiel 37)
10. The Gospel According to Luke

Also Known As . . .

☛ King David is sometimes known as the Sweet Singer of Israel because he authored many of the Psalms and was a noted musician. See if you can identify these Bible characters by their nicknames. (Some of these, by the way, are as off-the-wall and obscure as we could find—just for pleasure, of course. So don't feel bad about missing most of these.)

1. The Painted Woman
2. Mr. Encouragement
3. Tiny Taxman
4. The Wall Builder
5. Birthstone Man
6. Man One
7. Man Two
8. The Apple Woman
9. Mrs. Fool
10. Homicide Victim One
11. Seven Days Wonder
12. Mr. Fertility
13. Comforter and Joy
14. Timid Timmy
15. Mr. Schizo
16. Wise Guy
17. Mop Head
18. Earth Man
19. Henpecked King
20. Mr. and Mrs. Deceit
21. Mr. Marriage
22. Three Hot Men

Also Known As . . . (answers)

1. Jezebel, the wicked, idol-worshiping queen of Israel who "painted her face" (see 2 Kings 9:30)
2. Barnabas the apostle, who was a traveling companion of Paul and was known as the "son of encouragement" (see Acts 4:36—"son of consolation" in some translations)
3. Zacchaeus, the short tax collector who climbed a tree to see Jesus and was changed thereafter (Luke 19)
4. Nehemiah, who was in charge of rebuilding the walls of Jerusalem after the exile
5. Aaron, Israel's first high priest, whose priestly garment contained twelve stones that are the origin of the concept of birthstones
6. Adam (of course), the first man
7. Cain, Adam's first son (Did you remember that Cain, not Abel, was born first?)
8. Eve, the first to eat the forbidden fruit in the Garden of Eden; actually, the Bible doesn't say it was an apple. But tradition says apple, and who are we to argue with tradition?
9. Abigail, one of King David's wives, but first the wife (then widow) of the boorish and foolish Nabal (whose name literally means "fool")
10. Abel, murdered by his brother Cain
11. Zimri, the king of Israel who seized the throne, reigned for only seven days—then burned down the palace with himself inside
12. Abraham, who fathered his first son when he was age eighty-six (Genesis 16:16)
13. Abishag, the beautiful maiden brought to King David in his old age to be near him to warm his old bones (see 1 Kings 1)
14. Timothy, Paul's young follower, who was a devoted believer but somewhat reserved and shy (see 2 Timothy 1:7)
15. The demon-possessed man of the Gadarenes, who was healed by Jesus; the man—or rather, the demon(s) inside him—claimed to be called "Legion, for we are many" (see Mark 5:9).
16. Solomon the king, noted for his wisdom
17. Absalom, King David's handsome son, noted for his gorgeous mane of hair (see 2 Samuel 14:26)
18. Adam, the first man, formed by God from "the dust of the ground" (and, in fact, the name *Adam* in Hebrew means "earth")
19. Ahab, the wicked king of Israel, who let his idol-worshiping wife, Jezebel, lead him into even worse crimes
20. Ananias and Sapphira, the couple who lied to the apostle Peter about the money they donated to the church—and were then struck dead for their deceit (see Acts 5)
21. Solomon the king, who had hundreds of wives and concubines
22. Shadrach, Meshach, and Abednego, Daniel's three friends, thrown into the fiery furnace by King Nebuchadnezzar (see Daniel 3)

23. The Man Who Lost His Head over Dancing
24. Reaper Woman
25. The Cursing Prophet
26. Knee-Knocker
27. Fat Finger
28. Rainbow Threads
29. Red Sea Splitter
30. Dry Bones Man
31. Jew-Kicking King
32. King of the Dreams of Kings
33. The Giant-Killing Kid
34. Foxy Judge
35. Bear Baldy
36. In-Tents Couple
37. Woman Who Gives a Mean Haircut
38. Hot-Wheeled Prophet
39. Hairy Hunter
40. Beauty Pageant Queen of Iran
41. Baby-Killing King
42. Lead-Footed Charioteer

23. John the Baptist, who was beheaded after Herod's stepdaughter pleased Herod with her scintillating dance; her award for dancing: John the Baptist's head on a platter
24. Ruth, the faithful daughter-in-law of Naomi, who gleaned in the fields and was spotted there by her future husband, Boaz
25. Balaam, the false prophet of Moab who was summoned by the Moabite king to curse the Israelites (Numbers 22)
26. Belshazzar, the Babylonian king whose "knees knocked" when he saw the divine hand that appeared at his banquet and wrote on the wall; what it wrote was his message of doom (see Daniel 5).
27. Rehoboam, king of Judah and son of Solomon, who alienated many of the Israelites by boasting that his little finger was thicker than his father's thigh (speaking figuratively, that is) (see 1 Kings 12:10)
28. Joseph, Jacob's favorite son, who was given a "coat of many colors" by his doting father (see Genesis 37:3)
29. Moses, who parted the Red Sea so the Israelites could walk across and escape Pharaoh's army (see Exodus 14); more accurately, God parted the Red Sea, not Moses (or Charlton Heston).
30. Ezekiel, the prophet who had a vision of a valley of dry bones being brought to life by God (see Ezekiel 37)
31. Claudius, the Roman emperor who expelled the Jews from Rome (Acts 18:2)
32. Either Joseph (in Genesis) or Daniel (in Daniel), who interpreted the dreams of kings—in Joseph's case, the dreams of Pharaoh; in Daniel's case, the dreams of Nebuchadnezzar; in both cases, the men's interpretive powers resulted in their being raised to high rank.
33. David (of course), the shepherd boy who killed the giant Goliath and later became king of Israel
34. Samson, the judge of Israel who burnt the Philistines' crops by turning loose foxes with firebrands tied to their tail (Judges 15)
35. The prophet Elisha, who punished children who mocked his baldness by sending two bears upon them (2 Kings 2:23-24)
36. Aquila and Priscilla, Paul's friends and also, like Paul, tentmakers by profession
37. Delilah, Samson's Philistine girlfriend, who robbed Samson of his strength by cutting his long locks (Judges 16)
38. Elijah, the prophet who never died but was taken to heaven in a chariot of fire (2 Kings 2:11)
39. Esau, Jacob's hairy twin brother, whose favorite pastime was hunting (Genesis 25:27)
40. Esther, the Jewish woman who won the glamor competition to become queen of Persia (now known as Iran)
41. Herod, the wicked king of Judea who killed the boy infants of Bethlehem shortly after Jesus' birth
42. Jehu, the soldier and chariot driver who became king of Israel after being anointed by the prophet Elisha; the name *Jehu* has become a legendary name for a fast and furious driver (see 2 Kings 9:20).

43. Island Visionary
44. Lion Bait
45. Walking Corpse
46. Helpful Hooker
47. Tablet Man
48. Headless Apostle
49. Sister Act
50. Krazy King

Familiar Verse, Peculiar Order

☞ Placed in their proper order, the words are a familiar verse from the New Testament.

liberty is Lord of Spirit the is the there where

Four-Letter Words

☞ Each answer contains four letters (fear not—no profanity here).

1. What New Testament book tells the history of the early Christians?
2. What wicked king of Israel was married to the just-as-wicked Jezebel?
3. What "sea" mentioned in the Bible is actually a very salty landlocked lake?
4. John the Baptist referred to Jesus as the _____ of God.
5. What African country lay south of Egypt and was the home of Moses' wife?
6. Who was Jacob's first wife (before he married the prettier and better-loved Rachel)?
7. Who was the world's first murderer?
8. Which of the twelve tribes of Israel were Moses and Aaron descended from?

43. The apostle John, who recorded his visions in the book of Revelation while he was exiled on the isle of Patmos
44. Daniel, who was thrown (supposedly to his death) into a den of lions (Daniel 6:16)
45. Lazarus, who had already been entombed when Jesus caused him to rise from the dead (John 11)
46. Rahab, the Jericho prostitute who aided the Israelite spies in their capture of the city (Joshua 6:17)
47. Moses, who came down from Mount Sinai carrying the law on tablets of stone
48. James, who was the first of the apostles to die a martyr; he was executed by sword, by order of Herod (Acts 12:2).
49. Martha and Mary, two of Jesus' closest friends and followers and the sisters of Lazarus
50. Nebuchadnezzar, the Babylonian king who (as the prophet Daniel predicted) was driven from his palace insane and lived like a wild man (Daniel 4:33)

Familiar Verse, Peculiar Order (answer)

Where the Spirit of the Lord is, there is liberty. (2 Corinthians 3:17)

Four-Letter Words (answers)

1. Acts
2. Ahab (1 Kings 21:25)
3. Dead
4. Lamb (John 1:29)
5. Cush
6. Leah (Genesis 29)
7. Cain (who killed his brother Abel) (Genesis 4)
8. Levi

9. What, according to Paul, is greater than all the spiritual gifts?
10. According to Jesus, what falls on both the just and the unjust?
11. What was the Sabbath day made for?
12. What city received the longest of Paul's epistles?
13. What was Lot's wife turned into when she looked back on the doomed city of Sodom?
14. What Moabite woman was an ancestor of Jesus?
15. Who is the most important apostle in Acts?
16. Which author of a Gospel was referred to by Peter as "my son"?
17. Which of Noah's three sons were the Hebrews descended from?
18. Who was the first man in the Bible to die?
19. What was the apostle Paul's original name?
20. What substance in the Bible is often a symbol of bitterness?
21. What son was born to Adam and Eve after Cain had killed Abel?
22. What was the first month of the Jewish year?
23. What was hometown to the Philistine giant Goliath?
24. Who was made from the dust of the ground?
25. What direction of wind dried up the Red Sea so the Israelites could cross it?
26. What cruel Amalekite king was spared by Saul but chopped to pieces by Samuel?
27. What are the wise men at Jesus' birth sometimes called?
28. According to Jesus' parable, what does a foolish man build his house on?
29. What did Judas betray Jesus with?
30. What river (the longest in the world) is mentioned many times in the Bible, but never by name?
31. What are the streets of heaven paved with?
32. What was the disciple Matthew's other name?
33. What word, commonly used in the Bible and in Christian worship, means "so be it"?
34. What shape did the Holy Spirit take at Jesus' baptism?
35. What was the name of the first garden?
36. What is the most-mentioned pagan god in the Bible?
37. Who was Ruth's husband?
38. What nation was descended from Jacob's hairy twin brother, Esau?

9. Love (1 Corinthians 13)
10. Rain (Matthew 5:45)
11. Rest (Exodus 20)
12. Rome
13. Salt (Genesis 19:26)
14. Ruth (Matthew 1:5-16)
15. Paul
16. Mark (1 Peter 5:13); the expression "son" may be figurative.
17. Shem
18. Abel (Genesis 4)
19. Saul (Acts 7:58)
20. Gall (a bitter and poisonous herb) (Deuteronomy 32:32; Psalm 69:21)
21. Seth (Genesis 5:3-8)
22. Abib (Exodus 13:4; 23:15)
23. Gath (1 Samuel 17)
24. Adam (Genesis 2:7)
25. East (Exodus 14:21)
26. Agag (1 Samuel 15)
27. Magi
28. Sand (Matthew 7:26)
29. Kiss (Matthew 26:49)
30. Nile (which is usually just referred to as "the river")
31. Gold (Revelation 21:21)
32. Levi (Matthew 9:9; Mark 2:14)
33. Amen
34. Dove (John 1:32)
35. Eden (Genesis 2)
36. Baal (mentioned dozens of times in the Old Testament)
37. Boaz (Ruth 2-4)
38. Edom (Genesis 36)

39. What word, common in many Bible place names, means "house"?
40. Where did Jesus perform his first miracle, turning water into wine?
41. Which Gospel tells the story of the shepherds visiting the newborn Jesus?
42. What Israelite woman killed a Canaanite captain by driving a tent peg through his head?
43. In what Philistine city did Samson "bring the house down," killing many of the Philistines?
44. What prophet had a vision of a locust plague?
45. What did Naomi change her name to after she was widowed?
46. What nation worshiped a bloodthirsty god named Chemosh?
47. Who was the world's first drunk?
48. The Dead Sea is also called the _____ Sea.
49. Canaan was supposed to be a land flowing with _____ and honey.

Familiar Verse, Peculiar Order

☞ Placed in their proper order, the words are a familiar verse from Luke.

do Father know they forgive not them they what for

What's That Title Again?

☞ The books of the Bible were originally written in Hebrew (Old Testament) and Greek (New Testament)—and so were their titles. Some of the titles resemble our English translations—and some are not even close. Try your hand at guessing the English title for each Hebrew or Greek title listed here.

1. Apocalupsis (Hint: a book with many symbols)
2. Ekah (Hint: a very sad book)
3. Praxeis (Hint: Christian history)
4. Pros Philippesious (Hint: no, you probably don't need one for this)
5. Iakobou (Hint: an epistle)

39. Beth (as in Bethlehem, Bethel, Bethany, etc.)
40. Cana (John 2:1)
41. Luke (chapter 2)
42. Jael (Judges 4)
43. Gaza (Judges 16)
44. Joel (1:1–2:27)
45. Mara (which means "bitter," Ruth 1:20)
46. Moab (2 Kings 23:13)
47. Noah (who, after surviving the Flood, proceeded to plant a vineyard—and enjoy it) (Genesis 9:20-21)
48. Salt (which is appropriate—it is both lifeless and salty)
49. Milk (Exodus 3:8)

Familiar Verse, Peculiar Order (answer)

Father, forgive them, for they know not what they do. (Luke 23:34)

What's That Title Again? (answers)

1. Revelation
2. Lamentations
3. Acts
4. The Letter to the Philippians
5. The Letter of James

6. Wayyiqra (Hint: rituals and sacrifices)
7. Shopetim (Hint: great leaders and lots of wars)
8. Bemidbar (Hint: Hebrew wilderness wanderings)
9. Pros Ebraious (Hint: an epistle to no specific place)
10. Kata Loukan (Hint: the third of four)
11. Welleh Semot (Hint: Egyptian setting)
12. Dibre Hayyamim (Hint: kings and temples)
13. Elleh Haddebarim (Hint: Moses near the end)
14. Kata Markon (Hint: a familiar man's name)
15. Bereshith (Hint: early, early history)
16. Tehellim (Hint: often set to music)
17. Pros Romaious (Hint: to a large city)
18. Shir Hashirim (Hint: romance)
19. Pros Timotheon A (Hint: the second word gives this one away)
20. Iouda (Hint: one chapter only)
21. Masal (Hint: words for the wise)
22. Kata Mathaion (Hint: the first of four)
23. Pros Galatas (Hint: a letter)
24. Petrou A (Hint: one of the twelve apostles)
25. Melekhim (Hint: ruling class)
26. Pros Korinthious A (Hint: you don't need one for this)
27. Yonah (Hint: again, you don't need one)
28. Yehoshua (Hint: shorten the name)
29. Pros Philemona (Hint: one chapter)
30. Kata Ioannen (Hint: a common man's name)
31. Pros Ephesious (Hint: you don't need one)
32. Qohelet (Hint: a lot of wisdom)
33. Pros Titon (Hint: a young pastor)
34. Yoel (Hint: not needed)
35. Pros Kolossaeis (Hint: not needed)

Familiar Verse, Peculiar Order

☞ Placed in their proper order, the words are a familiar verse from Matthew.

the the are earth for inherit meek shall they blessed

---

6. Leviticus
7. Judges
8. Numbers
9. The Letter to the Hebrews
10. The Gospel according to Luke
11. Exodus
12. 1 and 2 Chronicles (which, in the Hebrew, were one book)
13. Deuteronomy
14. The Gospel according to Mark
15. Genesis
16. Psalms
17. The Letter to the Romans
18. The Song of Solomon
19. The First Letter to Timothy
20. The Letter of Jude
21. Proverbs
22. The Gospel according to Matthew
23. The Letter to the Galatians
24. The First Letter of Peter
25. 1 and 2 Kings (which, in the original Hebrew, were one book)
26. The First Letter to the Corinthians
27. Jonah
28. Joshua
29. The Letter to Philemon
30. The Gospel according to John
31. The Letter to the Ephesians
32. Ecclesiastes
33. The Letter to Titus
34. Joel
35. The Letter to the Colossians

Familiar Verse, Peculiar Order (answer)

Blessed are the meek, for they shall inherit the earth. (Matthew 5:5)

That Reminds Me of a Movie Title . . .

☛ When you see the film title *The Ten Commandments,* you think *Ah yes, a movie about Moses and the Exodus.* But are there film titles that *remind* you of a character or incident in the Bible? For example: Does *Gone with the Wind* remind you of someone? How about the prophet Elijah, taken to heaven in a whirlwind (2 Kings 2)?

Herewith we present—for the movie buff, for Bible readers, and for anyone else—movie titles, for which you will provide a biblical incident appropriate to the title.

1. *The Age of Innocence*
2. *Demolition Man*
3. *The Accused*
4. *Adam's Rib*
5. *Rain Man*
6. *You Only Live Twice*
7. *You Can't Take It with You*
8. *A Tale of Two Cities*
9. *Three Men and a Baby*
10. *Giant*
11. *Death on the Nile*
12. *Best Friends*
13. *Boys Town*
14. *Chariots of Fire*
15. *Dirty Dancing*
16. *Hair*
17. *Resurrection*
18. *My Favorite Wife*
19. *The Fugitive*
20. *Unfaithfully Yours*
21. *Betrayal*
22. *City Heat*
23. *Lifeboat*
24. *Sister Act*
25. *Medicine Man*
26. *Sleeping with the Enemy*
27. *Bringing Up Baby*
28. *Breaking Away*
29. *Come to the Stable*
30. *The Exorcist*

That Reminds Me of a Movie Title . . . (answers)

1. Adam and Eve in the Garden of Eden (Genesis 2–3)
2. Samson, the Hebrew strongman who killed hundreds of Philistines by toppling their crowded temple (Judges 16)
3. Jesus, of course, on trial before Pilate and Herod
4. Eve (naturally)
5. Noah, who survived the world's great flood (Genesis 7–8)
6. Lazarus, raised from the dead by Jesus (John 11). (Or, for that matter, Jesus himself)
7. The rich man in Jesus' parable of the beggar Lazarus and the rich man who died and went straight to hell (Luke 16)
8. The wicked cities of Sodom and Gomorrah, destroyed by God (Genesis 19)
9. The three wise men and the baby Jesus (naturally)
10. Goliath, the Philistine giant killed by the shepherd boy David (1 Samuel 17)
11. Moses killing the Egyptian overseer (Exodus 2:12)
12. David and Jonathan, the most famous friends in the Bible
13. The homosexually inclined city of Sodom (Genesis 18)
14. The prophet Elisha, who saw a vision of the Lord's chariots of fire (2 Kings 6:17)
15. The entrancing dance of Herod's stepdaughter, which pleased Herod so much that he offered her anything she wanted; she asked for the head of John the Baptist.
16. Samson, the Israelite judge whose strength lay in his long locks
17. Oh, come on. Don't you know?
18. Jacob, who labored for fourteen years in order to have Rachel as his wife (though she wasn't his *only* wife)
19. The prophet Elijah, on the run from wicked Queen Jezebel (1 Kings 19)
20. The prophet Hosea's unfaithful wife, Gomer
21. Judas Iscariot, who betrayed Jesus
22. Sodom and Gomorrah, destroyed by God because of their wickedness (Genesis 19)
23. Noah's ark, naturally
24. Rachel and Leah, the two sisters who both married Jacob
25. Luke, the physician and friend of Paul (Colossians 4:14)
26. Samson, the Israelite leader who consorted with the Philistine harlot Delilah
27. The infant Moses, taken up from the river by the daughter of Pharaoh (Exodus 2)
28. The Israelites' exodus from slavery in Egypt
29. The shepherds at Jesus' birth in Bethlehem
30. Jesus who expelled many demons from people

31. *The King and I*
32. *The Music Man*
33. *The Big Sleep*
34. *Don't Go Near the Water*
35. *The Rains Came*
36. *Marathon Man*
37. *Heaven Can Wait*
38. *The Good Son*
39. *Baby Boom*
40. *The Birth of a Nation*
41. *Bound for Glory*
42. *The Divorcee*
43. *The Empire Strikes Back*
44. *Kiss of Death*
45. *Lethal Weapon*
46. *The More the Merrier*
47. *Blood and Sand*
48. *Lady Sings the Blues*
49. *An Affair to Remember*
50. *Leap of Faith*
51. *Room at the Top*
52. *Little Murders*
53. *The Longest Day*
54. *The Man Who Loved Women*
55. *The Thin Man*
56. *Breathless*
57. *The Champ*
58. *Children of a Lesser God*
59. *A Cry in the Dark*

31. Joseph, the right-hand man at the court of Pharaoh (Genesis 40–50)
32. David, a noted musician and author of many of the psalms
33. The deep sleep of Adam, during which God took one of Adam's ribs and formed it into Eve (Genesis 2:21)
34. The plague of turning the Nile River into blood (Exodus 7)
35. Noah in the ark, of course
36. The prophet Elijah, who outran wicked King Ahab's horse-drawn chariot for many miles (1 Kings 18:46)
37. Lazarus, buried but then raised from the dead by Jesus (John 11)
38. Jesus, of course, the Son of God
39. Undoubtedly the judge Gideon, who had seventy sons (Judges 8:30)
40. The formation of the nation of Israel after the exodus from Egypt
41. The prophet Elijah, taken to heaven in a chariot of fire (2 Kings 2)
42. The Samaritan woman at the well, married and divorced five times (John 4)
43. The Egyptian army pursuing the Hebrews after they had left Egypt
44. Judas Iscariot's fateful kissing of Jesus
45. The jawbone of an ass—the weapon Samson used to kill a thousand Philistines (Judges 15:15)
46. King Solomon, with his seven hundred wives and three hundred concubines (1 Kings 11:3)
47. Moses killing the Egyptian overseer and hiding his body in the sand (Exodus 2:12)
48. Poor Naomi, downhearted after her husband and sons all died (Ruth)
49. The adulterous affair of David and Bathsheba; this resulted in the death of Bathsheba's husband, Uriah, and also a curse of bloodshed on David's household (2 Samuel 11–12). *Or,* how about the affair of Samson and Delilah?
50. The doubting disciple Thomas, who finally came to believe (John 20)
51. The Tower of Babel, which the people tried to build all the way to heaven—until God confused their languages, thus scuttling the project (Genesis 11)
52. Herod's slaughter of the infant boys of Bethlehem (Matthew 2:16)
53. Joshua and the Israelites' notorious victory over the Amorites, where "the sun stood still and the moon stayed" until the Amorites were crushed (Joshua 10)
54. Solomon with his hundreds of wives and concubines
55. Has to be John the Baptist, since you would expect anyone who lived on locusts and honey to be a bit gaunt (see Mark 1:6)
56. The newly formed (from dust) Adam—before God breathed "the breath of life" into him (Genesis 2:7)
57. David, who (according to the song of the Israelite women) had slain "tens of thousands" (as compared with poor King Saul, who had only slain thousands) (1 Samuel 18:7)
58. The priests of the false god Baal, who lost (obviously) in the contest between themselves and the Lord's prophet Elijah (1 Kings 18)
59. The young boy Samuel, whom the Lord called to at night (1 Samuel 3)

60. *Deliverance*
61. *Fantastic Voyage*
62. *A Double Life*
63. *The Great Lie*
64. *Jaws*
65. *The Marrying Kind*
66. *Possessed*
67. *The Man Who Knew Too Much*
68. *The Snake Pit*
69. *Indecent Proposal*
70. *Shadow of a Doubt*
71. *Till the Clouds Roll By*
72. *True Grit*
73. *Pillow Talk*
74. *The Razor's Edge*
75. *Rocky*
76. *The Rainmaker*
77. *The Old Man and the Sea*
78. *The Fallen Idol*
79. *Torn Curtain*
80. *Trading Places*

60. The Israelites' miraculous exodus from slavery in Egypt
61. Jonah, whose storm-tossed voyage got even more fantastic when he was thrown overboard and found himself in the belly of a fish
62. Lazarus, who lived, died, then was raised to life again by Jesus (John 11)
63. The lie Satan told to Eve: "And the serpent said unto the woman, Ye shall not surely die" (Genesis 3:4).
64. The Beast of the end times, which had seven heads, each with a lion's mouth (Revelation 13)
65. King Solomon, with his seven hundred wives (not to mention three hundred concubines) (1 Kings 11:3)
66. The Gadarene demon-possessed man, who had not just one demon but a whole "legion" of them (Luke 8)
67. The Lord's prophet Micaiah, who predicted (correctly) that wicked King Ahab would be killed in battle; for this unpleasant prediction, Ahab had him jailed and put on a diet of bread and water 1 Kings 22).
68. Pharaoh's palace—since Moses and Aaron and the Pharaoh's magicians were turning their rods into serpents (Exodus 7)
69. The lustful wife of the Egyptian official Potiphar, whose famous come-on to the virtuous Joseph was, "Lie with me" (Genesis 39).
70. The doubtful disciple Thomas, who could hardly believe Jesus had been raised from the dead (John 20:24-29)
71. Noah in the ark
72. David, the little shepherd boy who took on the Philistine giant Goliath (1 Samuel 17)
73. Strongman Samson, foolish enough to tell wicked Delilah, his mistress, the secret of his great strength (Judges 16)
74. Samson, again—*after* Delilah had learned his secret and used it against him
75. Peter, the disciple Jesus nicknamed "the Rock" (Matthew 16:18)
76. The prophet Elijah, who declared a drought in Israel for three years, then finally brought rain (1 Kings 17–18)
77. Noah, of course, who was already 350 years old at the time of the Flood (Genesis 9:28)
78. The Philistine god Dagon, whose idol was toppled by being in the presence of Israel's ark of the covenant (1 Samuel 5)
79. The great curtain in the temple, divinely ripped in half when Jesus died (Matthew 27:51)
80. Isaac's twin sons, Jacob and Esau—specifically, Jacob tricking his father out of Esau's inheritance by pretending to be Esau (Genesis 27:22); the old, blind Isaac fell for it.

Familiar Verse, Peculiar Order

☞ Placed in their proper order, the words are a familiar verse from the New Testament.

been faith grace have saved through you by

In a Nutshell: Books of the Bible, in Brief

☞ Sixty-six books in the Bible, and even assuming you can name them in order, do you know the basic theme (or story) in each one? Below, for each book of the Bible, is a "nutshell" condensed version. Name the book for each. (And, no, they aren't in the biblical order—what fun would that be?)

1. Israel in Egypt—and out
2. The faithful widow woman
3. Love songs
4. The end of this world, and the beginning of a new one
5. Letter to a slave owner
6. Letter to a lady
7. Wise sayings, good advice
8. Prophet in occupied Jerusalem—and in Egypt
9. Jesus' story, beginning before time began
10. Laws, sacrifices, laws, sacrifices
11. Samuel, Saul, David
12. One short chapter of prophecy against Edom
13. Jesus' story, including the wise men
14. The long letter with a love of love, and info on the resurrection of believers
15. The beginning of it all
16. Letter for Jewish Christians
17. The prophet in Babylon, seeing weird visions
18. Solomon's reign, the divided kingdom, the prophet Elijah
19. Samson, Gideon, and other leaders of Israel
20. Israel in the wilderness
21. The prophet to Nineveh, plus a great fish
22. Letter packing the most theology, written to the Eternal City
23. David's reign, plus page after page of family trees

Familiar Verse, Peculiar Order (answer)

By grace you have been saved through faith. (Ephesians 2:8)

In a Nutshell: Books of the Bible, in Brief (answers)

1. Exodus
2. Ruth
3. The Song of Solomon
4. Revelation
5. Philemon
6. 2 John
7. Proverbs
8. Jeremiah
9. John (which opens with "In the beginning was the Word. . . .")
10. Leviticus
11. 1 Samuel
12. Obadiah
13. Matthew
14. 1 Corinthians (with chapter 13 being the famous "love" chapter)
15. Genesis
16. Hebrews
17. Ezekiel
18. 1 Kings
19. Judges
20. Numbers
21. Jonah
22. Romans
23. 1 Chronicles

24. A prophet of repentance, with a locust plague
25. David and his family
26. Letter about faith plus good deeds
27. A prophecy of the great Day of the Lord
28. A prophecy regarding the Assyrians' cruelty
29. Pastoral advice to the pastor on the isle of Crete
30. Rebuilding the walls of Jerusalem after the exile in Babylon
31. Monarchs of Israel and Judah, captured by Assyrians and Babylonians
32. A letter of rejoicing and humility
33. A letter of freedom from the law and human rules
34. Prophecies that include a Messiah born in Bethlehem
35. A letter to persecuted Christians
36. The love letter
37. A good man suffering
38. The triviality of most human pursuits
39. The prophecy of justice
40. The conquest of Canaan
41. A dialogue between God and the prophet
42. The works of the apostles
43. The Jews of Persia saved from annihilation
44. How a young pastor can be a "man of God"
45. A letter about freedom from man-made rules and silly philosophizing
46. Jesus' story, short and simple
47. Weeping over Jerusalem destroyed
48. History from Solomon to the reign of Cyrus
49. A lot of Law, and the death of Moses
50. Religious reform after the return from the Exile
51. A letter against false teachers, and the coming of the Lord
52. Prophecy against wickedness, and many comforts concerning the coming Messiah
53. A brief letter to Gaius
54. A letter of Paul's gratitude and a defense of his integrity
55. The prophet with an unfaithful wife
56. A letter about unity in Christ and family harmony
57. Judgment on unfaithful rituals, and the promise of a new Elijah
58. A letter encouraging the young pastor, with a note on the inspiration of the Bible

24. Joel
25. 2 Samuel
26. James
27. Zephaniah (Note: Though several of the Old Testament prophets mention "the Day of the Lord," only Zephaniah calls it the *great* Day of the Lord, a key theme in the book.)
28. Nahum
29. Titus
30. Nehemiah
31. 2 Kings
32. Philippians
33. Galatians
34. Micah
35. 1 Peter
36. 1 John (which mentions love *many* times)
37. Job
38. Ecclesiastes
39. Amos
40. Joshua
41. Habakkuk
42. Acts
43. Esther
44. 1 Timothy
45. Colossians
46. Mark
47. Lamentations
48. 2 Chronicles
49. Deuteronomy
50. Ezra
51. 2 Peter
52. Isaiah
53. 3 John
54. 2 Corinthians
55. Hosea
56. Ephesians
57. Malachi
58. 2 Timothy

59. A letter praising the persecuted believers, with information about the coming of the Lord
60. Rebuilding the temple, with some curious visions
61. Jesus' story, including the shepherds
62. The glory of the rebuilt temple in Jerusalem
63. A letter about the man of lawlessness and the Second Coming
64. Hymns, songs, hymns, laments, songs, and more songs
65. A young righteous man in pagan courts
66. A very short letter about the sin and doom of godless men

Familiar Verse, Peculiar Order

☛ Placed in their proper order, the words are a familiar verse from the New Testament.

appear Christ judgment must of seat the all we before

Four-Letter Words (Part II)

1. Which apostle was the brother of James?
2. In what animal's carcass did Samson find a honeycomb?
3. In what animal shape did Aaron make the golden idol the Israelites worshiped while Moses was away?
4. What was Adam made of?
5. What bird did Noah send out of the ark after the Flood ceased?
6. What did King David's rebellious son Absalom have an abundance of?
7. What New Testament book refers to Satan and the angel Michael fighting over the body of Moses?
8. Which apostle wrote five books of the New Testament?
9. Who was the commander of David's armies?
10. Who wrote the book of Acts, in addition to writing one of the Gospels?
11. What was the ark of the covenant housed in before Solomon housed it in the temple?
12. What book of the Old Testament tells of the Jews' return from Babylon?

59. 1 Thessalonians
60. Zechariah
61. Luke
62. Haggai
63. 2 Thessalonians
64. Psalms
65. Daniel
66. Jude

Familiar Verse, Peculiar Order (answer)

We must all appear before the judgment seat of Christ.
(2 Corinthians 5:10)

Four-Letter Words (Part II) (answers)

1. John (Matthew 4:21)
2. Lion (Judges 14:8)
3. Calf (Exodus 32:4)
4. Dust (Genesis 2:7)
5. Dove (Genesis 8)
6. Hair (2 Samuel 14:26)
7. Jude (verse 9)
8. John (the Gospel, 1 John, 2 John, 3 John, and Revelation)
9. Joab (2 Samuel)
10. Luke
11. Tent (Exodus 40; also called "tabernacle" in some translations)
12. Ezra

13. What plague in Egypt was mingled with fire?
14. What was Saul the first of in Israel?
15. What musical instrument did King David play?
16. What Babylonian god's name is included in the name of King Nebuchadnezzar?
17. According to Jesus, what type of persons will always be among us?
18. What wintertime substance symbolizes purity and whiteness?
19. The book of Revelation is directed to seven Christian congregations in what region?
20. Who was the world's only righteous man when God chose to destroy the world?
21. What word, common in Bible place names, means "well"?
22. What prophet was a herdsman "two years before the earthquake"?
23. Which is the shortest of the four Gospels?
24. Who was bitten by a venomous snake but survived the bite?
25. What type of head did the prophet Elisha have?
26. What king, anointed by the prophet Elijah, slaughtered the idol-worshiping clan of King Ahab?
27. What bird did Jesus tell his followers to be as innocent as?
28. What water animal multiplied to produce the second plague on the Egyptians?
29. What evil king reigned only two years and was father of the righteous king Josiah?
30. What did Noah live in after he left the ark?
31. What coastal city supplied King David with cedar wood for building?
32. What did Jesus turn water into?
33. What instrument do the saints in heaven play?
34. Who was struck down by a vision of the Lord while on his way to persecute Christians?
35. What drink was offered to Jesus on the cross but refused by him?
36. According to John's Gospel, what existed before all else?
37. What Greek god was the apostle Barnabas mistaken for?
38. Who was the original nudist?
39. What mountain in Jerusalem is mentioned in the Bible more than any other mountain?
40. What did Jesus come to save people from?

13. Hail (Exodus 9:24); the meaning may be that the hailstorm also included lightning.
14. King
15. Harp (or in some translations, "lyre") (1 Samuel 16:23)
16. Nebo (Isaiah 46:1); various forms of the name were prevalent in the ancient world, including Nebo, Nebu, and Nabu.
17. Poor (Mark 14:7)
18. Snow (Matthew 28:3; Revelation 1:14)
19. Asia (which in those days was not the whole continent of Asia, but only the area we now call Turkey)
20. Noah (Genesis 6:8)
21. Beer (as in Beersheba)
22. Amos
23. Mark
24. Paul (Acts 28)
25. Bald (2 Kings 2); some children lived to regret their making fun of his condition.
26. Jehu (2 Kings 9)
27. Dove (Matthew 10:16)
28. Frog (Exodus 8)
29. Amon (2 Kings 21)
30. Tent (Genesis 9:21)
31. Tyre (2 Samuel 5:11)
32. Wine (John 2)
33. Harp (Revelation 14:2)
34. Paul (Acts 9)
35. Wine (Mark 15:23)
36. Word (John 1:1)
37. Zeus (or Jupiter, in some translations) (Acts 14:12); after Paul and Barnabas performed a healing at Lystra, the natives assumed the two men were the gods Hermes and Zeus.
38. Adam (Genesis 2:25—"naked . . . and not ashamed")
39. Zion
40. Sins (Matthew 1:21)

41. What roaring beast is Satan like, according to the New Testament?
42. What sister of Martha and Lazarus was a close friend of Jesus?
43. What Gospel author and friend of Paul's was called "the beloved physician"?
44. Who named the animals God created?
45. What beast did the apostle Paul claim to have been saved from?
46. What source of light is the law like for the devout believer?
47. What Christian leader was a Roman citizen?
48. Who asked God the question "Am I my brother's keeper?"
49. What everyday substance was changed into a plague of lice by Moses?
50. Who built a city called Enoch, east of Eden?

Familiar Verse, Peculiar Order

☞ Placed in their proper order, the words are a familiar verse from Luke.

commit Father hands I my into spirit your

Waiting for the "El"

☞ *El* in Hebrew means "God," which is why so many Old Testament names contain an "el" at either the beginning or the end of the word. (Names in Hebrew had to *mean* something, not just sound good. Daniel's name, for example, means "God is judge.") Each answer below contains an *el*. (A helpful hint in this section: Almost all the names are from the Old Testament instead of the New.)

1. What prophet was a thorn in the side of wicked King Ahab and Queen Jezebel?
2. What town in Israel has a name meaning "God's house"?
3. Who was John the Baptist's aged mother?
4. What prophet was noted as being bald?
5. What great leader of Israel anointed Saul and David as kings?
6. What was Jacob's new name after he wrestled all night with an angel?

41. Lion (1 Peter 5:8)
42. Mary (John 11:1)
43. Luke (Colossians 4:14)
44. Adam (Genesis 2:19)
45. Lion (2 Timothy 4:17)
46. Lamp (Psalms 119:105)
47. Paul (Acts 23:27)
48. Cain (Genesis 4:9)
49. Dust (Exodus 8:16-17)
50. Cain (Genesis 4:17)

Familiar Verse, Peculiar Order (answer)

Father, into your hands I commit my spirit (Luke 23:46)

Waiting for the "El" (answers)

1. Elijah (1 Kings); the name Elijah means "Yahweh is God."
2. Bethel; *beth* meaning "house," *el* meaning "God"
3. Elizabeth (Luke 1); her name means "God is my oath."
4. Elisha (2 Kings 2); his name means "God is salvation."
5. Samuel, a name meaning "name of God"
6. Israel (Genesis 32); the name means "wrestles with God."

7. According to one Old Testament prophet, there will come a day when young men will see visions and old men will dream dreams. Which prophet?

8. What was the original name of the young Israelite man named Belteshazzar?

9. What prophet's name means "God is strong"?

10. Who told Mary that her son was to be named Jesus?

11. What prophet did God tell to shave his head and beard?

12. Who was the mother of the Levitical priesthood?

13. What prophet was a very hairy man?

14. Which prophet, famous for his vision of the dry bones, was with the exiles in Babylon?

15. Which prophet predicted the outpouring of God's Spirit upon all people?

16. What prophet outran a king's chariot and a team of horses?

17. Who was forbidden to mourn the death of his beautiful wife?

18. Who told wayward King Saul that obeying God's voice was more important than sacrificing animals?

19. Who heard God's voice after running away from Queen Jezebel?

20. Who heard the voice of God as he watched four mysterious creatures flying under a crystal dome?

21. What famous rabbi was Paul's teacher?

22. What boy was called out of his sleep by the voice of God?

23. What upright young man was made ruler over the whole province of Babylon?

24. Who referred to Mary as the "mother of my Lord"?

25. What son of Abraham was supposed to have been against everyone, and everyone against him?

26. What priest had two wayward sons who slept with the women who worked at the entrance of the tabernacle?

27. What noble prophet's sons were notorious for taking bribes?

28. What soldier, David's oldest brother, picked at David for coming to the battle lines?

29. What prophet's word caused the Syrian soldiers to be struck blind?

30. What prophet triumphed when God consumed the offering on the altar and shamed the prophets of Baal?

31. What priest scolded a distressed woman because he thought she had been drinking at the tabernacle?

7. Joel (2:28)
8. Daniel (1:6-7); his name was changed while he was in Babylon. Daniel means "God is judge."
9. Ezekiel, whose name means "God strengthens"
10. Gabriel, the angel (Luke 1:26-31); Gabriel means "strong man of God."
11. Ezekiel (5:1-4)
12. Elisheba, wife of Aaron (Exodus 6:23)
13. Elijah (2 Kings 1:8)
14. Ezekiel
15. Joel
16. Elijah (1 Kings 18:46)
17. Ezekiel (24:16-18)
18. Samuel (1 Samuel 15:22)
19. Elijah (1 Kings 19:13)
20. Ezekiel (1:22-24)
21. Gamaliel (Acts 22:3), whose name means "reward of God"
22. Samuel (1 Samuel 3:2-10)
23. Daniel (2:48)
24. Elizabeth (Luke 1:41-43)
25. Ishmael (Genesis 16:12), whose name means "God hears"
26. Eli (1 Samuel 2:22)
27. Samuel's (1 Samuel 8:1-3)
28. Eliab (1 Samuel 17:28)
29. Elisha's (2 Kings 6:18-23)
30. Elijah (1 Kings 18)
31. Eli, who scolded Hannah, future mother of Samuel (1 Samuel 1:13-14)

32. What two men saw a chariot of fire drawn by horses of fire?
33. The angel of the Lord appeared to the banished Hagar and told her what to name her child. What was the child's name?
34. What was the name of the angel who appeared to Mary and to Zacharias?
35. Who had a vision of the Ancient of Days seated upon a throne?
36. According to Revelation, which angel fights against Satan?
37. Who made an axhead float on the water?
38. Which angel helped Daniel understand the future?
39. What prophet parted the Jordan River by striking it with his cloak?
40. According to Jude's epistle, who disputed with Satan over the body of Moses?
41. Who told Saul that rebellion was as bad as witchcraft?
42. What name (which applied to Jesus) means "God with us"?
43. What prophet was told to cut off his hair and scatter a third of it in the wind?
44. What prophet experienced a furious wind that split the hills and shattered the rocks?
45. What prophet had a vision of the four winds lashing the surface of the oceans?
46. Who had a vision of a river of fire?
47. Who lived by Kerith Brook, where he was fed by ravens?
48. What city was noted for its golden calf idols?
49. What prophet ordered a king to shoot arrows out of a window?
50. What priest was too indulgent toward his spoiled sons?
51. What prophet prophesied while accompanied by a minstrel?
52. Who was the prophet Samuel's father?
53. Who was the first of Israel's judges?

Familiar Verse, Peculiar Order

☞ Placed in their proper order, the words are a familiar verse from John.

am the and I life resurrection the

32. Elijah and Elisha (2 Kings 2:11)
33. Ishmael (Genesis 16:1-12)
34. Gabriel (Luke 1:5-38)
35. Daniel (7:9)
36. Michael (Revelation 12:7), whose name means "Who is like God?"
37. Elisha (2 Kings 6:4-7)
38. Gabriel (Daniel 8:15-26; 9:21-27)
39. Elijah (2 Kings 2:8-14)
40. Michael the archangel (Jude 9)
41. Samuel (1 Samuel 15:23)
42. Immanuel (Matthew 1:23)
43. Ezekiel (5:2)
44. Elijah (1 Kings 19:11)
45. Daniel (7:2)
46. Daniel (7:10)
47. Elijah (1 Kings 17:1-4)
48. Bethel; Dan and Bethel were the two cities chosen by Israel's King Jeroboam as worship centers to substitute for the temple of Jerusalem. Jeroboam set up calf idols in both towns (but since this is the "el" category, obviously Dan is not the correct answer).
49. Elisha (2 Kings 13:17)
50. Eli (1 Samuel 3:12-13)
51. Elisha (2 Kings 3:14-16)
52. Elkanah, a name meaning "God has possessed"
53. Othniel (Judges 3) (If you knew this one, consider yourself well-versed in the Old Testament.)

Familiar Verse, Peculiar Order (answer)

I am the resurrection, and the life. (John 11:25)

Also Known As . . . (Part II)

☛ See if you can identify these Bible characters by their nicknames. (Note: There are no repeat names from the previous set of "Also Known As" questions.)

1. Big Man Who Got Stoned
2. Eunuch Evangelizer
3. The Census Emperor
4. The Diplomatic Rabbi
5. Hard-hearted Egyptian
6. Temporary Water-Walker
7. Mediterranean Missionary
8. Jarring Soldier
9. Canaan Crusher
10. Long Liver
11. Unhappy Medium
12. Maid without a House
13. Blind Man's Bluff
14. Mother Bitterness
15. Spirit Broker
16. King Rash
17. Caravan Queen
18. Iron Horns
19. Leper Soldier
20. Queen Dynasty-Killer
21. Child Sacrifice (Almost)
22. Seducer Who Cried "Rape!"
23. Patricide Princes

Also Known As . . . (Part II) (answers)

1. Goliath, the Philistine giant killed by a stone from David's sling
2. Philip, the evangelist who witnessed to the Ethiopian eunuch (see Acts 8)
3. Augustus Caesar, the Roman emperor who ordered the imperial census, which resulted in Joseph and Mary going to Bethlehem (Luke 2)
4. Gamaliel, the rabbi who suggested that if the Christians were right in their beliefs, nothing could be done to stop the teaching (Acts 5)
5. Pharaoh, who in the book of Exodus is mentioned many times as having a "hard heart"
6. Peter, who walked on the water with Christ but lost faith and fell in (Matthew 14)
7. Paul, who spread the gospel throughout the Mediterranean area
8. Gideon, the judge who routed the Midianites by having his men shatter clay jars (Judges 7:19)
9. Joshua, who led the Israelites in their conquest of the land of Canaan
10. Methuselah, who, dying at age 969, was the longest-lived man in the Bible (Genesis 5:27)
11. The witch of Endor, who called up the ghost of Samuel at Saul's request but was fearful that she would be punished (1 Samuel 28)
12. Hagar, the handmaid of Sarah, Abraham's wife; she fled from Sarah into the wilderness after Sarah began to abuse her (Genesis 16; 21).
13. Jacob, who tricked his blind father, Isaac, into bestowing the inheritance on him instead of on his brother, Esau (Genesis 27)
14. Naomi, who became bitter after her husband and sons all died (book of Ruth)
15. Simon the sorcerer, who thought he could buy the Holy Spirit's power from the apostles (Acts 8)
16. Saul, Israel's first king, noted for his rash, headstrong deeds
17. The queen of Sheba, who came to Jerusalem with a huge caravan when she visited wise King Solomon (1 Kings 10)
18. The false prophet Zedekiah, who wore iron horns when he prophesied (wrongly) to King Ahab that Ahab would be victorious in battle (1 Kings 22)
19. Naaman, the commander of the Syrian army, who was healed of his leprosy by the prophet Elisha (2 Kings 5)
20. Athaliah, the wicked queen of Judah who destroyed all the royal family so she could continue her reign (2 Kings 11)
21. Isaac, who was (almost) sacrificed by his father, Abraham (Genesis 22)
22. The wife of Potiphar (Genesis 39); she tried repeatedly to seduce her husband's chief of staff, Joseph. Failing that, she claimed *he* tried to seduce *her.*
23. The sons of the Assyrian king Sennacherib, who murdered their father (the crime of patricide) when he was worshiping in the temple (2 Kings 19:36-37)

24. Iranian Genocide
25. Servant Song Man
26. Mr. Weepers
27. Prophet Overboard
28. Doubting Disciple
29. Star-gazing Wizards
30. Rich As Hell
31. Leper Lady
32. Loving Legionnaire
33. King of Fat
34. Mrs. Polygamy
35. Foxy Father-in-Law
36. Sheepish King
37. Flood Floater
38. Stoned Martyr
39. Treasury Traitor
40. Clock-watching King
41. Nazarene Nay-sayer
42. Freed Felon
43. Sightless Sorcerer
44. Salty Woman
45. Dr. Divorce

24. Haman, the Persian (Iranian) administrator who wanted to annihilate all the Jews in Persia (Esther 3) (Genocide is the crime of wiping out an entire nation or ethnic group.)

25. Isaiah the prophet, whose prophecies contain several predictions of a "suffering servant" who will come (Isaiah 41–44); these predictions are often referred to as the "Servant Songs."

26. Jeremiah, the "weeping" prophet, who wept over the idolatry of the Jews and also wrote the doleful book of Lamentations

27. Jonah, the Hebrew prophet who was thrown overboard and ended up (as you know) in the belly of a fish

28. Thomas, the disciple of Jesus who would not believe Jesus had risen from the dead until he had actually seen and touched him (John 20:24-29)

29. The wise men (or magi, or astrologers), who followed the star to find the newborn Jesus (Matthew 2)

30. The rich man in Jesus' parable (Luke 16); when he died he went straight to hell.

31. Miriam, the sister of Moses and Aaron, who was temporarily punished by the Lord by being struck with leprosy (Numbers 12:10)

32. Cornelius, the godly and charitable Roman soldier who was evangelized by the apostle Peter (Acts 10)

33. Eglon, the fat king of Moab, who was assassinated by the Hebrew judge Ehud; Eglon was so fat that Ehud's sword completely vanished inside the body (Judges 3:15-25).

34. The Samaritan woman at the well, who had been married five times and was living with another man (John 4:17)

35. Laban, Jacob's father-in-law; he tricked Jacob into laboring seven years in order to marry Rachel, then substituted her sister Leah. Jacob then had to labor another seven years to get the real Rachel (Genesis 29).

36. Mesha, the Moabite king noted as a shepherd (2 Kings 3:4)

37. Noah, of course

38. Stephen, the first man to die for the faith, stoned to death (Acts 7)

39. Judas, who betrayed Jesus and who was the treasurer among the disciples (John 12:6)

40. Hezekiah, the king who watched the Lord change the direction of shadows on the king's sundial (2 Kings 20:9-11)

41. Nathanael, a follower of Jesus, who at first doubted Jesus because he doubted that anything good could come out of Nazareth (John 1:46)

42. Barabbas, the criminal whom the Jerusalem mob asked to be set free instead of Jesus (Matthew 27:16)

43. Elymas, the evil court sorcerer on Cyprus who was cursed by Paul with blindness (Acts 13)

44. Lot's wife, who was turned into a pillar of salt because she turned and looked at the destroyed cities of Sodom and Gomorrah (Genesis 19)

45. Ezra the priest, who was horrified that Jews had intermarried with pagans and who ordered their divorce (Ezra 9)

Familiar Verse, Peculiar Order

☛ Placed in their proper order, the words are a familiar verse from the New Testament.

Christ with been crucified have I

Keep It Short!

☛ For several years the author worked for a publishing house that had this ironclad rule: *Never* abbreviate names of books of the Bible, since too many people aren't familiar enough with the Bible to know the standard abbreviations. Really? Try your skill on these—and note that we've thrown in some books from the Apocrypha just for fun. (Also, note that the briefest names—such as Mark and Acts and Ruth—are generally not abbreviated.)

1. Deut.
2. Col.
3. Lam.
4. Hag.
5. Lev.
6. Sus.
7. Rom.
8. Ps.
9. Hab.
10. Rev.
11. Josh.
12. Ex.
13. Jth.
14. Eph.
15. Heb.
16. Jon.
17. Ecclus.
18. Phil.
19. Philem.
20. Exod.
21. Neh.
22. Tob.
23. Dan.
24. Obad.

Familiar Verse, Peculiar Order (answer)

I have been crucified with Christ. (Galatians 2:20)

Keep It Short! (answers)

1. Deuteronomy
2. Colossians
3. Lamentations
4. Haggai
5. Leviticus
6. Susanna (from the Apocrypha, usually considered an addition to the book of Daniel)
7. Romans
8. Psalms
9. Habakkuk
10. Revelation
11. Joshua
12. Exodus
13. Judith (from the Apocrypha)
14 Ephesians
15. Hebrews
16. Jonah (no, not *John*)
17. Ecclesiasticus (from the Apocrypha, and not the same book as Ecclesiastes in the Old Testament)
18. Philippians
19. Philemon
20. Exodus (yes, both Ex. and Exod. are acceptable for Exodus)
21. Nehemiah
22. Tobit (from the Apocrypha)
23. Daniel
24. Obadiah

25. 2 Tim.
26. Prov.
27. Nah.
28. 1 Sam.
29. Bar.
30. Isa.
31. Mal.
32. 2 Thess.
33. Gen.
34. Ezek.
35. Zeph.
36. 1 Pet.
37. Eccles.
38. Matt.
39. S.S.
40. Num.

Familiar Verse, Peculiar Order

☞ Placed in their proper order, the words are a familiar verse from the New Testament.

are him conquerors loved than more through us we who

Four-Letter Words (Part III)

1. Who is mentioned first in the Bible as being very hairy?
2. What murderer was exiled to the land of Nod?
3. What evil king of Judah was killed by his servants?
4. What apostle preached to the intellectuals of Athens?
5. To whom did God say, "Who told thee that thou wast naked?"
6. According to one Old Testament prophet, there will come a day when young men will see visions and old men will dream dreams. Which prophet?
7. How many loaves of bread did Jesus use to feed the five thousand?
8. What is Satan the father of?

25. 2 Timothy
26. Proverbs
27. Nahum
28. 1 Samuel
29. Baruch (from the Apocrypha)
30. Isaiah
31. Malachi
32. 2 Thessalonians
33. Genesis
34. Ezekiel
35. Zephaniah
36. 1 Peter
37. Ecclesiastes
38. Matthew
39. Song of Solomon
40. Numbers

Familiar Verse, Peculiar Order (answer)

We are more than conquerors through him who loved us.
(Romans 8:37)

Four-Letter Words (Part III) (answers)

1. Esau (Genesis 27:11-23); he was Jacob's twin, even though Jacob
   was very smooth skinned.
2. Cain (Genesis 4:13-16)
3. Amon (2 Kings 21:23)
4. Paul (Acts 17:16-34)
5. Adam (Genesis 3:11)
6. Joel (2:28)
7. Five (Matthew 14:15-21)

9. What king of Israel was tormented by an evil spirit?

10. What New Testament writer ate a book that tasted good but gave him indigestion?

11. Solomon stated in Proverbs 18:22, "Whoso findeth a wife findeth a good thing." Who, in the New Testament, stated, "It is good for a man not to touch a woman"?

12. According to Isaiah, what is the food of the serpent?

13. Who was the first shepherd?

14. What Old Testament character must have been as strong as steel?

15. Who had a tearful farewell, with many kisses, at the city of Miletus?

16. What king of Israel claimed to be a devout worshiper of Baal in order to gather together Baal worshipers and butcher them?

17. What jealous king threw a javelin at David?

18. What apostle was almost done in by forty men waiting to ambush him at Jerusalem?

19. Who killed Amasa after holding his beard and kissing him?

20. Who was killed by God because he spilled out his seed on the ground?

21. By what other name was the tax collector Matthew known?

22. What empire's taxation led to Jesus being born in Bethlehem?

23. Who had Silas as a traveling companion on his second journey?

24. Mark 1:12-13 says that Jesus immediately went into the wilderness after his baptism and was there for forty days. Which Gospel claims that the day after his baptism he called Andrew and Peter to be his disciples?

25. What prophet had a vision of locusts with lions' teeth?

26. How did God keep the oceans clean?

27. What color was the cloth draped over the ark of the covenant?

28. According to Proverbs, what substance affects man like the bite of a snake?

29. What king disguised himself in order to consult with a sorceress?

30. What king led Israel into sin by allowing his evil wife to introduce Baal worship into the country?

8. Lies (John 8:44)
9. Saul (1 Samuel 16:14-23)
10. John (Revelation 10:9-10)
11. Paul (1 Corinthians 7:1)
12. Dust (Isaiah 65:25); Isaiah obviously was not an expert on reptiles.
13. Abel (Genesis 4:2)
14. Iron (Joshua 19:38); no joke, it's a man's name.
15. Paul (Acts 20:36-38)
16. Jehu (2 Kings 10)
17. Saul (1 Samuel 18:11)
18. Paul (Acts 23:21-23)
19. Joab (2 Samuel 20:9-10)
20. Onan (Genesis 38:9-10)
21. Levi (Luke 5:29-32)
22. Rome (Luke 2:1-7)
23. Paul (Acts 15–18)
24. John (1:35-42)
25. Joel (1:6)
26. Tide
27. Blue (Numbers 4:6)
28. Wine (Proverbs 23:32)
29. Saul (1 Samuel 28:8)
30. Ahab (1 Kings 16:29-33)

31. To whom did God say, "Why is thy countenance fallen? If thou doest well, shalt thou not be accepted?"
32. Who had surgery performed on him as he slept?
33. Which Gospel is the only one to mention the Roman soldiers piercing Jesus' body with a spear?
34. Who had a nephew that informed the Roman soldiers of a plot to kill a prisoner?
35. Who was commander of David's army?
36. What army commander was anointed by a prophet and told that he was to stamp out Ahab's dynasty?
37. What apostle told the early Christians that all believers were anointed by the Holy Spirit?
38. Who was the first man to build a city?
39. Who was the first person to practice wine making?
40. What righteous man started the practice of herding sheep?
41. What king received seventy human heads in baskets?
42. Who had a vision of an angel casting an enormous stone into the sea?
43. What book mentions the custom of giving a person one's shoe as a sign of transferring property?
44. What did Jesus eat after his resurrection to prove he was not a mere phantom?
45. Which prophet accused the people of Israel of selling the poor people for a pair of shoes?
46. What meat was eaten at the Passover meal?
47. According to Jeremiah, what kind of grape sets the children's teeth on edge?
48. Who hated his brother for taking away his birthright?
49. Who was the first man to murder his brother?
50. What village was home to the widow whose son Jesus raised from the dead?

Familiar Verse, Peculiar Order

☛ Placed in their proper order, the words are a familiar verse from John.

begotten for gave God he his loved only so son that the world

31. Cain (Genesis 4:6-7)
32. Adam (Genesis 2:21)
33. John (19:34)
34. Paul (Acts 23:16-22)
35. Joab (2 Samuel 8:16)
36. Jehu (2 Kings 9:1-11)
37. Paul (2 Corinthians 1:21)
38. Cain (Genesis 4:17)
39. Noah (Genesis 9:20-21)
40. Abel (Genesis 4:2)
41. Jehu (2 Kings 10:1-7)
42. John (Revelation 18:21)
43. Ruth (4:7)
44. Fish (Luke 24:38-43)
45. Amos (2:6)
46. Lamb (Exodus 12:1-20)
47. Sour, of course (Jeremiah 31:29)
48. Esau (Genesis 27:41)
49. Cain (Genesis 4:8)
50. Nain (Luke 7:11-15)

Familiar Verse, Peculiar Order (answer)

For God so loved the world, that he gave his only begotten Son. (John 3:16)

Keep It Short! (Again)

☛ Are you a "one-version" Bible reader, or do you read from several different translations? Are you aware of the differences among versions? Below are the standard abbreviations for the most popular versions. Which version does each abbreviation refer to?

1. TLB
2. KJV
3. RSV
4. NASB
5. TEV
6. GNB
7. JB
8. NEB
9. NAB
10. AV
11. NKJV
12. NIV
13. BIV

Familiar Verse, Peculiar Order

☛ Placed in their proper order, the words are a familiar verse from the New Testament.

be this conformed do not to world

Keep It Short! (Again) (answers)

1. *The Living Bible*
2. King James Version
3. Revised Standard Version
4. *New American Standard Bible*
5. Today's English Version
6. *Good News Bible* (which is simply an alternate name for the TEV)
7. *The Jerusalem Bible*
8. *The New English Bible*
9. *The New American Bible*
10. Authorized Version (another name for the King James Version)
11. New King James Version
12. New International Version
13. Biblically Illiterate Version (Trick! This one doesn't really exist!)

Familiar Verse, Peculiar Order (answer)

Do not be conformed to this world. (Romans 12:2)

Do You Remember?

☛ Would you like to see how much Bible trivia you can remember? Answer the questions (which you should have answered already in this section), and then see how well you rate on the scale on page xii.

1. Which of the twelve tribes of Israel were Moses and Aaron descended from?
2. Guess the English title for this Bible book's original Greek title: Yehoshua (Hint: shorten the name)
3. Guess this Bible book's name by this basic description: Letter packing the most theology, written to the Eternal City
4. Who asked God the question "Am I my brother's keeper?"
5. What upright young man was made ruler over the whole province of Babylon?
6. Guess this Bible person's real name by this nickname: Prophet Overboard
7. Guess the name of this Bible book by its abbreviation: Nah.
8. By what other name was the tax collector Matthew known?
9. Which Bible translation does this abbreviation refer to? AV
10. Who was the first man in the Bible to die?

Do You Remember? (answers)

1. Levi
2. Joshua
3. Romans
4. Cain (Genesis 4:9)
5. Daniel (2:48)
6. Jonah, the Hebrew prophet who was thrown overboard and ended up (as you know) in the belly of a fish
7. Nahum
8. Levi (Luke 5:29)
9. Authorized Version (another name for the King James Version)
10. Abel (Genesis 4)

PART 3

The Bible on the American Map

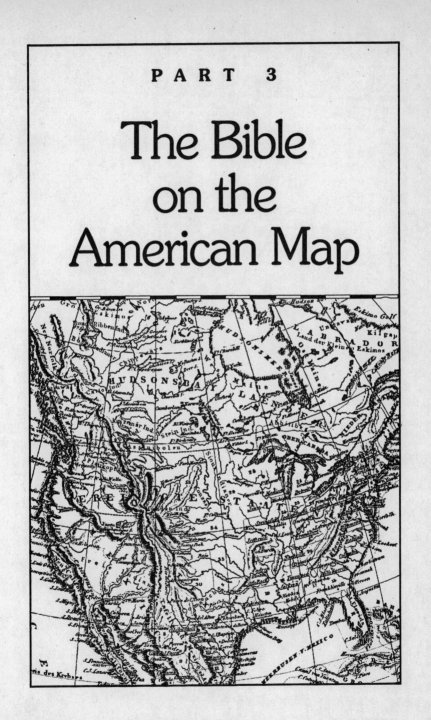

Test Your Bible IQ

☞ This quiz contains questions covering the topics in part 3, "The Bible on the American Map." Do your best, then turn the page to see how you did. If you are brave enough to see how your Bible IQ rates, turn to page xii for our scale.

1. What city with a biblical name do we associate with Elvis Presley?
2. Minnesota's capital city is named after which Bible character?
3. The Mennonite church has its archives in an Indiana town named for the Hebrew district of Egypt. What is the name of the town?
4. What Texas city has a name that means (in Latin) "body of Christ"?
5. St. Joseph, Michigan, lies on the shore of what lake?
6. Abilene, the name of a New Testament city, is also the city where President Eisenhower grew up. What state is it in?
7. San Clemente, California, is named for a friend of what New Testament figure?
8. A Tennessee town with a New Testament name is noted as the home of America's Nissan factory. Name the town.
9. What California city with a biblical name had Clint Eastwood as its mayor?
10. The Illinois city that was the birthplace of statesman William Jennings Bryan has a biblical name. What is it?

Test Your Bible IQ (answers)

1. Memphis
2. St. Paul
3. Goshen
4. Corpus Christi
5. Lake Michigan
6. Texas
7. Paul, who mentions Clement in Philippians 4:3
8. Smyrna
9. Carmel
10. Salem

Elvis Town, William Penn Town, Etc.

1. What major Minnesota city, named for a New Testament man, was originally named Pig's Eye?
2. Where is Hell in the U.S.?
3. What large New York city shares its name with a city in Sicily visited by Paul?
4. What is the only state to contain the name of a biblical person?
5. Zebulon, one of the twelve tribes of Israel, has namesake towns in which two southern states?
6. Jacob's Pillow Dance Festival takes its name from the story of Jacob sleeping on a stone pillow. In what state is the festival held?
7. Which three states have cities with the name Corinth?
8. What Pennsylvania city shares its name with the coastal plain of Israel?
9. Siloam Springs, named for a water source in Jerusalem, is in what southern state?
10. What large southern capital has a suburb named Lebanon?
11. What is the driest U.S. city with a biblical name?
12. What is the snowiest U.S. city with a biblical name?
13. What Egyptian city, mentioned in the New Testament, gives its name to a humid, low-lying city in Louisiana?
14. What California city is named for angels?
15. What city with a biblical name do we associate with Elvis Presley?
16. What city with a biblical name do we associate with William Penn?
17. What thriving southern capital has a suburb named Smyrna?
18. Babylon, Jericho, and Bethpage are found on what famous East Coast island?
19. Joppa, where Peter had his strange vision of unclean animals, has a namesake in what eastern state?
20. There are several Bethlehems in the U.S. Which state has the largest?
21. Sharon is the one biblically named suburb of a famous New England city surrounded by British place names. What is the city?
22. In Ohio, Shiloh is a suburb of what city?

Elvis Town, William Penn Town, Etc. (answers)

1. St. Paul
2. There isn't one, but there is a Hell's Canyon on the border between Idaho and Oregon.
3. Syracuse
4. Maryland; in fact, the state was not named for the biblical Mary, but for the English queen, Henrietta Maria. But since the colony of Maryland was originally settled by Roman Catholics, they no doubt made the connection between their new home and the Mary of the Bible.
5. Kentucky and North Carolina
6. Massachusetts
7. Mississippi, Texas, and New York
8. Sharon
9. Arkansas
10. Nashville, Tennessee
11. Probably Phoenix, Arizona, which receives only about seven inches of rain per year and has extremely low humidity
12. Probably Syracuse, New York, which receives over a hundred inches of snow each year—quite unlike the sunny biblical town of Syracuse on the Mediterranean island of Sicily
13. Alexandria
14. Los Angeles, of course
15. Memphis
16. Philadelphia, Penn's "city of brotherly love"—which is what the name *Philadelphia* means in Greek
17. Atlanta
18. Long Island
19. Maryland; Joppa is a Baltimore suburb.
20. Pennsylvania; Bethlehem has a population of about seventy thousand.
21. Boston
22. Dayton

23. Harrisburg, the capital of Pennsylvania, has a suburb named after what biblical region (and present-day nation)?
24. What Florida coastal city bears the same name as one of the apostle Paul's followers?
25. A Tennessee town with a New Testament name is noted as the home of America's Nissan factory. Name the town.
26. Greece, mentioned several times in the New Testament, lends its name to a town in what state?
27. In what state would you find New Canaan?
28. Egypt Lake is near what large Florida city?
29. The biblically named Alexandria and Bethesda are suburbs of what major eastern city?
30. The Roman god Jupiter, mentioned in Acts, has a city named for him in what state?
31. What dry, dusty Texas city is named for a pagan region in the New Testament?
32. What flat city on the Lake Michigan shoreline is named for a biblical mountain?
33. Mud Island is a recreation area in what large city named for a biblical port?
34. What landlocked desert city was named for a seaside town in the New Testament?
35. What California city, named for one of Jesus' disciples, probably has the mildest climate in North America?
36. What chilly, snowy New York city was named for a dry, hot city mentioned in Acts?
37. What city with a biblical name lies on the Delaware River?
38. What capital city with an Old Testament name lies on the Willamette River?
39. Ohio University is in a city with what biblical name?

Familiar Verse, Peculiar Order

☞ Placed in their proper order, the words are a familiar verse from Matthew.

are for God heart in see blessed shall the they pure

23. Lebanon
24. Titusville
25. Smyrna
26. New York
27. Connecticut
28. Tampa
29. Washington, D.C.
30. Florida
31. Abilene, mentioned in Luke 3:1
32. Zion, Illinois
33. Memphis
34. Phoenix
35. San Diego (in English, St. James)
36. Syracuse
37. Philadelphia, Pennsylvania
38. Salem, Oregon
39. Athens

Familiar Verse, Peculiar Order (answer)

Blessed are the pure in heart: for they shall see God. (Matthew 5:8)

Babylon, Bethlehem, New Bethlehem, Etc.

☛ There are hundreds—more accurately, *thousands*—of American places with a biblical name. In this section and those that follow you can test your acquaintance not only with the Bible but with the U.S. map.

1. What is the largest U.S. city with a biblical name?
2. What is the only U.S. capital named after a city in the Old Testament?
3. What California city with a biblical name had Clint Eastwood as its mayor?
4. The oldest town in the U.S. with a biblical name is what?
5. The pagan city Babylon lends its name to only one U.S. city. In what state would you find it?
6. In what state would you find a city named after ancient Israel's pagan neighbor, Moab?
7. What renowned Greek city, mentioned in Acts, lends its name to cities in several states?
8. Which state has both Bethlehem and New Bethlehem?
9. What state has a city named after Boaz, the husband of Ruth?
10. What Delaware resort town is popular as the summer haven for D.C. residents?
11. Which state has a city named Solomon?
12. Which state has a city containing the name of Naaman, the Syrian officer cured of leprosy?
13. Which state has the city of New Egypt?
14. The Sangre de Cristo Mountains (Spanish for "blood of Christ") are in what western state?
15. What is the only state with a city named Dothan, the dwelling place of the prophet Elisha?
16. Minnesota's capital city is named after which Bible character?
17. The city of Beersheba lends its name to only one U.S. city. In what state?
18. The New Testament city Philippi has only one U.S. counterpart. In what state?
19. Puerto Rico's capital is named after which of Jesus' disciples?

Babylon, Bethlehem, New Bethlehem, Etc. (answers)

1. Philadelphia, Pennsylvania
2. Salem, Oregon; Salem is mentioned in connection with the priest-king Melchizedek (Genesis 14), and the Israelites later assumed that Salem was the same as Jerusalem. The name means "peace," and it has been a popular name on the U.S. map.
3. Carmel
4. Salem, Massachusetts—named by its Puritan settlers
5. New York
6. Utah
7. Athens; there are at least eight in the U.S.
8. Pennsylvania
9. Alabama
10. Rehoboth Beach
11. Arizona
12. Delaware; the city is Naamans Gardens.
13. New Jersey
14. Colorado
15. Alabama
16. St. Paul
17. Tennessee; the town is Beersheba Springs.
18. West Virginia
19. St. John—which, in Spanish, is San Juan

20. Only one state has a city named after the first Christian martyr, St. Stephen. Which state?
21. Which southwestern state has a city named Trinity?
22. The city of Smyrna, mentioned in Revelation, gives its name to cities in three states. Which three?
23. Which two states have cities named Rome?
24. The New Testament village Emmaus lends its name to a town in which state?
25. In what state would you find Bethany, Bethel, and Bethlehem?
26. In what state is there a city named for John the Baptist?
27. Which two states have a Mars Hill, named for the place where Paul preached to the Athenians?
28. Two adjoining states have cities with similar names—Zion and Zionsville. What are the two states?
29. What East Coast state has a city named after an angel?
30. Which state has both a town and a college named for the New Testament city Berea?
31. Only one state has a Nebo, named for the mountain from which Moses saw the Promised Land. Which state?
32. In what state would you find Mount Sinai?
33. What Great Lakes state has the city of New Palestine?
34. Ephrata, an alternate name for the town of Bethlehem, would be found in which state?
35. Which state has the city of Pisgah, named for an important mountain in the Old Testament?
36. Which Middle Eastern nation lends its name to several U.S. cities?
37. Which southern state has a city named Hiram, an important figure in the story of Solomon?
38. Two of the U.S. Virgin Islands are named after apostles. Which two?
39. In what state would you find the Apostle Islands National Lakeshore?
40. What large southern California city is named for one of Jesus' disciples?
41. St. Simons Island is found on the coast of what southern state?
42. Utah has a national park named for a famous hill in Jerusalem. What is it?

20. South Carolina
21. Texas
22. Tennessee, Georgia, and Delaware
23. Georgia and New York
24. Pennsylvania
25. Connecticut
26. California; the city's name (in Spanish) is San Juan Bautista.
27. North Carolina and Maine
28. Illinois and Indiana
29. Maryland; the city is St. Michaels, named for the archangel Michael.
30. Kentucky
31. North Carolina
32. New York
33. Indiana
34. Washington
35. Ohio
36. Lebanon; there are at least five in the U.S.
37. Georgia
38. St. Thomas and St. John
39. Wisconsin; there are twelve islands, naturally.
40. San Diego—Spanish for St. James
41. Georgia
42. Zion

43. The oldest city in the U.S., St. Augustine, Florida, has a historic fort named for a New Testament character. Which one?
44. What Midwestern state has a town named Ephraim, founded by Moravian Christians from Norway?
45. What Illinois city with a biblical name was birthplace of two major figures in the 1925 "evolution" trial—attorney William Jennings Bryan and defendant John Scopes?
46. This North Carolina national forest with a biblical name is the site of Mount Mitchell, highest point east of the Mississippi River. What is it?
47. What San Francisco suburban city is named for one of the four Gospels?
48. What North Carolina town with a hyphenated name is named (partly) for a biblical city?
49. What city in Illinois with a biblical name has aroused controversy in the ongoing church-state issue?

Familiar Verse, Peculiar Order

☛ Placed in their proper order, the words are a familiar verse from the Old Testament.

the and earth beginning the God heavens the in created

Angel Mounds, Devil's Punch Bowl, Etc.

1. Where in the U.S. are the walls of Jerusalem?
2. Where can you see the parting of the Red Sea?
3. In what New England city would you find the exhibit *Light Unto My Path: Exploring the Bible in Sight and Sound?*
4. Where can you see the Ten Commandments carved in stone in letters five feet high (probably the grand example of a large-print Bible)?
5. The enormous Cathedral of St. John the Divine has a notable Bible Garden. What metropolis is it in?
6. The Oriental Institute, with artifacts from Assyria, Babylon, and Palestine, is in what Midwestern metropolis?

43. Mark; *Castillo de San Marcos* is Spanish for "Fort of St. Mark."
44. Wisconsin
45. Salem
46. Pisgah National Forest
47. San Mateo—Spanish for St. Matthew
48. Winston-Salem (Salem is the biblical part, of course)
49. Zion

Familiar Verse, Peculiar Order (answer)

In the beginning God created the heavens and the earth.
(Genesis 1:1)

Angel Mounds, Devil's Punch Bowl, Etc. (answers)

1. Eureka Springs, Arkansas; the late Gerald L. K. Smith pioneered the project of building replicas of Old Jerusalem sites in Arkansas. The walls, at present, are all that's been completed.
2. At Universal Studios in Hollywood, California, which re-creates the special effects used in the film *The Ten Commandments*
3. Boston
4. On a mountainside at Field of the Wood, North Carolina; a border around the Commandments measures the length of a football field.
5. New York City
6. Chicago

7. What state has the technological wonder called the St. Mary's River locks?

8. The awe-inspiring San Juan Mountains (named for St. John) are in what mountainous state?

9. The Kedron Valley sleigh ride center is named for a biblical brook. What state is Kedron Valley in?

10. Devil's Den State Park is in what southern state?

11. San Simeon, named for the Simeon in Luke's Gospel who blesses the child Jesus, is in what state (which happens to have a lot of "San" names)?

12. The land of Gilead is mentioned often in the Old Testament. Where is Mount Gilead State Park?

13. Ephraim, named for one of the tribes of Israel, was founded by Moravian settlers in which Great Lake state?

14. In what state is Bible Hill?

15. What New Hampshire town, named for an Old Testament site, was home of the poet Robert Frost?

16. Port Angeles, which means "port of angels," is on the coast of which Pacific state?

17. The St. Joseph River happens to be in the same state that has a St. Mary's River. Which state?

18. The reconstructed pioneer village of Little Norway is in a town named for the biblical Mount Horeb. What state is it in?

19. The Sangre de Cristo (Spanish for "blood of Christ") Mountains are in which southwestern state?

20. St. Peter's Fiesta is held each June in which state noted for its fishermen?

21. The Illinois city that was the birthplace of statesman William Jennings Bryan has a biblical name. What is it?

22. What large northeastern city is home to the Bible House, belonging to the American Bible Society?

23. Devil's Punch Bowl State Park is in which western state?

24. The Mennonite church has its archives in an Indiana town named for the Hebrew district of Egypt. What is the name of the town?

25. In what state is Devil's Hole State Park?

26. Sturbridge, Massachusetts, has a huge diorama depicting which New Testament town?

27. Mount Diablo (meaning "Devil's Mount") is in which state?

7. Michigan
8. Colorado
9. Vermont
10. Arkansas
11. California
12. Ohio
13. Wisconsin
14. Tennessee
15. Salem
16. Washington
17. Michigan
18. Wisconsin
19. New Mexico
20. Massachusetts
21. Salem
22. New York
23. Oregon
24. Goshen
25. New York
26. Bethlehem; the exhibit also has nativity scenes from all around the world.
27. California

28. Ohio has a state park named for which noted New Testament woman?

29. Ephrata, an alternate name in the Bible for Bethlehem, is the name of a town in which state?

30. The American Passion Play, depicting the last days of Jesus, is held in which university town in Illinois?

31. In what city near Chicago would you find Lord's Park?

32. Devil's Postpile National Monument is in which state?

33. In what state is the Titus Mountain Ski Area?

34. What California town is named for the New Testament city where believers were first called Christians?

35. What New England resort area has its Jericho House?

36. The town of Bethpage and also Bethpage State Park lie on what northeastern island?

37. Seamen's Bethel, a church dedicated to whalers and shaped like a ship, is in what Massachusetts town?

38. What is the only state to have both a St. Peter and a St. Paul?

39. What Massachusetts town with a biblical name was home to novelist Nathaniel Hawthorne?

40. Alexandria Bay, named for the Egyptian city of Alexandria mentioned in the Bible, is a resort center on the Canadian border. In what state?

41. St. Johnsbury is in what New England state?

42. Macedonia was the scene of Paul's first preaching in Europe. In what state would you find the Macedonia Brook State Park?

43. Virginia and West Virginia both have a "burg" named for an apostle. What is the name of the city?

44. The Bethel ski resort is in what chilly, mountainous state?

45. In what state are the Palestinian Gardens, an authentic scale model of the Holy Land at the time of Jesus?

46. New Canaan, originally called Canaan parish, is in what New England state?

47. What California town is named for the Holy Trinity?

48. The land of Moab was southeast of Israel. Where in the U.S. is Moab?

49. What Illinois city with a biblical name is connected with Abraham Lincoln?

50. What Missouri city is named for the place where Jesus ascended to heaven?

28. Mary—St. Mary's State Park
29. Washington
30. Bloomington
31. Elgin
32. California
33. New York
34. Antioch
35. Cape Cod
36. Long Island, New York
37. New Bedford
38. Minnesota
39. Salem
40. New York
41. Vermont
42. Connecticut
43. Petersburg
44. Maine
45. Mississippi; it is about twelve miles north of Lucedale in southern Mississippi. The twenty-acre park is designed on a scale of one yard to a mile.
46. Connecticut
47. Trinidad (*Trinidad* is the Spanish word for "Trinity")
48. Utah
49. New Salem
50. Bethany

51. In what southern state would you find the Bible Museum, with its collection of seven thousand antique Bibles?
52. In the Old Testament, Zoar is a city connected with Sodom and Gomorrah. In what state is the Zoar State Memorial?
53. Where is Bibletown?
54. Where would you see a parade in which all the floats tell a story from the Bible?
55. Where would you find the Shekinah Bible Gardens, with its recreations of Golgotha and Jesus' tomb?
56. New York has a town with an Old Testament name, noted for its harness racing. What is it?
57. The Black Hills Passion Play, depicting the last days of Jesus, is held in the town of Spearfish in which state?
58. In what east coast state would you find Jerusalem and Galilee—only a few miles apart?
59. What conservative southern college is home to the Bible Lands Museum?
60. The National Bible Museum, which includes biblical coins and papyrus plants in its collection, is in what state?
61. What Washington, D.C., site contains replicas of noted Holy Land shrines?
62. In what state is a very old Indian site known as Angel Mounds?

Familiar Verse, Peculiar Order

☞ Placed in their proper order, the words are a familiar verse from Matthew.

bread daily day give our this us

Eden, Eden Prairie, Edenton, Etc.

1. What D.C. church named for one of Jesus' disciples is known as "the Church of the Presidents"?
2. The New Testament city of Sardis has a namesake in only one U.S. state. Which one?
3. St. Matthews, Kentucky, is a suburb of what large city?
4. The well-known Cathedral Church of St. Peter and St. Paul in D.C. is better known by what name?

51. Arkansas; the museum, in Eureka Springs, also has a large collection of Bible manuscripts.
52. Ohio
53. Florida; it's a conference center at Boca Raton.
54. In Humboldt, Kansas, with its annual Biblesta Parade (the name is a combination of "Bible" and "fiesta"); all people on the floats must wear biblical costumes.
55. Near St. Cloud, Minnesota; the forty-acre park also has replicas of Herod's palace and the Jerusalem temple.
56. Goshen
57. South Dakota
58. Rhode Island; both are small fishing villages.
59. Bob Jones University in Greenville, South Carolina; the school also has a grand collection of art masterpieces on biblical themes.
60. Tennessee; it's in Gatlinburg, gateway to the Smoky Mountains.
61. Mount St. Sepulchre, part of the Franciscan Monastery at Fourteenth Street; it is sometimes called "The Holy Land of America."
62. Indiana

Familiar Verse, Peculiar Order (answer)

Give us this day our daily bread. (Matthew 6:11)

Eden, Eden Prairie, Edenton, Etc. (answers)

1. St. John's Episcopal
2. Georgia
3. Louisville
4. National Cathedral (or Washington Cathedral)

5. Annapolis, Maryland, has one of the oldest, most prestigious (and smallest) U.S. colleges, named for an apostle. What is the name of the school?

6. What southern city has St. Paul's Church, noted for being the church where Confederate President Jefferson Davis received the news that the Confederacy was about to fall?

7. California has a national park honoring a curious tree named for an Old Testament leader. What is the park's name?

8. What Texas city has a name that means (in Latin) "body of Christ"?

9. What D.C. suburb is named for a New Testament site where people were healed?

10. California has a famous geological "problem" named for one of the apostles. What is it?

11. St. John's Church, where Patrick Henry delivered his notorious "Give me liberty or give me death" speech, is in what southern capital?

12. The "fountain of youth" explorer Ponce de León is buried in what tropical city named for an apostle?

13. What large Florida resort town is named for a city in Russia that took its name from an apostle?

14. What West Virginia city (and its college) were founded by a Christian leader and named for a New Testament town?

15. Eden Prairie and Eden Valley are both in which Midwestern state?

16. If you were on the road to Damascus, what three states might you be headed for?

17. Which state has both an Eden and an Edenton?

18. Several states have a city named for St. Joseph, the husband of Mary. Which state has the largest?

19. Yellow Springs, Ohio, has a prestigious college named for the New Testament town where the name "Christian" was first used. What is the name of the college?

20. What Indiana town and its college are named for the Hebrews' dwelling place in Egypt?

21. Holy Family College is found in what large east coast city?

22. There is only one U.S. city named for Jesus' hometown. What state is it in?

23. A city name associated with Hebrew leader Joshua has several namesakes in the U.S. What is the city name?

5. St. John's College (founded 1696)
6. Richmond, Virginia
7. Joshua Tree National Monument
8. Corpus Christi
9. Bethesda, Maryland
10. The San Andreas Fault—*San Andreas* being Spanish for "St. Andrew"
11. Richmond, Virginia
12. San Juan (St. John), Puerto Rico
13. St. Petersburg
14. Bethany
15. Minnesota
16. Virginia, Georgia, or Maryland
17. North Carolina
18. St. Joseph, Missouri, with about seventy-six thousand people
19. Antioch
20. Goshen
21. Philadelphia
22. Michigan; the town's name is Nazareth, of course.
23. Jericho; there are at least three in the U.S.

24. In what state would you find Messiah College?
25. What state has the most cities named for New Testament characters?
26. In what state would you find Holy Apostles College?
27. What state has a city named Arab?
28. The city of Briarcliff Manor has The King's College, the king being Jesus Christ. What state is The King's College in?
29. The Old Testament town of Shiloh gave its name to a famous Civil War battlefield site in what southern state?
30. In what state would you find the University of Mary?
31. Babylon is a suburb of what large northeastern city?
32. *Evangel* is the New Testament word for "gospel." In what state would you find Evangel College?
33. Bethpage in the New Testament is associated with Jesus' triumphal entry into Jerusalem. What state has a city of Bethpage?
34. Christ College is found in a western state with dozens of biblical names. What state?
35. This biblical city name, found in several states, was actually an early Old Testament name for Jerusalem. What was the name?
36. Most people are surprised to learn that this large Texas city is named in the New Testament. What is it?
37. The hometown of Paul's friend Apollos is also the name for a Virginia suburb of D.C. What is it?
38. Antioch, California, is a suburb of what major city?
39. What city named in the New Testament is also the name of the site of the University of Georgia?
40. Bethlehem in Israel was and is a small town, but Bethlehem in this East Coast state has a population of about seventy thousand. Which state?

Familiar Verse, Peculiar Order

☛ Placed in their proper order, the words are a familiar verse from Psalms.

the declare glory God heavens the of

24. Pennsylvania
25. Probably California, which has the Spanish-named cities San Diego (James), San Jose (Joseph), San Marcos (Mark), San Simeon, San Mateo (Matthew), San Pablo (Paul), and San Juan Bautista (John the Baptist)
26. Connecticut
27. Alabama; it's pronounced with a long *a*, by the way (AY-rab).
28. New York
29. Tennessee
30. North Dakota
31. New York
32. Missouri
33. New York
34. California
35. Salem
36. Abilene
37. Alexandria
38. Oakland
39. Athens
40. Pennsylvania

Familiar Verse, Peculiar Order (answer)

The heavens declare the glory of God. (Psalm 19:1)

Moses Lake, Mount Carmel, Mount Olive, Etc.

1. Which southern state has towns named for traveling companions in the book of Acts—Paul and Silas?
2. The Devil's Playground (a geographical feature, not an amusement park) is in which western state?
3. Thyatira, the hometown of Lydia, has a namesake in what southeastern state?
4. Jacksonville, Florida, sits astride a river named for which apostle?
5. What prairie state has both a Lebanon and a New Lebanon (located quite a distance apart)?
6. Which state has an Emanuel County?
7. The town of Christ's Rock lies near the Chesapeake Bay in which state?
8. St. Joseph, Michigan, lies on the shore of what lake?
9. Tennessee has both a town and a famous Civil War battlefield named for an important Old Testament site. What was it?
10. There are counties named Trinity in which two states?
11. Shiloh, Bethel, and Mount Olive lie within a few miles of each other in which Great Lakes state?
12. Thaddeus, one of the lesser-known of Jesus' apostles, has a namesake town in what southern state?
13. Tabor, a mountain mentioned in connection with the judges Barak and Deborah, has a namesake in what plains state?
14. St. Elizabeth, St. Thomas, and St. James lie within a few miles of each other in which state?
15. The towns Bethlehem and St. Bethlehem are both in what southern state?
16. New Philadelphia and Philadelphia are both in what northeastern state?
17. The town of Joppa in Illinois lies on the banks of what major river?
18. What is the only state with a county named Lebanon?
19. The county of Titus lies in what state (which happens to have 254 counties)?
20. Elihu, one of Job's friends, has a namesake in which southern state?

Moses Lake, Mount Carmel, Mount Olive, Etc. (answers)

1. Alabama
2. California (appropriately)
3. Georgia
4. John—the St. John's River
5. Indiana
6. Georgia
7. Maryland
8. Lake Michigan
9. Shiloh; the town and battlefield in Tennessee are not, incidentally, anywhere near each other.
10. Texas and California
11. Ohio
12. Alabama
13. Iowa
14. Missouri
15. Tennessee
16. Pennsylvania
17. The Ohio
18. Pennsylvania
19. Texas
20. Kentucky

21. Salem County and the town of Salem are in what Atlantic coast state?
22. Moses Lake lies in which western state?
23. Mount Carmel and Pisgah, both named for biblical mountains, lie in Alabama on the banks of what wide river?
24. The Bible Museum, founded by the first bottler of Coca-Cola, is in what state?

Familiar Verse, Peculiar Order

☞ Placed in their proper order, the words are a familiar verse from Psalms.

he down me green in lie makes pastures

Hell's Gate, Devil's Lake, Devil's Tower, Etc.

1. St. Mary's Glacier is in what mountain state?
2. Arkansas has a lake named for what "mighty hunter" of the Old Testament?
3. What beach in Delaware has a New Testament name because it was formerly a revival center?
4. What biblically named city in Pennsylvania advertises itself as "America's Christmas City"?
5. The St. Andrew's State Recreation Area is in which state loaded with recreation areas?
6. In what state would you find Palestine?
7. Pauls Valley is a town in which oil-rich state?
8. The cedars of Lebanon are mentioned several times in the Bible. Where would you find Cedars of Lebanon State Park?
9. What well-watered (and snowy) state has the Mount Zion ski area?
10. Where is Devil's Lake?
11. In what state does the town of Cave Junction have Noah's Ark Wildlife Park?
12. Lofty Mount Nebo (11,877 feet high), named for the biblical mount, lies in what Rocky Mountain state?

21. New Jersey
22. Washington
23. The Tennessee River
24. Louisiana, in the city of Monroe; the museum is part of the Biedenharn Foundation, founded by Coca-Cola bottler Joseph Biedenharn.

Familiar Verse, Peculiar Order (answer)

He makes me lie down in green pastures. (Psalm 23:2)

Hell's Gate, Devil's Lake, Devil's Tower, Etc. (answers)

1. Colorado
2. Nimrod
3. Bethany Beach
4. Bethlehem (of course)
5. Florida
6. Texas
7. Oklahoma
8. Tennessee
9. Michigan
10. North Dakota and Wisconsin both have one.
11. Oregon
12. Utah

13. What Ohio city has Eden Park, originally called the Garden of Eden?
14. What state has both the Devil's Head ski area and the Devil's Lake State Park?
15. What large West Coast city has a district named San Pedro (Spanish for St. Peter)?
16. The town of Eureka Springs has a Bible Museum and a New Holy Land area. What state is it in?
17. What mountain state has the city of Trinidad (Spanish for Trinity), where the legendary Bat Masterson was sheriff?
18. Abilene, the name of a New Testament city, is also the city where President Eisenhower grew up. What state is it in?
19. The Ave Maria Grotto contains miniature replicas of sites in Jerusalem, Bethlehem, and Nazareth. In what state would you find this curious tourist attraction?
20. The Eden State Gardens are in which scenic state?
21. What Mississippi town—which shares its name with a New Testament city and a large Pennsylvania city—is still home to a large population of Choctaw Indians?
22. The Christus Gardens are in what scenic southern mountain range?
23. The town of Bethabara is mentioned only once in the New Testament. Where is the only Bethabara in the U.S.?
24. The San Marcos River and the city of San Marcos (both named for St. Mark) are in which southwestern state?
25. The San Miguel Mission, the oldest church in the U.S. still in use, is named for the archangel Michael. What southwestern capital city is it in?
26. The seven-story-high statue *Christ of the Ozarks* stands in which state?
27. *Las Cruces* is Spanish for "the crosses" and refers to the crosses over the graves of people massacred by Apaches. Where is the city of Las Cruces?
28. Fort St. Jean Baptiste (named for John the Baptist) is in what French-influenced state?
29. The Garden of Our Lord, with plants mentioned in the Bible, is in what Florida city?
30. In what southern capital would you find The Upper Room, named for the room where Jesus and the disciples had the Last Supper?

13. Cincinnati
14. Wisconsin
15. Los Angeles
16. Arkansas
17. Colorado
18. Texas
19. Alabama
20. Florida
21. Philadelphia
22. The Great Smoky Mountains
23. Bethabara Park in Winston-Salem, North Carolina
24. Texas
25. Santa Fe, New Mexico
26. Arkansas
27. New Mexico
28. Louisiana
29. Coral Gables
30. Nashville, Tennessee

31. In what biblically named city would you find the Christ Church Burial Ground, which has the grave of Benjamin Franklin?

32. St. Michael's Cemetery, named for the archangel Michael and containing the graves of early Spanish settlers, lies in which very old Florida city?

33. The Biblical Art Center, with a replica of Christ's tomb, is in what Texas metropolis?

34. St. John's College, one of the oldest colleges in the U.S., has its original campus in Maryland and a newer campus in which southwestern state?

35. While in Athens, Paul would inevitably have seen the Parthenon temple. In what southern city would you find a full-scale replica of the Parthenon?

36. The Great Passion Play, an enactment of the last days of Jesus, is held at Mount Oberamergau in which famous mountain range?

37. The Mount Pisgah Scenic Drive contains 10,400-foot Mount Pisgah, much higher than its biblical namesake. In what state is this Mount Pisgah?

38. Where is Hell's Gate?

39. What city and mountain range in California are named for an angel that plays a prominent role in the Gospels?

40. Emerald green St. Mary's Lake lies in what stunning national park?

41. The beautiful San Juan Islands, named for St. John, are found near the Canadian border in what state?

42. What large Pacific Coast city has a beautiful park named for the biblical Mount Tabor?

43. The city of Deadwood contains Mount Moriah Cemetery, named for the Old Testament mount and containing the graves of Wild Bill Hickok and Calamity Jane. What state is it in?

44. The island of Malta played an important role in Paul's voyage to Rome. In what state would you find Malta?

45. The Devil's Tower National Monument is in what state?

46. The Lake of Egypt recreation area lies in which prairie state?

47. Moses Lake—the name of both a city and a state park—are in what Pacific state?

48 What California city with an Old Testament name has a Biblical Garden?

31. Philadelphia, Pennsylvania
32. Pensacola
33. Dallas; the center also has a painting of Pentecost that measures 20 feet wide and 124 feet long.
34. New Mexico
35. Nashville, Tennessee
36. The Ozarks
37. Colorado
38. Idaho; it is a state park.
39. San Gabriel
40. Glacier National Park in Montana
41. Washington
42. Portland, Oregon
43. South Dakota
44. Montana
45. Wyoming
46. Illinois
47. Washington
48. Carmel

49. Where is the Devil's Kitchen—and *what* is it?
50. St. Mary's Square is in (strangely enough) the Chinatown section of which California city?

Familiar Verse, Peculiar Order

☛ Placed in their proper order, the words are a familiar verse from Psalms.

a in clean create God heart me O

St. Andrew, St. Stephen, St. Matthew, Etc.

1. The Greek island of Crete, mentioned in the New Testament, gives its name to a town in what landlocked state?
2. One of the tribes of Israel shares its name with a river and town in southern Virginia. Name the river and town.
3. What state has a St. Andrews, a St. Stephen, and a St. Matthew?
4. The expression "Beulah land" (*Beulah* actually means "married") occurs only in the book of Isaiah, and there is one city named Beulah in the U.S. What state is it in?
5. In what western state would you find the lofty Mount of the Holy Cross?
6. What western state has a Jordan River?
7. What large riverside city is named for an Egyptian port, mentioned by the prophets Isaiah, Jeremiah, and Ezekiel?
8. The hill from which Jesus ascended to heaven lends its name to several American cities. Name the hill.
9. What Alaska mountain range is named for the prophet Elijah?
10. What river named for an apostle flows from Maine into Canada?
11. What Pennsylvania city shares its name with the coastal plain of Israel?
12. A large New York city shares its name with a city in Sicily visited by Paul. What is it?

49. It's in Utah, and it's a canyon.
50. San Francisco

Familiar Verse, Peculiar Order (answer)

Create in me a clean heart, O God. (Psalm 51:10)

St. Andrew, St. Stephen, St. Matthew, Etc. (answers)

1. Nebraska
2. Dan River and Danville
3. South Carolina
4. North Dakota
5. Colorado
6. Utah
7. Memphis (Some Bible translations read Noph instead of Memphis, by the way.)
8. The Mount of Olives, also known as Mount Olive or Olivet
9. The Saint Elias Mountains—Elias being a variant form of Elijah
10. The St. John
11. Sharon
12. Syracuse

13. Zebulon, one of the twelve tribes of Israel, has namesake towns in which two southern states?
14. Which gulf state has counties named St. James, St. John the Baptist, and St. Mary?
15. San Clemente, California, is named for a friend of what New Testament figure?
16. The San Juan National Forest, named for the apostle John, is in which mountainous state?
17. What is the only state to have a town named for the apostle Philip?
18. St. Philip's Church is a much-photographed landmark in what historic southern city?
19. What city in Acts lends its name to a southwestern capital city?
20. The funeral of John F. Kennedy was held in what D.C. church named for an apostle?
21. Which state has two "beach" cities with Bible names?
22. Is Hell in the U.S.?
23. St. Mary's City was the first capital of what East Coast state?
24. In what southern state would you find Mars Hill, Mount Gilead, and Mount Olive?
25. What state has a capital whose name refers to the Lord's Supper and to baptism?
26. The Pisgah National Forest, named for a famous Old Testament mountain, is in what famous mountain range?

Familiar Verse, Peculiar Order

☛ Placed in their proper order, the words are a familiar verse from Exodus.

covet not neighbor's shall house you your

13. Kentucky and North Carolina
14. Louisiana; actually, they aren't counties, but *parishes*—Louisiana's equivalent of counties.
15. Paul, who mentions Clement in Philippians 4:3
16. Colorado
17. New Mexico; the town's Spanish name is San Felipe.
18. Charleston, South Carolina
19. Phoenix
20. St. Matthew's
21. Delaware has Bethany Beach and Rehoboth Beach.
22. No (geographically speaking), but there is a Hell's Canyon on the border between Idaho and Oregon. (Presumably if there is a Hell's Canyon, there must be a Hell.)
23. Maryland
24. North Carolina
25. California; *Sacramento* is the Spanish word for "sacrament," which does not actually appear in the Bible, though the Lord's Supper and baptism (which definitely are mentioned in the Bible) are considered sacraments.
26. The Appalachians of North Carolina

Familiar Verse, Peculiar Order (answer)

You shall not covet your neighbor's house. (Exodus 20:17)

Do You Remember?

☞ Would you like to see how much Bible trivia you can remember? Answer the questions (which you should have answered already in this section), and then see how well you rate on the scale on page xii.

1. The biblically named Alexandria and Bethesda are suburbs of what major eastern city?
2. In which state would you find Bethany, Bethel, and Bethlehem?
3. San Simeon, named for the Simeon in Luke's Gospel who blesses the child Jesus, is in what state (which happens to have a lot of "San" names)?
4. St. Matthews, Kentucky, is a suburb of what large city?
5. New Philadelphia and Philadelphia are both in what northeastern state?
6. The Devil's Tower National Monument is in what state?
7. A large New York city shares its name with a city in Sicily visited by Paul. What is it?
8. What city in Acts lends its name to a southwestern capital city?
9. Puerto Rico's capital is named after which of Jesus' disciples?
10. What California town is named for the New Testament city where believers were first called Christians?

Do You Remember? (answers)

1. Washington, D.C.
2. Connecticut
3. California
4. Louisville
5. Pennsylvania
6. Wyoming
7. Syracuse
8. Phoenix
9. St. John—which, in Spanish, is San Juan
10. Antioch

PART 4

A Bible Name for (Most) Celebrities

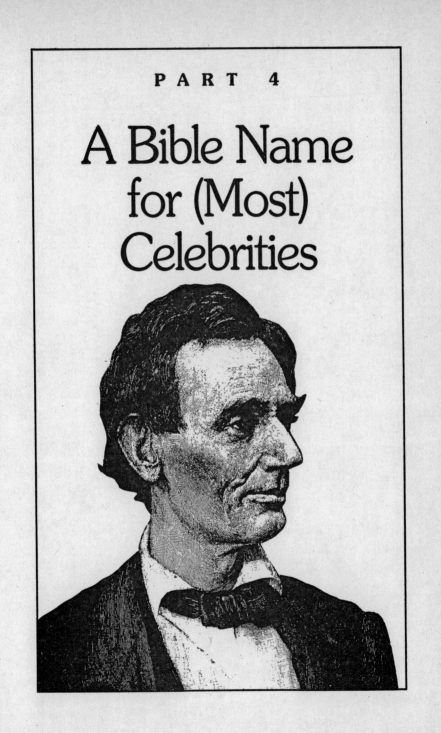

Nowhere is the Bible's influence more noticeable than in the giving of a name to a child. Wherever the church is, the Bible is, and where there are Bibles, there will be people named for the people in its pages. Names range from the common (John, James, Mary) to the bizarre (Eliphaz, Keren-happuch). Test your knowledge of biblical names by supplying the first names of the famous people listed here. This is a great section for "coasting"—after all, some of the most common names are biblical, so if you're stuck for an answer, you can always guess "John" or "James" for a man's name, or "Mary" or "Elizabeth" for a woman's. These are in no particular historical order, by the way, which we hope will add to the fun of guessing. Also, every category of famous people is included—political leaders, musicians, artists, authors, you name it.

Test Your Bible IQ

☛ This quiz contains questions covering the topics in part 4, "A Bible Name for (Most) Celebrities." Do your best, then turn the page to see how you did. If you are brave enough to see how your Bible IQ rates, turn to page xii for our scale.

1. _____ Jackson (U.S. president)
2. _____ Milton (English poet, author of *Paradise Lost*)
3. _____ Ewell Brown Stuart (Confederate general)
4. _____ Owens (American track star)
5. _____ Hamilton (first U.S. secretary of the treasury)
6. _____ Ustinov (British comedy actor)
7 _____ Malone (American basketball star in the 1970s and 1980s)
8. _____ McCartney (pop singer)
9. _____ Brady (Civil War photographer)
10. _____ Shelley (author of *Frankenstein*)

Test Your Bible IQ (answers)

1. Andrew
2. John
3. James (better known by his initials, J.E.B.)
4. Jesse
5. Alexander
6. Peter
7. Moses
8. Paul
9. Mathew (yes, the spelling is different)
10. Mary

A Great Source of Names: Stephen the Novelist, Elizabeth the Queen, and Many Others

1. _____ King (contemporary American horror novelist)
2. _____ Carter (U.S. president)
3. _____ and _____ Dorsey (American band leaders)
4. _____ Altizer (the "God is dead" theologian)
5. _____ Anka (pop singer)
6. _____ Arden (cosmetics queen)
7. _____ Stalin (Soviet leader)
8. _____ Warhol (offbeat American artist)
9. _____ Seeger (folk singer)
10. _____ Weissmuller (swimmer, actor)
11. _____ Franklin (colonial American leader)
12. _____ (the present queen of Great Britain)
13. _____ Williams (American playwright)
14. _____ Major (the British prime minister following Margaret Thatcher)
15. _____ Hawthorne (American novelist of the 1800s)
16. _____ Wyeth (contemporary American painter)
17. _____ Young (black political leader)
18. _____ Kaye (U.S. comedian)
19. _____ Kennedy (U.S. president)
20. _____ Kubler-Ross (expert on death and dying)
21. _____ McCartney (pop singer)
22. _____ Landry (football coach)
23. _____ Lawrence (British soldier, known as "Lawrence of Arabia")
24. _____ (medieval king of England)
25. _____ Adams (U.S. president)
26. _____ Hayes (U.S. marine and World War II hero)
27. _____ Mercer (songwriter)
28. _____ Webster (dictionary compiler)
29. _____ Jackson (U.S. president)
30. _____ Jackson (pop singer)
31. _____ Michener (contemporary author)
32. _____ Edwards (American theologian of the 1700s)

A Great Source of Names: Stephen the Novelist, Elizabeth the Queen, and Many Others (answers)

1. Stephen
2. James (better known as Jimmy, of course)
3. James and Thomas (better known as Jimmy and Tommy)
4. Thomas
5. Paul
6. Elizabeth (biblically, the mother of John the Baptist and kinswoman of the Virgin Mary, Luke 1)
7. Joseph
8. Andrew (better known as Andy)
9. Peter (better known as Pete)
10. John (better known as Johnny)
11. Benjamin
12. Elizabeth
13. Thomas (*much* better known as "Tennessee")
14. John
15. Nathaniel (see John 1:44-49)
16. Andrew
17. Andrew
18. Daniel (better known as Danny)
19. John
20. Elisabeth
21. Paul
22. Thomas (better known as Tom)
23. Thomas
24. John
25. John
26. Ira (yes, it really is a biblical name—2 Samuel 23:26)
27. John (better known as Johnny)
28. Noah
29. Andrew
30. Michael (the name of an angel—Daniel 10; Revelation 12)
31. James
32. Jonathan

33. _____ Mitchell (U.S. attorney general in the Nixon years)
34. _____ Mitchell (wife of 33)
35. _____ (another medieval English king)
36. _____ Carson (TV personality)
37. _____ Bryant (college football coach)
38. _____ Tyler Moore (TV personality)
39. _____ Goldwyn (movie producer)
40. _____ Lincoln (U.S. president)
41. _____ Adams (colonial American agitator)
42. _____ Addison (English essayist of the 1700s)
43. _____ Cabot (early explorer of America)
44. _____ Agee (American author of this century)
45. _____ Fenimore Cooper (American author of historical novels)
46. _____ James (American outlaw)
47. _____ C. Calhoun (Southern politician of the 1800s)
48. _____ Calvin (French theologian of the 1500s)
49. _____ (queen of England during Shakespeare's lifetime)
50. _____ Albright (American frontier preacher)
51. _____ Lennon (English pop singer)
52. _____ _____ Jackson (Confederate general)
53. _____ (king of England in the early 1600s)
54. _____ _____ Astor (American frontier entrepreneur)
55. _____ _____ Audubon (painter of birds)
56. _____ Taylor Barnum (American showman)
57. _____ Barrie (author of *Peter Pan*)
58. _____ Wilson (U.S. president)
59. _____ Wolfe (contemporary author)
60. _____ Frampton (British rock guitarist)
61. _____ Barrymore (American stage and movie actor)
62. _____ Burr (American statesman in the early years)
63. _____ Bellow (contemporary American author and Nobel prizewinner)
64. _____ Barbera (cartoonist, partner with William Hanna)
65. _____ Harvey (news commentator, "The Rest of the Story")

33. John
34. Martha
35. Stephen
36. John (better known as Johnny)
37. Paul (better known as "the Bear")
38. Mary
39. Samuel
40. Abraham
41. Samuel
42. Joseph
43. John
44. James
45. James
46. Jesse (the name of King David's father)
47. John
48. John
49. Elizabeth
50. Jacob
51. John
52. Thomas Jonathan (better known as "Stonewall")
53. James
54. John Jacob
55. John James
56. Phineas (yes, really—Exodus 6:25)
57. James
58. Thomas (better known by his middle name, Woodrow)
59. Thomas (better known as Tom)
60. Peter
61. John
62. Aaron
63. Saul
64. Joseph
65. Paul

66. _____ Hawking (contemporary physicist and author)
67. _____ Clemens (American author of the 1800s)
68. _____ Hayakawa (U.S. linguist and senator)
69. _____ Vincent Benet (American poet)
70. _____ Hendrix (rock guitarist)
71. _____ Bolivar (South American liberator in the 1800s)
72. _____ Hindemith (German composer of this century)
73. _____ Boone (American frontiersman)
74. _____ Hockney (contemporary English artist)
75. _____ Wilkes Booth (President Lincoln's assassin)
76. _____ Williams (American swimmer and movie actress)
77. _____ McDonald (lead singer in the rock group the Doobie Brothers)

Familiar Verse, Peculiar Order

☛ Placed in their proper order, the words are a familiar verse from Matthew.

are for persecuted are sake those righteousness' blessed who

Thomas the Actor, David the Commentator, and Many More

1. _____ Hoffa (U.S. labor leader)
2. _____ Brady (Civil War photographer)
3. _____ Hogan (American golfer)
4. _____ Cruise (contemporary film actor)
5. _____ Bowie (hero of the Texas revolution in the 1800s)
6. _____ Edgar Hoover (FBI head)
7. _____ Brown (American antislavery leader)
8. _____ Brinkley (TV newscaster and commentator)
9. _____ Huston (movie director)
10. _____ Britten (British classical composer)
11. _____ Jackson (civil rights activist)
12. _____ Buchanan (U.S. president)

66. Stephen
67. Samuel (better known as Mark Twain)
68. Samuel
69. Stephen
70. James (better known as Jimi)
71. Simon
72. Paul
73. Daniel
74. David
75. John
76. Esther
77. Michael

Familiar Verse, Peculiar Order (answer)

Blessed are those who are persecuted for righteousness' sake.
(Matthew 5:10)

Thomas the Actor, David the Commentator, and Many More (answers)

1. James (better known as Jimmy)
2. Mathew (yes, the spelling is different)
3. Benjamin (better known as Ben)
4. Thomas (better known as Tom)
5. James
6. John (but usually known simply by the initial J.)
7. John
8. David
9. John
10. Benjamin
11. Jesse
12. James

13. _____ Taylor (American actress)
14. _____ Jackson (baseball player)
15. _____ Streep (American actress)
16. _____ Jeffries (boxer)
17. _____ Bunyan (English preacher and author in the 1600s)
18. _____ _____ (the present pope, with two biblical names)
19. _____ Beard (U.S. cooking expert)
20. _____ Jones (author of *From Here to Eternity*)
21. _____ Jefferson (U.S. president)
22. _____ Carnegie (American millionaire)
23. _____ Joyce (Irish author)
24. _____ Keaton (silent-movie comedian)
25. _____ Carlyle (Scottish historian of the 1800s)
26. _____ Kennedy (father of a famous U.S. political family)
27. _____ More (English statesman, hero of *A Man for All Seasons*)
28. _____ Milton (English poet, author of *Paradise Lost*)
29. _____ Johnson (U.S. president after Lincoln)
30. _____ Swift (author of *Gulliver's Travels*)
31. _____ Newton (physicist, associated with an apple)
32. _____ Coolidge (U.S. president)
33. _____ Defoe (author of *Robinson Crusoe*)
34. _____ Jordan (basketball star)
35. _____ Sidney (English poet of the 1500s)
36. _____ Arness (TV personality)
37. _____ Simon (pop singer, or a U.S. senator)
38. _____ Van Buren (newspaper columnist)
39. _____ Ben-Gurion (premier of Israel)
40. _____ Thurber (American cartoonist and humorist)
41. _____ Disraeli (British prime minister in the 1800s)
42. _____ Clancy (contemporary American author)
43. _____ Hamilton (American founding father)
44. _____ Allen (Revolutionary War hero)
45. _____ Houston (a hero in Texas)
46. _____ Early (Confederate general)
47. _____ Updike (contemporary American novelist)
48. _____ Clark (World War II and Korean War leader)

13. Elizabeth
14. Joseph (better known as "Shoeless Joe")
15. Mary (better known as Meryl)
16. James
17. John
18. John Paul (*two* Bible names, wow!)
19. James
20. James
21. Thomas
22. Andrew
23. James
24. Joseph (better known as Buster)
25. Thomas
26. Joseph
27. Thomas
28. John
29. Andrew
30. Jonathan
31. Isaac
32. John (better known by his middle name, Calvin)
33. Daniel
34. Michael
35. Philip (the name of one of Jesus' twelve disciples *and* the name of a prominent New Testament evangelist)
36. James
37. Paul
38. Abigail (the name of one of King David's many wives)
39. David
40. James
41. Benjamin
42. Thomas (better known as Tom)
43. Alexander (yes, there's an Alexander in the New Testament—Mark 15:21; Acts 4:6)
44. Ethan (see 1 Kings 4:31)
45. Samuel
46. Jubal (If you know this one, consider yourself *extremely* well read. See Genesis 4:21)
47. John
48. Mark

49. _____ Crockett (American frontiersman)
50. _____ O'Connell (Irish liberation leader in the 1800s)

Familiar Verse, Peculiar Order

☞ Placed in their proper order, the words are a familiar verse from Matthew.

are for merciful obtain shall the blessed they mercy

Daniel the Senator, Asa the Cola Man, and Others

1. _____ _____ Jones (Revolutionary War naval hero)
2. _____ Taylor Coleridge (English Romantic poet)
3. _____ Pershing (American World War I hero)
4. _____ Conrad (English novelist, author of *Lord Jim*)
5. _____ Paine (colonial author of propaganda)
6. _____ Longstreet (Confederate general)
7. _____ Garfield (U.S. president in the 1880s)
8. _____ Steinbeck (American novelist)
9. _____ Stilwell (American leader in World War II)
10. _____ Ewell Brown Stuart (Confederate general)
11. _____ Moynihan (contemporary U.S. senator)
12. _____ Cassatt (American painter)
13. _____ Johnson (English literary leader in the 1700s)
14. _____ Gainsborough (English painter of *The Blue Boy*)
15. _____ Cranmer (English church leader in the 1500s)
16. _____ Pauling (contemporary U.S. scientist)
17. _____ Muhammad (American black Muslim leader)
18. _____ Smith (Scottish author of *The Wealth of Nations*)
19. _____ Edison (American inventor)
20. _____ Candler (founder of Coca-Cola)
21. _____ Lipton (tea merchant)
22. _____ Haydn (Austrian composer in the 1700s)
23. _____ Taylor (American pop singer)

49. David (better known as Davy)
50. Daniel

Familiar Verse, Peculiar Order (answer)

Blessed are the merciful: for they shall obtain mercy. (Matthew 5:7)

Daniel the Senator, Asa the Cola Man, and Others (answers)

1. John Paul
2. Samuel
3. John
4. Joseph
5. Thomas
6. James
7. James
8. John
9. Joseph
10. James (better known by his initials, J.E.B.)
11. Daniel
12. Mary
13. Samuel
14. Thomas
15. Thomas
16. Linus (yes, there's a Linus in the New Testament—2 Timothy 4:21)
17. Elijah
18. Adam
19. Thomas
20. Asa (the name of one of the kings of Judah)
21. Thomas
22. Joseph
23. James

24. _____ Caine (contemporary English actor)
25. _____ Tchaikovsky (Russian composer)
26. _____ Penney (founder of a department store chain)
27. _____ Mendelssohn (German composer)
28. _____ Cornell (American philanthropist, founder of a university)
29. _____ Sondheim (contemporary American musical composer)
30. _____ Bogdanovich (American movie director)
31. _____ Everly (half of a pop singing duo)
32. _____ Sheridan (Union general in the Civil War)
33. _____ Webster (American statesman in the early 1800s)
34. _____ Dukakis (former U.S. presidential candidate)
35. _____ Dinkins (New York mayor)
36. _____ Souter (Supreme Court justice)
37. _____ Harrison (U.S. president in the 1880s)
38. _____ Travolta (TV and movie actor)
39. _____ Whiteman (jazz band leader)
40. _____ Foster (American songwriter of the 1800s)
41. _____ Fahrenheit (German scientist of the 1700s)
42. _____ West (American painter in the late 1700s)
43. _____ Wesley (the founder of Methodism)
44. _____ Gauguin (French painter in the 1800s)
45. _____ Shelley (author of *Frankenstein*)
46. _____ Monroe (U.S. president)
47. _____ McCarthy (American novelist, died in 1989)
48. _____ Farragut (Union navy leader in the Civil War)
49. _____ _____ Goebbels (Nazi leader)
50. _____ Wilson (cartoonist who draws "Ziggy")
51. _____ Wambaugh (author of police novels)
52. _____ O'Neill (leader in the House)
53. _____ Goodman (TV and movie comic actor)
54. _____ Donahue (TV host)
55. _____ _____ Davis (movie actress)
56. _____ (pope from 1958 to 1963)
57. _____ McCarthy (U.S. senator in the 1950s)
58. _____ Mack (baseball player and manager)
59. _____ Mamet (American playwright and movie script writer)

24. Michael
25. Peter
26. James
27. Felix (yes, there's a Felix in the Bible—see Acts 23)
28. Ezra
29. Stephen
30. Peter
31. Philip (better known as Phil)
32. Philip
33. Daniel
34. Michael
35. David
36. David
37. Benjamin
38. John
39. Paul
40. Stephen
41. Gabriel (the name of an angel—Daniel 8: Luke 1)
42. Benjamin
43. John
44. Paul
45. Mary
46. James
47. Mary
48. David
49. Paul Joseph
50. Thomas (better known as Tom)
51. Joseph
52. Thomas
53. John
54. Phillip (better known as Phil)
55. Ruth Elizabeth (better known as Bette)
56. John
57. Joseph
58. Cornelius (better known as Connie—and the one Cornelius in the Bible is the Roman soldier in Acts 10)
59. David

60. _____ Eliot (American poet)
61. _____ Child (French cooking expert)
62. _____ Dryden (English poet in the 1600s)
63. _____ Morgan (Revolutionary War general)
64. _____ Arnold (English poet in the 1800s)
65. _____ Niven (English actor)
66. _____ Terry (American comics animator)
67. _____ von Hindenberg (German president in this century)
68. _____ Austin (leader of colonization in Texas)
69. _____ Carson (naturalist, author of *The Sea Around Us*)
70. _____ Demme (movie director)

Familiar Verse, Peculiar Order

☛ Placed in their proper order, the words are a familiar verse from Matthew.

and I fishers follow make me men of will you

Adlai the Statesman, Priscilla the King's Wife, and So On

1. _____ Newman (American movie actor)
2. _____ Hatfield (U.S. senator)
3. _____ Irving (American novelist)
4. _____ Madison (U.S. president)
5. _____ Hardy (English novelist of the 1800s)
6. _____ Helms (U.S. senator)
7. _____ Sununu (former White House staff member)
8. _____ Douglas (Abraham Lincoln's presidential opponent)
9. _____ Hancock (American Revolution leader)
10. _____ Lloyd George (British prime minister in this century)
11. _____ Stevenson (Illinois statesman and presidential candidate)
12. _____ Bedford Forrest (Confederate general)

60. Thomas (better known by his initials, T. S.)
61. Julia (yes, there's a Julia in the Bible—see Romans 16:15)
62. John
63. Daniel
64. Matthew
65. David
66. Paul
67. Paul
68. Stephen
69. Rachel
70. Jonathan

Familiar Verse, Peculiar Order (answer)

Follow me, and I will make you fishers of men. (Matthew 4:19)

Adlai the Statesman, Priscilla the King's Wife, and So On (answers)

1. Paul
2. Mark
3. John
4. James
5. Thomas
6. Jesse
7. John
8. Stephen
9. John
10. David
11. Adlai (yes, there is an Adlai in the Bible—see 1 Chronicles 27:29)
12. Nathan (notably, the prophet at the court of King David—2 Samuel 7)

13. _____ (pope from 1963 to 1978)
14. _____ Miller (contemporary English comic and director)
15. _____ Mott (religious leader in the early years of this century)
16. _____ Muni (movie actor in the 1930s)
17. _____ Muzorewa (Zimbabwe political leader)
18. _____ Namath (football star)
19. _____ Oakley (American rodeo sharpshooter)
20. _____ Ortega (Nicaraguan political leader)
21. _____ Owens (American track star)
22. _____ Vance (Carter administration notable)
23. _____ Papp (New York theatre producer)
24. _____ Bradley (Los Angeles mayor)
25. _____ Pearson (political columnist)
26. _____ Stookey (one-third of a pop music trio)
27. _____ Pound (offbeat American poet)
28. _____ Rayburn (longtime U.S. Congressman)
29. _____ Garroway (TV morning show host)
30. _____ Reed (American communist activist)
31. _____ Rockefeller (American millionaire who died in 1960)
32. _____ Cagney (movie actor)
33. _____ Rose (baseball star)
34. _____ Roth (contemporary American novelist)
35. _____ Smith (founder of the Virginia colony)
36. _____ Decatur (War of 1812 hero)
37. _____ Ritter (TV and movie comic)
38. _____ Roberts (movie actress)
39. _____ Belushi (movie actor)
40. _____ Gabriel (rock singer)
41. _____ Letterman (TV talk show host)
42. _____ Marshall (chaplain to the U.S. Senate and noted preacher)
43. _____ Montgomery (TV sitcom actress)
44. _____ Duke (tobacco tycoon and founder of a university)
45. _____ Watt (inventor of the steam engine)
46. _____ Mellon (millionaire industrialist and philanthropist)

13. Paul
14. Jonathan
15. John
16. Paul
17. Abel
18. Joseph (better known as Joe)
19. Phoebe (better known by her middle name, Anne, or Annie. The biblical Phoebe was a godly woman mentioned in Romans 16:1.)
20. Daniel
21. Jesse
22. Cyrus (the name of the Persian emperor in Ezra 1; Daniel 6)
23. Joseph
24. Thomas
25. Andrew (better known as Drew)
26. Paul
27. Ezra
28. Samuel
29. David
30. John
31. John
32. James
33. Peter (better known as Pete)
34. Philip
35. John
36. Stephen
37. John
38. Julia
39. James (or John)
40. Peter
41. David
42. Peter
43. Elizabeth
44. James
45. James
46. Andrew

47. _____ Strauss (pants manufacturer)
48. _____ Ward (founder of a mail-order firm and department store chain)
49. _____ Barber (American classical composer of this century)
50. _____ Presley (actress, wife of a deceased pop singer)

Familiar Verse, Peculiar Order

☛ Placed in their proper order, the words are a familiar verse from Matthew.

of the are earth salt the you

James the Film Idol, Mark the Guitarist, and Company

1. _____ Knopfler (leader of the rock group Dire Straits)
2. _____ Astin (American TV actor)
3. _____ Winthrop (founder of the Massachusetts Bay Colony in 1630)
4. _____ Cleveland (U.S. president)
5. _____ Alison (American race car driver who died in 1993)
6. _____ Birney (American TV actor)
7. _____ Foster Dulles (key figure in the Eisenhower administration)
8. _____ Cole (American painter in the early 1800s)
9. _____ Kenneth Galbraith (contemporary American economist)
10. _____ McCormick (American inventor of the reaper)
11. _____ Bowie (British rock star)
12. _____ Latrobe (architect partly responsible for designing the U.S. capitol)
13. _____ Stevens (vengeful U.S. House leader during the Reconstruction era)
14. _____ Brenner (American comic)
15. _____ Jay (first chief justice of the U.S. Supreme Court)

47. Levi (the name of one of Jacob's sons, and of one of the twelve tribes of Israel)
48. Aaron (better known by his middle name, Montgomery)
49. Samuel
50. Priscilla (in the New Testament, a godly friend of the apostle Paul)

Familiar Verse, Peculiar Order (answer)

You are the salt of the earth. (Matthew 5:13)

James the Film Idol, Mark the Guitarist, and Company (answers)

1. Mark
2. John
3. John
4. Stephen (better known by his middle name, Grover)
5. David (better known as Davey)
6. David
7. John
8. Thomas
9. John
10. Cyrus (in the Old Testament, a Persian emperor)
11. David
12. Benjamin
13. Thaddeus (the name of one of Jesus' twelve disciples)
14. David
15. John

16. _____ Flagg (cartoonist who created the "Uncle Sam" figure)
17. _____ Atlee (British prime minister in this century)
18. _____ Hamilton (first U.S. secretary of the treasury)
19. _____ Trumbull (American painter of historical pictures in the 1800s)
20. _____ Whitney (inventor of the cotton gin)
21. _____ Broderick (American movie actor)
22. _____ Javits (well-known New York senator for many years)
23. _____ Brown (American soul singer legend)
24. _____ Alden (one of the most famous *Mayflower* Pilgrims)
25. _____ Cranmer (English church leader in the 1500s, author of much of the *Book of Common Prayer*)
26. _____ Cleese (British comic and movie actor)
27. _____ Scheidemann (first chancellor of a democratic Germany)
28. _____ Cougar (American rock singer)
29. _____ Hull (U.S. navy leader during War of 1812)
30. _____ Wycliffe (English Bible translator in the Middle Ages)
31. _____ Crosby (one-fourth of a noted rock quartet)
32. _____ Benedict (American anthropologist, noted for studying southwestern Indian tribes)
33. _____ Kenny (Australian nurse who developed treatments for polio)
34. _____ Dean (American film idol of the 1950s)
35. _____ Lister (English scientist who pioneered in antiseptic surgery)
36. _____ Walton (founder of the Wal-Mart chain of stores)
37. _____ Falk (American comedy actor)
38. _____ Borodin (Russian composer in the 1800s)
39. _____ Wainwright (American military leader in World War II)
40. _____ Boswell (1700s literary figure in England, biographer of Samuel Johnson)
41. _____ Fogelberg (American pop singer)
42. _____ Ann Evans (English novelist in the 1800s)

16. James
17. Clement (yes, really—Philippians 4:3)
18. Alexander
19. John
20. Eli (the name of Samuel's mentor)
21. Matthew
22. Jacob
23. James
24. John
25. Thomas
26. John
27. Philip
28. John
29. Isaac
30. John
31. David
32. Ruth
33. Elizabeth
34. James
35. Joseph
36. Samuel (better known as Sam)
37. Peter
38. Alexander
39. Jonathan
40. James
41. Dan
42. Mary (much better known by her famous pen name, George Eliot)

43. _____ Forsythe (American TV actor)
44. _____ Gay (English composer in the 1700s, author of *The Beggar's Opera*)
45. _____ Chandler Harris (American author of the "Uncle Remus" stories)
46. _____ Galway (contemporary Irish flutist)
47. _____ Wooden (UCLA basketball coach)
48. _____ Herbert Lawrence (English novelist)
49. _____ Grey (American stage and movie comic)
50. _____ Williams (American composer of film music for *Star Wars, Jaws,* and many others)

Familiar Verse, Peculiar Order

☛ Placed in their proper order, the words are a familiar verse from Matthew.

world the of light are the you

Dinah the Crooner, Paul the Painter, and the Big Company

1. _____ Stern (classical violinist)
2. _____ Copland (American classical composer of this century)
3. _____ _____ Sousa (American marching band leader)
4. _____ Faure (French composer who died in the 1920s)
5. _____ Malkovich (movie actor)
6. _____ Shore (pop singer)
7. _____ O'Toole (movie actor)
8. _____ Lloyd Webber (contemporary theatrical composer)
9. _____ _____ Rubens (Flemish painter of the early 1600s)
10. _____ Keats (English Romantic poet)
11. _____ Haig (former Cabinet member)
12. _____ Steinbeck (American novelist)

43. John
44. John
45. Joel
46. James
47. John
48. David (better known by his initials, D. H.)
49. Joel
50. John

Familiar Verse, Peculiar Order (answer)

You are the light of the world. (Matthew 5:14)

Dinah the Crooner, Paul the Painter, and the Big Company (answers)

1. Isaac
2. Aaron
3. John Philip
4. Gabriel
5. John
6. Dinah (the name of the daughter of Jacob)
7. Peter
8. Andrew
9. Peter Paul
10. John
11. Alexander
12. John

13. _____ Moore (poet, author of "The Night before Christmas")
14. _____ Washington (wife of a U.S. president)
15. _____ Tyler (U.S. president)
16. _____ Gray (English poet in the 1700s)
17. _____ Tillich (German theologian in this century)
18. _____ J. Fox (TV and movie actor)
19. _____ Constable (English landscape painter)
20. _____ Polk (U.S. president)
21. _____ Stills (rock singer)
22. _____ Schneider (TV actor)
23. _____ Adams (wife of a U.S. president)
24. _____ Greenleaf Whittier (American poet of the 1800s)
25. _____ Currier (American lithography artist of the 1800s)
26. _____ Ives (American lithography artist of the 1800s)
27. _____ Crane (American novelist)
28. _____ Wolfe (British general in the French and Indian Wars)
29. _____ Arden (American comedy actress)
30. _____ Ustinov (British comedy actor)
31. _____ Johnson (American architect)
32. _____ Winfield (American actor)
33. _____ Knowles (American novelist)
34. _____ Royce (American philosopher)
35. _____ Cézanne (French painter in the 1800s)
36. _____ Beckett (offbeat Irish playwright of this century)
37. _____ Kosciusko (Polish general who aided colonists in the American Revolution)
38. _____ Richardson (English novelist of the 1700s)
39. _____ Klee (Swiss abstract artist)
40. _____ Hus (Czech religious reformer in the 1400s)
41. _____ L. Lewis (American labor leader)
42. _____ Campbell (American writer on mythology)
43. _____ Locke (English philosopher of the 1600s)
44. _____ Lean (English movie director of *Lawrence of Arabia* and many other classics)
45. _____ Mason (English movie actor)
46. _____ Theroux (American novelist)

13. Clement
14. Martha
15. John
16. Thomas
17. Paul
18. Michael
19. John
20. James
21. Stephen
22. John
23. Abigail
24. John
25. Nathaniel
26. James
27. Stephen
28. James
29. Eve
30. Peter
31. Philip
32. Paul
33. John
34. Josiah (the name of one of the better kings of Judah)
35. Paul
36. Samuel
37. Thaddeus (the name of one of Jesus' disciples)
38. Samuel
39. Paul
40. John
41. John
42. Joseph
43. John
44. David
45. James
46. Paul

47. _____ Inouye (U.S. senator from Hawaii)
48. _____ Becket (English archbishop in the Middle Ages, murdered in his cathedral by knights of King Henry II)
49. _____ Dewey (American educational philosopher)
50. _____ Russell (American political comic)
51. _____ Fogerty (leader of the rock group Creedence Clearwater Revival)

Familiar Verse, Peculiar Order

☛ Placed in their proper order, the words are a familiar verse from Genesis.

there and be God let light light said there was

Paul the Comic, Immanuel the Thinker, and the Whole Nine Yards

1. _____ Spitz (American swimmer, Olympic champion)
2. _____ Hartman (American actor and morning show host)
3. _____ O'Connor (American short story writer of this century)
4. _____ Hayes (American soul-rock singer)
5. Henry _____ Thoreau (American author of the 1800s)
6. _____ Francis Webster (American songwriter)
7. _____ Judd (retired member of a country female duo)
8. _____ Epstein (noted British sculptor of this century)
9. _____ Waller (American jazz musician and composer)
10. _____ Keaton (American movie comedy actor)
11. _____ McEnroe (American tennis champ in the 1980s)
12. _____ Washington (American jazz and blues singer)
13. _____ Kerr (British actress, popular in the 1960s and 1970s)
14. _____ McVie (a male member of the rock group Fleetwood Mac)

47. Daniel
48. Thomas
49. John
50. Mark
51. John

Familiar Verse, Peculiar Order (answer)

God said, Let there be light: and there was light. (Genesis 1:3)

Paul the Comic, Immanuel the Thinker, and the Whole Nine Yards (answers)

1. Mark
2. David
3. Mary (better known by her middle name, Flannery)
4. Isaac
5. David
6. Paul
7. Naomi (in the book of Ruth, Ruth's mother-in-law)
8. Jacob
9. Thomas (better known by his nickname, "Fats")
10. Michael
11. John
12. Dinah (in Genesis, the daughter of Jacob)
13. Deborah (in the book of Judges, Israel's only female judge)
14. John

15. _____ French (U.S. sculptor who designed the statue in the Lincoln Memorial)
16. _____ Ramey (contemporary American opera singer)
17. _____ Malone (American basketball star in the 1970s and 1980s)
18. _____ Raye (American comedy actress)
19. _____ Priestley (English chemist who discovered oxygen)
20. _____ Corbett (American boxing champ in the late 1800s)
21. _____ Lee Roth (rock singer)
22. _____ Grunewald (German religious painter in the 1400s)
23. _____ Stewart (American movie actor from the 1930s through the 1970s)
24. _____ Phillips (member of the pop group the Mamas and the Papas)
25. _____ Weir (Australian movie director)
26. _____ Hunt Morgan (scientist who developed chromosome theory of heredity)
27. _____ Williams (award-winning pop song lyricist)
28. _____ Yarrow (one-third of a folk-singing trio)
29. _____ Reynolds (English painter of the 1700s)
30. _____ Cole (pop singer, known by his nickname)
31. _____ Stuart Mill (English philosopher and economist in the 1800s)
32. _____ Ford (Irish movie director)
33. _____ Chadwick (British physicist who discovered the neutron)
34. _____ Janssen (TV's "Fugitive")
35. _____ Jolson (American songster)
36. _____ Fleming (scientist who discovered penicillin)
37. _____ Landon (popular TV actor)
38. _____ Abelard (controversial French theologian of the Middle Ages)
39. _____ Lorre (movie actor, popular in the 1940s and 1950s)
40. _____ Hobbes (English political philosopher in the 1600s)
41. _____ Lynde (comic actor in TV and movies)

15. Daniel
16. Samuel
17. Moses
18. Martha
19. Joseph
20. James
21. David
22. Matthias (in the book of Acts, the man who replaced Judas among the twelve disciples)
23. James
24. John
25. Peter
26. Thomas
27. Paul
28. Peter
29. Joshua
30. Nathaniel (better known as Nat, even better known as Nat "King" Cole)
31. John
32. John
33. James
34. David
35. Asa (better known as Al—his birth name was Asa Yoelson. Asa was the name of a king of Judah, by the way.)
36. Alexander
37. Michael
38. Peter
39. Peter
40. Thomas
41. Paul

42. _____ Kant (German philosopher of the 1700s)
43. _____ Rowan (half of a TV comedy team)
44. _____ Aquinas (medieval Catholic theologian, considered one of the great minds in Christian thought)
45. _____ Sellers (British movie comic)
46. _____ Knox (leader of the Reformation in Scotland in the 1500s)
47. _____ Selznick (movie producer, noted especially for *Gone with the Wind*)
48. _____ Smith (founder of the Mormon church)
49. _____ Macaulay (English historian in the 1800s)
50. _____ Wayne (legendary American movie actor)
51. _____ (prince, husband of Britain's Queen Elizabeth)
52. _____ (prince, second son of Queen Elizabeth)
53. _____ Garcia Marquez (Nobel prizewinning novelist from Colombia)
54. _____ Herndon (drummer with the country music group Alabama)

Familiar Verse, Peculiar Order

☞ Placed in their proper order, the words are a familiar verse from Exodus.

other before gods have me no shall you

42. Immanuel (in the Old Testament, a name meaning "God with us"—Isaiah 7:14)
43. Dan (not just a short form of Daniel, but the name of one of the twelve tribes of Israel)
44. Thomas
45. Peter
46. John
47. David
48. Joseph
49. Thomas
50. John (although his real name was Marion Morrison)
51. Philip
52. Andrew
53. Gabriel
54. Mark

Familiar Verse, Peculiar Order (answer)

You shall have no other gods before me. (Exodus 20:3)

Do You Remember?

☛ Would you like to see how much Bible trivia you can remember? Answer the questions (which you should have answered already in this section), and then see how well you rate on the scale on page xii.

1. _____ Anka (pop singer)
2. _____ _____ (the present pope, with two biblical names)
3. _____ Muhammad (American black Muslim leader)
4. _____ Douglas (Abraham Lincoln's presidential opponent)
5. _____ Cleese (British comic and movie actor)
6. _____ Lloyd Webber (contemporary theatrical composer)
7. _____ Smith (founder of the Mormon church)
8. _____ Lennon (English pop singer)
9. _____ Taylor (American actress)
10. _____ Caine (contemporary English actor)

Do You Remember? (answers)

1. Paul
2. John Paul (*two* Bible names, wow!)
3. Elijah
4. Stephen
5. John
6. Andrew
7. Joseph
8. John
9. Elizabeth
10 Michael

PART 5

Music,
Music,
Music

Test Your Bible IQ

☛ This quiz contains questions covering the topics in part 5, "Music, Music, Music." Do your best, then turn the page to see how you did. If you are brave enough to see how your Bible IQ rates, turn to page xii for our scale.

1. Fill in the blank for this lyric from a Christian song: "Stand up, stand up for Jesus, ye soldiers of the _____." (a thing)
2. Modern English composer William Walton wrote an oratorio *Belshazzar's Feast.* Which book of the Bible served as its basis?
3. Fill in the blank for this lyric from a Christian song: "All to _____ I surrender, all to him I freely give." (a name)
4. The following quote is from Handel's *Messiah.* Name the Bible book this is from: "For unto us a child is born, unto us a son is given, and the government shall be upon his shoulder."
5. Bernard Rogers's 1947 opera *The Warrior* deals with what strongman from the book of Judges?
6. Fill in the blank for this lyric from a Christian song: "Once in royal _____'s city stood a lowly cattle shed." (name of a king)
7. Richard Strauss' opera *Salome* features a notorious "dance of the seven veils." What famous New Testament character is the male lead in this opera?
8. The following quote is from Handel's *Messiah.* Name the Bible book this is from (and if you're good, the chapter and verse): "Worthy is the Lamb that was slain. Blessing and honor, glory and power be unto him that sitteth upon the throne."
9. Modern Italian composer Pizzeti chose two formidable women from the book of Judges as the subject for an opera. Who were they?
10. Fill in the blank for this lyric from a Christian song: "What child is this, who, laid to rest, on _____'s lap is sleeping?" (a person in the Gospels)

Test Your Bible IQ (answers)

1. Cross
2. Daniel; Belshazzar was the Babylonian ruler whose kingdom fell to the Persians immediately after his famous feast.
3. Jesus
4. Isaiah (9:6)
5. Samson
6. David
7. John the Baptist
8. Revelation (5:12-13)
9. *Deborah and Jael,* first performed in 1922
10. Mary

Ditty Time: The Bible in Song

☛ Christianity has been a singing religion since the very beginning, so it is natural that names and images from the Bible occur frequently in Christian songs—and in secular songs, for that matter. In fact, it is probably no overstatement to say that most people learn as much of the Bible's teaching from singing as they do from actually reading the Bible text. Below are passages (most of them familiar) from hymns and songs that mention a biblical name, place, or concept. (Biblical concepts can include *love, faith, grace, glory, peace,* etc.) Fill in the blanks if you can.

1. "Mine eyes have seen the _____ of the coming of the Lord." (an attribute of God)
2. "In _____ there is no east or west, in Him no south or north." (a name)
3. "Let there be _____ on earth, and let it begin with me." (an attribute)
4. "We are one in the _____, we are one in the Lord." (a divine name)
5. "We have heard the joyful sound: _____ saves! _____ saves!" (a name)
6. "O _____ haste, thy mission high fulfilling." (a place)
7. "Heaven came down and _____ filled my soul." (an attribute of God)
8. "Redeemed—how I love to proclaim it! Redeemed by the blood of the _____." (a name for Christ)
9. "I will sing the wondrous story of the _____ who died for me." (a name)
10. "Onward, _____ soldiers, marching as to war." (a name for believers)
11. "Stand up, stand up for Jesus, ye soldiers of the _____." (a thing)
12. "For all the _____ who from their labors rest." (a name applied to a group)
13. "Fight the good fight with all thy might! _____ is thy strength, and _____ thy might." (a name)
14. "Guide me, O thou great _____." (a name for God)
15. "I can hear my _____ calling, 'Take thy cross and follow me.'" (a name for Christ)
16. "_____ moves in a mysterious way, His wonders to perform." (a name)

Ditty Time: The Bible in Song (answers)

1. Glory
2. Christ
3. Peace
4. Spirit
5. Jesus
6. Zion
7. Glory
8. Lamb
9. Christ
10. Christian
11. Cross
12. Saints
13. Christ
14. Jehovah
15. Savior
16. God

17. "Savior, like a _____ lead us." (a title of Jesus)
18. "All the way my _____ leads me, what have I to ask beside?" (a name for Christ)
19. "Lead on, O _____ eternal, the day of march has come." (a title of God)
20. "Just a closer walk with thee, grant it, _____, is my plea." (a name)
21. "There shall be showers of _____, this is the promise of love." (a concept)
22. "Let us break _____ together on our knees." (a thing)
23. "Blest be the tie that binds our hearts in _____ love." (a name for believers)
24. "Come, _____ _____, dove divine." (a divine name)
25. "_____ is made the sure foundation, _____ the head and cornerstone." (a name)
26. "Built on the Rock, the _____ doth stand." (a name for believers)
27. "The church's one foundation is Jesus Christ her _____ ." (a name for Christ)
28. "We are one in the bond of _____." (a concept)
29. "God of grace and God of _____, on thy people pour thy power." (an attribute of God)
30. "_____ of our fathers, living still." (a concept)
31. "Lord, dismiss us with your _____ ." (a concept)
32. "Give of your best to the _____ ." (a name for Christ)
33. "Little is much, when _____ is in it." (a name)
34. "Must Jesus bear the _____ alone?" (a thing)
35. "Abide with me, fast falls the eventide. The darkness deepens, _____, with me abide." (a name for God)
36. "_____, perfect _____, in this dark world of sin." (a concept)
37. "We are climbing _____'s ladder." (an Old Testament character)
38. "In heavenly _____ abiding, no change my heart shall fear." (a concept)
39. "Open my eyes, illumine me, _____ divine." (a divine name)
40. "May the mind of Christ my _____ live in me from day to day." (a name for Christ)

17. Shepherd
18. Savior
19. King
20. Jesus
21. Blessing
22. Bread (referring to the bread of the Lord's Supper, of course)
23. Christian
24. Holy Spirit
25. Christ
26. Church
27. Lord
28. Love
29. Glory
30. Faith
31. Blessing
32. Master
33. God
34. Cross
35. Lord
36. Peace
37. Jacob
38. Love
39. Spirit
40. Savior

41. "Lord, lift me up and let me stand by faith on _____'s tableland." (a place)
42. "'Are ye able,' said the _____, 'to be crucified with me?'" (a name for Christ)
43. "Be thou my vision, O _____ of my heart." (a name for God)
44. "What a friend we have in Jesus, all our _____ and griefs to bear." (a concept)
45. "Take my life and let it be consecrated, _____, to thee." (a name for God)
46. "Take time to be _____, speak oft with the Lord." (an attribute of God)
47. "My _____, I love thee, I know thou art mine." (a name)
48. "Draw me nearer, blessed Lord, to the _____ where thou hast died." (a thing)
49. "When we walk with the Lord in the light of His Word, what a _____ he sheds on our way." (an attribute of God)
50. "_____ is the soul's sincere desire." (a concept)

Familiar Verse, Peculiar Order

☞ Placed in their proper order, the words are a familiar verse from Matthew.

so before light men your shine let

Joyful Noise: The Bible and the Great Composers

☞ Full of drama, both human and divine, the Bible has for centuries inspired the world's greatest composers, from Bach and Handel in the Baroque era to Andrew Lloyd Webber in our own day. Operas, choral works, and even instrumental works have drawn on the rich resources of the Bible's characters, stories, and themes. Test your knowledge of great music and the great Book. (And don't feel you have to be a music whiz to know the answers.)

1. The great choral work *Christ on the Mount of Olives* is by what famous German composer (who happened to be deaf)?

41. Heaven
42. Master
43. Lord
44. Sins
45. Lord
46. Holy
47. Jesus
48. Cross
49. Glory
50. Prayer

Familiar Verse, Peculiar Order (answer)

Let your light so shine before men. (Matthew 5:16)

Joyful Noise: The Bible and the Great Composers (answers)

1. Ludwig van Beethoven

2. George Frideric Handel took his words for the oratorio (large-scale choral work) *Israel in Egypt* from which book of the Bible?

3. The famous *German Requiem* differs from other requiems because its words are directly from the Bible, not from the Roman Catholic Mass. Who wrote the *German Requiem?*

4. Modern composer Arthur Honegger wrote a beautiful oratorio about which noted Old Testament king?

5. What German composer, familiar at Christmas time, wrote the oratorio *Joseph and His Brothers?*

6. What English composer, famous for his "Pomp and Circumstance" march used at graduations, wrote oratorios titled *The Apostles* and *The Kingdom?*

7. What Austrian composer, famous for his *Unfinished Symphony,* wrote the oratorio *Lazarus, the Feast of the Resurrection?*

8. The Austrian composer Joseph Haydn wrote a famous oratorio on the first few chapters of Genesis. What is the title of the work?

9. Modern English composer William Walton wrote an oratorio *Belshazzar's Feast.* Which book of the Bible served as its basis?

10. Charles Jennens composed the words (but not the music) for one of the most famous choral works in the world. What is it?

11. Felix Mendelssohn, famous for his *Midsummer Night's Dream* music, also wrote an oratorio about one of the apostles. Which one?

12. The greatest name in German opera also wrote a work for men's chorus titled *The Love Feast of the Apostles.* Who was the composer?

13. George Frideric Handel wrote a choral anthem that is still performed at British coronation ceremonies. What Old Testament priest is the subject of the anthem?

14. The great pianist Franz Liszt wrote a choral work about this New Testament woman who was related to Mary. Who was she?

15. Handel's *Messiah* is written in English, though the composer was German. But in what country did *Messiah* have its premiere performance?

2. Exodus
3. Johannes Brahms; the Requiem is not a mass, but an oratorio.
4. David; the title in French is *Le Roi David*—King David.
5. George Frideric Handel, more famous for his *Messiah*
6. Edward Elgar
7. Franz Schubert
8. *The Creation*
9. Daniel; Belshazzar was the Babylonian ruler whose kingdom fell to the Persians immediately after his famous feast.
10. *Messiah,* music by Handel; actually, Jennens merely arranged passages from the Bible.
11. *St. Paul*
12. Richard Wagner
13. Zadok
14. Elizabeth, mother of John the Baptist; the work's title is *The Legend of St. Elizabeth.*
15. Ireland; it was first performed in Dublin in 1742.

16. Ralph Vaughan Williams, one of the great names in twentieth-century music, wrote music for this Old Testament book about a suffering man. Which book?
17. *L'Enfance du Christ* ("The Childhood of Christ") is a choral work by a French composer famous for his *Symphonie Fantastique*. Who was he?
18. George Frideric Handel wrote oratorios dealing with two noted kings of Israel. Which ones?
19. French organist Cesar Franck wrote an oratorio about an admirable Old Testament woman. What was the title of this oratorio?
20. Benjamin Britten wrote a short opera *The Burning Fiery Furnace* based on an incident in what Old Testament book?
21. Handel wrote oratorios dealing with two great leaders in the book of Judges. Name them.
22. This Russian composer, who spent most of his life outside Russia after the Revolution, wrote a lovely choral work called *Symphony of Psalms*. Who was he?
23. *La Tour de Babel* is the French title for an opera by Cesar Franck. It may be the only opera ever written dealing with this story from Genesis. What story?
24. Felix Mendelssohn wrote an oratorio about what Old Testament prophet?
25. Composer Arnold Schoenberg, famous for his "atonal" music (which jars the ears of many people) wrote an opera about what two famous Old Testament brothers?
26. French composer Camille Saint-Saëns wrote a grand opera about two famous (or infamous) biblical lovers. Who were they?
27. Richard Strauss's opera *Salome* features a notorious "dance of the seven veils." What famous New Testament character is the male lead in this opera?
28. *Jesus Christ Superstar* and *Joseph and the Amazing Technicolor Dreamcoat* are pop operas with music by what noted composer?
29. What Christmas opera (originally written for television) concerns a crippled boy who meets the three wise men?
30. Modern composer Benjamin Britten wrote an entire opera about the most famous of Jesus' parables. Which parable?

16. Job
17. Hector Berlioz
18. Saul and Solomon
19. *Ruth*
20. Daniel
21. *Samson* and *Jephthah*
22. Igor Stravinsky, who died in 1971
23. The story of the Tower of Babel (If you can read French, this was an easy question.)
24. Elijah
25. Moses and Aaron
26. Samson and Delilah; the French title of the opera is *Samson et Dalila.*
27. John the Baptist
28. Andrew Lloyd Webber, who also wrote *Phantom of the Opera*
29. *Amahl and the Night Visitors* by Gian-Carlo Menotti
30. The Prodigal Son

31. The great French composer Charles Gounod wrote an opera titled (in French) *La Reine de Saba*. It concerns a famous woman in Solomon's life. Who?

32. Opera composer Rossini, famous for *The Barber of Seville*, also wrote an opera about a noted Hebrew liberator. Which one?

33. The great name in Italian opera, Giuseppe Verdi, wrote the opera *Nabuco*, which concerns a Babylonian king who plays a prominent role in the Bible. By what name do we know Nabuco?

34. Benjamin Britten wrote a curious biblical opera titled *Noye's Fludde*, in which the audience joins in to sing hymns. What Old Testament character is the opera about?

35. Richard Strauss wrote an opera that features a grisly scene of Herod's stepdaughter kissing the decapitated head of John the Baptist. What is the title of the opera?

36. George Frideric Handel wrote oratorios about three noted Old Testament women: a judge, an evil queen, and an emperor's wife. Who were they?

37. *The Seven Last Words of the Savior on the Cross* is a choral work by what great Austrian composer (famous for writing more than one hundred symphonies)?

38. Johann Sebastian Bach wrote several choral "Passions," with words drawn from the Gospels concerning Jesus' trial and crucifixion. Which Gospels' names did he attach to his two Passions?

39. In Luke's Gospel, Mary's speech that begins "My soul doth magnify the Lord" has been set to music by many composers. By what name do we call this?

40. English composer William Bennett is probably the only composer who has written a choral work about this scandalous woman found in the Gospels. Who was she?

Familiar Verse, Peculiar Order

☛ Placed in their proper order, the words are a familiar verse from John.

him is Pilate said to truth what

31. The queen of Sheba
32. Moses; the opera is *Moses in Egypt.*
33. Nebuchadnezzar
34. Noah; *Noye's Fludde* is an archaic form of "Noah's Flood."
35. *Salome*
36. Deborah, Athaliah, and Esther
37. Joseph Haydn
38. *St. Matthew Passion* and *St. John Passion*
39. *Magnificat,* the title being from the old Latin translation of the passage
40. *The Woman of Samaria,* which is the title of Bennett's oratorio; we also know her as "the woman at the well."

Familiar Verse, Peculiar Order (answer)

Pilate said to him, What is truth? (John 18:38)

Ditty Time:
The Bible in Song (Part II)

1. "O _____, let me walk with thee." (a name for Christ)
2. "I need thee every hour, most gracious _____." (a name for God)
3. "Sweet hour of _____, that calls me from a world of care." (a concept)
4. "Almost persuaded, now to believe; almost persuaded, _____ to receive." (a name)
5. "The _____ is waiting to enter your heart." (a name for Christ)
6. "_____ is tenderly calling thee home." (a name)
7. "Dear Lord and _____ of mankind, forgive our foolish ways!" (a name for God)
8. "Lord, I want to be a _____, in my heart." (a name for a believer)
9. "Just as I am, without one plea, but that thy _____ was shed for me." (a thing)
10. "Pass me not, O gentle _____, hear my humble cry!" (a name for Christ)
11. "Am I a soldier of the cross, a follower of the _____?" (a name for Christ)
12. "Lest I forget thy love for me, lead me to _____." (a place)
13. "All to _____ I surrender, all to him I freely give." (a name)
14. "Rise up, O men of _____, have done with lesser things." (a name)
15. "We gather together to ask the _____'s blessing." (a name)
16. "Praise God, from whom all _____ flow." (a concept)
17. "Joyful, joyful we adore thee, God of _____, Lord of love." (an attribute of God)
18. "Glorious things of thee are spoken, _____, city of our God." (a place)
19. "Rejoice, the Lord is _____!" (a title of God)
20. "O _____, our help in ages past." (a name)
21. "Ye servants of God, your _____ proclaim." (a name)

Ditty Time: The Bible in Song (Part II) (answers)

1. Master
2. Lord
3. Prayer
4. Christ
5. Savior
6. Jesus
7. Father
8. Christian
9. Blood
10. Savior
11. Lamb
12. Calvary
13. Jesus
14. God
15. Lord
16. Blessings
17. Glory
18. Zion
19. King
20. God
21. Master

22. "O for a thousand tongues to sing my great _____'s praise." (a name for Christ)
23. "All creatures of our God and _____." (a name for God)
24. "Crown him with many crowns, the _____ upon his throne." (a name for Christ)
25. "To God be the _____, great things he hath done." (an attribute of God)
26. "Come, thou almighty _____" (a title of God)
27. "Praise, my soul, the King of _____, to his feet thy tribute bring." (a place)
28. "Praise to the Lord, the _____, the King of creation." (a name for God)
29. "O worship the _____, all glorious above." (a title of God)
30. "All hail the power of Jesus name, let _____ prostrate fall." (a group of beings)
31. "Holy, holy, holy! Lord God _____!" (a name for God)
32. "Brethren, we have met to worship, to adore the _____ and God." (a name)
33. "Come, thou _____ of every blessing, tune my heart to sing thy grace." (a thing)
34. "I serve a risen _____, he's in the world today." (a name for Christ)
35. "O _____ my God, when I in awesome wonder . . ." (a name for God)
36. "Low in the grave he lay, Jesus my _____." (a name for Christ)
37. "Mine is the sunlight, mine is the morning born of the one light _____ saw play." (an Old Testament place)
38. "Christ, whose _____ fills the skies." (an attribute of God)
39. "This is my _____'s world." (a name for God)
40. "Christ the Lord is risen today, _____!" (a common biblical word denoting praise)
41. "Were you there when they crucified my _____?" (a name)
42. "O little town of _____, how still we see thee lie." (a place)

22. Redeemer
23. King
24. Lamb
25. Glory
26. King
27. Heaven
28. Almighty
29. King
30. Angels
31. Almighty
32. Lord
33. Fount
34. Savior
35. Lord
36. Savior
37. Eden
38. Glory
39. Father
40. Alleluia
41. Lord
42. Bethlehem

43. "Love divine, all loves excelling, joy of _____ to earth come down." (a place)
44. "What wondrous _____ is this, O my soul, O my soul?" (a concept)
45. "Hark! the herald angels sing, '_____ to the newborn King.'" (an attribute of God)
46. "Break thou the _____ of life, dear Lord, to me." (a thing)
47. "How firm a foundation, ye _____ of the Lord." (a name of a group)
48. "O come, O come, _____, and ransom captive Israel." (a name for Christ)
49. "There is a place of quiet rest, near to the heart of _____." (a name)
50. "The first Noel the _____ did say . . ." (a name)

Familiar Verse, Peculiar Order

☞ Placed in their proper order, the words are a familiar verse from the New Testament.

Alpha the am and and beginning end the I Omega

The Ultimate in Bible Music: Handel's *Messiah*

☞ George Frideric Handel's choral masterpiece *Messiah* is basically a very artful "quilting" job. Handel's collaborator, the lyricist Charles Jennens, stitched together passages from all over the Bible to create an enduring picture of Christ the Savior and Lord. Below are some of the famous airs and recitatives from *Messiah*. Try to identify the book of the Bible that each is from. (And if you're really good, you can identify the chapter and verse. . . .)

1. Comfort ye my people, saith your God. Speak ye comfortably to Jerusalem.
2. Who may abide the day of his coming, and who shall stand when he appeareth? For he is like a refiner's fire.
3. For unto us a child is born, unto us a son is given, and the government shall be upon his shoulder.

43. Heaven
44. Love
45. Glory
46. Bread
47. Saints
48. Immanuel
49. God
50. Angel

Familiar Verse, Peculiar Order (answer)

I am Alpha and Omega, the beginning and the end.
(Revelation 22:13)

The Ultimate in Bible Music: Handel's *Messiah* (answers)

1. Isaiah (40:1-2); this is the opening recitative, sung by a tenor.
2. Malachi (3:2)
3. Isaiah (9:6)

4. There were shepherds abiding in the field, keeping watch over their flock by night.
5. Come unto him, all ye that labor and are heavy laden, and he will give you rest.
6. Behold the Lamb of God that taketh away the sin of the world.
7. All they that see him laugh him to scorn.
8. Behold and see if there be any sorrow like unto his sorrow.
9. But thou didst not leave his soul in hell; nor didst thou suffer thy Holy One to see corruption.
10. Let all the angels of God worship him.
11. Thou shalt break them with a rod of iron; thou shalt dash them in pieces like a potter's vessel.
12. Hallelujah, for the Lord God omnipotent reigneth . . . King of kings, and Lord of lords!
13. I know that my redeemer liveth, and that he shall stand at the latter day upon the earth.
14. As in Adam all die, even so in Christ shall all be made alive.
15. If God be for us, who can be against us? Who shall lay anything to the charge of God's elect?
16. Worthy is the Lamb that was slain. Blessing and honor, glory and power be unto him that sitteth upon the throne.

Familiar Verse, Peculiar Order

☞ Placed in their proper order, the words are a familiar verse from the New Testament.

are but grace law not under under you

Ditty Time: The Bible in Song (Part III)

1. "On a hill far away stood an old rugged _____." (a thing)
2. "There is a balm in _____ to make the wounded whole." (a place)
3. "The great _____ now is here, the sympathizing Jesus." (a name for Jesus)

4. Luke (2:8)
5. Matthew (11:28)
6. John (1:29)
7. Psalm (22:7)
8. Lamentations (1:12)
9. Psalms (16:10)
10. Hebrews (1:6)
11. Psalm (2:9)
12. Revelation (19:6); from the famous "Hallelujah Chorus," of course.
13. Job (19:25)
14. 1 Corinthians (15:22)
15. Romans (8:31)
16. Revelation (5:12-13)

Familiar Verse, Peculiar Order (answer)

You are not under law, but under grace. (Romans 6:14)

Ditty Time: The Bible in Song (Part III) (answers)

1. Cross
2. Gilead
3. Physician

4. "I heard the voice of _____ say, 'Come unto me and rest.'" (a name)
5. "Burdens are lifted at _____." (a place in the Gospels)
6. "Blessed assurance, Jesus is mine! O what a foretaste of _____ divine!" (an attribute of God)
7. "What child is this, who, laid to rest, on _____'s lap is sleeping?" (a person in the Gospels)
8. "Standing on the promises of Christ my _____." (a title of Christ)
9. "Be still, my _____, the Lord is on thy side." (a thing)
10. "On _____'s bank the Baptist's cry announces that the Lord is nigh." (a river)
11. "My faith looks up to thee, thou Lamb of _____." (a place)
12. "Children of the heavenly _____ safely in his bosom gather." (a name for God)
13. "'Tis so sweet to trust in _____, just to take him at his word." (a name)
14. "My _____ is built on nothing less than Jesus' blood and righteousness." (a concept)
15. "Great is thy _____, O God my Father!" (an attribute of God)
16. "Amazing _____! How sweet the sound!" (an attribute of God)
17. "_____ of Ages, cleft for me, let me hide myself in thee." (a name for God)
18. "There's a wideness in God's _____ like the wideness of the sea." (an attribute of God)
19. "A mighty _____ is our God, a bulwark never failing." (a thing)
20. "When we all get to _____, what a day of rejoicing that will be." (a place)
21. "Come, _____ _____, heavenly dove." (a divine name)
22. "Go to dark _____, ye that feel the tempter's power." (a place in the Gospels)
23. "_____ of God, descend upon my heart." (a divine name)
24. "Heavenly sunlight, heavenly sunlight, flooding my soul with _____ divine." (an attribute of God)

4. Jesus
5. Calvary
6. Glory
7. Mary
8. King
9. Soul
10. Jordan
11. Calvary
12. Father
13. Jesus
14. Hope
15. Faithfulness
16. Grace
17. Rock
18. Mercy
19. Fortress
20. Heaven
21. Holy Spirit
22. Gethsemane
23. Spirit
24. Glory

25. "Alas, and did my _____ bleed, and did my Sovereign die?" (a title of Christ)
26. "There's a sweet, sweet _____ in this place." (a divine name)
27. "Joy to the world, the Lord is come, let earth receive her _____!" (a title of Christ)
28. "I wonder as I wander out under the sky how Jesus the _____ did come for to die." (a name for Christ)
29. "_____ from the realms of glory, wing your flight o'er all the earth." (a group of beings)
30. "There is a fountain filled with blood drawn from _____'s veins." (a name for Christ)
31. "O come all ye faithful, joyful and triumphant, O come ye, O come ye to _____." (a town)
32. "Go tell it on the mountain that _____ _____ is born!" (a name)
33. "Strong righteous man of _____, with borrowed peace we follow thee." (a place)
34. "I stand amazed in the presence of Jesus the _____." (a name)
35. "Yes, Jesus loves me! The _____ tells me so!" (a thing)
36. "I will sing of my _____ and his wondrous love to me." (a name for Christ)
37. "Take the name of _____ with you, child of sorrow and of woe." (a name)
38. "Fairest Lord Jesus, rule of all nature, O thou of _____ and man the Son." (a name)
39. "Jesus! What a friend for _____! Jesus! Lover of my soul!" (name of a group)
40. "'Man of sorrows'—what a name for the _____ _____ _____ who came." (a name for Christ)
41. "_____ covers it all, my past with its sin and stain." (a place)
42. "In the _____ of Christ I glory, towering o'er the wrecks of time." (a thing)
43. "When I survey the wondrous cross, on which the Prince of _____ died." (an attribute of God)
44. "And can it be that I should gain an interest in the _____'s blood." (a name for Christ)

25. Savior
26. Spirit
27. King
28. Savior
29. Angels
30. Immanuel
31. Bethlehem
32. Jesus Christ
33. Galilee
34. Nazarene
35. Bible
36. Redeemer
37. Jesus
38. God
39. Sinners
40. Son of God
41. Calvary
42. Cross
43. Glory
44. Savior

45. "What can wash away my sin? Nothing but the _____ of Jesus." (a thing)
46. "Come, thou Almighty _____." (a title of God)
47. "Praise the Lord! ye heavens, adore him; praise him, _____ in the height." (a group of beings)
48. "All people that on earth do dwell, sing to the _____ with cheerful voice." (a name for God)
49. "The God of _____ praise, who reigns enthroned above." (name of an Old Testament character)
50. "When all thy mercies, O my God, my rising _____ surveys . . ." (a thing)

Familiar Verse, Peculiar Order

☛ Placed in their proper order, the words are a familiar verse from Matthew.

   you causes eye it if out pluck right sin to your

Joyful Noise: The Bible and the Great Composers (Part II)

1. George Frideric Handel wrote a biblical oratorio that includes the characters Jonathan, David, and the Witch of Endor. What king of Israel is the oratorio named for?
2. American composer (and conductor) Leonard Bernstein named his Symphony no. 1 for an Old Testament prophet. Which one?
3. The great Austrian composer Gustav Mahler wrote *Symphony of a Thousand* and included in it a hymn, *Veni, Creator Spiritus*. What biblical person is this hymn addressed to?
4. The modern Italian composer Ottorino Respighi wrote a symphonic work titled *Belkis,* which deals with a foreign woman in King Solomon's life. What woman?
5. Carl Nielsen, the twentieth-century Danish composer, wrote an opera on what two kings of Israel?
6. Modern Italian composer Pizzeti chose two formidable women from the book of Judges as the subject for an opera. What is its title?

45. Blood
46. King
47. Angels
48. Lord
49. Abraham
50. Soul

Familiar Verse, Peculiar Order (answer)

If your right eye causes you to sin, pluck it out. (Matthew 5:29)

Joyful Noise: The Bible and the Great Composers (Part II) (answers)

1. Saul
2. Jeremiah
3. The Holy Spirit; *Veni, Creator Spiritus* is Latin for "come, creator Spirit," and refers to the Spirit in Genesis, "moving over the face of the waters."
4. The queen of Sheba; Belkis is the name (in Jewish legends) given to the queen, who is not actually named in the Bible.
5. *Saul and David,* first performed in 1902
6. *Deborah and Jael,* first performed in 1922

7. Probably the first opera written on a biblical subject happens to be (appropriately) on one of the earliest stories in the Bible. What is the name of the opera?

8. Appropriately enough, the *second* biblical opera on record concerns a pair of brothers. Who were they?

9. French composer César Franck wrote an oratorio about some of the most famous sayings of Jesus. What are they?

10. *Jesus of Nazareth* was an "almost"—an opera that was planned but never composed. Its composer abandoned the subject after many years, choosing instead to write about characters from German mythology. Who was the renowned German opera composer?

11. Italian opera composer Donizetti wrote the biblical opera *Il Diluvio Universale*. What man from Genesis is its main character?

12. What two noted Old Testament brothers are the subject of Felix Weingartner's 1914 opera?

13. *Israelites in the Wilderness,* based on Exodus, is an oratorio by one of Johann Sebastian Bach's talented sons. Which one?

14. Giacomo Meyer wrote an 1813 opera about one of Israel's judges who makes a rash vow. What is the title of the opera?

15. Bernard Rogers's 1947 opera *The Warrior* deals with what strongman from the book of Judges?

16. A biblical opera by French composer Etienne Mehul had the distinction of being Napoleon's favorite opera. What favorite son of Jacob is its subject?

17. A 1954 opera by Frenchman Darius Milhaud deals with a king of Israel and draws parallels between ancient and modern Israel. What king is the subject of the opera?

18. What New Testament character has been most frequently represented in operas? (Hint: He lost his head.)

19. What has supplied more stories for operas—the Old Testament or the New?

20. George Frideric Handel wrote many oratorios on biblical subjects, but only two had the words taken directly from the Bible. What were they?

21. What Czech composer famous for his *New World Symphony* also wrote the *Biblical Songs?*

7. *Adam and Eve*; the title in the original German is *Adam und Eva.* It was produced in 1678 by composer Johann Thiele.
8. *Cain and Abel,* a 1689 opera by Johann Philipp Fortsch
9. The Beatitudes
10. Richard Wagner, whose four-opera cycle *The Ring of the Nibelungs* was the subject he chose rather than the life of Jesus
11. Noah; translated into English, the opera's title is *The Universal Flood.*
12. Cain and Abel
13. Carl Philipp Emanuel Bach, often referred to as C. P. E. Bach, probably the most famous of Bach's sons
14. *Jephthah's Daughter,* which deals with Jephthah's sacrifice of his daughter in Judges 11
15. Samson
16. *Joseph,* written in 1807; Napoleon awarded the composer a medal
17. David
18. Probably John the Baptist; the story of his imprisonment by Herod and his beheading after the dance of Herodias's daughter has fascinated composers for centuries. Composers have been somewhat shy about writing operas about Jesus himself, since, traditionally, sacred subjects have not been considered appropriate for the opera house. Richard Strauss and Jules Massenet are just a few of the composers who have written about John the Baptist.
19. The Old, definitely; aside from the fact that the Old is much longer than the New, composers have been reluctant to portray the New Testament's main character, Christ, in opera. The Old Testament, on the other hand, is full of violent, sensuous people and stories that lend themselves well to operas—Saul, David, Samson, Moses, etc.
20. *Israel in Egypt,* which takes its words from Exodus, and *Messiah,* which takes its words from various parts of the Old and New Testaments
21. Antonin Dvorak; his "Largo" from the *New World Symphony* is probably his best-known work.

Familiar Verse, Peculiar Order

☞ Placed in their proper order, the words are a familiar verse from the book of Genesis.

keeper am brother's my I

Ditty Time:
The Bible in Song (Part IV)

1. "The King of love my _____ is, whose goodness faileth never." (a name for God)
2. "I sing the almighty _____ of God that made the mountains rise." (an attribute of God)
3. "Hail, thou once despised Jesus! Hail, thou Galilean _____." (a title for Jesus)
4. "Gentle _____ laid her child lowly in a manger." (name of a person in the Gospels)
5. "Once in royal _____'s city stood a lowly cattle shed." (name of a king)
6. "He rules the world with truth and _____, and makes the nations prove . . ." (an attribute of God)
7. "'Tis midnight, and on _____'s brow the star is dimmed that lately shone." (a hill)
8. "I serve a risen _____, he's in the world today." (a title for Jesus)
9. "The day of _____! earth tell it out abroad!" (an event in the Gospels)
10. "Joys are flowing like a river since the _____ has come." (a name for the Spirit)
11. "I love thy _____, Lord, the house of thine abode." (a thing)
12. "_____ of our fathers, living still in spite of dungeon, fire, and sword." (a concept)
13. "God hath spoken by his _____, spoken his unchanging Word." (a group of people)
14. "What can wash away my _____? Nothing but the blood of Jesus." (a thing)
15. "I lay my sins on Jesus, the spotless _____ of God." (a name for Christ)

Familiar Verse, Peculiar Order (answer)

Am I my brother's keeper? (Genesis 4:9)

Ditty Time: The Bible in Song (Part IV) (answers)

1. Shepherd
2. Power
3. King
4. Mary
5. David
6. Grace
7. Olive (referring to the Mount of Olives, of course)
8. Savior
9. Resurrection
10. Comforter
11. Kingdom
12. Faith
13. Prophets
14. Sin
15. Lamb

16. "Would you be free from your burden of sin? There's power in the _____." (a thing)
17. "Earnestly, tenderly, Jesus is calling, calling, O _____ come home." (a type of person)
18. "O _____ that will not let me go, I rest my weary soul in thee." (an attribute of God)
19. "More like the _____ I would ever be, more of his meekness, more humility." (a name for Jesus)
20. "There's within my heart a melody, _____ whispers sweet and low." (a name)
21. "_____, perfect _____, in this dark world of sin . . ." (a concept)
22. "Must Jesus bear the _____ alone, and all the world go free?" (a thing)
23. "The _____ has come, and he calls us to follow the track of the footprints he leaves on our way." (a name for Jesus)
24. "On _____'s stormy banks I stand and cast a wishful eye." (name of a river)
25. "Prepare the way, O _____, your Christ is drawing near." (a place)
26. "O victory in Jesus, my _____ forever!" (a name for Christ)
27. "From _____ above to earth I come to bring good news to everyone." (a place)
28. "Silent night, holy night, _____ ___ _____, love's pure light." (a name for Jesus)
29. "Earth has many a noble city; _____ dost all excel." (a town)
30. "When Christ's appearing was made known, King _____ trembled for his throne." (name of a king)
31. "Christ is alive! Let Christians sing; His _____ stands empty to the sky." (a thing)
32. "We walk by _____ and not by sight." (a concept)
33. "When _____, full of power and grace, went forth throughout the land." (name of a New Testament person)
34. "I sing a song of the _____ of God, patient and brave and true." (a group of people)
35. "Lord, dismiss us with thy blessing, fill our hearts with joy and _____." (a concept)

16. Blood
17. Sinner
18. Love
19. Master
20. Jesus
21. Peace
22. Cross
23. Master
24. Jordan
25. Zion
26. Savior
27. Heaven
28. Son of God
29. Bethlehem
30. Herod
31. Cross
32. Faith
33. Stephen
34. Saints
35. Peace

36. "God of the prophets, bless the prophets' heirs! Elijah's mantle o'er _____ cast." (name of an Old Testament character)

37. "Come, thou incarnate _____, by heaven and earth adored." (a name for Christ)

38. "From all that dwell below the skies let the _____'s praise arise!" (a name for God)

39. "Thy mercies how tender, how firm to the end; our Maker, Defender, _____, and Friend!" (a name for God)

40. "O bless the Lord, my soul, His _____ to thee proclaim!" (an attribute of God)

41. "I'll praise my _____ while I've breath." (a name for God)

42. "Lift up your heads, ye mighty gates; behold the _____ of glory waits." (a title for God)

43. "As _____ with travel was weary one day, at night on a stone for a pillow he lay." (name of an Old Testament character)

44. "The head that once was crowned with thorns is crowned with _____ now." (an attribute of God)

45. "Creator _____, by whose aid the world's foundations first were laid." (a divine name)

46. "Blessed city, heavenly _____, vision dear of peace and love." (an Old Testament town)

47. "O holy city, seen of _____, where Christ, the Lamb, doth reign." (name of an apostle)

48. "Judge eternal, throned in splendor, Lord of lords and _____ _____ _____." (a title for Christ)

49. "Hail to the Lord's anointed, great _____'s greater Son!" (name of an Old Testament character)

50. "Ye watchers and ye holy ones, bright seraphs, _____, and thrones." (a group of angels)

Familiar Verse, Peculiar Order

☛ Placed in their proper order, the words are a familiar verse from Psalms.

forsaken God hast me my thou my why God

36. Elisha
37. Word (from verse 2 of "Come, Thou Almighty King")
38. Creator
39. Redeemer (from the final verse of "O Worship the King")
40. Grace
41. Maker
42. King
43. Jacob (from an old English carol)
44. Glory
45. Spirit
46. Salem
47. John
48. King of kings
49. David
50. Cherubim

Familiar Verse, Peculiar Order (answer)

My God, my God, why hast thou forsaken me? (Psalm 22:1)

Do You Remember?

☞ Would you like to see how much Bible trivia you can remember? Answer the questions (which you should have answered already in this section), and then see how well you rate on the scale on page xii.

1. Fill in the blank for this lyric from a Christian song: "Open my eyes, illumine me, _____ divine." (a divine name)
2. Charles Jennens composed the words (but not the music) for one of the most famous choral works in the world. What is it?
3. Fill in the blank for this lyric from a Christian song: "Praise God, from whom all _____ flow." (a concept)
4. The following quote is from Handel's *Messiah*. Name the Bible book this is from (and if you're good, the chapter and verse): "I know that my redeemer liveth, and that he shall stand at the latter day upon the earth."
5. Fill in the blank for this lyric from a Christian song: "What can wash away my sin? Nothing but the _____ of Jesus." (a thing)
6. Italian opera composer Donizetti wrote the biblical opera *Il Diluvio Universale*. What man from Genesis is its main character?
7. Fill in the blank for this lyric from a Christian song: "Hail to the Lord's anointed, great _____'s greater Son!" (name of an Old Testament character)
8. The great choral work *Christ on the Mount of Olives* is by what famous German composer (who happened to be deaf)?
9. Fill in the blank for this lyric from a Christian song: "All hail the power of Jesus name, let _____ prostrate fall." (a group of beings)
10. The modern Italian composer Ottorino Respighi wrote a symphonic work titled *Belkis,* which deals with a foreign woman in King Solomon's life. What woman?

Do You Remember? (answers)

1. Spirit
2. *Messiah,* music by Handel; actually, Jennens merely arranged passages from the Bible.
3. Blessings
4. Job (19:25)
5. Blood
6. Noah; translated into English, the opera's title is *The Universal Flood.*
7. David
8. Ludwig van Beethoven
9. Angels
10. The queen of Sheba; Belkis is the name (in Jewish legends) given to the queen, who is not actually named in the Bible.

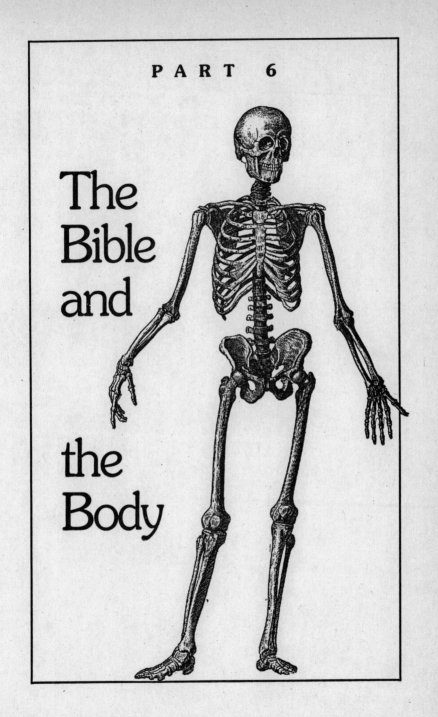

PART 6

The
Bible
and

the
Body

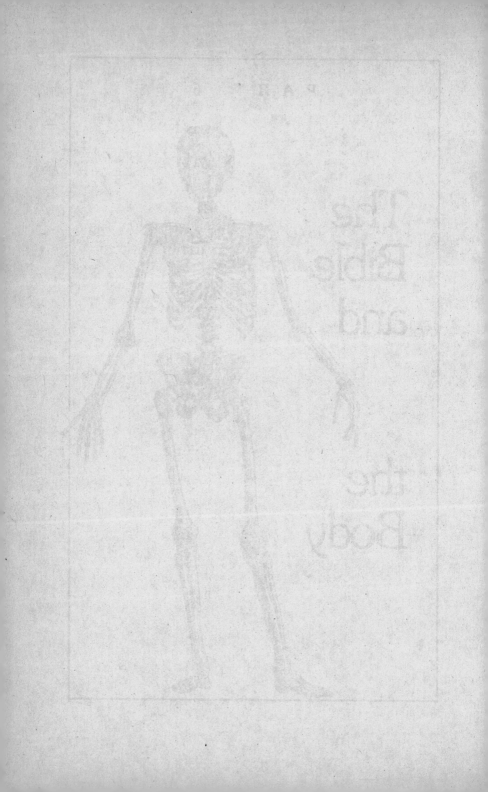

Test Your Bible IQ

☛ This quiz contains questions covering the topics in part 6, "The Bible and the Body." Do your best, then turn the page to see how you did. If you are brave enough to see how your Bible IQ rates, turn to page xii for our scale.

1. What did Jesus put in the eyes of the blind man at the pool of Siloam?
2. Who says in his heart, "There is no God"?
3. What praise-filled book ends with the words "Let every thing that hath breath praise the Lord"?
4. Which New Testament letter talks about the importance of "bridling" the tongue?
5. Who made a gift of two hundred Philistine foreskins to his future father-in-law?
6. What famous king had a curious dream of seven fat cows being devoured by seven scrawny cows?
7. According to Paul, what group of people comprises Christ's body?
8. What murdered man's blood cried out from the earth?
9. Which book of the Old Testament contains the "eye for eye" rule?
10. According to Paul, when a person speaks with the gift of tongues, who is he speaking to?

Test Your Bible IQ (answers)

1. Mud (John 9:1-7)
2. The fool (Psalm 14:1)
3. Psalms (150:6)
4. James (1:26)
5. David (1 Samuel 18:27); Saul had required this for David to marry Saul's daughter Michal, hoping that David would be killed in trying to acquire the foreskins.
6. The pharaoh of Egypt; his dream (which symbolized seven good years followed by seven years of famine) was interpreted by Joseph (Genesis 41).
7. The church, that is, Christians (Colossians 1:24)
8. Abel's, after being killed by his brother Cain (Genesis 4:10)
9. Exodus (21:24)
10. God (1 Corinthians 14:2)

Let's Get Physical:
The Anatomy Lesson

1. God foretold that Eve's offspring would strike the serpent's head. What part of man's body would the serpent strike?
2. When a Hebrew man swore an oath to another man, where would he place his hand?
3. What happened to the children who made fun of Elisha's bald head?
4. Who had a belly and thighs of brass?
5. What epistle says that blessing and cursing should not come out of the same mouth?
6. What did Jesus put in the eyes of the blind man at the pool of Siloam?
7. According to Revelation, what is inscribed on the triumphant Christ's thigh?
8. For what crime could a man have his shoe taken away and his face spit in?
9. What son of Saul was murdered by two servants who stabbed him in the belly and carried his severed head to David?
10. What happened when Paul placed his hands on the believers at Ephesus?
11. Which disciple was reluctant to have Jesus wash his feet?
12. Which prophet comforted the people of Israel with these words: "Thou shalt suck the breast of kings"?
13. What prophet saw a little cloud like a man's hand?
14. What king of Judah suffered from a crippling foot disease?
15. Who put a golden chain around Joseph's neck?
16. What king executed John the Baptist after his stepdaughter asked for John's head on a platter?
17. Who cut off the ear of Malchus, the high priest's servant?
18. What rebel against David was beheaded, with his head thrown over the city wall?
19. What king received seventy human heads in baskets?
20. What beheaded prophet was buried by his disciples?
21. Whose palace had a hand that wrote on the wall?
22. What book has a devoted lover praising a woman's beautiful feet?
23. What venomous creature bit Paul on the hand but did not harm him?

Let's Get Physical: The Anatomy Lesson (answers)

1. The heel (Genesis 3:15)
2. Under the other man's thigh (see Genesis 24:2; 47:29); if this seems a bit odd, consider: Being near the man's reproductive organs, the meaning of the oath was something like, "Swear by my descendants."
3. They were torn apart by two bears (2 Kings 2:23-25).
4. Not really a "who" but a "what"—the five-metal statue in the dream of King Nebuchadnezzar of Babylon, interpreted by the prophet Daniel (Daniel 2:32)
5. James (3:10)
6. Mud (John 9:1-7)
7. "King of Kings, and Lord of Lords" (Revelation 19)
8. Refusing to marry the widow of his deceased brother (Deuteronomy 25:9)
9. Ishbosheth, slain by Recab and Baanah (2 Samuel 4:5-8)
10. They spoke in tongues and proclaimed the gospel (Acts 19:1-7).
11. Peter (John 13:6-9)
12. Isaiah (60:16); he was speaking figuratively, not literally.
13. Elijah (1 Kings 18:44); the cloud was the sign that the three-year drought in Israel was at an end.
14. Asa (1 Kings 15:23)
15. Pharaoh (Genesis 41:42); this was a sign of elevation to high office.
16. Herod (Mark 6:14-28); he had been so entranced by the girl's dance that he offered to give her anything she asked.
17. Peter (John 18:10), who was zealous to keep Jesus from being arrested; Jesus then healed the man's ear.
18. Sheba (2 Samuel 20:22)
19. Jezreel (2 Kings 10:7); they were the heads of evil King Ahab's family members, a dynasty that Jehu effectively eliminated.
20. John the Baptist (Matthew 14:11-12)
21. Belshazzar's, the king of Babylon (Daniel 5:5); the hand wrote a message that predicted Babylon's downfall.
22. The Song of Solomon (7:1)
23. A viper (Acts 28:3-6)

24. Who had a vision of a prostitute with a city's name engraved on her head?

25. What did Jesus place in the ears of a deaf man when healing him?

26. According to Jesus, what bodily organ should you pluck out if it causes you to sin?

27. According to the prophet Ezekiel, which ruler tried to foretell the future by looking at animal livers?

28. What evil queen "painted her face" before meeting with the rebel king Jehu?

29. What did Elisha's servant see after Elisha prayed that his eyes would be opened?

30. What Old Testament book begins, "Let him kiss me with the kisses of his mouth: for thy love is better than wine"?

31. What pitiful man's face turned foul (red) with weeping?

32. What miraculous thing happened to Moses' hand?

33. Who tore a lion apart with his bare hands?

34. What blind father recognized Jacob's voice but was deceived by his glove-covered hands?

35. What Old Testament book says that anyone who scorns his parents will have his eyes pecked out by ravens?

36. What gruesome object did the Philistines fasten in the temple of Dagon?

37. Who saw the "back" of God, since he could not bear to see him face to face?

38. Is the human posterior ever mentioned in the Bible?

39. What wife of King David gave him a tongue lashing for dancing in the streets and exposing himself to the town's women?

40. Though God has no body, the Bible refers many times (figuratively) to his face, hands, mouth, etc. Which part is mentioned most often?

41. What book of the Old Testament is most concerned with human anatomy?

42. According to the Law, if a man is attacked by another man, what part of the assailant's body is forbidden for the woman to touch?

43. According to Jesus, what part of the body are we not to swear an oath by?

24. John (Revelation 17:5)
25. His fingers (Mark 7:33)
26. Your eye (Mark 9:47)
27. The king of Babylon (Ezekiel 21:21); surprisingly enough, "reading" omens through animals' organs was fairly common in the ancient world (and still is in some areas).
28. Jezebel, widow of evil King Ahab (2 Kings 9:30)
29. An angelic army (2 Kings 6:15-17)
30. The Song of Solomon (1:2)
31. Job's (16:16)
32. It became leprous, then became normal again (Exodus 4:7).
33. Samson (Judges 14:5-6)
34. Isaac, who was deceived by his wily son Jacob (Genesis 27:22); the gloves were intended to make Isaac believe that he was touching the hands of Jacob's hairy-bodied brother, Esau.
35. Proverbs (30:17)
36. The head of Israel's king, Saul, whom they had defeated in battle (1 Chronicles 10:10)
37. Moses (Exodus 33:23)
38. Yes, twice, both times referring to captives who were shamed by publicly having their buttocks exposed (2 Samuel 10:4; Isaiah 20:4)
39. Michal (2 Samuel 6); David replied that he was dancing spontaneously and joyously because the ark of the covenant had been returned to the Israelites.
40. Eyes; the eyes of the Lord are mentioned almost a hundred times in the Bible, mostly in the Old Testament.
41. Undoubtedly the Song of Solomon, which dwells on details of the two lovers' lips, cheeks, breasts, thighs, eyes, hair, hands, feet, etc.
42. His genitals; her punishment for doing so is to have her hand cut off (Deuteronomy 25:11).
43. The head (Matthew 5:36)

44. What part of the body are we supposed to cut off if it causes us to sin?
45. According to the Law, why couldn't the Israelites build an altar with steps leading up to it?

Familiar Verse, Peculiar Order

☛ Placed in their proper order, the words are a familiar verse from the New Testament.

God hearts in of peace rule the your let

Matters of the Heart

1. Who told his mistress "all his heart" and lost his hair (and eyesight and freedom) as a result?
2. What evil Old Testament king had his heart repeatedly hardened by God?
3. When a man looks at a woman with lust in his heart, what sin has he committed?
4. Whose wife "despised him in her heart" because he was dancing merrily in the streets and exposing a little too much flesh?
5. What handsome prince "stole the hearts of the men of Israel"?
6. Who told the Israelites to "circumcise the foreskins of their hearts"?
7. What pagan king's heart was "merry with wine"?
8. Which Old Testament book commands, "Thou shalt not hate thy brother in thine heart"?
9. According to Paul, what sort of people had been given up to the lusts of their own hearts?
10. To whom did God say, "The Lord looketh on the heart"?
11. What did God do when he perceived that man's heart was "only evil continually"?
12. Who claimed to be "meek and lowly in heart"?
13. According to Jesus, where is a person's heart?
14. Who takes away the Word sown in people's hearts?
15. What king was "a man after God's own heart"?

44. The hand, according to Jesus (Matthew 5:30)
45. For fear that, by walking up the steps, they might indecently expose themselves (Exodus 20:26)

Familiar Verse, Peculiar Order (answer)

Let the peace of God rule in your hearts. (Colossians 3:15)

Matters of the Heart (answers)

1. Samson, who, unfortunately, told Delilah "all his heart" (Judges 16)
2. The pharaoh at the time of Moses (Exodus 7:3)
3. Adultery (Matthew 5:28)
4. David, whose wife Michal thought his dancing was undignified (2 Samuel 6:16)
5. David's son Absalom, who led a rebellion against his father (2 Samuel 15:6)
6. Moses (Deuteronomy 10:16), who was speaking figuratively, of course
7. The Persian king Ahasuerus (Esther 1:10)
8. Leviticus (19:17); this is a remarkable verse, since Leviticus is mostly concerned with offerings and sacrifices.
9. Homosexuals (Romans 1:24)
10. Samuel, who was in the process of choosing a king for Israel (1 Samuel 16:7)
11. Decided to destroy the earth with a flood (Genesis 6:5)
12. Jesus (Matthew 11:29)
13. Where his treasure is (Matthew 6:21)
14. Satan (Mark 4:15)
15. David (1 Samuel 13:14)

16. Who was sent by God "to turn the hearts of the fathers to the children"?
17. According to Hosea, which two vices "take away the heart"?
18. What pagan king lost his mind and had his heart changed from a man's to a beast's?
19. Whose heart "fainted" when he heard that his long-lost son was still alive?
20. Who kept in her heart all the things people said about her newborn child?
21. Who entered Judas's heart to urge him to betray Jesus?
22. Which prophet said, "Rend your heart and not your garments"?
23. Who says in his heart, "There is no God"?
24. Who offered sacrifices on the possibility that his children had cursed God in their hearts?
25. What kind of heart is the Lord near to?
26. What book says that even in laughter the heart is sorrowful?
27. What rebel was killed by three darts, shot into his heart by Joab?
28. What book says that the Lord's people have become as heartless as ostriches in the desert?
29. According to Malachi, what prophet will come back to turn the hearts of the children to their fathers?
30. Who said that the Old Testament Law allowed divorce because of people's hardness of heart?
31. What prophet claimed that God would make a new covenant that would be written on men's hearts?
32. What will happen to the pure in heart, according to Jesus?

Familiar Verse, Peculiar Order

☛ Placed in their proper order, the words are a familiar verse from Luke.

earth and glory God highest in on peace the to

16. John the Baptist (Luke 1:17)
17. "Whoredom and wine" (Hosea 4:11)
18. Nebuchadnezzar of Babylon (Daniel 4:16)
19. Jacob, father of Joseph (Genesis 45:26)
20. Mary, Jesus' mother (Luke 2:51)
21. Satan (John 13:2)
22. Joel (2:13); he was referring to the practice of rending (tearing) the garments to express grief and claiming that it was more important to grieve inwardly than outwardly.
23. The fool (Psalm 14:1)
24. Job (1:5)
25. A broken one (Psalm 34:18)
26. Proverbs (14:13)
27. Absalom, David's son (2 Samuel 18:14)
28. Lamentations (4:3)
29. The prophet Elijah (Malachi 4:6)
30. Jesus (Matthew 19:8)
31. Jeremiah (31:33)
32. They will see God (Matthew 5:8).

Familiar Verse, Peculiar Order (answer)

Glory to God in the highest, and on earth peace. (Luke 2:14)

Breathing Lessons

1. Who had the only known case of halitosis in the Bible?
2. What happened when the risen Jesus "breathed on" his disciples?
3. What Jewish fanatic was "breathing out threatenings and slaughter against the disciples of the Lord," but later became an apostle?
4. What prophet had a vision of a valley of dry bones, brought to life when God breathed into them?
5. What lump of dust came to life when God breathed into it?
6. What military leader went into Canaan and "utterly destroyed all that breathed, as the Lord commanded"?
7. What chilly weather phenomenon did Job think came from the breath of God?
8. What praise-filled book ends with the words "Let every thing that hath breath praise the Lord"?
9. What prophet warned against worshiping gold and silver idols that have no breath in them?
10 In Luke's Gospel, what did Jesus say before he breathed his last?
11. Which apostle claimed that all Scripture is "God-breathed"?
12. In the book of Revelation, what people were brought to life when God breathed into them?
13. Who, according to 2 Thessalonians, will Christ overthrow by the breath of his mouth?
14. In the King James Version, what phrase is used to mean "breathed his last breath"?
15. Which sensuous Old Testament book describes a lover whose breath has the fragrance of apples?
16. Which prophet described God blowing on the fires of hell to kindle the blaze?
17. According to Mark's Gospel, what did Jesus do just before he breathed his last?

Breathing Lessons (answers)

1. Job, who lamented that his wife found his breath "offensive" (or "strange," depending on the translation you're reading (Job 19:17)
2. They received the Holy Spirit (John 20:22).
3. Saul, later called Paul (Acts 9:1)
4. Ezekiel (37:5)
5. Adam, the first man (Genesis 2:7)
6. Joshua (10:40); we have to assume that this refers to people, not to absolutely *everything* that breathed.
7. Frost (Job 37:10)
8. Psalms (150:6)
9. Habakkuk (2:19)
10. "Father, into thy hands I commend my spirit" (Luke 23:46).
11. Paul, writing to Timothy (2 Timothy 3:16); some translations have "inspired" instead of "God-breathed," though in fact "God-breathed" is a perfect translation of the Greek wording.
12. The two witnesses, who had been killed by the Beast from the Abyss (Revelation 11:11)
13. The man of lawlessness, who will appear at the end times (2 Thessalonians 2:8)
14. "Gave up the ghost" (Genesis 25:8 and many other places)
15. The Song of Solomon (7:8)
16. Isaiah (30:33), who was describing the fire of Tophet, an Old Testament name for the place of destruction
17. Cried out in a loud voice (Mark 15:37)

Familiar Verse, Peculiar Order

☞ Placed in their proper order, the words are a familiar verse from Luke.

as be Father is just merciful your merciful

Tongues, Tied and Untied

1. What great leader of Israel considered himself "slow of tongue"?
2. Who healed a mute man by touching his tongue?
3. What New Testament man was made temporarily tongue-tied because he doubted the words of an angel?
4. Which parable of Jesus features a rich man in hell, begging for someone to cool his tongue with a drop of water?
5. At what place did the "confusion of tongues" occur?
6. Which New Testament letter addresses the issue of speaking in tongues?
7. Where were the apostles when "tongues of fire" rested upon them?
8. In which Gospel does Jesus prophesy that his followers will speak with "new tongues"?
9. At what Roman soldier's home did the Holy Spirit lead the people to speak in tongues?
10. What Israelite leader selected his army by choosing men who drank water by lapping it up with their tongues like a dog?
11. What king compared the tongue to a bow that shoots bitter arrows?
12. What king (and poet) compared the deceitful tongue to a sharp razor?
13. Which New Testament letter talks about the importance of "bridling" the tongue?
14. What prophetic book describes men gnawing their own tongues in pain?
15. According to Psalm 140, what animal's tongue does an evil man's tongue resemble?
16. Where was Paul when he laid hands on twelve men and they spoke in tongues?

Familiar Verse, Peculiar Order (answer)

Be merciful, just as your Father is merciful. (Luke 6:36)

Tongues, Tied and Untied (answers)

1. Moses (Exodus 4:10)
2. Jesus, of course (Mark 7:33)
3. Zacharias, father of John the Baptist (Luke 1)
4. The parable of the rich man and Lazarus the beggar (Luke 16:24)
5. At Babel (Genesis 11); until that time, men had all spoken one common language.
6. 1 Corinthians (12; 14)
7. In Jerusalem at Pentecost (Acts 2)
8. Mark (16:17)
9. Cornelius (Acts 10)
10. The judge Gideon (Judges 7:5)
11. David (Psalm 64:3)
12. David (Psalm 52:2)
13. James (1:26)
14. Revelation (16:10)
15. A serpent's (Psalm 140:3)
16. Ephesus (Acts 19:6)

17. Which apostle wrote, "Let us not love in word, neither in tongue; but in deed and in truth"?
18. Who called the tongue "a fire, a world of iniquity"?
19. Following Paul's advice to Timothy, what type of men should not be "doubletongued"?
20. According to Paul, when a person speaks with the gift of tongues, who is he speaking to?
21. What prophet proclaimed, "The Lord God hath given me the tongue of the learned"?
22. What earthy Old Testament book says, "Honey and milk are under thy tongue; and the smell of thy garments is like the smell of Lebanon"?
23. According to Proverbs, the tongue of what type of person is like "choice silver"?
24. What king's last public speech included these words: "The spirit of the Lord spake by me, and his word was in my tongue"?
25. According to the book of Job, the wicked man will be slain by what animal's tongue?
26. What New Testament author uses the symbol of a ship's rudder to describe the power of the human tongue?

Familiar Verse, Peculiar Order

☞ Placed in their proper order, the words are a familiar verse from Matthew.

are Christ living of Son the God the you the

17. John (1 John 3:18)
18. James (3:6)
19. Deacons (1 Timothy 3:8)
20. God (1 Corinthians 14:2)
21. Isaiah (50:4)
22. The Song of Solomon (4:11)
23. The just (Proverbs 10:20)
24. David (2 Samuel 23:2)
25. A viper's (Job 20:16)
26. James (3:4)

Familiar Verse, Peculiar Order (answer)

You are the Christ, the Son of the living God. (Matthew 16:16)

Covenant Surgery:
The Rite of Circumcision

☞ Does this sound like a distasteful subject? Perhaps, but circumcision is mentioned quite often in the Bible, notably because it was a sign of the Hebrews' covenant with God. In the New Testament, circumcision was a divisive issue because some Christian believers insisted that all new converts must be circumcised. Test your familiarity with this practice and its place in the biblical narrative.

1. At what age were Hebrew boys to be circumcised?
2. At what advanced age was the patriarch Abraham circumcised?
3. Who circumcised her own son and placed the foreskin at her husband's feet?
4. When the Old Testament refers to "the uncircumcised," which nation were they usually referring to?
5. Which prophet said, "Circumcise yourselves to the Lord, and take away the foreskins of your heart"?
6. What Christian martyr told the Jews that they were "uncircumcised in heart and ears"?
7. Which apostle boasted of his Jewish heritage by claiming he was "circumcised on the eighth day"?
8. With what aged man did God institute the practice of circumcision?
9. What king committed suicide to avoid being abused by "the uncircumcised"?
10. Were the Jews allowed to perform circumcision on the Sabbath?
11. Who told Christians that circumcision (and the covenant it represented) was an inward matter, not an outward?
12. What apostle fraternized with non-Jews until pressured to separate from them by the "circumcision group"?
13. According to Paul, what is much more important to the believer than circumcision?
14. What son of Abraham was circumcised at age thirteen?
15. Who was the first person to be circumcised when eight days old, as God's commandment had decreed?
16. What group of men were attacked while they were still recovering from circumcision?
17. Who described himself as having "uncircumcised lips"?

Covenant Surgery: The Rite of Circumcision (answers)

1. Eight days (Genesis 17:12)
2. Ninety-nine (Genesis 17:24)
3. Moses' wife, Zipporah (Exodus 4:25)
4. The Philistines, but also to non-Jewish people in general
5. Jeremiah (4:4)
6. Stephen (Acts 7:51)
7. Paul (Philippians 3:5)
8. Abraham (Genesis 17)
9. Saul (1 Samuel 31:4), who was about to be captured by the Philistines
10. Yes (John 7:22)
11. Paul (Romans 2:29)
12. James (Galatians 2:12); James was under pressure from the Jewish Christians who insisted that all Christians must be circumcised.
13. Faith (Galatians 5:6)
14. Ishmael (Genesis 17:25)
15. Abraham's son Isaac (Genesis 21:4)
16. The clan of Shechem, who had submitted to circumcision under pressure from Jacob's sons; the sons attacked the Shechemites while they were still recovering (Genesis 34).
17. Moses (Exodus 6:12)

18. What Jewish feast required that any man partaking of it must be circumcised?
19. What leader circumcised the Hebrew men after they settled in the land of Canaan?
20. What strongman offended his parents by seeking out a wife among the uncircumcised Philistines?
21. By what name do we know the child who was originally named Zacharias after his circumcision?
22. Who made a gift of two hundred Philistine foreskins to his future father-in-law?
23. Which book of the Old Testament refers to a "hill of the foreskins."
24. Which Old Testament book refers to uncircumcised fruit trees?
25. Who told the people of Israel, "Circumcise therefore the foreskin of your heart, and be no more stiffnecked"?
26. What prophet lamented that the people of Israel had "uncircumcised ears"?
27. Who considered himself the apostle to the uncircumcised?
28. Which epistle mentions a spiritual circumcision, "the circumcision made without hands"?
29. What Greek companion of Paul aroused controversy because Paul refused to have him circumcised?
30. What prophet warned that a day was coming when God would punish the circumcised as well as the uncircumcised?
31. In what city was a famous Christian council which decided the issue of whether Christian converts had to undergo the Jewish rite of circumcision?
32. What half-Jewish, half-Greek follower of Paul was circumcised by Paul?
33. What prophet predicted a time when the uncircumcised would never again set foot in Jerusalem?

Familiar Verse, Peculiar Order

☛ Placed in their proper order, the words are a familiar verse from Matthew.

and are for hunger righteousness those
who blessed thirst

18. The Passover (Exodus 12:44-48)
19. Joshua (5:2-3)
20. Samson (Judges 14:3)
21. John the Baptist (Luke 1:59)
22. David (1 Samuel 18:25-27); Saul had required this for David to marry Saul's daughter Michal, hoping that David would be killed in trying to acquire the foreskins.
23. Joshua (5:3); the name of the hill (in some Bible translations) is Gibeath Haaraloth.
24. Leviticus (19:23)
25. Moses (Deuteronomy 10:16)
26. Jeremiah (6:10)
27. Paul (Galatians 2)
28. Colossians (2:11)
29. Titus (Galatians 2:3)
30. Jeremiah (9:25)
31. Jerusalem (Acts 15)
32. Timothy (Acts 16:3)
33. Isaiah (52:1)

Familiar Verse, Peculiar Order (answer)

Blessed are those who hunger and thirst for righteousness. (Matthew 5:6)

Fat of the Land, and Other Fat

☞ In the diet-conscious, weight-conscious 1990s, inevitably we must consider what the Bible has to say about the dreaded (and tempting) subject of *fat*.

1. The first mention of fat in the Bible is connected with a murder victim. Who was he?
2. What Old Testament book (full of dietary regulations) forbids the eating of fat?
3. What pagan king is the first fat man mentioned in the Bible?
4. Which parable of Jesus mentions killing a fattened calf for a grand feast?
5. Which Old Testament book says that a meal of vegetables eaten in harmony is better than a meal of fattened calf eaten in strife?
6. According to the Law, what type of animal fat could be used for household purposes (but not for eating)?
7. What prophet predicted a time when the fat of Israel would waste away?
8. What famous king had a curious dream of seven fat cows being devoured by seven scrawny cows?
9. According to the book of Job, what sort of man has a fat neck and a bulging waistline?
10. In Ezekiel's parable of God judging between the fat sheep and the lean sheep, who were the fat sheep?
11. What dabbler in the occult cooked a fattened calf and gave it to a distraught King Saul?
12. What prophet condemned the rich of Israel for lying on ivory beds and dining on fattened calves?
13. What leader mocked the Israelites foolish enough to sacrifice fat to false gods?
14. In Samuel's famous warning to King Saul, what is more pleasing to God than a sacrifice of fat?
15. What priest of Israel was chastised for allowing his greedy sons to grow fat on the people's sacrificial animals?
16. According to Ezekiel, what guests would be invited to dine on the blood and fat of aristocrats?
17. What New Testament epistle warns rich people that they are fattening themselves for a day when they will be slaughtered?

Fat of the Land, and Other Fat (answers)

1. Abel, murdered by his jealous brother Cain; Abel found favor with God by offering God the fat (that is, the choice part) from his flocks of sheep (Genesis 4).
2. Leviticus (3:17); this was not, by the way, based on a fear of fat in the diet (something the Israelites had no surplus of anyway), but, rather, based on the concept that the fat (the choice part) belonged to God.
3. Eglon, the king of Moab who was stabbed to death by the Israelite judge Ehud (Judges 3)
4. The parable of the Prodigal Son (Luke 15); the happy father, rejoicing at his son's return, ordered the calf killed.
5. Proverbs (15:17)
6. The fat found in a dead animal (Leviticus 7:24); the fat from a living animal (one specifically slaughtered for food, that is) had to be given up as a sacrifice.
7. Isaiah (17:4)
8. The pharaoh of Egypt; his dream (which symbolized seven good years followed by seven years of famine) was interpreted by Joseph (Genesis 41).
9. The wicked man (Job 15:27)
10. The leaders of Israel—specifically, the priests and prophets who had not cared for the people (Ezekiel 34:20)
11. The witch (spiritualist) of Endor; she had, at Saul's command, summoned up the ghost of Samuel. Samuel's prophecy of doom for Saul distressed him, and the witch insisted that the king eat to regain his strength (1 Samuel 28:20-25).
12. Amos (6:4)
13. Moses (Deuteronomy 32:38)
14. Obedience (1 Samuel 15:22)
15. Samuel's mentor Eli, whose greedy sons were Hophni and Phinehas (1 Samuel 2:29)
16. The birds and wild animals (Ezekiel 39:18); Ezekiel was prophesying judgment on the cruel rulers of mankind.
17. James (5:5)

18. Which parable of Jesus mentions the preparation of fattened cows and calves for a meal?
19. What type of meat, normally forbidden in diets, is condemned as unclean in the Old Testament?

Familiar Verse, Peculiar Order

☞ Placed in their proper order, the words are a familiar verse from the New Testament.

shaken are be a cannot kingdom receiving that we

Let's Get Physical: The Anatomy Lesson (Part II)

1. Whose teeth are set on edge when the fathers eat sour grapes?
2. In what place will people "gnash their teeth"?
3. Which king had a jealous eye?
4. What would make the Israelites' ears tingle?
5. Who prayed to God that his eyes and ears would be open and attentive to the people's prayers?
6. What prophet mentions a lustful woman infatuated with men's privates?
7. What elderly man was promised that he would father a child from his own body?
8. Which New Testament epistle refers to the body as a tent?
9. According to Paul, what group of people comprises Christ's body?
10. Who refers to the hair on his body standing on end?
11. Which part of the body tests words?
12. Who said (on several occasions), "He who has ears, let him hear"?
13. Where did the Lord plant "trees pleasing to the eye"?
14. Which two Old Testament books give instructions on what a man is to do after he has a nocturnal emission?
15. Who was God addressing when he told someone there was not a healthy spot on their body?

18. The parable of the wedding feast (Matthew 22)
19. Pork, of course (Leviticus 11:7); but the Law did not condemn pork as unclean for diet-related reasons. The Israelites were not plagued with an overabundance of fat or cholesterol.

Familiar Verse, Peculiar Order (answer)

We are receiving a kingdom which cannot be shaken. (Hebrews 12:28)

Let's Get Physical: The Anatomy Lesson (Part II) (answers)

1. The children's (Ezekiel 18:2); Ezekiel makes this statement as if it were a common proverb among the people—then goes on to say that it is no longer true.
2. Hell (Matthew 8:12; 13:42; 24:51); "gnashing the teeth" is an indication of anguish and rage.
3. Saul, who kept his jealous eye on David (1 Samuel 18:9)
4. The news about the disaster the Lord brought upon Jerusalem (2 Kings 21:12)
5. Solomon, at the dedication of the new temple in Jerusalem (2 Chronicles 6:40); note that when we refer to "his" eyes and ears, we are referring to God's, not Solomon's.
6. Ezekiel, who is speaking figuratively; the "woman" is actually Jerusalem, which (spiritually speaking) has left her true husband (God) and has become promiscuous (worshiping false gods) (Ezekiel 23:20).
7. Abraham (Genesis 15:4)
8. 2 Peter (1:13); the idea is that a tent, like our earthly body, is only a temporary dwelling.
9. The church, that is, Christians (Colossians 1:24)
10. Job's friend Eliphaz (4:15); this is the only place in the Bible referring to flesh crawling.
11. The ear, of course (Job 12:11)
12. Jesus (Matthew 11:15; Mark 4:23; and many others)
13. The Garden of Eden, naturally (Genesis 2:9)
14. Leviticus (15:16; 22:4) and Deuteronomy (23:10)
15. The nation of Israel (Isaiah 1:6); he was speaking figuratively, not literally.

16. What New Testament man had been accustomed to having his hands and feet chained?
17. What is the only book of the Bible to refer to semen?
18. Who walked with a limp after an angel threw his hip out of joint?
19. What part of the body was usually broken to help a crucified man die quicker?
20. Who is the only man mentioned as wearing armor on his legs?
21. Where is Jesus now seated?
22. What apostle was struck on the mouth by order of the Jewish high priest?
23. What Christian was prone to tummy trouble?
24. Who complained to God about his faltering lips?
25. What sort of lips does the Lord detest?
26. Whose face was like "the face of an angel"?
27. According to Ecclesiastes, what brightens a man's face?
28. What prophet lamented that he was a man of "unclean lips"?
29. How did God cure this prophet's unclean lips?
30. According to Jesus, what do we do when someone strikes us on the right cheek?
31. Whose face shone like the sun?
32. Whose face turned deathly pale when he saw a ghostly hand writing on the wall?
33. Who was promised that their eyes would "be opened" if they would disobey God?
34. Which book of the Old Testament contains the "eye for eye" rule?
35. According to Jesus, what people loaded heavy burdens onto men's shoulders but would not help them carry them?
36. What Christian's preaching caused the Jews to gnash their teeth in rage?
37. What part of a proud person's body is "stiff"?
38. When the Old Testament says that King Asa became "diseased in his feet," what body part might actually be referred to?

16. The demon-possessed man whom Jesus healed (Mark 5:4)
17. Leviticus (15:16; 22:4)
18. Jacob (Genesis 32:22-30)
19. The legs (John 19:31)
20. The Philistine giant Goliath (1 Samuel 17:6)
21. At the "right hand of God" (Romans 8:34)
22. Paul, who then referred to the priest as a "whitewashed wall" (Acts 23:2-3)
23. Timothy (1 Timothy 5:23); Paul urged him to take a little wine for his ailment.
24. Moses (Exodus 6); this may have meant he had a speech impediment, or simply that he was not eloquent.
25. Lying lips (Proverbs 12:22)
26. Stephen, the first Christian martyr (Acts 6:15)
27. Wisdom (Ecclesiastes 8:1)
28. Isaiah (6:5)
29. An angel touched Isaiah's lips with a coal from the temple's altar (Isaiah 6:6-7); this is a vision, not an actual burning of flesh.
30. Turn the left cheek toward him (Matthew 5:39)
31. Jesus, on the Mount of Transfiguration, when he was with Elijah and Moses (Matthew 17:2)
32. Belshazzar, the Babylonian king whose doom was being foretold by the hand (Daniel 5:6)
33. Adam and Eve, who believed the serpent's lie (Genesis 3:5-7)
34. Exodus (21:24)
35. The Pharisees; he was speaking figuratively—not actual physical burdens, but rules and regulations that were too difficult to live by (Matthew 23:4).
36. Stephen (Acts 7:54)
37. The neck; the expression "stiff-necked" occurs many, many times in the Bible.
38. Possibly his genitals (1 Kings 15:23); in several places the Old Testament politely uses the word *feet* when the genitals may be intended (see Ruth 3:8, for example).

Familiar Verse, Peculiar Order

☛ Placed in their proper order, the words are a familiar verse from Genesis.

alone be for it man not is the to good

Bloody Mess

☛ The Bible isn't squeamish about the subject of blood. This shouldn't be too surprising since the people in Bible times lived close to the land. They were familiar with the slaughtering of animals for food and ritual and also familiar (alas!) with frequent violence and brutality that led to the shedding of human blood. Interestingly, the loss of blood, an idea that most people find unpleasant, was transformed by Jesus' death into a symbol of love and forgiveness.

1. According to Job, what bird feeds blood to its young?
2. What river was turned into blood?
3. What woman was "drunk with the blood of the saints"?
4. What Roman official killed some Galileans and mixed their own blood with their sacrifices?
5. What wicked king shed so much blood that he "filled Jerusalem from one end to another"?
6. What murdered man's blood cried out from the earth?
7. What queen had her blood spattered on King Jehu's horses?
8. What bloodsucking creature is, in Proverbs, held up as an example of something that can never be satisfied?
9. How was the woman with the issue of blood healed by Jesus?
10. What book mentions making robes white by washing them in blood?
11. Who did Moses anoint with the blood of a ram?
12. What ritual is a reminder of Christ's body and blood?
13. What was the affliction of the woman who touched the hem of Jesus' robe?
14. According to Moses, what color is a grape's blood?
15. What New Testament letter says, "It is not possible that the blood of bulls and of goats should take away sins"?
16. Whom did Paul cure of a "bloody flux"?

Familiar Verse, Peculiar Order (answer)

It is not good for the man to be alone. (Genesis 2:18)

Bloody Mess (answers)

1. The eagle (Job 39:30)
2. The Nile (Exodus 7:20)
3. The great harlot (Revelation 17:6), who probably represents Rome
4. Pilate (Luke 13:1)
5. Manasseh (2 Kings 21:16)
6. Abel's, after being killed by his brother, Cain (Genesis 4:10)
7. Jezebel (2 Kings 9:33)
8. The leech (Proverbs 30:15)
9. She touched the hem of his garment (Matthew 9:20-22).
10. Revelation 7:14; the blood of the Lamb makes them clean.
11. Aaron and his sons (Leviticus 8:23)
12. The Lord's Supper (Luke 22:19)
13. An issue of blood (Mark 5:27-29)
14. Red (Deuteronomy 32:14)
15. Hebrews (10:4)
16. The father of Publius (Acts 28:8)

17. What pierced Jesus' side so that blood and water flowed out?
18. What people were frightened away when they mistook the redness of the morning sun on water for blood?
19. What guilty man said, "I have sinned in that I have betrayed the innocent blood"?
20. What prophet said, "Woe to him that buildeth a town with blood"?
21. What king was Shimei cursing when he said, "Thou bloody man"?
22. In Revelation, what caused the green grass on earth to be burned up?
23. What beloved king was not allowed to build the Lord's temple because he was a man of blood?
24. Where did Jesus encounter a woman who had had an unnatural flow of blood for many years?
25. Whose wife referred to him as a "bloody husband"?
26. Which Old Testament book is the bloodiest?
27. Who was "clothed with a vesture dipped in blood"?
28. What was the name of the field purchased by Judas's thirty pieces of silver?
29. Who washed his hands to show he was innocent of shedding Jesus' blood?
30. Which Gospel says that Jesus sweated drops of blood?
31. Which apostle claimed that he was standing by when the blood of the martyr Stephen was shed?
32. To whom did God give the command, "Whoso sheddeth man's blood, by man shall his blood be shed"?
33. Which of Joseph's eleven brothers advised the others not to shed his blood?
34. Who, following the Lord's advice, turned the rivers of Egypt to blood?
35. According to the law of Moses, what person was supposed to avenge a murder?
36. What did Israel suffer because of Saul shedding the blood of the Gibeonites?
37. What wicked king died so that his blood ran out of the chariot he was riding in?
38. What wicked queen fell to her death, with her blood spattering on the walls?
39. Which New Testament book has the most to say about blood?

17. The spear of the Roman soldier (John 19:34)
18. The Moabites (2 Kings 3:22)
19. Judas Iscariot (Matthew 27:4)
20. Habakkuk (2:12)
21. David (2 Samuel 16:7)
22. Blood, hail, and fire poured on the earth (Revelation 8:7)
23. David (1 Chronicles 22:8)
24. Capernaum (Matthew 9:20)
25. Moses' wife, Zipporah, who said, "Surely a bloody husband art thou to me" (Exodus 4:25). This was connected with the mysterious incident of her circumcising their son.
26. Undoubtedly Leviticus, since it deals with the sacrificial system in Israel; blood is mentioned more than eighty times.
27. The rider on the white horse, called the Word, undoubtedly referring to Christ (Revelation 19:13)
28. The field of blood (Matthew 27:8)
29. Pilate (Matthew 27:24)
30. Luke (22:44)
31. Paul (Acts 22:20)
32. Noah (Genesis 9:6)
33. Reuben, who advised, instead, throwing him into a pit in the wilderness (Genesis 37:22)
34. Moses and Aaron (Exodus 7)
35. The "avenger of blood" (Numbers 35), a person (presumably a close relative) who was responsible for killing the murderer
36. A three-year famine (2 Samuel 21:1)
37. Ahab (1 Kings 22:35)
38. Jezebel, Ahab's wife (2 Kings 9:33)
39. The Letter to the Hebrews, which has a lot to say about the sacrificial system in the temple and the sacrifice of Jesus' blood

40. When Jesus mentioned the shedding of righteous blood, what man from Genesis did he hold up as an example of righteousness?

41. How many years had the woman had the issue of blood before Jesus healed her?

42. Whose blood, according to Jesus, had been shed since the foundation of the world?

43. In which Gospel does Jesus say that people must eat his flesh and drink his blood in order to have eternal life?

44. What heavenly body will be turned to blood, according to Acts?

45. Which apostle told a group of Jews, "Your blood be on your own heads. Henceforth I will go to the Gentiles"?

46. In which epistle does Paul say we are "justified" by the blood of Jesus?

47. Which epistle of Paul mentions "redemption through his blood"?

48. What sign did God tell Moses would convince the people of his divine mission?

49. What was daubed with blood so that the Lord's angel of death would bypass the homes of the Israelites?

50. What rebel against King David was killed and "wallowed in blood in the midst of the highway"?

51. Whom did David tell his son Solomon should be executed because he had shed blood in peacetime as well as in wartime?

52. The book of Nahum is directed against a certain "bloody city." Which great pagan city is it?

53. Who asked the question, "Will I eat the flesh of bulls, or drink the blood of goats?"?

54. What was the name of the places where people who had unintentionally shed blood could flee to?

Familiar Verse, Peculiar Order

☞ Placed in their proper order, the words are a familiar verse from Matthew.

seed heaven a is kingdom like of mustard the

40. Abel, who was killed by his brother, Cain (Matthew 23:35)
41. Twelve (Mark 5:25)
42. The prophets' (Luke 11:50)
43. John (6:53-56); he was speaking symbolically, of course.
44. The moon (Acts 2:20); presumably this means the moon will turn blood red.
45. Paul (Acts 18:6)
46. Romans (5:9)
47. Ephesians (1:7) and Colossians (1:14)
48. Pouring water on dry ground and having it turn to blood (Exodus 4:9)
49. Their door frames (Exodus 12:22)
50. Amasa, captain of the rebel forces under David's son Absalom (2 Samuel 20:12)
51. Joab, the commander in chief (1 Kings 2:5-7)
52. Nineveh, the capital of Assyria; the Assyrians were regarded by the Hebrews (and everyone else) as extremely cruel.
53. God (Psalm 50:13)
54. The cities of refuge (Numbers 35; Deuteronomy 19), six of them in all; these were provided to protect a person until his case could be properly tried. They were *not* designed to protect willful murderers.

Familiar Verse, Peculiar Order (answer)

The kingdom of heaven is like a mustard seed. (Matthew 13:31)

Do You Remember?

☞ Would you like to see how much Bible trivia you can remember? Answer the questions (which you should have answered already in this section), and then see how well you rate on the scale on page xii.

1. Who saw the "back" of God, since he could not bear to see him face-to-face?
2. Who offered sacrifices on the possibility that his children had cursed God in their hearts?
3. Which apostle claimed that all Scripture is "God-breathed"?
4. At what place did the "confusion of tongues" occur?
5. What Greek companion of Paul aroused controversy because Paul refused to have him circumcised?
6. Which Old Testament book says that a meal of vegetables eaten in harmony is better than a meal of fatted calf eaten in strife?
7. Where did the Lord plant "trees pleasing to the eye"?
8. Which Gospel says that Jesus sweated drops of blood?
9. Whose palace had a hand that wrote on the wall?
10. Who said that the Old Testament Law allowed divorce because of people's hardness of heart?

Do You Remember? (answers)

1. Moses (Exodus 33:23)
2. Job (1:5)
3. Paul, writing to Timothy (2 Timothy 3:16); some translations have "inspired" instead of "God-breathed," though in fact "God-breathed" is a perfect translation of the Greek wording.
4. At Babel (Genesis 11); until that time, men had all spoken one common language.
5. Titus (Galatians 2:3)
6. Proverbs (15:17)
7. The Garden of Eden, naturally (Genesis 2:9)
8. Luke (22:44)
9. Belshazzar's, the king of Babylon (Daniel 5:5); the hand wrote a message that predicted Babylon's downfall.
10. Jesus (Matthew 19:8)

PART 7

What's My Name?

Test Your Bible IQ

☞ This quiz contains questions covering the topics in part 7, "What's My Name?" Do your best, then turn the page to see how you did. If you are brave enough to see how your Bible IQ rates, turn to page xii for our scale.

1. Paul's first traveling companion was Barnabas. Who was the second? (Hint: five letters)
2. What son of David was noted for his luxurious mane of hair? (Hint: starts with A)
3. Who tore a lion apart with his bare hands? (Hint: six letters)
4. Who told God that Job would curse him to his face? (Hint: five letters)
5. What's this Bible character's name? S_____: Only one of him, and a great man, a kingmaker, influential in the lives of David and Saul (Hint: six letters)
6. Guess the familiar name of this Bible character's original Greek form: Mathaios.
7. Who asked Jesus the famous question "What is truth?" (Hint: six letters)
8. What Bible character has a famous Charlton Heston movie with the same name? (Hint: six letters)
9. What's this Bible character's name? C_____: Only one in the Bible, a real killer (Hint: four letters)
10. What smooth-skinned man disguised himself so well that he passed himself off as his hairy brother? (Hint: five letters)

Test Your Bible IQ (answers)

1. Silas (Acts 15:36-41)
2. Absalom (2 Samuel 14:25-26)
3. Samson (Judges 14:5-6)
4. Satan (Job 1:11; 2:5)
5. Samuel
6. Matthew
7. Pilate (John 18:38)
8. Ben-Hur, one of Solomon's twelve food commissioners (1 Kings 4:8); he was not an important person, but his name certainly lives on.
9. Cain, who murdered his brother Abel
10. Jacob, brother of the hirsute Esau (Genesis 27:1-29)

Five-Letter Names

☛ By an interesting coincidence, several of the Bible's most famous people have five-letter names—Jesus, Moses, Aaron, David, Peter, James, and Jacob. Test your Bible knowledge on the questions below, keeping in mind that each answer has only five letters.

1. What gleeful king danced with all his might when the ark of the covenant was brought to Jerusalem?
2. Which disciple, busy at his daily work, was caught naked by Jesus?
3. Who laughed when she heard she would bear a son in her old age?
4. What Old Testament character's name means "laughter"?
5. At 969 years, Methuselah was the longest-lived man. Who came in second at 962 years?
6. Paul's first traveling companion was Barnabas. Who was the second?
7. What malicious king of Moab sent the prophet Balaam to curse Israel?
8. What shepherd boy, the youngest of eight sons, was anointed king by Samuel in front of his brothers?
9. What king wanted to see miracles when the arrested Jesus was sent to him?
10. What king of Tyre sent cedar logs and craftsmen to King David?
11. What king of Israel reigned only seven days and killed himself by burning down his palace around him?
12. What king of Moab was famous as a sheep farmer?
13. What leader did God ask, "How long will this people provoke me?"
14. God protected the wily Jacob by sending a dream of warning that Jacob should not be pursued or harmed. Who received this dream?
15. What prophet was told by God to name his son Lo-ammi?
16. What boy ran into the Philistine camp to confront their best warrior?
17. What new name did Jesus give to Simon?
18. Who ran into the midst of the Israelites carrying incense to stop a plague?

Five-Letter Names (answers)

1. David (2 Samuel 6:14)
2. Peter (John 21:7); "naked" here probably does not mean *totally* nude, but, more likely, wearing a mere loincloth—the biblical equivalent of being caught in one's undies.
3. Sarah, Abraham's wife (Genesis 18:10-12)
4. Isaac (Genesis 21:3-6)
5. Jared (Genesis 5:20)
6. Silas (Acts 15:36-41)
7. Balak (Numbers 22:2-6)
8. David (1 Samuel 16:6-13)
9. Herod (Luke 23:8)
10. Hiram (2 Samuel 5:11)
11. Zimri (1 Kings 16:15, 18)
12. Mesha (2 Kings 3:4)
13. Moses (Numbers 14:11)
14. Laban, Jacob's father-in-law (Genesis 31:29)
15. Hosea (1:9)
16. David (1 Samuel 17:48-49)
17. Peter (John 1:42)
18. Aaron (Numbers 16:46-48)

19. What hooker became a heroine for saving the life of Joshua's spies and was so honored in later days that she is listed in the genealogy of Jesus?
20. What wayward Old Testament woman had children named Lo-ruhamah, Lo-ammi, and Jezreel?
21. What king of Judah had to be hidden as a boy to protect him from the wrath of wicked Queen Athaliah?
22. What was the name of Sarah's Egyptian maid?
23. What cruel king lied to the wise men about his desire to worship the infant Jesus?
24. What king of Persia issued the decree that the people of Judah could rebuild their temple?
25. What king, mentioned 1118 times in the Bible, is the second most mentioned man (after Jesus, of course)?
26. What Hebrew leader, with 740 mentions, ranks third?
27. What priest ranks fourth with a total of 339 references?
28. Which of Jesus' disciples is mentioned the most times in the New Testament?
29. This Egyptian-born Hebrew leader predicted the coming of a prophet like himself.
30. What blind father recognized Jacob's voice but was deceived by his glove-covered hands?
31. What Old Testament woman bore a child at age ninety and is the most mentioned woman in the Bible (fifty-six mentions)?
32. What traveling companion of Paul was considered a prophet?
33. What fugitive prophet slept in the bottom of a ship as it rolled in a storm?
34. What apostle addressed the Pentecost crowd in a loud voice?
35. Who slept on a stone pillow at Bethel and dreamed about angels?
36. What clever woman hoodwinked her father-in-law out of a signet ring and bracelets?
37. What military man slept at David's door while he was home on furlough?
38. What New Testament woman had the same name as an old kingdom of Asia?
39. What king had ten concubines that were sexually assaulted by his wayward son?

19. Rahab (Joshua 2; 6); in the King James Version, Rahab is called a "harlot"; more recent translations usually say "prostitute."
20. Gomer, unfaithful wife of the prophet Hosea (Hosea 1)
21. Joash (2 Kings 11:2)
22. Hagar (Genesis 16:1)
23. Herod (Matthew 2:7-8)
24. Cyrus (Ezra 1:1-4)
25. David
26. Moses
27. Aaron
28. Peter, who is mentioned 166 times—slightly less than Paul, who was an apostle but not one of the original Twelve
29. Moses (Deuteronomy 18:15)
30. Isaac (Genesis 27:22)
31. Sarah
32. Silas (Acts 15:32)
33. Jonah (1:5)
34. Peter (Acts 2:14)
35. Jacob (Genesis 28:11-15)
36. Tamar (Genesis 38:17-18)
37. Uriah, Bathsheba's husband (2 Samuel 11:9)
38. Lydia (Acts 16:14)
39. David (2 Samuel 16:21-22)

40. Who called herself Marah, a name meaning "bitter"?
41. Who plotted to have the entire Hebrew nation completely exterminated?
42. What Roman official gave Paul a centurion as a guard and told the centurion to allow Paul freedom to see whomever he wished?
43. Who carried five smooth stones as his weapons?
44. What former member of the Egyptian court killed an Egyptian official?
45. What good king of Judah was murdered by his court officials?
46. Who pretended to be a madman in order to escape from King Achish?
47. What smooth-skinned man disguised himself so well that he passed himself off as his hairy brother?
48. Who ordered his daughter-in-law Tamar burned because she had acted like a prostitute?
49. According to Paul, who masquerades as an angel of light?
50. What son of David forced his half-sister to have sexual relations with him?

Familiar Verse, Peculiar Order

☛ Placed in their proper order, the words are a familiar verse from John.

must again born be you

Brother "Ah" and Father "Ab"

☛ Many Old Testament names contain "Ab" or "Ah"—the reason being that the people of Old Testament times chose names carefully, every name having a meaning, and the meaning often had something to do with fathers and brothers. Test your knowledge of Old Testament characters, keeping in mind that each name here contains an "ab" or "ah," usually (but not always) at the beginning of the name.

1. What wicked king of Israel was Jezebel's husband?
2. What Hebrew patriarch had a name meaning "father of a multitude"?

40. Naomi (Ruth 1:19-21)
41. Haman, minister of Persia (Esther)
42. Felix (Acts 24:23)
43. David (1 Samuel 17:40)
44. Moses (Exodus 2:12)
45. Joash (2 Kings 12:20-21)
46. David (1 Samuel 21:12–22:1)
47. Jacob, brother of the hirsute Esau (Genesis 27:1-29)
48. Judah (Genesis 38:24)
49. Satan (2 Corinthians 11:14)
50. Amnon (2 Samuel 13:1-14); it might be accurate to describe King David's family as "dysfunctional."

Familiar Verse, Peculiar Order (answer)

You must be born again. (John 3:7)

Brother "Ah" and Father "Ab" (answers)

1. Ahab, whose name combines both "ah" and "ab," the name meaning something like "father's brother"
2. Abraham, whose name is appropriate for the founder of the Hebrews

3. What wife of David was once married to Nabal, whose name means "fool"?

4. What rambunctious, violent son of the judge Gideon proclaimed himself king and murdered seventy of his brothers?

5. What court counselor of David joined in the ill-fated conspiracy of David's son Absalom and later hanged himself?

6. What prophet predicted that Jeroboam would rule over the ten tribes that broke away from David's dynasty's rule?

7. What high priest managed to escape Saul's slaughter of eighty-four priests?

8. Who followed Rehoboam as king of Judah?

9. What young Shunammite maiden served as King David's "bed warmer" in his old age?

10. What soldier was a cousin of King Saul and commander in chief of his army?

11. What rebellious son of David had the (ironic) name meaning "father is peace"?

12. Which one of David's "mighty men" has a name meaning "brother of mother"?

13. Which of David's "mighty men" was a slingshot expert?

14. What priest gave David Goliath's sword when David was fleeing from Saul?

15. What noted Jewish woman was Abihail the father of?

16. What son of Aaron the priest was struck down for "offering strange fire" to the Lord?

17. What cousin of David was the commander of the mighty men known as "the Thirty"?

18. What name did Jesus use for God?

19. What priest who served faithfully under David was banished by David's son Solomon?

20. What man was given the ark of the covenant for safe keeping after it was returned from the Philistines?

21. What son of King Jeroboam died in childhood, as prophesied by the prophet Ahijah?

22. What two kings of Israel had wives named Ahinoam?

23. What false prophet was executed by King Nebuchadnezzar by being roasted in a fire?

24. Who was the commander in chief of David's armies?

3. Abigail, whose name means "father of rejoicing"
4. Abimelech, whose name means "father is king"
5. Ahitophel, whose name means (appropriately) "brother of folly"
6. Ahijah, meaning "brother of Yah [God]"
7. Abiathar, meaning "father of abundance"
8. Abijah, meaning "father is Yah [God]"
9. Abishag, meaning (strangely enough) "the father errs"
10. Abner, the son of Ner, whose name means (surprise!) "Ner is father"
11. Absalom
12. Ahiam (2 Samuel 23:33)
13. Ahiezer (1 Chronicles 12:2-3), meaning "brother is help"
14. Ahimelech ("brother is king")
15. Esther, who became queen of Persia; *Abihail* means "father has power."
16. Abihu (Leviticus 10:1-3), which means "my father"
17. Abishai, whose name's meaning is uncertain
18. Abba, which is Aramaic for "dear Father" (Mark 14:36)
19. Abiathar ("father gives abundance"); Abiathar was banished because he supported Adonijah, Solomon's brother and rival for the throne of Israel.
20. Abinadab ("father is generous")
21. Abijah ("Yah [God] is father")
22. Saul (1 Samuel 14:50) and David (1 Samuel 25:43); the name means "brother is pleasant." These are not the same woman, by the way.
23. Ahab ("brother's father") (Jeremiah 29:20-23); this is not the same as King Ahab.
24. Joab, meaning "Yah [God] is father"

25. What son of David was noted for his luxurious mane of hair?
26. What soldier murdered a man while kissing him?
27. What older brother of David scoffed at the idea that little David would kill Goliath?
28. Whose death caused David to order the people of Israel to tear their clothes?
29. Who received a letter from David, telling him to put Uriah in the heat of battle?
30. Who had his name changed (by God) from a name meaning "exalted father" to a name meaning "father of multitudes"?
31. Who had intercourse on a rooftop with all his father's concubines?
32. In which epistles did Paul tell Christians to call God "Abba, Father"?

Familiar Verse, Peculiar Order

☞ Placed in their proper order, the words are a familiar verse from Matthew.

against cannot divided house a itself stand

What's My Name Now?

☞ The Old Testament was written in Hebrew and the New Testament in Greek—two very different languages. Thus Old Testament names translate somewhat differently in the New Testament. Look at the Old Testament names below and see if you know the New Testament form each name takes. (Note: These questions are based on the King James Version. Some contemporary translations—for the sake of clarity—use the Hebrew names in the New Testament.)

1. Elijah
2. Joshua
3. Hannah
4. Miriam
5. Zechariah
6. Simeon
7. Johanan

25. Absalom ("father is peace") (2 Samuel 14:26)
26. Joab, David's commander in chief, who murdered Amasa (2 Samuel 20:9)
27. Eliab ("El [God] is father") (1 Samuel 17:28)
28. Abner's (2 Samuel 3:31); "rending the garment" was an ancient symbol of grief and mourning.
29. Joab ("Yah [God] is father") (2 Samuel 11:4, 15); David had Uriah killed so he could marry Uriah's wife, Bathsheba.
30. Abraham, who was originally named Abram (Genesis 17:5)
31. Absalom ("father is peace") (2 Samuel 16:22)
32. Romans (8:15) and Galatians (4:6)

Familiar Verse, Peculiar Order (answer)

A house divided against itself cannot stand. (Matthew 12:25)

What's My Name Now? (answers)

1. Elias
2. Jesus (yes, really!)
3. Anna
4. Mary
5. Zacharias
6. Simon
7. John

8. Judah
9. Boaz
10. Rehoboam
11. Zadok
12. Uzziah
13. Hezekiah
14. Zerubbabel
15. Jeremiah
16. Isaiah
17. Hananiah
18. Messiah
19. Eleazar
20. Jacob

Familiar Verse, Peculiar Order

☛ Placed in their proper order, the words are a familiar verse from the New Testament.

creature if any be a Christ he in is man new

Six-Letter Names

☛ So many of the great names in the Bible seem to have five letters—Jesus, Moses, David, Peter, etc. But think of the "big names" that have six letters—Joseph, Elijah, Isaiah, Samson, many others. Each answer for the following question has six letters.

1. Who is the only man mentioned in the Bible as being naturally bald?
2. What Jewish girl became queen of Persia?
3. Who parted the Jordan by striking it with his mantle?
4. What prophet of Moab had a talking donkey?
5. What prophet walked around naked for three years?
6. Who nagged at her husband David for dancing wildly in the streets?
7. What godly king began his reign at age eight and led a major reform movement in Judah?
8. What names does the New Testament give to the magicians in Pharaoh's court in the time of Moses?

8. Judas
9. Booz
10. Roboam
11. Sadoc
12. Ozias
13. Ezekias
14. Zorobabel
15. Jeremy, or Jeremias
16. Isaiah
17. Ananias
18. Messias
19. Lazarus
20. James

Familiar Verse, Peculiar Order (answer)

If any man be in Christ, he is a new creature. (2 Corinthians 5:17)

Six-Letter Names (answers)

1. Elisha the prophet (2 Kings 2:23)
2. Esther (Esther 2:17)
3. Elijah (2 Kings 2:8-14)
4. Balaam (Numbers 22:21-33)
5. Isaiah (20:3)
6. Michal (2 Samuel 6:20)
7. Josiah (2 Kings 22–23)
8. Jannes and Jambres (2 Timothy 3:8)

9. The Ammonites' bloodthirsty god was widely known in Israel because of the horrible practice of sacrificing children to him. What was the name of this god?
10. What devout young man was placed in a lions' den?
11. Who tore a lion apart with his bare hands?
12. Who trapped five Canaanite kings in the cave where they were hiding?
13. What prophet was a very hairy man?
14. Who defied her royal husband and was replaced by a foreign woman?
15. What woman did Peter raise from the dead?
16. Who built ancient Babylon?
17. What prophetess was the sister of two great leaders and was once afflicted with leprosy for being rebellious?
18. What New Testament prophet predicted a worldwide famine?
19. What prophet outran a king's chariot and a team of horses?
20. The people of Lystra were so dazzled by Paul and Barnabas that they called them by the names of two Greek gods. What name did they call Paul?
21. Who was food storage supervisor in Egypt when famine came?
22. What king of Judah was killed at the Battle of Megiddo by the forces of Egypt?
23 Who was absent when the risen Jesus appeared to the apostles?
24. Who was sent by the king of Moab to put a curse on Israel?
25. Who told Saul that obeying God's voice was more important than sacrificing animals?
26. Who slew a thousand men with the jawbone of an ass?
27. According to Paul, who was made a curse for our sins?
28. What loving woman, a concubine of King Saul, watched over the corpses of her slaughtered children, protecting them from birds and animals?
29. Which apostle brought Nathanael to meet Jesus?
30. To what woman did Jesus declare, "I am the resurrection and the life"?
31. What prophet made an axhead float on the water?
32. What doting mother made her absent son a new coat each year?

9. Molech (Leviticus 18:21; 1 Kings 11:7; 2 Kings 23:10; Amos 5:26)
10. Daniel (6:16)
11. Samson (Judges 14:5-6)
12. Joshua (10:16-27)
13. Elijah (2 Kings 1:8)
14. Vashti, queen of Persia who was replaced by the Jewish girl Esther (Esther 1:11)
15. Dorcas (Acts 9:36-41)
16. Nimrod (Genesis 10:8-10)
17. Miriam (Exodus 15; Numbers 12)
18. Agabus (Acts 11:28)
19. Elijah (1 Kings 18:46)
20. Hermes (Mercury in some Bible translations) (Acts 14:12)
21. Joseph (Genesis 41)
22. Josiah (2 Kings 23:29-30)
23. Thomas (John 20:24)
24. Balaam (Numbers 22:1-6)
25. Samuel (1 Samuel 15:22)
26. Samson (Judges 15:15)
27. Christ (Galatians 3:13)
28. Rizpah (2 Samuel 21:1-10)
29. Philip (John 1:43-46)
30. Martha, the sister of Lazarus and Mary (John 11:24-26)
31. Elisha (2 Kings 6:4-7)
32. Hannah, the mother of Samuel (1 Samuel 2:19)

33. Who drew the army of Ai out of the city while another group ambushed the city and destroyed it?
34. What prophet experienced a furious wind that split the hills and shattered the rocks?
35. Who begged her sister for some mandrake plants, hoping they would help her bear children?
36. What grandson of Noah was cursed for his father's sins?
37. What Roman official in Jerusalem bowed to the wishes of an uncontrollable mob?
38. What Roman soldier treated Paul kindly on his voyage to Rome?
39. What prophet had a vision of a lion with eagle's wings?
40. Who criticized her famous brother Moses for being married to an Ethiopian woman?

Familiar Verse, Peculiar Order

☛ Placed in their proper order, the words are a familiar verse from Psalms.

feet a is lamp my to word your

Five-Letter Names (Part II)

1. Who was the only apostle we know for sure was married?
2. Who kept Paul in prison, hoping Paul would try to bribe him for release?
3. Which apostle was sleeping between two soldiers when he was miraculously delivered from prison?
4. What cousin of Saul was commander of the king's troops?
5. What soldier, David's oldest brother, needled David for coming to the battle lines?
6. What holy man was anointed by an immoral woman?
7. Which pagan goddess had a notorious temple at Ephesus?
8. Who anointed the tabernacle with oil?
9. Who was carried up to the highest point of the Jerusalem temple?
10. What priests—two of Aaron's sons—were killed because they offered "strange fire" to the Lord?

33. Joshua (8:12-22)
34. Elijah (1 Kings 19:11)
35. Rachel, who was envious that her sister Leah was bearing children while she wasn't (Genesis 30:14)
36. Canaan, the son of Ham, who had dishonored his father (Genesis 9:25)
37. Pilate (Matthew 27:23-24)
38. Julius (Acts 27:1-3)
39. Daniel (7:4)
40. Miriam (Numbers 12:1)

Familiar Verse, Peculiar Order (answer)

Your word is a lamp to my feet. (Psalm 119:105)

Five-Letter Names (Part II) (answers)

1. Peter, who is mentioned as having a mother-in-law (which means he must have had a wife also) (Mark 1:30)
2. Felix (Acts 24:26)
3. Peter (Acts 12:6)
4. Abner (1 Samuel 14:50)
5. Eliab (1 Samuel 17:28)
6. Jesus (Luke 7:37-38)
7. Diana (or Artemis, in some translations) (Acts 19:27-28)
8. Moses (Exodus 40:9)
9. Jesus (Matthew 4:5)
10. Nadab and Abihu (Numbers 3:4); no one is quite sure what the "strange fire" was, although it probably means that the offering was done improperly in some way.

11. What high priest had John and Peter arrested after the two disciples had healed a lame man?
12. What disciple angrily cut off the ear of the high priest's servant when Jesus was arrested?
13. What priest anointed Solomon as king?
14. What magician came to be baptized by Philip?
15. Who was the first apostle to be martyred?
16. What businesswoman was baptized by Paul and Silas?
17. To whom did Jesus say, "Feed my lambs"?
18. What brother of Jesus does Paul call an apostle?
19. What apostle, a traveling companion of Paul, was sometimes called Silvanus?
20. Who cursed a fig tree for not bearing fruit?
21. Who told God that Job would curse him to his face?
22. What king confessed to God that he had done wrong in taking a census of Israel?
23. Who saw the back of God, since he could not bear to see him face to face?
24. What two people walked on water in the midst of a storm?
25. What disciple did Satan enter into?
26. What prophet called the city of Nineveh the "mistress of witchcrafts"?
27. What fish-shaped god of the Philistines was disgraced when his statue was broken by the presence of the ark of the covenant?
28. Who amazed the people of Samaria with his conjuring tricks?
29. Who, according to tradition, wrote the book of Psalms?
30. Who put a bronze snake on a pole in order to heal snakebite victims?
31. What ruler was eaten by worms before he died?
32. What shepherd (and former prince) married the shepherd girl Zipporah?
33. Who told his followers they would have the power to handle deadly snakes?
34. What future king claimed that he had grabbed lions by the throat and beaten them to death?
35. According to 1 Peter, what person is like a ravenous lion?
36. What prophet had his shade-producing vine eaten by a worm?

11. Annas (Acts 4:6-7)
12. Peter (Matthew 26:51; John 18:10)
13. Zadok (1 Kings 1:45-46)
14. Simon (the sorcerer; Acts 8:12-13)
15. James (Acts 12:1-2)
16. Lydia (Acts 16:14-15)
17. Peter (John 21:15-19)
18. James (Galatians 1:19)
19. Silas (1 Thessalonians 1:1); "Silas" is apparently the short form of "Silvanus."
20. Jesus (Mark 11:21)
21. Satan (Job 1:11; 2:5)
22. David (2 Samuel 24:10)
23. Moses (Exodus 33:23)
24. Jesus and Peter (Matthew 14:22-32)
25. Judas (Luke 22:3-4)
26. Nahum (3:4)
27. Dagon (Judges 16:23; 1 Samuel 5:1-5)
28. Simon the sorcerer (Acts 8:9)
29. David, Asaph, and many others
30. Moses (Numbers 21:8-9)
31. Herod (Acts 12:23)
32. Moses (Exodus 2:16-21)
33. Jesus (Mark 16:18)
34. David (1 Samuel 17:35)
35. Satan (1 Peter 5:8)
36. Jonah (4:7)

37. What almost-slaughtered son asked his father the naive question "Where is the lamb for a burnt offering?"
38. Who had a vision of a sheet filled with all sorts of unclean birds and other animals?
39. Who used rods of poplar, hazel, and chestnut wood to make genetic changes in his cattle?
40. What king appointed an overseer to watch after the fruits of the olive trees and sycamores?
41. What prophet spoke of people who sow a wind and reap a whirlwind?
42. What two long-dead men were with Jesus when a shining cloud covered them?
43. What runaway boarded a ship that the Lord struck with a strong wind?
44. What Christian woman worshiped with a group that met by a river?
45. What prophet asked his shipmates to cast him into the sea?
46. Who is mentioned as the ancestor of those who play the harp and organ?
47. Who fashioned a golden calf idol for the Israelites?
48. What king was the youngest of eight brothers?
49. Who said that we must change and become like children?
50. Whose wives included Abigail, Bathsheba, Michal, Maacah, Haggith, and Eglah?

Familiar Verse, Peculiar Order

☞ Placed in their proper order, the words are a familiar verse from John.

am of bread I life the

37. Isaac, who was on the verge of being sacrificed by his father Abraham (Genesis 22:7)
38. Peter (Acts 10:9-13)
39. Jacob (Genesis 30:37-39); this is probably the first recorded example of genetic engineering.
40. David (1 Chronicles 27:28)
41. Hosea (8:7)
42. Moses and Elijah (Matthew 17:15)
43. Jonah (1:4)
44. Lydia (Acts 16:13-14)
45. Jonah (1:12)
46. Jubal (Genesis 4:21)
47. Aaron (Exodus 32:4)
48. David (1 Samuel 17:12-14)
49. Jesus (Matthew 18:3)
50. David (2 Samuel 12:8)

Familiar Verse, Peculiar Order (answer)

I am the bread of life. (John 6:35)

Where Have You Been?

☞ We inevitably associate people with certain places—Mark Twain with Missouri and the Mississippi River, for example. The questions here involve three or four places that had a famous Bible character associated with them. You name the person. For example: Bethlehem, Nazareth, Jerusalem. The answer: Jesus, of course, who was born in Bethlehem, grew up in Nazareth (and was rejected there), and taught and died in Jerusalem. (These questions are not intended for the faint of heart. But if you do well on these, give yourself a Bible pat.)

1. Egypt, Midian, Sinai
2. Ur, Canaan, Egypt
3. Tarsus, Rome, Ephesus, Jerusalem
4. Jerusalem, the Jordan River, Herod's palace
5. Capernaum, Bethsaida, Joppa, Babylon
6. Anathoth, Jerusalem, Egypt
7. Tishbe, Samaria, Cherith Brook
8. Bethlehem, Hebron, Jerusalem
9. Jerusalem, Babylon, Persia
10. Tarshish, Joppa, Nineveh
11. Moresheth, Samaria, Jerusalem
12. Ramathaim, Shiloh, Mizpah, Ramah
13. Jericho, Ai, Gibeon, Hebron
14. Zorah, Timnah, the Valley of Sorek, Gaza

Familiar Verse, Peculiar Order

☞ Placed in their proper order, the words are a familiar verse from the New Testament.

Christ the God himself in to reconciling was world

Where Have You Been? (answers)

1. Moses (who was born in Egypt, married in Midian, and received the Law on Sinai)
2. Abraham (born in Ur, moved to Canaan, lived in Egypt for a while)
3. Paul (born in Tarsus, traveled to Rome and Ephesus, studied and taught in Jerusalem)
4. John the Baptist (born in Jerusalem, baptized people in the Jordan, imprisoned and executed in Herod's palace)
5. Peter (who lived in Capernaum and Bethsaida, had his famous vision in Joppa, and traveled as a missionary to "Babylon" [which may be a code name for Rome])
6. Jeremiah (a native of Anathoth, ministered in Jerusalem, was carried away to Egypt)
7. Elijah (native of Tishbe, prophesied in Samaria, was fed by ravens at Cherith)
8. David (native of Bethlehem, established his capitals at Hebron and Jerusalem)
9. Daniel (native of Jerusalem, exiled in Babylon, then in Persia)
10. Jonah (who headed for Tarshish, departed from Joppa, prophesied in Nineveh)
11. Micah (native of Moresheth, prophesied against both Samaria and Jerusalem)
12. Samuel (born in Ramathaim, served in Shiloh, Mizpah, and Ramah)
13. Joshua (these were all cities he and his armies captured or destroyed)
14. Samson (born in Zorah, married in Timnah, met Delilah at Sorek, imprisoned at Gaza)

Familiar Verse, Peculiar Order (answer)

God was in Christ reconciling the world to himself.
(2 Corinthians 5:19)

Names, Common and Uncommon

☛ There are many personal names in the Bible, ranging from the common (John, David, James, Paul, Samuel) to the very uncommon (Shishak, Shear-Jashub, Abednego). Many of the Bible names were shared by more than one person—in some cases, a *lot* more than one. Below are questions about people in the Bible. We give you the first letter of the name, followed by a count of how many people in the Bible had that name—plus a clue about one (or more) of the people with that name.

1. D_____: A king of Israel and the only Bible man bearing this name (which is now, curiously, a common name throughout the world)
2. Z_____: The name of thirty-three different men in the Bible, but most notably an Old Testament prophet who has a book bearing his name.
3. A_____: Moses' brother and the only man in the Bible with this name
4. J_____: Three men in the Bible had this name, but one—the One—is the best-known man of all.
5. A_____: The name of four men in the Old Testament, none of them very important—although one was one of the judges in the book of Judges
6. U_____: Six of them in the Bible, the most famous being the husband of Bathsheba, who was later married to David
7. P_____: Four of them in the New Testament, one of them an apostle—and still a fairly common man's name
8. M_____: Only one of these in the Bible, an apostle of Jesus—but a common name nowadays
9. A_____: Eight of them in the Old Testament, none too important—except one of them was Samuel's son
10. S_____: Only two in the Bible, one a king, one an apostle—both very important
11. J_____: Only one in the Bible, noted as patient and long-suffering
12. J_____: Thirteen (count 'em!) in the Bible, the most notable being the Old Testament prophet who has a book named for him

Names, Common and Uncommon (answers)

1. David
2. Zechariah (thirty-three Zechariahs in the Bible—amazing!)
3. Aaron
4. Jesus (Yes, there are actually two other Jesuses in the Bible.)
5. Abdon
6. Uriah
7. Philip
8. Matthew
9. Abijah
10. Saul (which, if you recall, was Paul's original name)
11. Job
12. Joel

13. S_____: Only one of him, and a great man, a kingmaker, influential in the lives of David and Saul
14. J_____: Five of them in the New Testament, including an apostle—with a name that is still very common
15. P_____: Only one of him, but he dominates much of the New Testament
16. H_____: Four of them in the Old Testament, the most famous being king when Isaiah was active
17. J_____: Five of them in the New Testament, including an apostle and a brother of Jesus
18. A_____: Only one of him—thank goodness, since he was one of Israel's worst kings
19. Z_____: Nine of them in the Bible, none too important, except perhaps the one who was priest in David's time
20. S_____: One of the most common New Testament names—nine in all, most notably one of Jesus' disciples
21. M_____: Only one in the Bible, and the dominant figure in the Bible's first five books
22. M_____: Thirteen in all—one of the most common Old Testament names, but none of any significance
23. M_____: A common woman's name in the New Testament (six in all), one that has stayed popular for ages
24. M_____: Only one in the New Testament, but now one of the most common names for a man
25. N_____: Three of them in the Bible, most notably the one who helped rebuild Jerusalem after the Babylonian exile
26. N_____: Two of them, but one an almost total unknown, the other being the Old Testament's famous "rainy day" man
27. A_____: Only one, which is appropriate, since he was "the original" of us all
28. I_____: Only one, not too famous himself, but noted as the son of Abraham and the father of Jacob
29. J_____: Ten of them in the Old Testament, the best-known being the "weeping prophet" who has a long book named for him
30. T_____: One of the most common man's names now, but only one of him in the New Testament, a doubting disciple

13. Samuel
14. John
15. Paul
16. Hezekiah
17. James
18. Ahab
19. Zadok
20. Simon (which was Peter's original name)
21. Moses
22. Mattaniah
23. Mary
24. Mark
25. Nehemiah
26. Noah
27. Adam
28. Isaac
29. Jeremiah
30. Thomas

31. J_____: A common name in both Testaments—twelve men in all—a son of Jacob, a close connection of Jesus, and still a common name for men

32. A_____: Only one in the Old Testament, but a dominant character, the original settler in Canaan

33. S_____: Only one, the first Christian martyr, but a common man's name today

34. P_____: Only one in the New Testament, Jesus' most outspoken disciple

35. S_____: Only one in the Old Testament, the Bible's famous long-haired strongman

36. J_____: Five of them in the Old Testament, none outstanding except the king who wiped out Baal worship—and Ahab's family in the process

37. E_____: Four of them in all, but the most famous was the outspoken Old Testament prophet who was a thorn in the side of bad king Ahab

38. E_____: A common woman's name nowadays, but only one of them in the Bible

39. R_____: Only one of them in the Old Testament, Jacob's favorite wife

40. R_____: Four of them in all, none too well-known except for Moses' Midianite father-in-law

41. A_____: Five of them, the name serving for both men and women, but the most notable being the father of Esther

42. J_____: Four of them in the Bible, the most famous being Moses' right-hand man, with a book of the Bible named for him

43. J_____: Eleven of them in the Old Testament—none of any note, except the Levite who explained the Law as Ezra read it

44. J_____: Eight of them, the most famous being Jacob's son whose name was held by the largest of the twelve tribes of Israel

45. D_____: Two in the Bible, the most famous being a female judge of Israel—and a common name for women today

46. J_____: Fifteen in the Old Testament, the best-known being David's best friend

31. Joseph
32. Abraham
33. Stephen
34. Peter
35. Samson
36. Jehu
37. Elijah
38. Elizabeth
39. Rachel
40. Reuel (which is given as an alternate name for Jethro, the better-known name of Moses' father-in-law)
41. Abihail
42. Joshua
43. Jozabad (*eleven* of them—amazing!)
44. Judah
45. Deborah
46. Jonathan

47. N_____: Five of them in all, the most famous being the prophet who confronted David with his adultery
48. R_____: A common woman's name today, but only one in the Bible, with a book named for her
49. D_____: Four of them in the Old Testament, notably the handsome young prophet carried into captivity to Babylon, hobnobbing with King Nebuchadnezzar
50. L_____: Only one in the New Testament, the author of a Gospel and traveling companion of Paul

Familiar Verse, Peculiar Order

☛ Placed in their proper order, the words are a familiar verse from Matthew.

as debtors our forgive our us debts forgive we

What's That Character's Name Again?

☛ Many names of Bible characters may appear very strange to us in their original Hebrew or Greek form. Try guessing the familiar names of these Bible characters.

1. Yoseph
2. Timotheos
3. Aharon
4. Hevel
5. Yitshak
6. Shelomoh
7 Yehonathan
8. Yonah
9. Ioannes
10. Stephanos
11. Yehudhah
12. Yirmeyahu
13. Markos
14. Iakobos
15. Miryam

47. Nathan
48. Ruth
49. Daniel
50. Luke

Familiar Verse, Peculiar Order (answer)

Forgive us our debts, as we forgive our debtors. (Matthew 6:12)

What's That Character's Name Again? (answers)

1. Joseph (We thought we'd start with an easy one.)
2. Timothy
3. Aaron
4. Abel
5. Isaac
6. Solomon
7. Jonathan
8. Jonah
9. John
10. Stephen
11. Judah
12. Jeremiah
13. Mark
14. James
15. Mary

16. Mathaios
17. Dawidh
18. Yehoshua
19. Yoshiyahu
20. Ioudas
21. Shaul
22. Petros
23. Yishay
24. Moseheh
25. Ya'akov
26. Ahashwerosh
27. Zakhaios
28. Zekharyahu
29. Gidhon
30. Sephanyah
31. Iesous
32. Yov
33. Adham
34. Andreas
35. Bartholomaios
36. Binyamin
37. Izevel
38. Eliyahu
39. Pilatos
40. Ovadhyah
41. Akylos
42. Kornelios
43. Hizkiyah
44. Sheth
45. Shemuel
46. Hanokh
47. Shimshon
48. Koresh
49. Yehezkel
50. Yishmael

16. Matthew
17. David
18. Joshua
19. Josiah
20. Jude
21. Saul
22. Peter
23. Jesse
24. Moses
25. Jacob
26. Ahasuerus (or Xerxes, in some newer translations of the book of Esther)
27. Zacchaeus
28. Zechariah
29. Gideon
30. Zephaniah
31. Jesus
32. Job
33. Adam
34. Andrew
35. Bartholomew
36. Benjamin
37. Jezebel
38. Elijah
39. Pilate
40. Obadiah
41. Aquila
42. Cornelius
43. Hezekiah
44. Seth
45. Samuel
46. Enoch
47. Samson
48. Cyrus
49. Ezekiel
50. Ishmael

Familiar Verse, Peculiar Order

☛ Placed in their proper order, the words are a familiar verse from Psalms.

I is Lord my not shall shepherd the want

Six-Letter Names (Part II)

1. What muscle man burned the Philistines' grain by tying torches to the tails of foxes?
2. Who was the first polygamist in the Bible?
3. What apostle was Peter's brother?
4. What king of Judah was stricken with leprosy?
5. Who killed the Syrian king Ben-Hadad by smothering him with a wet cloth?
6. Jacob wept with love and joy over what beautiful woman?
7. Who evangelized the Ethiopian eunuch?
8. Who was commissioned by an angel to save Israel from the raiding Midianites?
9. What friend of Paul was one of the many Jews expelled from Rome by order of Emperor Claudius?
10. What two prophets were separated by horses of fire?
11. Who had his lips touched by a live coal held by an angel?
12. Who was the oldest of Jacob's brood of twelve sons?
13. What Persian queen upset the king and his cronies by refusing to appear before them at their drunken banquet?
14. Who heard God's voice after running away from Queen Jezebel?
15. What Canaanite commander was murdered by Jael, who drove a tent peg into his skull?
16. What pagan prophet was trapped against a wall by an angel with a drawn sword?
17. What sorcerer, an opponent of Paul, was struck blind?
18. What judge had seventy sons?
19. What Hebrew military leader was told by God to cripple his enemies' horses?
20. Who prophesied to the Shunammite woman that, though her husband was too old, she would bear a child?

Familiar Verse, Peculiar Order (answer)

The Lord is my shepherd; I shall not want. (Psalm 23:1)

Six-Letter Names (Part II) (answers)

1. Samson (Judges 15:4-5)
2. Lamech, the great-grandson of Cain (Genesis 4:19)
3. Andrew
4. Uzziah (2 Kings 15:5)
5. Hazael (2 Kings 8:7, 15)
6. Rachel (Genesis 29:11)
7. Philip (Acts 8:26-39)
8. Gideon (Judges 6:11-23)
9. Aquila (Acts 18:2)
10. Elijah and Elisha (2 Kings 2:11)
11. Isaiah (6:5-7)
12. Reuben (Genesis 35:23)
13. Vashti, whose place was taken later by the Jewish girl Esther (Esther 1)
14. Elijah (1 Kings 19:13)
15. Sisera (Judges 4:21-22)
16. Balaam (Numbers 22:24)
17. Elymas (Acts 13:7-12)
18. Gideon (Judges 8:30)
19. Joshua (11:6)
20. Elisha (2 Kings 4:13-17)

21. In the division of Canaan among Israel's twelve tribes, which tribe got the raw deal of being allotted the desert land in the south?

22. Which son of Jacob lost his rights as the firstborn son because he slept with his father's concubine?

23. This man's mother was visited by the angel of the Lord, who told her she would have a son who would be dedicated as a Nazirite. Who was he?

24. What devout elderly man blessed the infant Jesus in the temple at Jerusalem?

25. Who irritated his brothers by telling them of his dreams?

26. Who wept because her husband's other wife taunted her for being childless?

27. The prophet Ezekiel saw a woman weeping for what pagan god?

28. Who died giving birth to Jacob's youngest son, Benjamin?

29. Which disciple was probably a twin?

30. What prophet, fleeing from wicked Queen Jezebel, hid in a cave?

31. What godly king removed the horse idols that the kings of Judah had dedicated to the worship of the sun?

32. Who had a miraculous well opened up for him after he worked up a thirst in battle?

33. Who was Jacob's favorite of his twelve sons?

34. What prophet said that Ahab's descendants would be eaten by birds?

35. Who had a dream telling him to flee to Egypt to escape the violence of King Herod?

36. What synagogue leader had his daughter raised from the dead by Jesus?

37. Who asked Jesus the famous question "What is truth?"

38. What wealthy man took Jesus' body and buried him in his own family's tomb?

39. What Jewish Christian was a friend of Paul and, like Paul, a tentmaker by trade?

40. Which Roman official accused Paul of having gone insane with too much studying?

21. Simeon; eventually most of the tribe disappeared.
22. Reuben (Genesis 35:22; 49:3-4)
23. Samson (Judges 13:1-20)
24. Simeon (Luke 2:25-35)
25. Joseph (Genesis 37:2-11); to be specific, his dreams all showed them bowing down to him—which didn't exactly please them.
26. Hannah, who later was the mother of Samuel (1 Samuel 1:6-7)
27. Tammuz (Ezekiel 8:14)
28. Rachel (Genesis 35:16-18)
29. Thomas (John 11:16)
30. Elijah (1 Kings 19:9)
31. Josiah (2 Kings 23:11)
32. Samson (Judges 15:18-20)
33. Joseph (Genesis 37:3)
34. Elijah (1 Kings 21:24)
35. Joseph, husband of Mary (Matthew 2:13)
36. Jairus (Mark 5)
37. Pilate (John 18:38)
38. Joseph (of Arimathea) (John 19:38)
39. Aquila (Acts 18:2)
40. Festus (Acts 26:24)

Familiar Verse, Peculiar Order

☛ Placed in their proper order, the words are a familiar verse from Psalms.

and Babylon down of rivers sat the we by wept

My Son "Ben"

☛ A good many names in the Bible begin or end with *ben*—the Hebrew word for "son." Test your knowledge of the ben men in the Bible.

1. Who was the youngest of Jacob's twelve sons?
2. What Bible character has a famous Charlton Heston movie with the same name?
3. When Rachel gave birth to Benjamin, she did not name him Benjamin but gave him a name meaning "son of my sorrow." What was the name?
4. What king of Syria was smothered to death, fulfilling a prophecy of the prophet Elisha?
5. What child of an incestuous union was ancestor of the Ammonite tribe?
6. What gory place near Jerusalem was connected with child sacrifice and sorcery?
7. Who was Jacob's oldest son?

Familiar Verse, Peculiar Order

☛ Placed in their proper order, the words are a familiar verse from the Old Testament.

am I me send here

Names, Common and Uncommon (Part II)

1. M_____: Twenty of them in all—one of the most common names in the Bible, but not one of them noteworthy

Familiar Verse, Peculiar Order (answer)

By the rivers of Babylon, we sat down and wept. (Psalm 137:1)

My Son "Ben" (answers)

1. Benjamin
2. Ben-Hur, one of Solomon's twelve food commissioners (1 Kings 4:8); he was not an important person, but his name certainly lives on.
3. Ben-Oni (Genesis 35:18); Rachel died, and Jacob immediately gave the son a more pleasant name.
4. Ben-Hadad; he was smothered by Hazael, who succeeded him as king (2 Kings 8:7-15). Ben-Hadad means "son of Hadad," Hadad being a Syrian storm god.
5. Ben-ammi, whose name means "son of my people" (Genesis 19:38); he was the child of Abraham's nephew Lot and Lot's younger daughter.
6. The valley of Ben-Hinnom—that is "valley of the son of Hinnom"; no one knows exactly who Hinnom (or his son) was, but the valley was mentioned many times in connection with horrible rituals.
7 Reuben, whose name means "see, a son" (Genesis 29:32)

Familiar Verse, Peculiar Order (answer)

Here am I; send me. (Isaiah 6:8)

Names, Common and Uncommon (Part II) (answers)

1. Maaseiah (If you knew this, give yourself an A+ in Bible knowledge.)

2. M_____: Only one in the Bible, the last book of prophecy in the Old Testament

3. H_____: Twelve men with this unusual name in the Old Testament

4. C_____: Two of these mentioned in the New Testament, one of them being a Roman emperor

5. C_____: Only one in the Bible, a real killer

6. N_____: Two of them in the Bible, one being an Old Testament prophet with a book named for him

7. G_____: Only one of these, one of the really *big* men in the Old Testament

8. E_____: Eight of these in the Bible, the best-known being a son of the priest Aaron

9. D_____: Only one of these, one of the world-famous wicked women of the Old Testament

10. C_____: Only one, an emperor of Persia

11. B_____: Only one, the husband of the Moabite woman who was an ancestor of Jesus

12. J_____: David's father and the only person in the Bible with this name

13. J_____: Only one in the Bible, a godly king of Judah

14. B_____: Three of them in the Old Testament, one of them being Jeremiah's friend and secretary

15. G_____: Only one of these, one of the greatest of the judges of Israel

16. B_____: Only one of them, one of the great evangelists of the New Testament, a friend of Paul

17. S_____: Israel's wise king and the only person with this distinguished name

18. A_____: Three of these in the New Testament—a good Christian, a backsliding Christian, and a priest

19. A_____: Only two in the Bible, one being a Hebrew prophet with a book named for him

20. E_____: Two of them in the Old Testament, one being the great priest and leader at the time of the return from Babylon

21. S_____: Only one of these, one of Paul's traveling companions

22. D_____: A common name today, but only one of these in the Bible, one of Jacob's twelve sons

2. Malachi
3. Hashabiah
4. Claudius
5. Cain
6. Nahum
7. Goliath
8. Eleazar
9. Delilah
10. Cyrus
11. Boaz
12. Jesse
13. Josiah
14. Baruch
15. Gideon
16. Barnabas
17. Solomon
18. Ananias
19. Amos
20. Ezra
21. Silas
22. Dan

23. N_____: Only one of these, the name of Ruth's mother-in-law
24. J_____: Only one, the man who was swallowed by a huge fish
25. O_____: Thirteen men with this name in the Old Testament—including the author of the shortest Old Testament book
26. H_____: Only one of these, the name of Samuel's mother
27. J_____: Only one of these, the father of the twelve tribes of Israel
28. M_____: Two of them in the Old Testament—one of Jacob's sons and a wicked king of Judah
29. E_____: Only one of these, the Jewish girl who married the king of Persia
30. S_____: Sixteen of these in the Old Testament—none too important, although one was a king of Israel
31. J_____: Two of these in the Bible, the famous one being a wicked queen of the Old Testament
32. E_____: Only one of these, one of the greatest of the Hebrew prophets
33. A_____: Only one of these, a great king's rebellious son
34. I_____: Only one, the most read of the Hebrew prophets, with a book named after him
35. P_____: Only one, a devout woman and a friend of Paul's
36. M_____: Twenty-one of these (yes, that many!) in the Bible, none of any importance
37. M_____: Only one of these in the Bible, and for a reason: it's a mouthful, the longest name in the whole Bible
38. T_____: Only one of these, a disciple of Paul, with two New Testament epistles bearing his name
39. J_____: Only one of these, a New Testament woman whose name is fairly common today
40. N_____: Only one of these in the New Testament, a Christian man who has the same name as a flower
41. R_____: Only one of these, an Old Testament woman, mother of two famous twins

23. Naomi
24. Jonah
25. Obadiah
26. Hannah
27. Jacob
28. Manasseh
29. Esther
30. Shallum
31. Jezebel
32. Ezekiel
33. Absalom
34. Isaiah
35. Phoebe
36. Meshullam (If you knew this answer, treat yourself to a lavish dinner.)
37. Maher-shalal-hash-baz (see Isaiah 8:1-3)
38. Timothy
39. Joanna
40. Narcissus
41. Rebecca

42. A_____: Two of these in the Old Testament, one a wife of David, the other a sister of David
43. M_____: Only one of these, a friend of Jesus', and today a common name for a woman
44. A_____: Peter's brother and the only man in the Bible with this name (now fairly common)
45. A_____: Only one of these, a great Christian leader whose name reminds us of a Greek god
46. C_____: Only one of these in the Old Testament, which is just as well, since his name in Hebrew means "dog"
47. C_____: Only one of these, a New Testament man who was a Roman soldier
48. E_____: Five of these in the Old Testament, the most famous being Samuel's father
49. E_____: The original woman and the only Bible person with this name
50. A_____: Only one in the Old Testament, which is appropriate, since he died young and left no children
51. A_____: There are twenty-two in the Old Testament, one of them a king of Judah (who was better known by the name Uzziah)

Familiar Verse, Peculiar Order

☛ Placed in their proper order, the words are a familiar verse from the New Testament.

door and at behold knock stand the I

42. Abigail
43. Martha
44. Andrew
45. Apollos
46. Caleb
47. Cornelius
48. Elkanah
49. Eve
50. Abel
51. Azariah

Familiar Verse, Peculiar Order (answer)

Behold, I stand at the door, and knock. (Revelation 3:20)

Do You Remember?

☞ Would you like to see how much Bible trivia you can remember? Answer the questions (which you should have answered already in this section), and then see how well you rate on the scale on page xii.

1. What king wanted to see miracles when the arrested Jesus was sent to him? (Hint: five letters)
2. Who had his name changed (by God) from a name meaning "exalted father" to a name meaning "father of multitudes"? (Hint: starts with A)
3. What Jewish girl became queen of Persia? (Hint: six letters)
4. What magician came to be baptized by Philip? (Hint: five letters)
5. Name the famous Bible person associated with these places: Tarshish, Joppa, Nineveh.
6. What's this Bible character's name? A_____: Only one of him—thank goodness, since he was one of Israel's worst kings (Hint: four letters)
7. Guess the familiar name of this Bible character's original Hebrew form: Yov.
8. Who irritated his brothers by telling them of his dreams? (Hint: six letters)
9. What's this Bible character's name? N_____: Only one of these, the name of Ruth's mother-in-law (Hint: five letters)
10. What wayward Old Testament woman had children named Lo-ruhamah, Lo-ammi, and Jezreel? (Hint: five letters)

Do You Remember? (answers)

1. Herod (Luke 23:8)
2. Abraham, who was originally named Abram (Genesis 17:5)
3. Esther (Esther 2:17)
4. Simon (the sorcerer; Acts 8:12-13)
5. Jonah (who headed for Tarshish, departed from Joppa, prophesied in Nineveh)
6. Ahab
7. Job
8. Joseph (Genesis 37:2-11); to be specific, his dreams all showed them bowing down to him—which didn't exactly please them.
9. Naomi
10. Gomer, unfaithful wife of the prophet Hosea (Hosea 1)

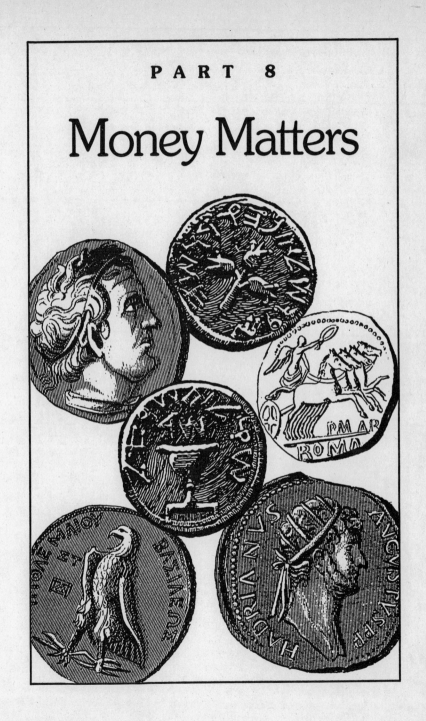

PART 8

Money Matters

Test Your Bible IQ

☞ This quiz contains questions covering the topics in part 8, "Money Matters." Do your best, then turn the page to see how you did. If you are brave enough to see how your Bible IQ rates, turn to page xii for our scale.

1. Whom did Jesus send fishing in order to get money for taxes?
2. To whom did Jesus say, "If thou wilt be perfect, go and sell that thou hast, and give to the poor"?
3. Who paid an enormous amount of silver to buy a cave to bury his beloved wife in?
4. What (formerly) rich man sat in a pile of ashes?
5. Who stated that, being a poor man, he couldn't possibly marry Saul's daughter?
6. Which of Jesus' disciples had charge of the group's money?
7. What young king pleased the Lord by praying for wisdom instead of for wealth?
8. Who sold their brother into slavery for twenty pieces of silver?
9. Which book of the Bible says that money is the root of all evil?
10. In only one place in the Bible is a coin's appearance referred to. Whose face was on it?

Test Your Bible IQ (answers)

1. Peter (Matthew 17:24-27)
2. The rich young ruler (Matthew 19:21)
3. Abraham, who bought the cave of Machpelah to bury Sarah in (Genesis 23)
4. Job (2:8)
5. David, who did indeed marry Saul's daughter (1 Samuel 18:23)
6. Judas (John 13:29)
7. Solomon, who ended up being both rich *and* wise (1 Kings 3:10-13)
8. Jacob's sons, who sold Joseph to the Ishmaelites (Genesis 37:28)
9. The Bible doesn't say that; what Paul said was that "the love of money is the root of all evil" (1 Timothy 6:10).
10. Caesar's, meaning that it was a Roman coin, the one discussed by Jesus and the Pharisees (Matthew 22:18-21)

The Root of All Evil

1. What treacherous man do we associate with thirty pieces of silver?
2. What disciple found a coin in the mouth of a fish?
3. What was the common unit of currency in the Old Testament?
4. What treacherous prostitute received a hefty amount of silver for betraying a Hebrew strongman?
5. What land was the richest source of gold?
6. What word, which today means "ability," was a unit of currency in biblical times?
7. What Assyrian king received thirty-eight tons of silver as tribute money from Ahaz of Israel?
8. What did the chief priests buy with the silver Judas returned to them?
9. Where did the Israelites keep their money?
10. In what parable of Jesus are servants given money to invest?
11. What priest of Judah placed a money collection box near the temple's altar?
12. What New Testament prophet told Roman soldiers to be content with their pay and to avoid taking money by force?
13. Whom did Jesus send fishing in order to get money for taxes?
14. In the parable of Lazarus and the rich man, what does Abraham say to the rich man who wants to keep his relatives out of hell?
15. What bird does Jeremiah compare to a man who gains riches by unjust means?
16. What prophet condemned the idle rich on their beds of ivory?
17. What character in a parable wasted his money on prostitutes?
18. In the time of the judges, what man stole eleven hundred pieces of silver from his own mother?
19. What people were so affluent that they put gold chains around their camels' necks?
20. What saintly king had a fleet built to sail for gold, though the ships never sailed?
21. Which of Jesus' parables mentions a rich man dressed in purple robes?
22. What (formerly) rich man sat in a pile of ashes?

The Root of All Evil (answers)

1. Judas Iscariot, the disciple who betrayed Jesus for that amount (Matthew 26:15)
2. Peter (Matthew 17:27)
3. The shekel, which is today the name of the unit of currency in Israel
4. Delilah, who betrayed Samson and received eleven hundred pieces of silver from each of the Philistine nobles (Judges 16:5)
5. Ophir, mentioned several times in the Old Testament; it was probably in what is today called Arabia.
6. The *talent;* no one knows exactly what a talent was worth, though it was much larger than a shekel.
7. Tiglath-Pileser (2 Kings 16:7-8)
8. A field to bury strangers in (Matthew 27:6-7)
9. The banks of the Jordan (No, this isn't a serious question.)
10. The parable of the talents (Matthew 25:14-30)
11. Jehoiada (2 Kings 12:9)
12. John the Baptist (Luke 3:14)
13. Peter (Matthew 17:24-27)
14. He tells him that the people have Moses and the prophets (Luke 16:27-29).
15. A partridge that hatches eggs it does not lay (Jeremiah 17:11)
16. Amos (6:4)
17. The Prodigal Son (Luke 15:30)
18. Micah (Judges 17:1-4); this is *not* the same as the prophet Micah, by the way.
19. The Midianites (Judges 8:26); considering that the bandit Midianites gained most of their wealth by robbing others while on camelback, this was probably appropriate.
20. Jehoshaphat (1 Kings 22:48)
21. The parable of the rich man and Lazarus (Luke 16:19)
22. Job (2:8)

23. What figure is portrayed in these words by Isaiah: "He made his grave with the wicked, and with the rich in his death"?
24. What woman in the time of the judges had dedicated eleven hundred shekels of silver to the making of idols?
25. Where was the first piggy bank?
26. What wealthy Christian woman made her living selling purple dye?
27. What wealthy woman had a son that died of a sunstroke?
28. What wealthy man had fourteen thousand sheep?
29. What wealthy man buried Jesus in his own tomb?
30. Which apostle proclaimed, "I have coveted no man's silver, or gold, or apparel"?
31. Who healed a crippled beggar who was asking for money?
32. Who tried to buy the gifts of the Holy Spirit with money?
33. Who told his followers not to bother carrying money with them?
34. What did Judas do with the thirty pieces of silver he received for betraying Jesus?
35. What did Jesus use to drive the money changers out of the temple?
36. What wicked king of Israel tried to buy a man's family estate by offering him money?
37. Who sold their brother into slavery for twenty pieces of silver?
38. What financial practice (the foundation of capitalism) was forbidden in the Old Testament Law?
39. Who is the first rich man mentioned in the Bible?
40. According to Psalm 19, what is much more desirable than fine gold?
41. According to Proverbs, what is more valuable than either gold or silver?
42. What prophet invited people who had no money to come and dine at the Lord's feast?
43. What prophet lamented that Israel's prophets and priests did their work strictly for money?
44. Which New Testament epistle warns against Christian congregations showing favoritism to the rich?
45. Who sat and watched rich people casting large amounts of money into the temple treasury?
46. What husband-and-wife pair was struck dead for lying to the apostles about a church contribution?

23. The Suffering Servant (Isaiah 53:9); this was, of course, a prophecy of Christ
24. Micah's mother (Judges 17:2-4)
25. In the temple at Jerusalem; it was a chest, ordered by King Joash, who had a hole bored in the lid to keep priests from stealing funds from it (2 Kings 12).
26. Lydia (Acts 16:14)
27. The woman of Shunam (2 Kings 4:18-20), the hostess for the prophet Elisha
28. Job (42:12)
29. Joseph of Arimathea (Matthew 27:59-60)
30. Paul (Acts 20:33)
31. Peter (Acts 3:6)
32. Simon the sorcerer (Acts 8:18-20)
33. Jesus (Matthew 10:9)
34. Returned it to the priests and threw it down in the temple (Matthew 27:3-5)
35. A whip made out of cords (John 2:15)
36. Ahab, who tried to buy the vineyard of Naboth (1 Kings 21:2)
37. Jacob's sons, who sold Joseph to the Ishmaelites (Genesis 37:28)
38. Usury—that is, lending money at interest (Deuteronomy 23:19)
39. Abraham (Genesis 13:2), who "was very rich in cattle, in silver, and in gold"
40. The commands of the Lord (Psalm 19:10)
41. Wisdom (Proverbs 16:16)
42. Isaiah (55:1)
43. Micah (3:11)
44. James (2:2-4)
45. Jesus (Mark 12:41)
46. Ananias and Sapphira, who sold some property and gave the money to the apostles, but lied about the amount they received (Acts 5:1-11)

47. What corrupt Roman official detained Paul in jail, hoping for a bribe of money?
48. Which book of the Bible says that money is the root of all evil?
49. What people burned their occult books and calculated their price at fifty thousand silver coins?
50. What agitator made a killing selling silver statues of a pagan goddess?

Familiar Verse, Peculiar Order

☞ Placed in their proper order, the words are a familiar verse from the New Testament.

to Christ live for is me

Po' Folks

1. What man, deeply moved by meeting Jesus, gave half his goods to the poor?
2. What pagan conqueror carried off all the people of Jerusalem except the poorest?
3. Which Old Testament book forbids charging interest on loans to the poor?
4. What were Poor Man's Bibles?
5. Who told King David a parable of a poor man who had his one pet lamb taken away from him by a rich man?
6. Which New Testament epistle warns churches against treating rich folks better than poor folks?
7. What festival of the Jews featured giving gifts to the poor?
8. What wise king said, "Better is a poor and a wise child than an old and foolish king"?
9. To whom did Jesus say, "If thou wilt be perfect, go and sell that thou hast, and give to the poor"?
10. Which of Jesus' disciples protested Jesus' anointing with oil, saying that the money spent on the oil could have been given to the poor?
11. The Christians in Greece took up a love offering for the poor Christians in what city?

47. Felix (Acts 24:25-26)
48. The Bible doesn't say that; what Paul said was that "the love of money is the root of all evil" (1 Timothy 6:10).
49. The people of Ephesus (Acts 19:19), who apparently had been rather caught up in the New Age movement
50. Demetrius, the silversmith of Ephesus, who made images of the temple of the goddess Artemis (Acts 19:24)

Familiar Verse, Peculiar Order (answer)

For me to live is Christ. (Philippians 1:21)

Po' Folks (answers)

1. The tax collector Zacchaeus (Luke 19:8)
2. Nebuchadnezzar (2 Kings 24:14)
3. Exodus (22:25)
4. Picture books widely used in the Middle Ages in place of the Bible. Used by the illiterate, they were probably the earliest books to be printed.
5. Nathan the prophet, who was condemning David's adultery with Bathsheba (2 Samuel 12)
6. James (2:2-4)
7. Purim, which is told of in the book of Esther
8. Solomon, who (according to tradition) is the author of Ecclesiastes (4:13)
9. The rich young ruler (Matthew 19:21)
10. Judas Iscariot (John 12:4-5)
11. Jerusalem (Romans 15:26)

12. Who said, "Though I bestow all my goods to feed the poor, and though I give my body to be burned, and have not charity, it profiteth me nothing"?
13. Who had a dream of seven poor cattle coming out of the Nile River?
14. Who stated that, being a poor man, he couldn't possibly marry Saul's daughter?
15. What judge of Israel protested that he wasn't fit to lead because he came from a poor family?
16. What commendable deed was done by a poor widow Jesus saw in the temple?
17. Which prophet accused the people of Israel of selling the poor people for a pair of shoes?
18. What Christian woman was noted for helping the poor in the early church?
19. Matthew 5:3 has Jesus saying, "Blessed are the poor in spirit." What does he say in Luke 6:20?
20. What did Elisha miraculously supply a poor widow with?
21. Deuteronomy 15:4 says "There shall be no poor among you." What does Deuteronomy 15:11 say?

Familiar Verse, Peculiar Order

☛ Placed in their proper order, the words are a familiar verse from Matthew.

Caesar is Caesar's render unto what

The Root of All Evil (More of It)

1. Who were the first wealthy men to set eyes on Jesus?
2. What king of Israel became legendary for both his wealth and his wisdom (and a lot of wives, to boot)?
3. What man did Jesus tell to sell all his possessions and give the proceeds to the poor?
4. According to Jesus, what is easier than a rich man entering the kingdom of heaven?
5. Who was given money to say that Jesus' disciples had stolen his body from the tomb?

12. Paul (1 Corinthians 13:3)
13. The pharaoh in Joseph's time (Genesis 41)
14. David, who did indeed marry Saul's daughter (1 Samuel 18:23)
15. Gideon (Judges 6)
16. She put two mites (coins) in the temple treasury, even though this was almost all she owned (Mark 12:42)
17. Amos (2:6)
18. Dorcas (Acts 9:36, 39)
19. "Blessed are you poor."
20. Large quantities of oil (2 Kings 4:1-7)
21. "The poor shall never cease out of the land."

Familiar Verse, Peculiar Order (answer)

Render unto Caesar what is Caesar's. (Matthew 22:21)

The Root of All Evil (More of It) (answers)

1. Probably the wise men; since they brought expensive gifts (gold, frankincense, myrrh) and had traveled a long way, they were undoubtedly well-heeled.
2. Solomon
3. The rich young nobleman, who is not mentioned by name (Matthew 19:16-22); the young man did not take Jesus up on his offer.
4. A camel going through the eye of a needle (Matthew 19:24)
5. The Roman soldiers (Matthew 28:12-15)

6. What church was becoming smug and lazy because of its wealth?
7. Who paid an enormous amount of silver to buy a cave to bury his beloved wife in?
8. Who surprised his brothers by returning the money they had paid him for food?
9. Omri, king of Israel, paid six thousand pieces of silver to buy the land on which to build which famous city?
10. What pagan military officer was willing to pay thirty thousand pieces of silver and six thousand pieces of gold to be cured of leprosy?
11. When Joseph sent his eleven brothers back to Canaan, which brother did he supply with three hundred pieces of silver and five changes of clothes?
12. During the Syrians' siege of Samaria, what peculiar food was selling for the outrageous price of eighty pieces of silver?
13. Which book of the Bible contains the lament of a wealthy man who was not satisfied with his money?
14. What good king of Judah was stupid enough to display his treasures to the ambassadors from Babylon?
15. According to Ecclesiastes, what two amusements can't be had without money?
16. Who uttered the famous words "Woe to you who are rich"?
17. Which Old Testament book offers this wise advice: "He that loveth silver shall not be satisfied with silver; nor he that loveth abundance"?
18. Does the Bible approve of a graduated tax system?
19. According to Psalms, what type of money lender would be considered pure enough to enter the Lord's temple?
20. What prophet condemned the rich of Israel for selling out the poor for money?
21. In which book of prophecy would you find these words: "The silver is mine, and the gold is mine, saith the Lord of hosts"?
22. What neighbor nation of Israel is most often condemned for being a nation of wheeler-dealers in money?
23. According to 1 Timothy, what type of man should not be a lover of money?
24. Which of Jesus' disciples had charge of the group's money?
25. According to Proverbs, what type of money dwindles away?

6. The church of Laodicea (Revelation 3:14-18)
7. Abraham, who bought the cave of Machpelah to bury Sarah in (Genesis 23)
8. Joseph, who sent his brothers back to Canaan not only with a full supply of food, but with the money they had paid him for it (Genesis 42:25-28)
9. Samaria, which he made the capital of his kingdom (1 Kings 16:24)
10. Naaman the Syrian, who was eventually cured by the prophet Elisha (2 Kings 5:5)
11. Benjamin, who was his only *full* brother of the large brood (Joseph and Benjamin being the two sons of Jacob and Rachel) (Genesis 45:22)
12. A donkey's head (2 Kings 6:25); we have to assume that the Samaritans were on the verge of starvation.
13. Ecclesiastes (2:8-11), which supposedly was written by rich King Solomon
14. Hezekiah (Isaiah 39:2); later on, the Babylonians attacked Jerusalem and carried off all the treasure.
15. Wine and feasting (Ecclesiastes 10:19)
16. Jesus (Luke 6:24)
17. Ecclesiastes (5:10)
18. Apparently not, since Exodus 30:11-16 describes a tax in which the rich and the poor pay the same amount; also, the idea of the tithe—that is, a tenth—being given is equal for everyone, regardless of income.
19. One who had not charged interest (Psalm 15:1, 5); consider that when you look at the interest rate on your credit card statement.
20. Amos (8:6)
21. Haggai (2:8)
22. The people of the seacoast city of Tyre, which was renowned in ancient times for being a city of merchants; it is mentioned dozens of times in the Old Testament.
23. A church's bishop (or "overseer" or "leader," depending on the translation you have) (1 Timothy 3:3); for that matter, *no* Christian is supposed to be a lover of money.
24. Judas (John 13:29)
25. Money earned dishonestly (Proverbs 13:11)

26. What soothsaying slave girl made a great deal of money for her owners?

27. Which New Testament epistle advises us to keep our lives free from the love of money, and be satisfied with what we have?

28. What type of people were the Jews allowed to lend money to with interest?

29. What emperor held a grand feast to show off his vast wealth?

30. What eighty-year-old rich man lamented that he could no longer taste food nor hear the voices of singers?

31. Who was the *shortest* wealthy man in the Bible?

32. In Jesus' parable of the sower and the seed, what symbolizes the people whose love of money keeps them from becoming believers?

33. What prophet lamented that the people of Israel had made their wealth by cheating their customers?

34. What was one of the unfortunate results of good King Jehoshaphat of Judah becoming wealthy?

35. What nasty Persian official boasted to his friends how wealthy he was?

36. What young king pleased the Lord by praying for wisdom instead of for wealth?

37. The book of Proverbs states, "Give me neither poverty nor riches." What, instead, is requested?

38. In Jesus' parable, what happened to the rich man who had to build bigger storehouses to keep all his wealth?

39. Who did Paul praise for being generous as rich people, even though they were poor?

40. Which of the psalms contains the can't-take-it-with-you philosophy?

41. Which New Testament epistle of Paul's instructs the rich to be "rich in good works"?

42. What great city, famous for its wealth (and vice), is destroyed in the book of Revelation?

43. Who confronted King David with an incriminating parable about a rich man who takes away a poor man's prized possession?

44. What foreign visitor was deeply impressed with King Solomon's wealth?

26. The fortune-teller of Philippi; she lost her ability when Paul exorcised the demon that gave her this ability (Acts 16:18).
27. Hebrews (13:5)
28. Foreigners—that is, non-Jews (Deuteronomy 23:20); they could not charge interest to a fellow Jew.
29. Ahasuerus, the Persian king who later married the Jewish girl Esther (Esther 1:4)
30. Barzillai, a good friend of King David (2 Samuel 19:32-35)
31. Probably Zacchaeus, the wealthy tax collector of Jericho who was so short he had to climb a tree to see Jesus passing through (Luke 19:1-10)
32. The seeds that fall among the thorns, the thorns symbolizing wealth (Matthew 13:18-23)
33. Hosea, who mentions using false scales to falsify business transactions (Hosea 12:7)
34. He married off one of his children to the family of wicked King Ahab of Israel (2 Chronicles 18:1)
35. Haman, the official who plotted to have all the Jews exterminated (Esther 5:11)
36. Solomon, who ended up being both rich *and* wise (1 Kings 3:10-13)
37. "My daily bread" (Proverbs 30:8)
38. He died (Luke 12:16-21).
39. The Christians in Macedonia (2 Corinthians 8:1-3)
40. Psalm 49; all twenty verses are directed against the foolishness of trusting in riches. Most of the psalm dwells on the idea that even the rich man must die, leaving his wealth to someone else.
41. 1 Timothy (6:17-18)
42. Babylon (which may be a sort of code name for the city of Rome) (Revelation 18:19)
43. The prophet Nathan, who was chastising David for his adultery with Bathsheba, whose husband had been killed at David's command (2 Samuel 12)
44. The queen of Sheba, who was herself rather well-heeled (1 Kings 10:7)

45. Which New Testament book says that a rich man's wealth will vanish like a wildflower withering?
46. What name do the Gospels use for the god of money?
47. The original Greek text of the New Testament mentions a coin called an *assarion*. How does the English Bible translate this?
48. When Paul wrote "The love of money is the root of all evil," the Greek word translated "money" actually refers to a metal. Which one?
49. In only one place in the Bible is a coin's appearance referred to. Whose face was on it?
50. According to Jeremiah, a rich man should not boast of his riches but should boast of what?

Familiar Verse, Peculiar Order

☛ Placed in their proper order, the words are a familiar verse from the New Testament.

and devil from flee he resist the will you

45. James (1:10-11)
46. Mammon, who is not really a god, though Jesus uses the words "Ye cannot serve God and mammon" (Matthew 6:24).
47. "Penny" in most modern versions (see Matthew 10:29; Luke 12:6); the King James Version (reflecting its British origin) has "farthing." An *assarion,* a penny, and a farthing all refer to a very small coin.
48. Silver; the Greek word is *philarguria,* "love of silver."
49. Caesar's, meaning that it was a Roman coin, the one discussed by Jesus and the Pharisees (Matthew 22:18-21)
50. His relationship with the Lord (Jeremiah 9:23-24)

Familiar Verse, Peculiar Order (answer)

Resist the devil, and he will flee from you. (James 4:7)

Do You Remember?

☛ Would you like to see how much Bible trivia you can remember? Answer the questions (which you should have answered already in this section), and then see how well you rate on the scale on page xii.

1. What treacherous prostitute received a hefty amount of silver for betraying a Hebrew strongman?
2. Who told King David a parable of a poor man who had his one pet lamb taken away from him by a rich man?
3. What name do the Gospels use for the god of money?
4. What wealthy Christian woman made her living selling purple dye?
5. Which of Jesus' disciples protested Jesus' anointing with oil, saying that the money spent on the oil could have been given to the poor?
6. What pagan military officer was willing to pay thirty thousand pieces of silver and six thousand pieces of gold to be cured of leprosy?
7. What New Testament prophet told Roman soldiers to be content with their pay and to avoid taking money by force?
8. Deuteronomy 15:4 says "There shall be no poor among you." What does Deuteronomy 15:11 say?
9. What great city, famous for its wealth (and vice), is destroyed in the book of Revelation?
10. What wealthy man buried Jesus in his own tomb?

Do You Remember? (answers)

1. Delilah, who betrayed Samson and received eleven hundred pieces of silver from each of the Philistine nobles (Judges 16:5)
2. Nathan the prophet, who was condemning David's adultery with Bathsheba (2 Samuel 12)
3. Mammon, who is not really a god, though Jesus uses the words "Ye cannot serve God and mammon" (Matthew 6:24)
4. Lydia (Acts 16:14)
5. Judas Iscariot (John 12:4-5)
6. Naaman the Syrian, who was eventually cured by the prophet Elisha (2 Kings 5:5)
7. John the Baptist (Luke 3:14)
8. "The poor will never cease to be in the land."
9. Babylon (which may be a sort of code name for the city of Rome) (Revelation 18:19)
10. Joseph of Arimathea (Matthew 27:59-60)

PART 9

Groups, Gatherings, and So On

Test Your Bible IQ

☛ This quiz contains questions covering the topics in part 9, "Groups, Gatherings, and So On." Do your best, then turn the page to see how you did. If you are brave enough to see how your Bible IQ rates, turn to page xii for our scale.

1. Consider the following grouping, then pick out the one element in the group that is not biblically correct. Roman officials: Julius Caesar, Augustus, Pilate, Sergius Paulus
2. What two sisters of Bethany had a brother named Lazarus and were close friends of Jesus?
3. What do these have in common: Eliphaz, Zophar, Bildad?
4. Genesis 10 contains the famous "table of nations," which shows how the different nations of the world were descended from three men. What notable man were these three the sons of?
5. What two military men are the most famous friends in the Bible (and possibly the most famous male friends in the world)?
6. What do these have in common: shekel, denarius, mite?
7. Guess this famous Bible character's name using his or her relatives' names: Brother was Jacob, mother was Rebecca, father was Isaac.
8. Consider the following grouping, then pick out the one element in the group that is not biblically correct. Saintly women: Mary Magdalene, Jezebel, Ruth, Lydia
9. An earthquake at Philippi eventually led to the release of two Christians from prison there. Who were they?
10. Which of the twelve disciples was "the disciple whom Jesus loved"?

Test Your Bible IQ (answers)

1. Julius Caesar
2. Mary and Martha (Luke 10:38-42; John 11)
3. Job's three friends (who were also poor comforters)
4. Noah; the sons were Shem, Ham, and Japheth.
5. David and Jonathan, whose deep friendship is recounted in 1 and 2 Samuel; consider David's lament for the dead Jonathan: "Thy love to me was wonderful, passing the love of women" (2 Samuel 1:26).
6. Coins used in the Bible
7. Esau
8. Jezebel was a wicked queen in the Old Testament.
9. Paul and Silas (Acts 16:25-27)
10. He is not named, but since he is mentioned only in John's Gospel (John 13:23; 19:26; 20:2; 21:7), readers have traditionally believed that it must be John himself, exercising a little modesty by not mentioning himself by name.

Mentioned in the Bible—Not!

☞ Would you recognize the name of a person, place, or thing *not* mentioned in the Bible? Consider the following groupings, then pick out the one element in the group that is not biblically correct.

1. Disciples of Jesus: James, Matthias, Thomas, Philip
2. Kings: Hezekiah, Josiah, Solomon, Manassas
3. Fruit of the Spirit: tolerance, peace, kindness, self-control
4. Apostles: Paul, Barnabas, Elymas, Peter
5. Old Testament nations: Iraq, Assyria, Persia, Egypt
6. Biblical birds: the bat, the eagle, the stork, the parrot
7. New Testament people: James, John, Jethro, Judas
8. Prophets: Agabus, Elijah, Malachi, Moloch
9. Cities: Philadelphia, Bethlehem, Salem, Jersey City
10. Roman officials: Julius Caesar, Augustus, Pilate, Sergius Paulus
11. Sons of Jacob: Benjamin, Asher, Gad, Ishmael
12. Judges of Israel: Samson, Reuben, Gideon, Barak
13. Sons of King David: Zadok, Absalom, Solomon, Nathan
14. Cities: Bethany, Jericho, Tyre, Rhoda
15. Rivers: the Nile, the Tigris, the Jordan, the Jabbok
16. Cities that received epistles from Paul: Corinth, Laodicea, Rome, Galatia
17. Books written by Moses: Deuteronomy, Exodus, Genesis, Lamentations
18. Parables of Jesus: the blind men and the elephant, the wise and foolish virgins, the Good Samaritan, the lost sheep
19. Names of the devil: the tempter, the father of lies, the prince of demons, the burning one
20. Authors of New Testament epistles: Titus, Paul, Peter, James
21. Kings: Amon, Saul, Artemis, Pekah
22. Animals: donkey, dog, deer, Tasmanian devil
23. Food: manna, locusts, bagels, raisins
24. Historical books: Judges, 2 Samuel, Daniel, 2 Chronicles
25. Epistles: 1 Peter, Acts, Hebrews, Jude
26. People in Genesis: Nimrod, Joseph, Moses, Isaac
27. Suicides: Samson, Judas, Zimri, Herod
28. People who were executed: James, Jesus, Mark, Stephen
29. Wealthy men: Job, Joseph of Arimathea, Zacchaeus, Lazarus

Mentioned in the Bible—Not! (answers)

1. Matthias; he is an *apostle* in the book of Acts but not one of Jesus' original twelve disciples.
2. Manassas; there is a *Manasseh* who was a king. Manassas was a battle of the Civil War.
3. Tolerance is not in the list (Galatians 5).
4. Elymas was a sorcerer in the book of Acts.
5. Iraq; this is a fairly modern name. The area of modern Iraq was called Mesopotamia, Assyria, or Babylon in the Old Testament.
6. The parrot; the bat (surprise!) is mentioned in the Old Testament and is named in a list of birds, so apparently the Hebrews classed it as a bird simply because it flies.
7. Jethro is Moses' father-in-law in the Old Testament.
8. Moloch was the god of the Ammonites.
9. Jersey City (If you missed this, take a long vacation with a reliable atlas.)
10. Julius Caesar
11. Ishmael was a son of Abraham.
12. Reuben was one of Jacob's twelve sons.
13. Zadok was a priest in David's day. (In case you said to yourself, *Wasn't Nathan a prophet in the court of David?* the answer is, "Yes, he was, but David also had a son named Nathan.")
14. Rhoda was a woman in the book of Acts.
15. The Nile, believe it or not; though the river is *referred to* many times in the Bible, it is never actually mentioned by name. Usually it is simply called "the river."
16. Galatia—which isn't a city, but an entire *province* of the Roman Empire; Laodicea (though there is no Epistle to the Laodiceans in the Bible) did receive a letter from Paul, mentioned in Colossians 4:16. If you answered this correctly, buy yourself the rich dessert of your choice.
17. Lamentations was, according to tradition, written by Jeremiah.
18. The blind men and the elephant
19. The burning one
20. Titus has a New Testament epistle bearing his name, but the epistle is *from* Paul *to* Titus.
21. Artemis is a Greek goddess mentioned in the New Testament.
22. Tasmanian devil—and shame on you if you missed this!
23. Bagels are not mentioned in the Bible, though certainly they have a long association with Judaism.
24. Daniel is considered a prophetic book, though it does contain some historical narrative.
25. Acts is a historical book of the New Testament, not an epistle.
26. Moses is not mentioned until the book of Exodus.
27. Herod
28. Mark
29. Lazarus was a beggar in one of Jesus' parables.

30. Men who performed healing miracles: Elijah, Isaiah, Elisha, Jesus
31. Sexual practices forbidden: homosexuality, incest, rape, deep kissing
32. Tribes: Israelites, Moabites, Mennonites, Levites
33. Birds: hoopoe, toucan, cuckoo, peacock
34. Towns visited by Jesus: Nazareth, Jerusalem, Jericho, Corinth
35. People in the Gospels: Herod, Elisabeth, Isaac, Lazarus
36. Women: Gomer, Rachel, Joanna, Aquila
37. Military men: Gamaliel, Cornelius, Gideon, Jonathan
38. Tribes: Hittites, Jebusites, Danites, Campbellites
39. Holidays: Tabernacles, Pentecost, Easter, Passover
40. Nations: Egypt, Syria, Turkey, Ethiopia
41. New Testament epistles: 1 John, 2 Peter, 3 Timothy, 3 John
42. Prophets: Nathan, Micaiah, Jeremiah, Ahab
43. Foods: melons, pumpkins, cucumbers, onions
44. Angels: Gabriel, Michael, Zuriel
45. Capital crimes: adultery, Sabbath breaking, murder, drunk driving
46. Men who lived long lives: Adam, Abel, Methuselah, Jared
47. Jewish political groups: Herodians, Epicureans, Pharisees, Sadducees
48. Biblical cities that still exist: Damascus, Athens, Nazareth, Nineveh
49. People who were murdered: Abel, Paul, Absalom, Abner
50. Names for the Holy Spirit: Advocate, Channeler, Comforter, Counselor

Familiar Verse, Peculiar Order

☛ Placed in their proper order, the words are a familiar verse from a letter of Paul's.

a as child I a I spoke child was when

30. Isaiah
31. Deep kissing (Now *really,* did anyone miss this?)
32. Mennonites are a Protestant denomination that originated in Europe in the 1500s.
33. Toucans, native to America, are not mentioned in the Bible. The peacock, native to India, is mentioned, apparently because some were imported to the Middle East (see 1 Kings 10:22; 2 Chronicles 9:21).
34. Corinth, in Greece, was visited by Paul but not by Jesus.
35. Isaac is in Genesis.
36. Aquila was a male friend of Paul and was the husband of Priscilla. Gomer (surprise!) was the unfaithful wife of the prophet Hosea.
37. Gamaliel, a rabbi, was Paul's teacher.
38. Campbellites were members of an American religious group in the 1800s.
39. Easter is not mentioned in the Bible as a holiday, even though its key event (the resurrection of Jesus) *is* the most important event in the Bible.
40. Turkey was known in New Testament times as Asia, not Turkey.
41. 3 Timothy; there is a 1 and a 2 Timothy, but not a 3.
42. Ahab was a wicked king of Israel, not a prophet.
43. Pumpkins, native to America, were not known in Bible times.
44. Zuriel
45. Drunk driving, of course (Did anyone think there were automobiles in Bible times?)
46. Abel, murdered by his brother Cain, apparently died quite young. The others lived over nine hundred years each.
47. Epicureans were a Greek philosophical group, mentioned in Acts 17:18.
48. Nineveh, the capital of Assyria, has been a ruin for centuries.
49. Paul; according to a tradition later than the New Testament, Paul was executed (not murdered) by order of Emperor Nero.
50. Channeler is a term from New Age teaching, not from the Bible.

Familiar Verse, Peculiar Order (answer)

When I was a child, I spoke as a child. (1 Corinthians 13:11)

Couples, Pairs, Duos, Twosomes, Etc.

1. Who were the first twins?
2. Who were the first foreign missionaries?
3. Solomon led the way in constructing the first temple in Jerusalem. Who led in the building of the second temple?
4. What two women ran from Jesus' empty tomb to tell the disciples what had happened?
5. What two sisters of Bethany had a brother named Lazarus and were close friends of Jesus?
6. What two kings are mentioned as the authors of Proverbs?
7. What two women of Philippi are asked by Paul to stop their quarreling?
8. Which two Hebrew prophets had a fruitful mentor relationship?
9. What two Hebrew women did God make houses for?
10. What two men were to instruct the people involved in the construction of the tabernacle?
11. What two tribes of Israel were descended from an Egyptian woman?
12. What two apostles were put into prison in Jerusalem for preaching the gospel?
13. Who died after lying to Peter about the value of the possessions they had sold?
14. Who remained in the prison at Philippi even after an earthquake opened the prison doors?
15. What two women brought about the execution of John the Baptist?
16. What two brothers killed Hamor and Shechem for seducing their sister, Dinah?
17. What priests—two of Aaron's sons—were killed because they offered "strange fire" to the Lord?
18. What two gluttonous priests were notorious for keeping the sacrificial meat for themselves?
19. What was the name of the two stones worn in the high priest's breastplate and used to determine God's will?
20. What two men were high priests during David's reign?
21. Who were the sons of Zebedee?
22. Who, in Romans 16, did Paul refer to as apostles?

Couples, Pairs, Duos, Twosomes, Etc. (answers)

1. Jacob and Esau (Genesis 25:23-26)
2. Paul and Barnabas (Acts 13)
3. Zerubbabel and Joshua (Ezra 3)
4. Mary and Mary Magdalene (Matthew 28:18)
5. Mary and Martha (Luke 10:38-42; John 11)
6. Solomon and Lemuel (Proverbs 1:1; 31:1)
7. Euodias and Syntyche (Philippians 4:2)
8. Elijah and Elisha
9. Puah and Shiprah, the Hebrew midwives (Exodus 1:20-21)
10. Bezaleel and Aholiab (Exodus 35:30-35)
11. Manasseh and Ephraim; their father, Joseph, was married to Asenath of Egypt (Genesis 41:50-52).
12. Peter and John (Acts 4:3)
13. Ananias and Sapphira (Acts 5:1-10)
14. Paul and Silas (Acts 16:25-28)
15. Herodias and her daughter (Mark 6:22-27)
16. Levi and Simeon (Genesis 34:25-26)
17. Nadab and Abihu (Numbers 3:4)
18. Hophni and Phinehas (1 Samuel 2:17)
19. Urim and Thummim (Exodus 28:30)
20. Abiathar and Zadok (2 Samuel 20:25)
21. James and John
22. Andronicus and Junias

23. What kinds of objects were around the hem of the high priest's robe?
24. What husband-wife couple helped Paul establish the church in Corinth?
25. What two apostles were met by a priest of Zeus, who tried to offer sacrifices to them?
26. Who requested special places for themselves in Jesus' kingdom?
27. According to the Law, what sort of handicapped people should we not curse?
28. Who brought Greeks to Jesus?
29. Whom did Jesus say he would make into fishers of men?
30. What two men saw a chariot of fire drawn by horses of fire?
31. What two people walked on water in the midst of a storm?
32. What two sinful cities were destroyed by fire and brimstone from heaven?
33. Who appeared with Jesus at his miraculous transfiguration?
34. What were the names of the magicians in Pharaoh's court in the time of Moses?
35. The people of Lystra were so dazzled by Paul and Barnabas that they called them by the name of two Greek gods. What were the names?
36. When children laughed at Elisha for his baldness, what appeared that mangled the children?
37. What father-son soldier duo did David say were stronger than lions?
38. An earthquake at Philippi eventually led to the release of two Christians from prison there. Who were they?
39. Who escaped from Absalom's men by hiding in a well?
40. Who healed a lame man at the Jerusalem temple's Beautiful Gate?
41. Who were Perez and Zerah?
42. What elderly couple produced a child in accordance with the words of an angel?
43. What two servants of Pharaoh were in prison with Joseph?
44. Who told the repentant people of Israel to go home and enjoy sweet drinks?
45. Whose death caused the people of Jabesh-Gilead to fast for seven days?
46. Who fled from Iconium when they heard of a plot to stone them?

23. Bells and pomegranates (Exodus 28:33-34)
24. Priscilla and Aquila (Acts 18:2)
25. Paul and Barnabas (Acts 14:13)
26. James and John (Mark 10:35-37)
27. The blind and the deaf (Leviticus 19:14)
28. Philip and Andrew (John 12:20-22)
29. Peter and Andrew (Mark 1:16-17)
30. Elijah and Elisha (2 Kings 2:11)
31. Jesus and Peter (Matthew 14:22-32)
32. Sodom and Gomorrah (Genesis 19:24)
33. Elijah and Moses (Matthew 17:1-9)
34. Jannes and Jambres (2 Timothy 3:8); these are not, by the way, named in Exodus. The names in 2 Timothy are from Jewish folklore.
35. Zeus and Hermes (also called Jupiter and Mercury in some Bible translations) (Acts 14:12)
36. Two she-bears (2 Kings 2:24)
37. Saul and Jonathan (2 Samuel 1:23)
38. Paul and Silas (Acts 16:25-36)
39. Ahimaaz and Jonathan (2 Samuel 17:17-21)
40. Peter and John (Acts 3:2-7)
41. Twin sons of Judah and his daughter-in-law Tamar (Genesis 38:29-30)
42. Elisabeth and Zacharias (Luke 1:7-9, 13, 18)
43. The chief butler and chief baker (Genesis 40)
44. Nehemiah and Ezra (Nehemiah 8:10)
45. Saul's and his son Jonathan's (1 Samuel 31:13)
46. Paul and Barnabas (Acts 14:5-6)

47. What two male friends wept together?
48. Who buried Isaac?
49. What patriarch and his father-in-law heaped up stones as a sign of their covenant together?
50. Who played the leading roles in the 1951 movie *David and Bathsheba?*

Familiar Verse, Peculiar Order

☞ Placed in their proper order, the words are a familiar verse from John.

good am and I my I the know sheep shepherd

Common Bonds

☞ If you see the names "Saul, David, Solomon" and are asked "What do these have in common?" you (of course) reply, "They're all kings of Israel." Test your knowledge of the common bonds in each of the following groups.

1. Gold, frankincense, myrrh
2. Moses, Elijah, Jesus
3. Eliphaz, Zophar, Bildad
4. Ahaz, Manasseh, Zedekiah
5. Moab, Edom, Ammon
6. Assyria, Babylonia, Persia
7. Isaiah, Jeremiah, Ezekiel
8. Nebuchadnezzar, Cyrus, Sargon
9. Frogs, hail, lice, boils
10. Molech, Baal, Ashtoreth
11. Turning water to wine, giving sight to the blind, making the lame walk
12. Cain, Abel, Seth
13. Matthew, Mark, Luke, John (Don't even *think* of missing this one.)
14. Proverbs, Ecclesiastes, Song of Solomon
15. Shem, Ham, Japheth
16. Absalom, Solomon, Adonijah, Amnon
17. The Prodigal Son, the lost sheep, the unjust steward

47. David and Jonathan (1 Samuel 20:41) (This was long, long before the heyday of "sensitive men.")
48. The quarreling brothers Esau and Jacob (Genesis 35:29)
49. Jacob and Laban (Genesis 31:44-52)
50. Gregory Peck and Susan Hayward

Familiar Verse, Peculiar Order (answer)

I am the good shepherd, and I know my sheep. (John 10:14)

Common Bonds (answers)

1. The gifts brought by the wise men to the newborn Jesus
2. The three men who were together on the Mount of Transfiguration (Matthew 17)
3. Job's three friends (who were also poor comforters)
4. Kings of Judah—to be specific, *wicked* kings of Judah
5. Neighbor nations of Israel
6. Empires that controlled Israel at various times
7. The three "major" prophets of the Old Testament—so called because their books were longer than those of the other ("minor") prophets
8. Pagan emperors who played an important role in Israel's history
9. Four of the plagues God sent upon Egypt in Moses' time
10. Gods worshiped by Israel's neighbor nations (and sometimes by the Israelites as well)
11. Three of Jesus' many miracles
12. The three sons of Adam and Eve
13. The four Gospels (If you missed this, shame on you! Force yourself to attend first-grade Sunday school class.)
14. The three Old Testament books that are attributed to Solomon
15. The three sons of Noah
16. Four sons of King David
17. Three of Jesus' parables

18. Philippi, Ephesus, Rome, Corinth
19. 1 Timothy, 2 Timothy, Titus
20. Joseph, Benjamin, Reuben, Judah
21. Hosea, Jonah, Joel, Habakkuk
22. Peter, Andrew, James, John
23. Pharisees, Sadducees, Zealots
24. Pentecost, Tabernacles, Passover
25. Aquila, Priscilla, Apollos
26. Ahab, Jeroboam, Omri
27. The New International Version, *The New English Bible,*
    The Jerusalem Bible
28. Tigris, Euphrates, Jordan
29. Olivet, Zion, Carmel, Sinai
30. Aaron, Zadok, Abiathar
31. Abigail, Michal, Bathsheba
32. Mary Magdalene, Martha, Joanna
33. Micah, Amos, Nahum
34. Pork, shellfish, rabbit, bats
35. Simeon, Levi, Reuben
36. Solomon, Job, the rich young ruler, Joseph of Arimathea
37. Delilah, Jezebel, Athaliah
38. Stealing, murdering, coveting, lying
39. Pontius Pilate, Claudius, Festus
40. Jerusalem, Tirzah, Samaria
41. Thomas, Philip, Matthew, Bartholomew
42. Hebrew, Aramaic, Greek
43. Luke, Silas, Barnabas
44. Lazarus, Jairus's daughter, the widow of Nain's son
45. Sargon, Sennacherib, Pul
46. Zechariah, Haggai, Malachi
47. Cedar, olive, oak, palm
48. Leviathan, Behemoth, Rahab
49. Nebuchadnezzar, Evil-Merodach, Belshazzar
50. Samson, Deborah, Gideon

18. Four cities whose churches received epistles from Paul
19. The three Pastoral Epistles of Paul, so called because Paul gives advice on pastoring a Christian congregation
20. Four of Jacob's twelve sons
21. Four of the minor prophets of the Old Testament
22. Four of Jesus' disciples—specifically, the four who were fishermen
23. Three Jewish factions in New Testament times
24. Jewish religious festivals
25. Friends of Paul and fellow evangelists
26. Three kings of Israel—specifically, *wicked* kings
27. Three contemporary Bible translations
28. Rivers in the Bible
29. Mountains in the Bible
30. Priests of Israel
31. Wives of King David
32. Women followers of Jesus
33. Three of the Old Testament's minor prophets
34. "Unclean" animals that the Israelites were not allowed to eat—that is, not kosher (We can't imagine there was much demand for bat meat anyway.)
35. Three of the twelve tribes of Israel
36. Rich men of the Bible
37. Wicked women of the Old Testament
38. Things forbidden in the Ten Commandments
39. Roman officials mentioned in the New Testament
40. Capitals of the kingdom of Israel
41. Four of Jesus' disciples
42. The three languages in which the Bible was written
43. Traveling companions of the apostle Paul
44. Three people Jesus raised from the dead
45. Kings of Assyria
46. Three Old Testament prophets—specifically, the three who were active after the Jews' return from exile in Babylon
47. Trees mentioned in the Bible
48. Legendary animals, all mentioned in the book of Job
49. Kings of Babylon
50. Judges of Israel

Familiar Verse, Peculiar Order

☛ Placed in their proper order, the words are a familiar verse from John.

place a and for go I prepare you

Pedigrees and Generation Gaps

☛ Genealogies—family trees, that is—were very important among the Jews. Small wonder that several very long genealogies appear in Scripture. While these aren't considered the most lively reading in the Bible, the genealogies are rather interesting for the light they shed on certain key people (Jesus being the supreme example).

1. Which of the four Gospels opens with Jesus' family tree?
2. What noted Old Testament man does that genealogy begin with?
3. Which other Gospel contains Jesus' family tree?
4. And which Old Testament man is the beginning of that genealogy?
5. Which historical book in the Old Testament devotes nine long, tedious chapters to the family tree of the Israelites?
6. In Matthew's genealogy of Jesus, which immoral woman is an ancestor?
7. Do the Gospels' genealogies of Jesus trace his descent through Mary or Joseph?
8. Matthew's Gospel traces Jesus' ancestry through King David's son Solomon. How does Luke's Gospel differ?
9. Genesis 10 contains the famous "table of nations," which shows how the different nations of the world were descended from three men. What notable man were these three the sons of?
10. Which of these three sons were the Jews descended from?
11. Which Old Testament book, full of battle scenes, shows the clans of the twelve tribes and how they divided up the land of Canaan?
12. Which of the twelve tribes was given no tract of land, but was assigned the duties of being priests and ministers?

Familiar Verse, Peculiar Order (answer)

I go and prepare a place for you. (John 14:3)

Pedigrees and Generation Gaps (answers)

1. Matthew (1:1-17)
2. Abraham, who is considered the father of the Hebrews (Matthew 1:2)
3. Luke (3:23-38)
4. Adam (and you can't go any further than that) (Luke 3:38)
5. 1 Chronicles, which begins with Adam and goes on to the family of King David
6. Tamar, the daughter-in-law of Judah—and also the mother of two of his sons (Matthew 1:3)
7. Joseph (Luke 3:23; Matthew 1:16); the Jews traced descent through the male, never the female—even though Joseph was Jesus' father only in the legal sense.
8. In Luke's genealogy, the line is traced through David's son Nathan, not Solomon. Matthew's account is concerned to show that Jesus' ancestors included all the kings of Judah, who are descended from Solomon. (See Luke 3:31.)
9. Noah; the sons were Shem, Ham, and Japheth.
10. Shem, from whom we get the word *Semite* (and hence the word *anti-Semitic*)
11. Joshua (13–21)
12. The Levites (the tribe of Levi, that is), the tribe that Moses and Aaron (the first high priest of Israel) were from

Familiar Verse, Peculiar Order

☛ Placed in their proper order, the words are a familiar verse from Job.

my know lives Redeemer that I

Friends in High (and Low) Places

1. What Old Testament patriarch was called a "friend of God"?
2. What Roman official was accused by a Jewish mob of not being Caesar's friend?
3. Who was "a friend of tax collectors and sinners"?
4. What friend of Jesus was so beloved that Jesus raised him from the dead?
5. Who spoke to God face to face, "as a man speaketh to his friend"?
6. What king of Israel was accused of loving his enemies and hating his friends?
7. What suffering man received little comfort from his three talkative friends?
8. Which Old Testament book claims that "there is a friend that sticketh closer than a brother"?
9. What two military men are the most famous friends in the Bible (and possibly the most famous male friends in the world)?
10. What two unscrupulous rulers became friends after they both met Jesus?
11. Who had his Philistine wife given to his best man?
12. What pitiful man lamented, "My friends scorn me: but mine eye poureth out tears unto God"?
13. Which New Testament epistle warns that friendship with the world is enmity with God?
14. Who said, "Greater love hath no man than this, that a man lay down his life for his friends"?
15. What lecherous son of David had a calculating friend who devised a scheme for raping his half sister?
16. What loyal friend of King David saved the king by foiling the rebellion of David's son Absalom?
17. Who warned his followers that they would be betrayed by even their friends and relatives?

Familiar Verse, Peculiar Order (answer)

I know that my Redeemer lives. (Job 19:25)

Friends in High (and Low) Places (answers)

1. Abraham (2 Chronicles 20:7; James 2:23)
2. Pilate, who was jeered by the Jews who wanted Christ crucified (John 19:12)
3. Jesus, of course (Luke 7:34)
4. Lazarus (John 11)
5. Moses (Exodus 33:11)
6. David, who was so accused because of the grief he showed over his rebellious son Absalom (2 Samuel 19:6)
7. Job, whose friends were Zophar, Eliphaz, and Bildad
8. Proverbs (18:24)
9. David and Jonathan, whose deep friendship is recounted in 1 and 2 Samuel; consider David's lament for the dead Jonathan: "Thy love to me was wonderful, passing the love of women" (2 Samuel 1:26).
10. Herod and Pilate (Luke 23:12)
11. Samson (Judges 14:20); some translations simply refer to this person as "friend," though in the context it more specifically means "friend and best man."
12. Job (16:20)
13. James (4:4)
14. Jesus (John 15:13)
15. Amnon, whose friend Jonabad concocted the scheme for Amnon to seduce Tamar (2 Samuel 13)
16. Hushai (2 Samuel 15–16), who entered Absalom's inner circle as an agent provocateur, giving advice to Absalom that he knew would help David
17. Jesus (Luke 21:16)

18. Who warned the Israelites against letting friends seduce them into worshiping false gods?
19. Who scolded Job's three friends for not speaking the whole truth about God?
20. According to Proverbs, what type of person causes best friends to go their separate ways?
21. What prophet predicted that friends would eat each other's flesh during a siege of Jerusalem?
22. What prophet warned against trusting a friend, a neighbor, or even a spouse?
23. To what treacherous man did Jesus say, "Friend, wherefore art thou come?" before his arrest?
24. In Jesus' parable of the man calling upon his friend at midnight, what was the man asking to borrow?
25. What passionate Old Testament book has a woman referring to her beloved as simply her "friend"?
26. What prophet had Baruch as both his secretary and his best friend?
27. Which of the twelve disciples was "the disciple whom Jesus loved"?

Familiar Verse, Peculiar Order

☛ Placed in their proper order, the words are a familiar verse from Matthew.

and are build church I my Peter rock this on will you

Common Bonds (Part II)

1. The Good Samaritan, the talents, the sheep and the goats
2. Son of God, Son of Man, Savior, Lord, Mediator
3. *The Ten Commandments, King of Kings, The Greatest Story Ever Told*
4. Beelzebub, Satan, the father of lies, the tempter
5. Hail, locusts, darkness, death of the firstborn
6. Samson, Paul, Joseph, Jeremiah, Peter

18. Moses (Deuteronomy 13:6-9)
19. God (Job 42:7)
20. A whisperer (Proverbs 16:28)
21. Jeremiah (19:9)
22. Micah (7:5)
23. Judas Iscariot (Matthew 26:50)
24. Three loaves of bread (Luke 11:5)
25. The Song of Solomon (5:16)
26. Jeremiah
27. He is not named, but since he is mentioned only in John's Gospel (John 13:23; 19:26; 20:2; 21:7), readers have traditionally believed that it must be John himself, exercising a little modesty by not mentioning himself by name.

Familiar Verse, Peculiar Order (answer)

You are Peter, and on this rock I will build my church. (Matthew 16:18)

Common Bonds (Part II) (answers)

1. Parables of Jesus
2. Names and titles used for Jesus
3. Movies based on the Bible
4. Names used for the devil
5. Four of the plagues God sent upon Egypt in Moses' time
6. People put into prison

7. The witch of Endor, Simon the sorcerer, Elymas, Jannes, Jambres
8. Martin Luther, William Tyndale, William Barclay, J. B. Phillips
9. The poor in spirit, the meek, the merciful, the peacemakers
10. The Word, the Lamb of God, the Bread of Life, the true Vine
11. Carmel, Pisgah, Horeb, Ararat
12. Jericho, Cana, Bethany, Bethsaida
13. Judas Iscariot, Saul, Zimri, Ahitophel
14. Stoning, burning, crucifixion, beheading
15. The wise men, the shepherds, Simeon, Anna
16 Shekel, denarius, mite
17. Harp, cymbals, trumpet, tambourine
18. Love, joy, peace, long-suffering, kindness
19. Healing, prophecies, tongues, discerning of spirits
20. Rose of Sharon, lily, crocus
21. Red, Dead, Galilee
22. Cyprus, Malta, Crete, Sicily
23. Judea, Samaria, Galilee
24. Uzziah, Naaman, Gehazi, Miriam
25. Nebuchadnezzar, Pharaoh, Joseph, Pilate's wife
26. Shadrach, Meshach, Abednego
27. Rachel, Leah, Bilhah, Zilpah
28. Manna, quail, pillar of fire, pillar of cloud
29. Adam, Eve, the serpent, God
30. The unjust judge, the wise and foolish virgins, the mustard seed
31. Paul, Peter, James, John, Jude
32. Enoch, Elijah, Jesus
33. Gad, Asher, Benjamin, Naphtali
34. The cupbearer, the baker, Pharaoh
35. Potiphar's wife, Rahab, Tamar
36. Nadab, Baasha, Elah, Ahaziah
37. 1 Chronicles, 2 Chronicles, Ezra
38. Solomon, Agur, Lemuel
39. Tobit, Judith, 1 Maccabees, Wisdom of Solomon
40. Raven, dove, eagle, stork
41. Zeus, Hermes, Artemis
42. Ephesus, Smyrna, Philadelphia, Laodicea

7. Practitioners of witchcraft
8. Noted Bible translators
9. Four types of people who will be blessed, according to the Beatitudes
10. Titles for Jesus, used only in John's Gospel
11. Noted mountains
12. Cities visited by Jesus
13. People who committed suicide
14. Means of execution mentioned in the Bible
15. People associated with the newborn Jesus
16. Coins used in the Bible
17. Musical instruments used in the Bible
18. Fruit of the Spirit
19. Gifts of the Spirit
20. Flowers mentioned in the Bible
21. Seas in the Bible—although the Dead Sea and the Sea of Galilee are actually landlocked lakes, not true seas
22. Islands in the Bible
23. The three Roman divisions of the Holy Land
24. People with leprosy
25. People who dreamed
26. Daniel's three friends in Babylon, thrown into the fiery furnace
27. The mothers of Jacob's twelve sons
28. God's provisions for the Israelites after the Exodus
29. The four beings in the Garden of Eden who were capable of speech
30. Three of Jesus' parables
31. Authors of epistles in the New Testament
32. Men taken to heaven by God
33. Four of the twelve tribes of Israel
34. Those whose dreams were interpreted by Joseph
35. Naughty ladies
36. Kings of Israel
37. Books supposed to have been written by Ezra
38. The authors of the book of Proverbs
39. Books of the Apocrypha (which do not appear in all Bibles, but in some versions are placed between the Old and New Testaments)
40. Birds mentioned in the Bible (Oddly enough, the bat is also listed as a bird in the Bible.)
41. Greek gods mentioned in Acts
42. Four of the seven churches addressed in the book of Revelation

43. Peter's mother-in-law, the Gadarene demoniac, the centurion's servant, two blind men of Jericho
44. The Beast, seven bowls of wrath, the four horsemen, the New Jerusalem
45. Job, Proverbs, Ecclesiastes
46. Nehemiah, Esther, Daniel
47. Obadiah, Philemon, 2 John, 3 John, Jude
48. Paul's conversion, Pentecost, Peter's vision at Joppa, the council at Jerusalem
49. The Creation, Noah's ark, the Tower of Babel, the sacrifice of Isaac
50. David, Asaph, the sons of Korah

Familiar Verse, Peculiar Order

☞ Placed in their proper order, the words are a familiar verse from John.

world of is kingdom this not my

Next of Kin

☞ Would you recognize famous Bible characters by hearing their relatives named?
   For example: Wife was Eve, sons were Cain and Abel. Answer: Adam (of course)

1. Sons were Shem, Ham, and Japheth
2. Father was Jesse, brother was Eliab, wife was Michal
3. Brother was Aaron, sister was Miriam, son was Gershom
4. Mother was Mary, cousin was John the Baptist, brother was James
5. Brother was John, father was Zebedee
6. Father was Manoah, mistress was Delilah
7. Father was David, mother was Bathsheba, son was Rehoboam
8. Husband was Boaz, mother-in-law was Naomi, son was Obed
9. Husband was Ahasuerus, cousin was Mordecai
10. Father was Kish, son was Jonathan

43. People healed by Jesus
44. Symbols in the book of Revelation
45. Three Wisdom books of the Old Testament
46. Books whose action takes place in Persia (A large part of the book of Daniel also takes place in Babylon. If you knew this one, award yourself the Wisdom of Persia medal.)
47. The shortest books in the Bible, all only one chapter each
48. Events in Acts
49. Events in Genesis
50. Authors of the Psalms

Familiar Verse, Peculiar Order (answer)

My kingdom is not of this world. (John 18:36)

Next of Kin (answers)

1. Noah
2. David
3. Moses
4. Jesus
5. James the apostle
6. Samson
7. Solomon
8. Ruth
9. Esther
10. Saul the king

11. Father was Terah, wife was Sarah, son was Isaac
12. Husband was Jacob, sister was Leah, father was Laban
13. Father was Jacob, sons were Ephraim and Manasseh
14. Sisters were Martha and Mary
15. Mother was Hannah, father was Elkanah
16. Brother was Moses, sister was Miriam, son was Eleazar
17. Best friends were Bildad, Zophar, and Eliphaz
18. Husband was Abraham, son was Isaac
19. Mother was Rachel, brother was Joseph, father was Jacob
20. Brothers were Aaron and Moses
21. Wife was Jezebel, father was Omri, son was Ahaziah
22. Father was Ahaz, son was Manasseh
23. Father was Abraham, son was Jacob
24. Brother was Jacob, mother was Rebecca, father was Isaac
25. Mother was Hagar, father was Abraham
26. Father was Jacob, wife was Mary
27. Brother was Andrew
28. Brothers were Abel and Seth
29. Grandfather was Methuselah, father was Lamech
30. Wives were Bathsheba, Abigail, Ahinoam
31. Father was Gilead, mother was a prostitute
32. Sons were Adonijah, Nathan, Amnon, and Absalom
33. Wife was Gomer, father was Beeri
34. Brothers were James, Joses, Simon, and Judas
35. Mother was Elisabeth, father was Zacharias
36. Father was Zebedee, brother was James
37. Wife was Herodias, father was Herod the king
38. Mother was Eunice, grandmother was Lois
39. Daughters were Jemimah, Keziah, and Keren-happuch
40. Father was Amon, sons were Jehoahaz and Zedekiah

Familiar Verse, Peculiar Order

☞ Placed in their proper order, the words are a familiar verse from the New Testament.

against be can for God if us us who be

11. Abraham
12. Rachel
13. Joseph (the one in Genesis, not the one in the New Testament)
14. Lazarus, whom Jesus raised from the dead
15. Samuel
16. Aaron
17. Job
18. Sarah
19. Benjamin
20. Miriam
21. Ahab
22. Hezekiah the king
23. Isaac
24. Esau
25. Ishmael
26. Joseph (in the New Testament)
27. Peter
28. Cain
29. Noah
30. David
31. Jephthah the judge
32. David (These weren't *all* of David's sons, by the way. He had many more.)
33. The prophet Hosea
34. Jesus (see Matthew 13:55)
35. John the Baptist
36. John the disciple
37. Herod Antipas (not the Herod at the time of Jesus' birth, but the second Herod, who executed John the Baptist and met with the arrested Jesus)
38. Timothy, the follower of Paul
39. Job
40. Josiah the king

Familiar Verse, Peculiar Order (answer)

If God be for us, who can be against us? (Romans 8:31)

Mentioned in the Bible—Not! (Part II)

☛ Would you recognize the name of a person, place, or thing *not* mentioned in the Bible? Consider the following groupings, then pick out the one element in the group that is not biblically correct.

1. Cities in the Holy Land: Bethlehem, Babylon, Bethany, Bethel
2. Miracles of Jesus: healing the blind, multiplying bread and fish, withering a fig tree, turning wine to water
3. Animals: hyena, leopard, fox, tiger
4. Saintly men: Job, Joab, Josiah, Joseph of Arimathea
5. Rulers: Titus, Felix, Pilate, Festus
6. People in Exodus: Pharaoh, Aaron, Jacob, Moses
7. Emperors: Ahasuerus, Augustus, Nebuchadnezzar, Nero
8. Unmarried men: Paul, Solomon, Jesus, Jeremiah
9. People who did not practice circumcision: Hebrews, Egyptians, Philistines, Syrians
10. Precious stones: ruby, topaz, emerald, diamond
11. Metals: steel, gold, bronze, copper
12. Gentile Christians in the New Testament: Paul, Stephen, John, Luke
13. People in the Gospels: Luke, Lazarus, Nicodemus, Simeon
14. Saintly women: Mary Magdalene, Jezebel, Ruth, Lydia
15. Men who worked miracles: Moses, Elijah, Peter, Stephen
16. Incredibly wicked people: Ahab, Herod, Noah, Er
17. Old Testament women: Rachel, Miriam, Rahab, Judith
18. Church officers named in the New Testament: priest, deacon, elder, pastor
19. Pagan cities: Ur, Nineveh, Damascus, Cairo
20. Books whose authors are unknown: Proverbs, Hebrews, Esther, Ruth
21. Drinks: wine, milk, beer, water
22. Precious stones: amethyst, lapis lazuli, turquoise, rhinestone
23. Musical instruments: lyre, drum, psaltery, autoharp
24. People in Acts: Pilate, Ananias, Cornelius, Sergius Paulus
25. Gardens: Eden, Gethsemane, Kew
26. Countries of Europe: Greece, France, Spain, Italy
27. Places in Jerusalem: Mount Zion, the temple, the pool of Bethesda, Jesus' birthplace

Mentioned in the Bible—Not! (Part II) (answers)

1. Babylon is in the Bible, but not in the Holy Land.
2. Turning wine to water; Jesus turned water into wine on one occasion.
3. Tiger
4. Joab, David's army captain, was loyal but hardly a saint.
5. Titus, a follower of Paul, was a pastor, but not a ruler.
6. Jacob is in the book of Genesis.
7. Nero, a Roman emperor, is not mentioned in the Bible.
8. Solomon had hundreds of wives.
9. Philistines are unique in the Old Testament for not practicing circumcision. They are referred to many times as "the uncircumcised."
10. Diamonds are not mentioned in the Bible.
11. Steel is not mentioned in the Bible, though iron is mentioned many times. (You may want to argue about this one, particularly if you're using the King James Version, which mentions "steel" in Job 20:24, Jeremiah 15:12, and a few other verses. But Bible scholars and archaeologists agree that the proper translation in these verses is probably "bronze," not "steel." Newer Bible translations reflect this change.)
12. Only Luke was a non-Jew.
13. Luke was the author of a Gospel but does not actually appear in the Gospels.
14. Jezebel was a wicked queen in the Old Testament.
15. Stephen was a New Testament saint, but he is not recorded as working any miracles.
16. Noah was the one righteous man on earth when the Lord decided to flood the world. For information on wicked Er, see Genesis 38.
17. Judith is a character in the Apocrypha, not the Old Testament.
18. Jewish priests are mentioned many times in the New Testament, but *not* as an office of the church.
19. Cairo, Egypt, is not mentioned in the Bible.
20. Proverbs is attributed to Solomon, Lemuel, and Agur.
21. Beer
22. Rhinestone, of course
23. The autoharp is a very modern instrument. The psaltery, by the way, was a sort of ancient autoharp with ten strings.
24. Pilate appears in the Gospels but not in Acts. He is *mentioned* several times in Acts.
25. Kew Gardens are in England, not in the Bible.
26. France
27. Jesus was born in Bethlehem, not Jerusalem.

28. Giants: Og, Goliath, Rephaim, Zacchaeus
29. Books that mention the end times: Revelation, Daniel, 1 Corinthians, Jonah
30. Birds: mockingbird, ostrich, owl, pelican
31. People: Greeks, Ethiopians, Arabs, Gypsies
32. Occupations: scribe, tennis instructor, farmer, carpenter
33. Evangelists: Philip, Paul, Silas, Billy
34. Towns in Israel that are named in the Bible: Joppa, Tel Aviv, Jerusalem, Nazareth
35. People in the books of Kings: Saul, Elijah, Ahab, Josiah
36. Epistles written to individuals: Titus, Philemon, Jude, 2 Timothy
37. Notable women: Ruth, Bathsheba, Deborah, Elisha
38. Movies based on the Bible: *King David, King of Kings, Quo Vadis, Samson and Delilah*
39. Wicked people in the life of Jesus: Barabbas, Herod, Caiaphas, Simeon
40. Regions of the Holy Land: Ponderosa, Galilee, Samaria, Judea
41. Books named for their main character: Matthew, Joshua, Ezra, Ruth
42. Books that feature Satan as a character: Matthew, Job, Luke, Exodus
43. Disciples of Jesus: Nicodemus, Thomas, Andrew, Philip
44. Ancestors of Jesus: David, Abraham, Adam, Cain
45. Old Testament prophets: Nahum, Aaron, Balaam, Malachi
46. Modern Bible versions: *The Living Bible,* New International Version, Today's English Version, Geneva Bible
47. Divisions of the Old Testament: Law, Prophets, Writings, Epistles
48. Animals used in the Jews' sacrifices: lambs, goats, pigeons, hogs
49. Friends of Jesus: Martha, Simon the leper, Lazarus, Caiaphas
50. Tribes of Israel: Ephraim, Edom, Manasseh, Zebulun

Familiar Verse, Peculiar Order

☞ Placed in their proper order, the words are a familiar verse from the New Testament.

Adam in alive all as be Christ die all in made shall so even

28. The tax collector Zacchaeus was notably *short*. (Remember the Sunday school song, "Zacchaeus was a wee little man, a wee little man was he"?)
29. Jonah
30. Mockingbirds are found only in America.
31. Gypsies
32. Tennis instructor (and don't admit to anyone that you missed this)
33. Billy is *not* in the Bible.
34. Tel Aviv was, in Bible times, nothing more than sand dunes.
35. Saul dies at the end of 1 Samuel.
36. Jude is an epistle *from* Jude, not *to* him.
37. Elisha was a *male* prophet.
38. *Quo Vadis* features some Bible characters (notably Paul and Peter), but the story is not actually based on the Bible.
39. Simeon blessed the infant Jesus in the temple (see Luke 2).
40. Ponderosa was the name of the ranch on TV's *Bonanza*. (But you knew that, didn't you?)
41. Matthew is *not* the main character in the Gospel of Matthew. Jesus is.
42. Exodus does not mention Satan.
43. Nicodemus
44. Cain
45. Aaron was a priest but not a prophet.
46. The Geneva Bible was published in 1553.
47. Epistles are in the New Testament, not the Old.
48. Hogs were not used, since they were among the "unclean" animals listed in Leviticus.
49. Caiaphas was the Jewish chief priest who condemned Jesus.
50. Edom was a separate nation from Israel, descended from Jacob's brother Esau.

Familiar Verse, Peculiar Order (answer)

As in Adam all die, even so in Christ shall all be made alive. (1 Corinthians 15:22)

Do You Remember?

☛ Would you like to see how much Bible trivia you can remember? Answer the questions (which you should have answered already in this section), and then see how well you rate on the scale on page xii.

1. Consider the following grouping, then pick out the one element in the group that is not biblically correct. Names of the devil: the tempter, the father of lies, the prince of demons, the burning one
2. What was the name of the two stones worn in the high priest's breastplate and used to determine God's will?
3. What do these have in common: Frogs, hail, lice, boils?
4. Which of the twelve tribes was given no tract of land but was assigned the duties of being priests and ministers?
5. Who said, "Greater love hath no man than this, that a man lay down his life for his friends"?
6. What do these have in common: Cyprus, Malta, Crete, Sicily?
7. Guess this famous Bible character's name using his or her relatives' names: Mother was Hagar, father was Abraham.
8. Consider the following grouping, then pick out the one element in the group that is not biblically correct. Towns in Israel that are named in the Bible: Joppa, Tel Aviv, Jerusalem, Nazareth
9. Who died after lying to Peter about the value of the possessions they had sold?
10. What two unscrupulous rulers became friends after they both met Jesus?

Do You Remember? (answers)

1. The burning one
2. Urim and Thummim (Exodus 28:30)
3. Four of the plagues God sent upon Egypt in Moses' time
4. The Levites (the tribe of Levi, that is), the tribe that Moses and Aaron (the first high priest of Israel) were from
5. Jesus (John 15:13)
6. Islands in the Bible
7. Ishmael
8. Tel Aviv was, in Bible times, nothing more than sand dunes.
9. Ananias and Sapphira (Acts 5:1-10)
10. Herod and Pilate (Luke 23:12)

PART 10

Keeping the Faith

Test Your Bible IQ

☞ This quiz contains questions covering the topics in part 10, "Keeping the Faith." Do your best, then turn the page to see how you did. If you are brave enough to see how your Bible IQ rates, turn to page xii for our scale.

1. According to the Letter to the Hebrews, what is required if sins are to be forgiven?
2. When does the Sabbath officially begin?
3. Where did Jesus send the unclean spirits who had possessed a man?
4. Where was Jesus when he prayed that he would not have to be executed?
5. Who advised husbands and wives not to go overboard on sexual abstinence, since it might lead to temptation?
6. Whom did God tell that Job was a perfect and upright man?
7. Who was the only king of Israel referred to as a "man of God"?
8. What sort of lips are an abomination to the Lord?
9. What king offered up a long prayer of dedication in the new temple in Jerusalem?
10. How many of each clean beast did Noah take into the ark?

Test Your Bible IQ (answers)

1. The shedding of blood (Hebrews 9:22)
2. On Friday evening (sundown), ending Saturday evening
3. Into a herd of pigs (Mark 5:13)
4. In the Garden of Gethsemane (Matthew 26:36)
5. Paul (1 Corinthians 7:5)
6. Satan (Job 1:8)
7. David (2 Chronicles 8:14)
8. Lying lips (Proverbs 12:22)
9. Solomon (1 Kings 8); this is probably one of the most-read prayers in the Bible
10. Seven; he took two each of the unclean beasts (Genesis 7:2)

Unforgiven (and Forgiven)

1. What young man confessed his riotous living to his forgiving father?
2. According to Jesus, how many times are we supposed to forgive someone?
3. What is the one sin that cannot be forgiven?
4. Who asked the prophet Elisha's forgiveness for worshiping in the temple of the god Rimmon?
5. Who was the first man recorded as forgiving those who wronged him?
6. To whom did Jesus say, "Your sins are forgiven"?
7. Who was Jesus' immediate predecessor in preaching the forgiveness of sins?
8. In which Gospel does Jesus say from the cross, "Father, forgive them; for they know not what they do"?
9. According to the Letter to the Hebrews, what is required if sins are to be forgiven?
10. Which Old Testament book is concerned with offering animal sacrifices for the forgiveness of sins?
11. According to Deuteronomy, what sin cannot be forgiven?
12. Who begged David's forgiveness for her husband's boorish behavior?
13. What book of the Bible mentions forgiveness the most times?
14. What abused prophet prayed that God would not forgive his enemies' many plots against him?
15. What happens to people who will not forgive their enemies?
16. According to Jesus, what was poured out for the forgiveness of men's sins?
17. According to Mark's Gospel, what activity should we cease from until we have forgiven our brothers?
18. What woman loved much because she had been forgiven much?

Familiar Verse, Peculiar Order

☛ Placed in their proper order, the words are a familiar verse from the Old Testament.

the of beginning fear is Lord of the wisdom the

Unforgiven (and Forgiven) (answers)

1. The Prodigal Son (Luke 15:18)
2. Seventy times seven (Matthew 18:21-22); Peter had assumed (wrongly) that seven times was adequate.
3. Blasphemy against the Holy Spirit (Matthew 12:31)
4. Naaman, the Syrian soldier whom Elisha healed of leprosy (2 Kings 5:18)
5. Joseph, who had been so badly treated by his brothers (Genesis 50:17)
6. The paralytic man whom he healed (Matthew 9:2)
7. His kinsman John the Baptist (Mark 1:4)
8. Luke (23:34)
9. The shedding of blood (Hebrews 9:22)
10. Leviticus, which means forgiveness many, many times
11. Leading others into idolatry (Deuteronomy 29:16-20)
12. Abigail, the wife of surly Nabal; after Nabal died, Abigail became one of David's many wives (1 Samuel 25:28).
13. Psalms, the Bible's prayer book, mentions it more than ten times.
14. Jeremiah (18:23)
15. They will not be forgiven by God (Matthew 6:15).
16. His blood (Matthew 26:28)
17. Praying (Mark 11:25)
18. The immoral woman who anointed Jesus' feet with precious ointment (Luke 7:36-46)

Familiar Verse, Peculiar Order (answer)

The fear of the Lord is the beginning of wisdom. (Psalm 111:10)

One Day out of Seven: The Sabbath

☛ We take our seven-day week for granted, forgetting that it was the Hebrews who gave the world the concept of a seven-day week with one day of rest (now, thankfully, extended to two days for most people). Test your knowledge of the Sabbath day.

1. Who instituted the Sabbath day rest?
2. Which of the Ten Commandments says that the Sabbath day must be kept holy?
3. What was the penalty in Israel for working on the Sabbath?
4. When does the Sabbath officially begin?
5. What kind of work was a man doing on the Sabbath that led him to be put to death?
6. What Jewish leader was deeply offended when he saw people engaging in trade on the Sabbath in Jerusalem?
7. According to Matthew's Gospel, what Sabbath healing caused the Pharisees to plot to kill Jesus?
8. Whom did Jesus heal in a synagogue on the Sabbath?
9. What miraculous food were the Israelites allowed to gather for only six days a week?
10. What Old Testament books were read in the synagogues on the Sabbath?
11. What was the normal offering made on the Sabbath day?
12. Which of the psalms is called "a song for the Sabbath day"?
13. Who criticized Jesus for healing on the Sabbath?
14. What led the early Christians to start observing the first day of the week as holy instead of the seventh day?

Familiar Verse, Peculiar Order

☛ Placed in their proper order, the words are a familiar verse from Matthew.

you as love neighbor yourself shall your

Tempting Situations

1. Who tempted Abraham by asking him to sacrifice his son Isaac?

One Day out of Seven: The Sabbath (answers)

1. God did, by resting on the seventh day after six days' labor (Genesis 2:2-3). Interestingly enough, the word *sabbath* itself does not occur in the book of Genesis.
2. The fourth (Exodus 20:8-11)
3. Death (Exodus 31:14); actually, we know of only one person who was actually put to death for this offense.
4. On Friday evening (sundown), ending Saturday evening
5. Gathering sticks (Numbers 15:32-36); this occurred while the Israelites were in the wilderness.
6. Nehemiah (13:15)
7. The healing of the man with the withered hand (Matthew 12:10-14)
8. A crippled woman (Luke 13:10-13)
9. The manna in the wilderness (Exodus 16); on the sixth day they were supposed to gather enough to see them through the seventh day.
10. The books of Moses (the first five books) (Acts 15:21)
11. Two lambs (Numbers 28:9-10)
12. Psalm 92; interestingly, it does not mention the Sabbath.
13. The Pharisees, who apparently regarded healing as work, which was forbidden on the Sabbath (Luke 13:14)
14. The fact that Jesus' resurrection had been on the first day of the week (Acts 2:1; 1 Corinthians 16:1-2)

Familiar Verse, Peculiar Order (answer)

You shall love your neighbor as yourself. (Matthew 22:39)

Tempting Situations (answers)

1. God did (Genesis 22:1). Apparently the word *tempt* here means "test."

2. Who tempted Jesus with the question "Is it lawful for a man to put away his wife?"
3. How many days was Jesus tempted by Satan? (Hint: the temptation took much longer than the Gospels seem to indicate.)
4. Who advised husbands and wives not to go overboard on sexual abstinence, since it might lead to temptation?
5. According to James, what does the man who endures temptation receive?
6. "Lead us not into temptation" is from what famous Bible passage?
7. Who tempted Jesus by asking him to show a sign from heaven?
8. To whom did Jesus say, "Thou shalt not tempt the Lord thy God?"
9. According to James, we are not tempted by God, but by what?
10. Which New Testament letter mentions that Jesus was like all human beings in that he was subject to temptation?
11. Which letter claims that God will always show us a way out of temptation?
12. What woman died after she tempted the Spirit of the Lord?

Familiar Verse, Peculiar Order

☛ Placed in their proper order, the words are a familiar verse from Matthew.

but is flesh is the the weak willing spirit

Perfect, or Practically Perfect

1. Whose pagan wives turned him away from God, so that "his heart was not perfect with the Lord his God"?
2. Who said, "Be ye therefore perfect, even as your Father which is in heaven is perfect"?
3. What pitiful man, sorely tested by Satan, was "perfect and upright"?

2. The Pharisees (Mark 10:2)
3. Forty (Mark 1:13)
4. Paul (1 Corinthians 7:5)
5. The crown of life (James 1:12)
6. The Lord's Prayer (Matthew 6:13)
7. The Pharisees and the Sadducees (Matthew 16:1)
8. Satan (Luke 4:12)
9. Our own lusts (James 1:13-14); no mention of Satan!
10. Hebrews (2:18)
11. 1 Corinthians (10:13)
12. Sapphira, who with her husband, Ananias, had lied to the apostles (Acts 5)

Familiar Verse, Peculiar Order (answer)

The spirit is willing, but the flesh is weak. (Matthew 26:41)

Perfect, or Practically Perfect (answers)

1. King Solomon (1 Kings 11:4)
2. Jesus (Matthew 5:48)
3. Job (1:1)

4. What Old Testament man was "perfect in his generations" and one who "walked with God"?
5. Who was able to preach boldly after Aquila and Priscilla taught him "the way of God more perfectly"?
6. To whom did Jesus say, "If thou wilt be perfect, go and sell that thou hast, and give to the poor"?
7. Which prophet said, "Thou wilt keep him in perfect peace, whose mind is stayed on thee"?
8. Which king's heart was "perfect with the Lord all his days"?
9. Who warned Christians against thinking that they could be perfect by their own efforts alone?
10. Who predicted he would be "perfected" on the third day?
11. Which book of the Law commands people to use "perfect" weights and measures so they will deal honestly?
12. Who wept and begged the Lord to remember that he had served him with a perfect heart?
13. Whom did God tell that Job was a perfect and upright man?
14. What city was called "The perfection of beauty, the joy of the whole earth"?

Familiar Verse, Peculiar Order

☛ Placed in their proper order, the words are a familiar verse from Matthew.

all and go disciples make nations of

Men of God, by Calling

☛ How many men in the Bible are called "man of God"? Surprisingly, very few. Test your knowledge of the select handful who received that name.

1. Who is the first man in the Bible to be called "man of God"?
2. What strongman's birth was foretold by a man of God with a face like an angel?
3. Which of Paul's young followers did he refer to as a "man of God"?
4. Who referred to Jesus as a man of God?

4. Noah (Genesis 6:9)
5. Apollos (Acts 18:24-26)
6. The rich young ruler (Matthew 19:21)
7. Isaiah (26:3)
8. Asa's (1 Kings 15:14)
9. Paul (Galatians 3:3)
10. Jesus (Luke 13:32); apparently his meaning was this: with his resurrection on the third day, his work would be completed.
11. Deuteronomy (25:15)
12. King Hezekiah (2 Kings 20:3)
13. Satan (Job 1:8)
14. Jerusalem (Lamentations 2:15)

Familiar Verse, Peculiar Order (answer)

Go and make disciples of all nations. (Matthew 28:19)

Men of God, by Calling (answers)

1. Moses (Deuteronomy 33:1)
2. Samson (Judges 13:6)
3. Timothy (1 Timothy 6:11)
4. No one; surprisingly, Jesus is never called this.

5. What aged priest received a visit from a man of God, who prophesied doom for the priest's greedy, lecherous sons?
6. What man of God told King Rehoboam of Judah not to make war on the other tribes of Israel?
7. What fiery prophet of the Lord was called "man of God"?
8. Who was the only king of Israel referred to as a "man of God"?
9. According to Paul, what did God give us so that "the man of God may be perfect"?
10. What future king sought out Samuel, the "man of God," in order to find out where his lost donkeys were?
11. What king received a bad case of arthritis when a man of God prophesied against him?
12. What king spared the tomb of a man of God when he was desecrating tombs at a pagan shrine?
13. What prophet received forty camel loads of luxury goods from the dying king of Syria?
14. What mighty prophet of the Old Testament told the king of Israel's military men, "If I be a man of God, then let fire come down from heaven, and consume thee and thy fifty"?
15. What man of God healed a pagan military leader of leprosy by having him dip himself seven times in the Jordan River?

Familiar Verse, Peculiar Order

☛ Placed in their proper order, the words are a familiar verse from Luke.

exalted he himself humbles who be will

Abominable Abominations

☛ The word *abomination* occurs often in the Bible and refers to something that (in the words of my six-year-old cousin) "makes God go 'Ugh!'" Generally we find the word associated with idolatry, the worship of the created object rather than the Creator.

1. What people considered it an abomination to eat with Hebrews?
2. Which Old Testament book declares that it is an abomination for a man to wear women's clothing (or vice versa)?

5. Eli, Samuel's mentor and father of the corrupt Hophni and Phinehas (1 Samuel 2:27-36)
6. The prophet Shemaiah (1 Kings 12:22)
7. Elijah (1 Kings 17:18)
8. David (2 Chronicles 8:14)
9. The Scriptures (2 Timothy 3:16-17)
10. Saul (1 Samuel 9:6)
11. Jeroboam; he was offering incense on a pagan altar when the prophet came. When Jeroboam stretched out his hand and said, "Arrest him!" the king's hand withered (1 Kings 13:1-4).
12. Josiah, whose birth and deeds had been foretold by this very man of God (2 Kings 23:16-18)
13. Elisha; he received the gifts from the king Ben-Hadad, who wanted the prophet to foretell whether he would die or not (2 Kings 8:7-9).
14. Elijah, who was being pursued by wicked King Ahaziah's soldiers (2 Kings 1:10)
15. Elisha, who cured the Syrian king Naaman (2 Kings 5)

Familiar Verse, Peculiar Order (answer)

He who humbles himself will be exalted. (Luke 14:11)

Abominable Abominations (answers)

1. The Egyptians (Genesis 43:32)
2. Deuteronomy (22:5)

3. To which prophet did God say, "Incense is an abomination unto me"?
4. In which Gospel does Jesus say, "That which is highly esteemed among men is abomination in the sight of God"?
5. What woman was "the mother of harlots and abominations of the earth"?
6. What city will not have any abomination within it?
7. Whose wages would be considered an abomination if offered to the Lord?
8. What loathsome god was "the abomination of the Ammonites"?
9. What sort of lips are an abomination to the Lord?
10. Whose sacrifice is an abomination to the Lord?
11. What innocent occupation was considered an abomination by the Egyptians?
12. What sort of seafood is supposed to be an abomination?
13. What was the punishment for the abomination of homosexual intercourse?
14. King Ahaz of Judah committed what abomination with his own son?
15. What godly king expelled the sorcerers, who were an abomination to the Lord?
16. What were the Israelites supposed to do with the idols of other nations?
17. What kind of animal is it an abomination to sacrifice to the Lord?
18. Saul's military prowess made Israel an abomination to what people?
19. What kind of prostitutes, an abomination to the Lord, flourished under Solomon's son?
20. What wise king built pagan temples for his foreign wives?
21. What kind of scale is an abomination to the Lord?
22. What kind of heart is an abomination to the Lord?
23. Who predicted "the abomination of desolation" standing in the Jerusalem temple?

3. Isaiah (1:13)
4. Luke (16:15)
5. Babylon, the scarlet woman (Revelation 17:5)
6. The New Jerusalem (Revelation 21:27)
7. A prostitute's (Deuteronomy 23:18)
8. The god Milcom (or Molech, in some translations) (1 Kings 11:5)
9. Lying lips (Proverbs 12:22)
10. The sacrifice of the wicked (Proverbs 15:8)
11. Shepherding (Genesis 46:34)
12. Anything without fins and scales (Leviticus 11:10)
13. Death (Leviticus 20:13)
14. Sacrificed him to a pagan god (2 Kings 16:2-3)
15. Josiah (2 Kings 23:24)
16. Burn them (Deuteronomy 7:25)
17. One with a blemish of any kind (Deuteronomy 17:1)
18. The Philistines (1 Samuel 13:4)
19. Male shrine prostitutes (1 Kings 14:24)
20. Solomon (1 Kings 11)
21. A false one (Proverbs 11:1)
22. A proud heart (Proverbs 16:5)
23. Jesus (Matthew 24:15)

Familiar Verse, Peculiar Order

☞ Placed in their proper order, the words are a familiar verse from Matthew.

whom am beloved I in is my pleased Son this well

"Teach Us to Pray"

1. Who is the first person in the Bible who prayed?
2. Who prayed while in the belly of a sea beast?
3. According to Jesus' Sermon on the Mount, what type of people should we pray for?
4. What blinded strongman prayed to the Lord for vengeance on the cruel Philistines?
5. What woman prayed silently with her lips moving, so that she appeared to be drunk?
6. In what book of the New Testament is incense a symbol of believers' prayers?
7. According to the Letter of James, what should church elders do in addition to praying for a sick person?
8. What barren woman conceived after her husband prayed for her?
9. Who prayed to be saved from the wrath of his peeved twin brother?
10. What king is quoted as saying, "Pray to the Lord to take the frogs away from me and my people"?
11. What king offered up a long prayer of dedication in the new temple in Jerusalem?
12. What distraught prophet prayed for the Lord to take his life?
13. What book of the Bible mentions prayer the most times?
14. According to Isaiah, why does the Lord not heed certain prayers?
15. What dying king prayed for wellness so that the Lord extended his life another fifteen years?
16. According to Paul, how often are we supposed to pray?
17. What prophet prayed that enemy soldiers would be struck with blindness?
18. In the Letter of James, which Old Testament prophet is held up as a good role model for praying?

Familiar Verse, Peculiar Order (answer)

This is my beloved Son, in whom I am well pleased. (Matthew 3:17)

"Teach Us to Pray" (answers)

1. Abraham (Genesis 20:17)
2. The prophet Jonah, of course (Jonah 2:1)
3. People who persecute us (Matthew 5:44)
4. Samson (Judges 16:28); the prayer was answered.
5. Hannah, the mother of Samuel (1 Samuel 1)
6. Revelation (5:8; 8:4)
7. Anoint him with oil (James 5:14)
8. Rebekah, the wife of Isaac (Genesis 25:21)
9. Jacob; he feared the wrath of Esau, whom he had cheated out of their father's blessing (Genesis 32:11).
10. Pharaoh, who was speaking to Moses after God had sent the plague of frogs on Egypt (Exodus 8:8)
11. Solomon (1 Kings 8); this is probably one of the most-read prayers in the Bible.
12. Elijah, on the run from the wrath of wicked Queen Jezebel (1 Kings 19:4)
13. Psalms—which is appropriate, since many of the psalms are in fact prayers
14. Because "your hands are full of blood" (Isaiah 1:15)
15. Hezekiah (Isaiah 38:2-5)
16. Continually (1 Thessalonians 5:17)
17. Elisha (2 Kings 6:18)
18. Elijah (James 5:17)

19. According to Acts, what time of day was prayer time in the temple?
20. What martyr prayed, as his last words, "Lord Jesus, receive my spirit"?
21. What Roman military man was renowned for his prayers and his works of charity?
22. What sin of Israel so displeased God that the people asked for Samuel to pray for them?
23. Who was noted for withdrawing to pray in lonely places?
24. According to Jesus, what group of hypocrites were noted for making lengthy prayers in public?
25. What pitiful man claimed that his prayers had always been pure?
26. Who is the chief author of Psalms, the great prayer book of the Bible?
27. What king prayed for Jerusalem to be delivered from the cruel conqueror Sennacherib of Assyria?
28. What prophet was told by God not to pray for the people of Judah?
29. What Old Testament book laments that God has covered himself with a cloud, so that no prayer can penetrate?
30. What pagan king issued a decree that people were not to pray to God, but to the king?
31. What apostle stopped on a beach to pray with some friends?
32. Who was visited by the angel Gabriel while in prayer?
33. Who was praying on a rooftop when he received a weird vision of a sheet carrying unclean animals?
34. In the early church, what activity often accompanied prayer?
35. Whom did God spare after his brother prayed for him?
36. What king prayed for the Lord to end the plague the king had brought upon Israel?
37. According to Jesus, what kinds of people pray in the streets?
38. Which two Gospels contain the Lord's Prayer?
39. What evil man asked Peter and John to pray that he wouldn't be punished?
40. What apostle received a vision while he was praying in the temple at Jerusalem?
41. Where was Paul when his companions prayed for daylight to come?

19. Three in the afternoon (Acts 3:1)
20. Stephen (Acts 7:59)
21. Cornelius the centurion (Acts 10)
22. They asked for a king to rule over them (1 Samuel 12:19).
23. Jesus (Luke 5:16)
24. The teachers of the Law (Mark 12:38-40)
25. Job (16:17)
26. David; of the 150 psalms, 73 are attributed to him.
27. Hezekiah (2 Kings 19:14-19)
28. Jeremiah (7:16; 14:11)
29. Lamentations (3:44)
30. Darius, king of Persia (Daniel 6)
31. Paul (Acts 21:5)
32. Daniel (Daniel 9:21)
33. Peter (Acts 10)
34. Fasting
35. Aaron; he was saved by the prayer of Moses. Aaron had angered God by building the golden calf idol the Israelites worshiped while Moses was on Sinai (Deuteronomy 9:20).
36. David; he had caused the plague by taking a census of Israel (2 Samuel 24).
37. Hypocrites (Matthew 6:5)
38. Matthew (6:9-13) and Luke (11:2-4)
39. Simon the magician of Samaria, who had tried to buy the power of the Holy Spirit from the apostles (Acts 8:9-24)
40. Paul (Acts 22:17); the vision was a warning that there was a conspiracy in Jerusalem to kill Paul.
41. On a storm-tossed ship in the middle of the ocean (Acts 27:27-30)

42. Where was Jesus when he prayed that he would not have to be executed?
43. What elderly woman spent her days fasting and praying in the temple?
44. In Jesus' parable of the hypocrite's prayer, what two types of men were praying in the temple?
45. When Jesus ran the money changers out of the temple, he claimed they had changed "the house of prayer" into what?
46. According to Paul, what sort of person should wear a head covering while praying?
47. What type of people were brought to Jesus so he could pray for them?
48. According to Paul, who helps us when we don't know how to pray?
49. Where was Jesus praying when the Holy Spirit descended upon him?
50. According to Paul, when a person speaks in tongues, what should he pray for?

Familiar Verse, Peculiar Order

☛ Placed in their proper order, the words are a familiar verse from Exodus.

false against bear neighbor you not shall witness your

Cleanliness Is Next to Godliness

☛ *Clean* and *unclean* are words that crop up often in the Bible, particularly in the Old Testament, with its code of kosher foods and other restrictions on small details of life.

1. To whom did Jesus give power to cast out unclean spirits?
2. How many of each clean beast did Noah take into the ark?
3. What Old Testament book contains the "kosher code"?
4. After a woman had given birth to a son, how many days was she ritually unclean?
5. How many days after giving birth to a daughter?
6. When Jesus said to his disciples, "You are not all clean," who was the unclean one?

42. In the Garden of Gethsemane (Matthew 26:36)
43. The prophetess Anna, who was eighty-four years old when she saw the infant Jesus (Luke 2:36-37)
44. A Pharisee (the hypocrite) and a tax collector (the repentant sinner) (Luke 18:10)
45. "A den of robbers" (Luke 19:46)
46. Women; men, on the other hand, are *not* to cover their heads during prayer (1 Corinthians 11).
47. Little children (Matthew 19:13)
48. The Holy Spirit (Romans 8:26)
49. The river Jordan, at the time of his baptism (Luke 3:21-22)
50. That he will be able to interpret what he has just uttered (1 Corinthians 14:13)

Familiar Verse, Peculiar Order (answer)

You shall not bear false witness against your neighbor.
(Exodus 20:16)

Cleanliness Is Next to Godliness (answers)

1. The twelve disciples (Matthew 10:1)
2. Seven; he took two each of the unclean beasts (Genesis 7:2).
3. Leviticus (11:1-23), which lists the animals that may (and may not) be eaten
4. Seven days (Leviticus 12:2)
5. Fourteen days (Leviticus 12:5)
6. Judas Iscariot (John 13:11)

7. Which apostle received a strange vision of a huge sheet filled with unclean animals?

8. According to the law of Moses, what is needed to cleanse out the blood of a murdered man?

9. According to Paul, what is the opposite of uncleanness?

10. According to Jesus, when an unclean spirit leaves a man, where does it go?

11. What, according to the New Testament, cleanses us from all sin?

12. According to the law of Moses, what could a man do with a wife in whom he had found some uncleanness?

13. What godly king cleansed Jerusalem by burning the bones of false priests on their altars?

14. What substance, according to Job, could wash a man's hands squeaky clean?

15. Which apostle said, "I know, and am persuaded by the Lord Jesus, that there is nothing unclean of itself"?

16. What pagan king did the prophet Elisha cleanse from leprosy?

17. Who cleansed ten lepers but received a thank you from only one of them?

18. According to the Psalms, what plant is used for cleansing a person?

19. What sea creatures were unclean (and forbidden as food)?

20. What prophet lamented that he was a man of unclean lips, living among an unclean people?

21. What prophet predicted that the Israelites would eat unclean things in Assyrian exile?

22. What did the prophet Amos mean by the phrase "cleanness of teeth"?

23. Whom did Jesus criticize for being obsessive about cleaning their dishes but not their own souls?

24. Who took the body of the crucified Jesus and wrapped it in a clean linen cloth?

25. In Revelation, what city is the habitation of every kind of unclean thing?

26. Whose armies are dressed in clean white linen robes?

27. Where did Jesus send the unclean spirits who had possessed a man?

28. Who had a vision of unclean spirits shaped like frogs, coming out of the mouth of a dragon?

7. Peter, who was being told by God that the clean (Jews) and unclean (Gentiles) are both loved by God (Acts 10)
8. The blood of the one who murdered him (Numbers 35:33)
9. Holiness (1 Thessalonians 4:7: "For God hath not called us unto uncleanness, but unto holiness")
10. Into "dry places" (or "desert places" in some translations) (Matthew 12:43)
11. The blood of Jesus (1 John 1:7)
12. Divorce her (Deuteronomy 24:1)
13. Josiah (2 Chronicles 34:15)
14. Melted snow (Job 9:30)
15. Paul, who was commenting on dietary restrictions (Romans 14:14)
16. Naaman the Syrian (2 Kings 5)
17. Jesus (Luke 17:14)
18. Hyssop (Psalm 51:7)
19. Anything without fins or scales (thus ruling out shellfish) (Leviticus 11:12)
20. Isaiah, after his vision of the Lord in the temple (Isaiah 6:5)
21. Hosea (9:3)
22. Famine—that is, the teeth are clean because nothing has been eaten (Amos 4:6).
23. The scribes and Pharisees (Matthew 23:25)
24. Joseph of Arimathea (Matthew 27:59)
25. Babylon (Revelation 18:2)
26. The Lord's (Revelation 19:14)
27. Into a herd of pigs (Mark 5:13)
28. John (Revelation 16:13)

29. What type of persons were forced to walk around in public crying out, "Unclean! Unclean!"
30. What prophet was commissioned by the Lord to teach Israel the difference between clean and unclean?
31. What prophet predicted a fountain in Jerusalem that would cleanse people from their sins?

Familiar Verse, Peculiar Order

☛ Placed in their proper order, the words are a familiar verse from Luke.

a be sinner God me merciful to

29. Lepers (Leviticus 13:45)
30. Ezekiel (44:23)
31. Zechariah (13:1)

Familiar Verse, Peculiar Order (answer)

God be merciful to me a sinner. (Luke 18:13)

Do You Remember?

☛ Would you like to see how much Bible trivia you can remember? Answer the questions (which you should have answered already in this section), and then see how well you rate on the scale on page xii.

1. Who begged David's forgiveness for her husband's boorish behavior?
2. What miraculous food were the Israelites allowed to gather for only six days a week?
3. How many days was Jesus tempted by Satan? (Hint: the temptation took much longer than the Gospels seem to indicate.)
4. Who was able to preach boldly after Aquila and Priscilla taught him "the way of God more perfectly"?
5. What future king sought out Samuel, the "man of God," in order to find out where his lost donkeys were?
6. What people considered it an abomination to eat with Hebrews?
7. According to the Letter of James, what should church elders do in addition to praying for a sick person?
8. What prophet lamented that he was a man of unclean lips, living among an unclean people?
9. To whom did Jesus say "Your sins are forgiven"?
10. According to Matthew's Gospel, what Sabbath healing caused the Pharisees to plot to kill Jesus?

Do You Remember? (answers)

1. Abigail, the wife of surly Nabal; after Nabal died, Abigail became one of David's many wives (1 Samuel 25:28).
2. The manna in the wilderness (Exodus 16); on the sixth day they were supposed to gather enough to see them through the seventh day.
3. Forty (Mark 1:13)
4. Apollos (Acts 18:24-26)
5. Saul (1 Samuel 9:6)
6. The Egyptians (Genesis 43:32)
7. Anoint him with oil (James 5:14)
8. Isaiah, after his vision of the Lord in the temple (Isaiah 6:5)
9. The paralytic man whom he healed (Matthew 9:2)
10. The healing of the man with the withered hand (Matthew 12:10-14)

PART 11

All Over the Bible Map

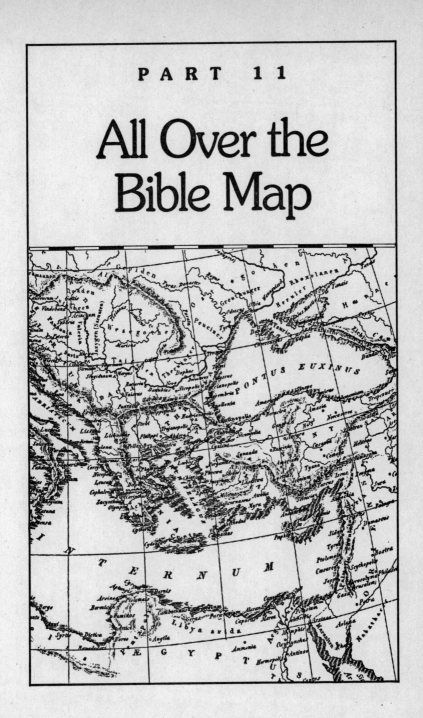

Test Your Bible IQ

☛ This quiz contains questions covering the topics in part 11, "All Over the Bible Map." Do your best, then turn the page to see how you did. If you are brave enough to see how your Bible IQ rates, turn to page xii for our scale.

1. Which is the only Gospel to mention the land of Egypt?
2. According to tradition, the cruel Roman emperor Domitian had which apostle exiled on the island of Patmos?
3. What village was home to Jesus' friends Lazarus, Martha, and Mary?
4. Which Hebrew prophet was sent by God to preach to the Assyrians?
5. In what river was Jesus baptized by John?
6. What neighboring country of Israel was descended from Jacob's hairy twin brother, Esau?
7. What world conqueror carried away furnishings from the Jerusalem temple and put them in the temple at Babylon?
8. What prophet of Moab had a talking donkey?
9. Did Paul write the Letter to the Romans before or after he came to Rome?
10. What wicked city was destroyed by fire from heaven?

Test Your Bible IQ (answers)

1. Matthew; his is the only Gospel that tells of Joseph, Mary, and Jesus fleeing to Egypt.
2. John, author of Revelation
3. Bethany (John 11)
4. Jonah, who convinced the people of Nineveh, the Assyrian capital, to repent
5. The Jordan (Matthew 3)
6. Edom (Genesis 25:30; 36:1); Edom was another name for Esau, just as Jacob's other name was Israel.
7. Nebuchadnezzar (2 Chronicles 36:7)
8. Balaam (Numbers 22:21-33)
9. Before
10. Sodom (Genesis 19)

Pharaoh Land: Egypt

☛ Of Israel's many neighbor nations, none is more intriguing than Egypt. From the early chapters of Genesis on through the New Testament, this mighty pagan nation was never far from the thoughts of the Bible authors. Test your knowledge of the mighty empire of Egypt, keeping in mind that things haven't changed much—just look at your daily newspaper to see how the hostilities continue.

1. Who was the first Hebrew to leave his famine-struck country to seek sustenance in Egypt?
2. The pharaoh bestowed the name Zaphenath-Paneah on what Hebrew leader?
3. In the book of Revelation, which city "spiritually is called Sodom and Egypt"?
4. Who told Joseph to carry Mary and the newborn Jesus to Egypt?
5. What Hebrew name is Egypt known by in the Old Testament?
6. What servant of Abraham and Sarah was an Egyptian?
7. According to Proverbs, what sort of fine cloth comes from Egypt?
8. Which pharaoh killed Israel's good king Josiah in battle?
9. What was the name of the Hebrew slaves' ghetto in Egypt?
10. What king of Israel married a daughter of the pharaoh?
11. What villainous king made Joseph, Mary, and the child Jesus flee to Egypt?
12. Who was the son of Abraham and his Egyptian maidservant?
13. What Hebrew liberator killed an Egyptian and buried his body in the sand?
14. Which apostle was accused of being an Egyptian terrorist?
15. Whose heart was hardened by God?
16. What author of a large section of the Bible never once mentions Egypt?
17. What king extended the boundary of Israel all the way to Egypt?
18. What New Testament martyr gave a long account of Israel and Egypt before he was stoned to death?
19. Whom did Moses say good-bye to before he went back to Egypt?

Pharaoh Land: Egypt (answers)

1. Abraham (Genesis 12:10)
2. Joseph (Genesis 41:45)
3. Jerusalem (Revelation 11:8)
4. An angel (Matthew 2:13)
5. Mizraim (Genesis 10:6); Mizraim was one of the sons of Ham, Noah's son.
6. Hagar, the mother of Ishmael (Genesis 16:1)
7. Linen (Proverbs 7:16)
8. Neco (2 Kings 23:29)
9. Goshen (Exodus 9:26)
10. Solomon (1 Kings 3:1)
11. Herod (Matthew 2:15)
12. Ishmael (Genesis 16), whose mother was Hagar
13. Moses (Exodus 2)
14. Paul, who was confused with an Egyptian agitator (Acts 21:38)
15. The pharaoh's (Exodus 4:21)
16. Paul; Egypt is mentioned constantly in the Old Testament, and also in the Gospels, but not in Paul's letters.
17. Solomon (1 Kings 4:21)
18. Stephen (Acts 7)
19. His Midianite father-in-law, Jethro (Exodus 4:18)

20. What Israelite king had wisdom that "excelled all the wisdom of Egypt"?
21. What Old Testament prophet predicted, "Egypt shall be a desolation"?
22. The great river of Egypt is never named in the Bible, but merely referred to as "the stream." What is the name of the river?
23. What famous peninsula lies between Egypt and Israel?
24. The Egyptian city of Noph (its name in the Bible) is also known by another name (which happens to be a large city in Tennessee). What is it?
25. What Hebrew leader married the daughter of the priest of the Egyptian city of On?
26. Whose wife was considered gorgeous by the men of Egypt?
27. What tribe of people sold Joseph as a slave to the Egyptians?
28. What four pharaohs are mentioned by name in the Bible?
29. Who interpreted the pharaoh's strange dreams?
30. Egypt was noted for its many gods. Which ones are mentioned by name in the Bible?
31. The "river of Egypt" was the boundary between which two regions?
32. Which prophet uttered the surprising words "Blessed be Egypt my people"?
33. What prophet was carried off to Egypt after Jerusalem was captured by Babylonians?
34. What Egyptian wife made passes at her Hebrew slave?
35. What official of Solomon's fled to Egypt and later became king of Israel?
36. What pharaoh stripped Jerusalem of its temple treasures?
37. What book of the Bible refers to the practice of mummification?
38. What form of pagan worship did the Hebrews carry with them out of Egypt?
39. Who was the slave of an Egyptian named Potiphar?
40. Who told the Egyptians that his beautiful wife was in fact his sister?
41. Who was given a land "from the river of Egypt to the great river, the river Euphrates"?
42. What prophet accused the Jews of "committing fornication with the Egyptians thy neighbors"?

20. Solomon (1 Kings 4:30)
21. Joel (3:19)
22. The Nile, of course; it is probably not named because it is *the* river of Egypt, the only one of any importance.
23. The Sinai Peninsula
24. Memphis
25. Joseph (Genesis 41:45)
26. Abraham's—his wife was Sarah (Genesis 12:14).
27. The Midianites (Genesis 37:36)
28. Shishak (1 Kings 11:40), So (2 Kings 17), Neco (2 Kings 23), and Hophra (Jeremiah 44:30); curiously, the very important pharaohs of Joseph's and Moses' times are never named.
29. Joseph (Genesis 41)
30. None are; this is curious, since the Bible mentions the false gods of most of the other surrounding nations.
31. Canaan and Egypt (Genesis 15:18)
32. Isaiah (19:25)
33. Jeremiah (chapter 43)
34. The wife of Potiphar, who made amorous advances to Joseph (Genesis 39)
35. Jeroboam (1 Kings 11–12)
36. Shishak (1 Kings 14)
37. Genesis, which mentions the embalming of Joseph (50:3)
38. Calf worship (Exodus 32)
39. Joseph, Jacob's son (Genesis 39)
40. Abraham, husband of Sarah (Genesis 12)
41. Abraham (Genesis 15:18)
42. Ezekiel (16:26)

43. Which is the only Gospel to mention the land of Egypt?
44. What king established calf worship in Israel after living for a while among the pagan Egyptians?
45. What pharaoh probably has the shortest royal name in the Bible?
46. According to the Letter to the Hebrews, who "esteemed the reproach of Christ greater riches than the treasures in Egypt"?
47. What sea did God dry up so the Israelites could cross it?
48. What two servants of the pharaoh had their mysterious dreams interpreted by Joseph?
49. What modern musical play is based on the adventures of Joseph in Egypt?
50. What king made a fatal attempt to stop the Egyptian forces at Megiddo?
51. What thirty-year-old Hebrew supervised a food storage program in Egypt?
52. Were there Egyptians present when the Holy Spirit descended at Pentecost?
53. Which book of the Bible opens by telling of "a new king over Egypt, which knew not Joseph"?
54. What great composer of choral music wrote *Israel in Egypt,* with words taken from Exodus?
55. What was the important occupation of the two Hebrew women named Puah and Shiprah?
56. What wealthy king of Israel purchased horses from Egypt?
57. Which prophet quotes God as saying, "When Israel was a child, then I loved him, and called my son out of Egypt"?
58. What Hebrew child was hidden in a basket in a river to protect him from an Egyptian decree?
59. What king of Judah was carried off to Egypt and died there?
60. To whom did God say, "I have surely seen the affliction of my people which are in Egypt"?
61. What king took away Egypt's possessions in Palestine?
62. What was the first plague God sent against the Egyptians?
63. In the book of Judges, who led the Israelites against the Egyptians?
64. Who was embalmed in Egypt after dying at the age of 110?
65. What was the last plague God sent against the Egyptians?
66. From what direction did God send the wind that parted the Red Sea?

43. Matthew; his is the only Gospel that tells of Joseph, Mary, and Jesus fleeing to Egypt.
44. Jeroboam (1 Kings 12:28)
45. So (2 Kings 17:4)
46. Moses (Hebrews 11:26)
47. The Red Sea (Exodus 14)
48. The butler and the baker (Genesis 40)
49. *Joseph and the Amazing Technicolor Dreamcoat*
50. Josiah (2 Kings 23)
51. Joseph (Genesis 41)
52. Yes (Acts 2:10)
53. Exodus
54. George Frideric Handel, more famous for his *Messiah*
55. They were the midwives who delivered the Hebrew babies in the land of Egypt (Exodus 1).
56. Solomon (1 Kings 10:28)
57. Hosea (11:1)
58. Moses (Exodus 2)
59. Jehoahaz, son of Josiah (2 Kings 23:34)
60. Moses (Exodus 3:7)
61. The king of Babylon (2 Kings 24:7)
62. Turning the river to blood (Exodus 7:14-24)
63. No one; this was one period of Israel's history when the Egyptians were not invading Israel.
64. Joseph (Genesis 50:26)
65. Killing the firstborn (Exodus 11)
66. The east (Exodus 14:21)

67. When the Hebrews left Egypt, whose bones did they carry with them?
68. Who sent his ten sons to find food in Egypt?
69. What king received a wedding present of a Canaanite city whose inhabitants had been slaughtered by the pharaoh?
70. What two sons (whose names were two of the tribes of Israel) were sons of Joseph and his Egyptian wife?
71. What prophet predicted that Egyptians would slaughter each other?
72. How many years did the Hebrews wander in the wilderness after leaving Egypt?
73. Who fled to Egypt to escape the wrath of Solomon?
74. What objects did the Egyptians force the Hebrews to create without straw?
75. What miracle of Aaron's were the Egyptian magicians able to duplicate?
76. What did Moses toss into the air to create the plague of boils on the Egyptians?
77. What caused Jeroboam to leave Egypt and return to Israel, where he became a king?
78. What son of Noah were the Egyptians descended from?
79. When hail fell on Egypt, what was the only region not affected?
80. What pagan king taunted the Israelites for believing the Egyptians would aid them?

Familiar Verse, Peculiar Order

☞ Placed in their proper order, the words are a familiar verse from Matthew.

shall alone bread live man not by

67. Joseph's (Exodus 13:19)
68. Jacob (Genesis 42)
69. Solomon, who married Pharaoh's daughter (1 Kings 9)
70. Ephraim and Manasseh (Genesis 46:20)
71. Isaiah (19:2)
72. Forty (Joshua 5:6)
73. Jeroboam (1 Kings 11:40)
74. Bricks (Exodus 5:7)
75. Turning a staff into a snake (Exodus 7)
76. Soot (Exodus 9:10)
77. The death of Solomon (1 Kings 11:40)
78. Ham (Genesis 10:6)
79. Goshen, the district where the Hebrew slaves lived (Exodus 9:26)
80. Sennacherib, king of Assyria (2 Kings 18)

Familiar Verse, Peculiar Order (answer)

Man shall not live by bread alone. (Matthew 4:4)

Doing As the Romans Do

☛ Christianity began and spread when the Roman Empire ruled much of Europe, the Middle East, and north Africa. Test your knowledge of Rome and its important place in the New Testament.

1. What paranoid king, appointed to his post by the Romans, ordered the massacre of babies in Bethlehem?
2. What Rome-appointed ruler was called "that fox" by Jesus?
3. What noted Jerusalem landmark was renovated and enlarged by King Herod?
4. Who had the apostle James executed by the sword?
5. Who followed Pontius Pilate as Roman governor in Palestine?
6. What Roman ruler ordered a census of the empire?
7. What was the name of the Jewish agitators who wanted to revolt against Roman rule?
8. When Jesus said, "Render unto Caesar what is Caesar's," which Roman ruler was he referring to?
9. According to tradition, what Roman emperor was responsible for executing both Paul and Peter?
10. This Jewish princess, mentioned in Acts 25 and present at Paul's trial, was noted for being the mistress of the Roman general Titus, who later became emperor. Who was she?
11. Which Roman ruler expelled the Jews from Rome?
12. Which is the only Gospel to mention Roman emperors by name?
13. According to tradition, the cruel Roman emperor Domitian had which apostle exiled on the island of Patmos?
14. Which Roman governor hoped to receive a bribe from the apostle Paul?
15. Whom did the Roman soldiers force to carry Jesus' cross?
16. What Christian was the empire's director of public works in the city of Corinth?
17. Which apostle was a flunky for the Roman government?
18. What "wee little man" was a dishonest tax collector for the Romans before his conversion?
19. What demon had a Roman military name?
20. What early Christian convert was a Roman centurion?
21. What part of the Roman military diet was offered to Jesus when he was on the cross?

Doing As the Romans Do (answers)

1. Herod, known to history (for some strange reason) as "Herod the Great" (Matthew 2:13-18)
2. Herod Antipas, son of Herod the Great
3. The temple
4. Herod Agrippa, grandson of Herod the Great (Acts 12:1-2)
5. Felix (Acts 24)
6. Caesar Augustus (Luke 2)
7. The Zealots
8. Emperor Tiberius
9. Nero, who committed suicide in A.D. 68
10. Bernice; Titus had to abandon her after he became emperor.
11. Claudius (Acts 18:2)
12. Luke's; he mentions Augustus (2:1) and Tiberius (3:1).
13. John, author of Revelation
14. Felix (Acts 24:26)
15. Simon of Cyrene (Matthew 27:32)
16. Erastus (Romans 16:23)
17. Matthew, the tax collector (Matthew 9:9)
18. Zacchaeus of Jericho (Luke 19:2)
19. Legion (Mark 5:9)
20. Cornelius (Acts 10)
21. Sour wine (or "vinegar" in some older translations) (Matthew 27:48)

22. Which Gospel tells of a compassionate Roman centurion who asked Jesus to heal a favorite slave?

23. What New Testament epistle was sent to the owner of a runaway slave?

24. What were former slaves called in the Roman Empire?

25. In what epistle did Paul urge that Christians pray for the Roman rulers?

26. At what city with a Roman name did Peter proclaim that Jesus was the Messiah?

27. What Roman-appointed governor was struck down by a fatal illness in the midst of an amphitheater?

28. What Roman construction was admired by Jesus' disciples?

29. Which Christian leaders were Roman citizens?

30. Which Roman governor tried to make himself popular with the Jews by persecuting the Christians?

31. Which of Jesus' disciples was a Zealot, an agitator against Roman rule?

32. At the time of Jesus' trial, who was in prison for being a notorious political agitator?

33. In the book of Revelation, what "code name" is used to refer to the persecuting Roman Empire? (Hint: it's the name of an ancient empire.)

34. The book of Revelation also mentions the number of hills Rome was built on. How many?

35. What Roman gods are mentioned in the New Testament?

36. When Paul preached in Athens, his audience included people who followed two popular philosophies in the Roman Empire. What were the two?

37. Who was emperor while Paul languished in prison in Caesarea for two years?

38. Which apostle was chained to a praetorian guard?

39. Though the New Testament was written in Greek, what was the basic language used throughout the Roman Empire?

40. Who spoke of "twelve legions of angels"?

41. In what epistle does Paul describe the "whole armor of God," modeling it after the Roman soldier's equipment?

42. Which epistle mentions that some of the early Christians were in fact slaves?

43. In what city did Paul face an angry mob in a Roman theater?

22. Luke (7:2)
23. Philemon, who was the owner of Onesimus
24. Libertines, or freedmen (Acts 6:9)
25. 1 Timothy (2:1-3)
26. Caesarea Philippi (Mark 8:27-29)
27. Agrippa (Acts 12:21-23)
28. The renovated temple in Jerusalem (Mark 13)
29. Paul and Silas (Acts 16:38)
30. Herod Agrippa (Acts 12:1)
31. Simon (Luke 6:15)
32. Barabbas (Matthew 27:17)
33. Babylon (Revelation 14-18)
34. Seven
35. Jupiter and Mercury (Acts 14:12) and Diana (Acts 19:24) (These are the Roman names. Some translations of the Bible use the Greek names for these gods: Zeus, Hermes, and Artemis.)
36. Stoics and Epicureans (Acts 17:18)
37. Claudius
38. Paul (Acts 28:16, 20)
39. Latin
40. Jesus (Matthew 26:53)
41. Ephesians
42. Philippians (4:22)
43. Ephesus (Acts 19:29)

44. The Parthian Empire was the long-standing enemy of the Roman Empire. Which New Testament book mentions the Parthians?
45. What sort of woman does the book of Revelation compare Rome to?
46. The Roman general Titus destroyed the Jerusalem temple in the year A.D. 70. Who predicted this?
47. Which epistle mentions the presence of saints in "Caesar's household"?
48. What Jewish group expressed fear that Jesus' miracles would result in Rome destroying the temple and the entire Jewish religion?
49. What two men were thrown into prison for advocating practices against Roman custom?
50. What cruel punishment was about to be inflicted on Paul when he announced he was a Roman citizen?

Familiar Verse, Peculiar Order

☞ Placed in their proper order, the words are a familiar verse from Psalms.

a all lands Lord make noise the unto ye joyful

Ancient Places, Modern Names

☞ Here are the contemporary names of some noted biblical sites. Some bear a passing resemblance to their biblical name—and some definitely do not. Try to identify the biblical name for each place.

1. Natzeret (This is an easy one, so you don't need a hint.)
2. Kafr Kanna (Hint: Jesus' first miracle)
3. Be'ersheva (No hint needed)
4. Beit Lehem (Easy)
5. Heshban (Hint: Amorite city)
6. Nablus (Hint: an important city for the Samaritans)
7. Al-Iskandaria (Hint: an Egyptian city, home of Apollos)
8. Yafo (Hint: Peter's vision on the rooftop)
9. Tveriya (Hint: a New Testament place named for a Roman emperor)

44. Acts (2:9); there were Parthians in Jerusalem on the day of Pentecost.
45. A prostitute (Revelation 17)
46. Jesus (Luke 21)
47. Philippians (4:22)
48. The Sanhedrin (John 11:48)
49. Paul and Silas (Acts 16:21)
50. Scourging (or flogging, in some translations) (Acts 22:25)

Familiar Verse, Peculiar Order (answer)

Make a joyful noise unto the Lord, all ye lands. (Psalm 100:1)

Ancient Places, Modern Names (answers)

1. Nazareth
2. Cana
3. Beersheba
4. Bethlehem
5. Heshbon
6. Shechem
7. Alexandria
8. Joppa
9. Tiberias

10. Kfar Nahum (Hint: Jesus did some healing there)
11. Migdal (Hint: a female follower of Jesus)
12. Yam Kinneret (Hint: a noted body of water in the Gospels)
13. Ashkelon
14. Ein Gedi (Hint: a spring connected with David)
15. Beit-el (Hint: Jacob's dream on a stone pillow)
16. Jerash (Hint: a man demon-possessed)
17. Thessaloniki
18. Akhisar (Hint: Lydia, the seller of purple)
19. Amman, Jordan (Hint: chief city of the Ammonites)
20. Antakya (Hint: associated with Paul)
21. Izmir (Hint: mentioned in Revelation)
22. Alashehir, Turkey (Hint: its ancient name is that of a large American city.)
23. Iran (Hint: no, too easy)
24. Kavalla (Hint: the place where Paul first set foot in Europe)
25. Zerqa (Hint: a river, noted because Jacob wrestled an angel nearby)
26. El-Quebeibeh (Hint: a village associated with Jesus after his resurrection)
27. Kaysariyeh (Hint: a New Testament town, built to honor Rome)
28. Athina (Hint: a capital of a country)
29. Kriti (Hint: a large island where Paul landed)
30. Korinthos (Hint: no, too easy)
31. Ghazzeh (Hint: a Philistine town)
32. Jebel Fuquah (Hint: mountain where King Saul died)
33. Jebel Musa (Hint: Moses and the Law)
34. Es-sur (Hint: Hiram was its king.)
35. Sebastiyeh (Hint: capital of the northern kingdom of Israel)
36. Nein (Hint: Jesus raised the dead.)
37. Verria (Hint: Paul knew some noble-minded Christians there.)
38. Banias (Hint: the place where Peter confessed Jesus as the Messiah)
39. El-Khalil (Hint: David's capital before he moved to Jerusalem)
40. Konya (Hint: visited by Paul and Barnabas)
41. Dimasq (Hint: Paul on the road)
42. Sart (Hint: mentioned in Revelation)
43. Rhodhos (Hint: island where Paul stopped)

10. Capernaum
11. Magdala (as in Mary Magdalene)
12. The Sea of Galilee
13. Surprise! The ancient Philistine city still has the same name.
14. En Gedi
15. Bethel
16. Gerasa (as in the Gerasene demoniac)
17. Thessalonica
18. Thyatira (As we noted, some of the names don't even faintly resemble the modern names.)
19. Rabbah
20. Antioch
21. Smyrna
22. Philadelphia
23. Persia
24. Neapolis
25. The Jabbok
26. Emmaus
27. Caesarea
28. Athens
29. Crete
30. Corinth
31. Gaza
32. Gilboa
33. Mount Sinai
34. Tyre
35. Samaria
36. Nain
37. Berea
38. Caesarea Philippi
39. Hebron
40. Iconium
41. Damascus
42. Sardis
43. Rhodes

44. Ras el-Kharrubeh (Hint: Jeremiah's hometown)
45. Esdud (Hint: major Philistine city)
46. Ele-Azariya (Hint: home to Mary, Martha, and Lazarus)
47. Shakhat (Hint: someone who helped Jesus carry his cross)
48. Eski Hissar (Hint: had a community of lazy Christians)
49. Baffa (Hint: where Paul met the governor of Cyprus)
50. Philippis (Hint: Do you really need one?)

Familiar Verse, Peculiar Order

☛ Placed in their proper order, the words are a familiar verse from Exodus.

God in Lord name not of shall take your the the vain you

B on the Bible Map

☛ How familiar are you with places in the Bible? All the answers to the questions below begin with *B*.

1. What expansive empire was a constant thorn in Israel's side? (Hint: King Nebuchadnezzar)
2. What small town was the birthplace of both David and Jesus?
3. All human beings spoke a common language until the Lord confused their tongues at what place?
4. What town was usually named as being the southern limit of Israel?
5. What tribe (and region) of Israel was named for the youngest of Jacob's twelve sons?
6. What pagan god's name appears in more than twelve place names in the Old Testament?
7. What region was ruled by King Og, noted for possessing an iron bed?
8. The name Beer occurs in many place names in the Old Testament. What important feature of human life is a Beer (in Hebrew)?
9. What city in Greece was visited by Paul, who found many devout believers there?

44. Anathoth
45. Ashdod
46. Bethany
47. Cyrene
48. Laodicea
49. Paphos
50. Philippi, of course

Familiar Verse, Peculiar Order (answer)

You shall not take the name of the Lord your God in vain.
(Exodus 20:7)

B on the Bible Map (answers)

1. Babylon
2. Bethlehem
3. Babel (Genesis 11)
4. Beersheba; the phrase "from Dan to Beersheba" occurs several times in the Bible, and means, roughly, "all Israel, from the northern tip to the southern tip."
5. Benjamin
6. Baal, the Canaanite fertility god whose name is, roughly translated, "master"; his name occurs in Baal Hermon, Baalath Beer, Baal Tamar, etc.
7. Bashan
8. A well—very important, especially in a dry country like Israel
9. Berea (Acts 17)

10. What village was home to Jesus' friends Lazarus, Martha, and Mary?
11. What Galilean city was home to the disciples Peter, Andrew, and Philip?
12. At what place on the Jordan was Jesus baptized by John?
13. What town was the dwelling place of Naomi and her daughter-in-law Ruth?
14. Where did Jacob have his dream of a stairway to heaven?
15. Which village did Jesus pass through on his Palm Sunday journey to Jerusalem?
16. Where was Moses buried?
17. What city was cursed by Jesus because of its unbelief?
18. In what Philistine city were the bodies of the slain Saul and Jonathan put on display?
19. What town was the center of a calf-worshiping cult in Israel?
20. What is the meaning of the *Beth* in the many Bible place names containing the word?
21. What kingdom was ruled by King Nebuchadnezzar?
22. In what village did Jesus heal a blind man?
23. What is the most-mentioned *B* place in the Bible?
24. *Beer Lahai Roi* means "Well of the Living One who sees me." What pitiful woman was greeted by an angel at this place?
25. What pagan nation is mentioned about 250 times in the Bible?
26. What tribe (and region) of Israel joined with the tribe of Judah when the ten other tribes separated from the kingdom?

Familiar Verse, Peculiar Order

☞ Placed in their proper order, the words are a familiar verse from Matthew.

deliver evil not from but temptation us lead us into

10. Bethany (John 11)
11. Bethsaida (John 1:44; 12:21)
12. Bethany—some translations say *Bethabara* (John 1:28)—which, from all we know, is not the same Bethany mentioned in question 10
13. Bethlehem
14. Bethel (Genesis 28:19)
15. Bethphage (Matthew 21:1)
16. Beth-peor (Deuteronomy 34:6)
17. Bethsaida (Luke 10:13)
18. Bethshan (1 Samuel 31:10)
19 Bethel (1 Kings 12), where King Jeroboam set up his infamous calf idols
20. It means "house"; it is found in Bethlehem, Bethel, Bethany, etc.
21. Babylon
22. Bethsaida (Mark 8)
23. Bethel; only Jerusalem is mentioned more often. It is possible that more than one place named Bethel is referred to.
24. Hagar, who was fleeing from the wrath of her mistress, Abraham's wife Sarah (Genesis 16:14)
25. Babylon
26. Benjamin

Familiar Verse, Peculiar Order (answer)

Lead us not into temptation, but deliver us from evil. (Matthew 6:13)

Mammoth Empires:
Babylon, Assyria, Persia

☛ Due to its location, the Holy Land in Bible times had numerous dealings (mostly unpleasant) with the two great empires to the east (Assyria and Babylon) and, later, with the slightly more humane empire even further east, Persia. Israel, the small kingdom in a strategic location, had some colorful (and usually violent) run-ins with these three imperial giants. Test your knowledge of these empires in the Bible, keeping in mind that things haven't changed completely—after all, Babylon, Assyria, and Persia occupied the land that is now Iraq and Iran.

1. What Old Testament book is set in the capital city of Persia?
2. What renowned king of Assyria was murdered at worship by his two sons?
3. What renowned Babylonian ruler went insane while walking on the roof of his palace?
4. This Babylonian god is mentioned by Jeremiah as being filled with terror after the fall of Babylon. What was his name?
5. What nation saw 185,000 of its soldiers slaughtered by an angel of the Lord?
6. What Persian king was considered to be God's anointed one?
7. What king of Babylon burned Jerusalem?
8. Which book of the Bible advises dashing the babies of Babylon against stones? (No, it doesn't seem like a "love thy neighbor" sort of action, does it?)
9. Who held the first "world's fair"?
10. Who built ancient Babylon?
11. What king of Judah was blinded and imprisoned because he defied Babylonian authority?
12. The ancient city of Ur lay in what country?
13. What Babylonian king, prominent in the Bible, built the impressive Hanging Gardens of Babylon, one of the Seven Wonders of the World?
14. Who had enemies that wrote smear letters about him to the Persian king?
15. What king of Babylon, driven from his palace, lived in the wilderness and let his hair grow long and shaggy?

Mammoth Empires: Babylon, Assyria, Persia (answers)

1. Esther, which takes place at the royal court at Susa
2. Sennacherib (2 Kings 19:37)
3. Nebuchadnezzar (Daniel 4:28-33)
4. Merodach (Jeremiah 50:2)
5. Assyria (2 Kings 19:35)
6. Cyrus (Isaiah 45:1); presumably he was called this because he allowed the Jews to return from Persia to Palestine.
7. Nebuchadnezzar (2 Kings 25:9)
8. Psalms (137:8-9)
9. King Ahasuerus of Persia; Esther 1:4 states that he "showed the riches of his glorious kingdom and the honour of his excellent majesty many days, even an hundred and fourscore days." That's 180 days of display.
10. Nimrod (Genesis 10:8-10)
11. Zedekiah (2 Kings 25:6-7)
12. Babylon; it was Abraham's home before he moved to Canaan. The city has been excavated by archaeologists.
13. Nebuchadnezzar; the acclaimed gardens are not mentioned in the Bible but were famous throughout the ancient world.
14. Zerubbabel (Ezra 4:6-16)
15. Nebuchadnezzar (Daniel 4:33)

16. What king was criticized by the prophet Isaiah for showing Judah's treasure to Babylonian ambassadors?
17. Where was the first beauty contest in the Bible, and who won?
18. Who rebuilt Babylon on a grand scale?
19. What evil king of Israel rode into battle in a chariot but was fatally wounded by an Assyrian arrow?
20. Who knelt toward Jerusalem and prayed, looking out of his eastern window in Babylon?
21. When the Assyrians deported the people of Israel, how many of the twelve original tribes were left?
22. What Persian queen upset the king and his aides by refusing to appear before them at their drunken banquet?
23. What nation had Nebo as one of its gods?
24. What king issued an edict ending the exile of the Jews?
25. What Babylonian king had a dream of a tree where every bird found shelter?
26. Who scandalized the godly by having an Assyrian-style altar made for the Jerusalem temple?
27. What nation's ambassadors were taken on a tour of the palace by King Hezekiah?
28. What king of Israel was imprisoned for defying Assyrian authority?
29. Who served as a cupbearer in Persia's royal palace?
30. What king of Israel had much of his territory taken away by the Assyrian king?
31. What great city does Isaiah predict will become like a helpless widow?
32. Who taxed the Israelites in order to pay off Pul, the king of Assyria?
33. After the death of the sinister Persian prime minister Haman, who received the Persian king's signet ring?
34. What king of Assyria sent foreigners to settle in Israel after the Israelites had been taken away to exile?
35. What city in Revelation was seen as a place that would never again hear the voices of brides and grooms?
36. What Assyrian king brought about the fall of Samaria and the deportation of the Israelites to other countries?
37. What Jewish girl married a Persian emperor and helped save her exiled people from extermination?

16. Hezekiah (2 Kings 20:12-18)
17. The one at the court of Persian ruler Ahasuerus; the winner was Esther (Esther 2).
18. Nebuchadnezzar (Daniel 4:30)
19. Ahab (1 Kings 22:34-38)
20. Daniel (6:10)
21. One—Judah (2 Kings 17:18)
22. Vashti, wife of King Ahasuerus (Esther 1)
23. Babylon (Isaiah 46:1)
24. Cyrus of Persia (2 Chronicles 36:22-23)
25. Nebuchadnezzar (Daniel 4:12)
26. King Ahaz (2 Kings 16:10-17)
27. Babylon's (2 Kings 20:14-15)
28. Hoshea (2 Kings 17:4)
29. Nehemiah (1:1; 2:1)
30. Pekah (2 Kings 15:29)
31. Babylon (Isaiah 47:8-9)
32. King Menahem (2 Kings 15:19-20)
33. Mordecai, Esther's kinsman (Esther 8:2-13)
34. Esar-haddon (Ezra 4:2)
35. Babylon (Revelation 18:23)
36. Shalmaneser (2 Kings 17:3-6)
37. Esther, who married King Ahasuerus and saved the Jews from the plot of the wicked Haman

38. What Assyrian field commander tried to intimidate King Hezekiah by speaking propaganda to the people of Jerusalem?
39. When the Jews were allowed to defend themselves against the Persians, how many Persians were killed?
40. Who plotted to have the entire Hebrew nation completely exterminated?
41. What king of Judah was blinded and taken away in chains to Babylon?
42. Nehemiah waited until this Persian king was softened up with wine before he asked the king to let the Jews return to their homeland. Who was the king?
43. What four faithful young men refused to eat the rich foods of the king of Babylon?
44. What festival was to be a memorial of the Jews' salvation from the wicked Persian Haman?
45. What king of Israel paid tribute money to King Shalmaneser of Assyria?
46. What Hebrew patriarch was originally from Babylon?
47. Who prophesied that Assyria would become a desolate roosting place for all sorts of strange night birds?
48. What evil king of Judah was humbled and repentant after being taken to Babylon in chains?
49. What king removed the gold from the doors of the temple and gave it to the king of Assyria?
50. What king of Persia issued the decree that the people of Judah could rebuild their temple?
51. Which apostle, according to tradition, preached in Assyria and Persia and died a martyr in Persia?
52. What upright young man was made ruler over the whole province of Babylon?
53. What Babylonian king caused famine in Jerusalem?
54. What prophet advised building a signal fire as a sign of the coming invasion of Babylon?
55. What Assyrian king attacked the Philistines and Egyptians, leading Isaiah to walk around naked for three years?
56. What prophet in Babylon wore sackcloth while seeking the Lord?
57. Who laid a tax on the whole Persian empire?
58. The city of Babylon is located on what great river of the Middle East?

38. Rabshakeh (2 Kings 18:17-37); Bible scholars still debate over whether Rabshakeh was the man's actual name or merely a title (which proves that scholars enjoy debating over things that have no significance whatsoever).
39. Seventy-five thousand (Esther 9:15-16)
40. Haman, minister of Persia (Esther)
41. Zedekiah (2 Kings 25:7)
42. Artaxerxes (Nehemiah 2:1)
43. Daniel, Shadrach, Meshach, and Abednego (Daniel 1:3-16)
44. Purim (Esther 9:28), which is still a major holiday for Jews
45. Hoshea (2 Kings 17:3-4)
46. Abraham, who was from "Ur of the Chaldees" (Genesis 11:28); Ur was in the area that was considered (later) a part of the Babylonian empire.
47. Zephaniah (2:14)
48. Manasseh (2 Chronicles 33:10-13)
49. Hezekiah (2 Kings 18:16)
50. Cyrus (Ezra 1:1-4)
51. Jude; nothing in the Bible indicates this, but the tradition arose fairly early.
52. Daniel (2:48)
53. Nebuchadnezzar (2 Kings 25:1-3)
54. Jeremiah (6:1)
55. Sargon (Isaiah 20); Isaiah's action was supposed to be a sign to the people who trusted in the power of Egypt and Philistia to hold off the Assyrian power. In effect, the message was, "OK, the Philistines and Egyptians are being led away naked into exile—so what do you think will inevitably happen to us?"
56. Daniel (9:3)
57. King Ahasuerus (Esther 10:1)
58. The Euphrates

59. What prophet, famous for his vision of the dry bones, was with the exiles in Babylon?
60. What was another name in ancient times for the Babylonian empire?
61. In what country were the Jews when they fasted after learning of an executive order to have them all killed?
62. The arrogant Babylonian king Belshazzar, drunk at his feast, committed an outrage when he asked for new drinking vessels to be brought in. What were these vessels that led to so much trouble for the king?
63. Where, according to tradition, did the wise men in the Christmas story come from?
64. What Persian gods are mentioned in the Bible?
65. Which Hebrew prophet was sent by God to preach to the Assyrians?
66. What Persian king conquered the Babylonian empire?
67. The city of Susa (or Shushan) was the capital of what empire?
68. Who was sent by the Persian king to reorganize the temple services in Jerusalem?
69. In the New Testament period, what empire occupied the area formerly called Persia?
70. Who visited the church at Babylon?
71. What Assyrian king received thirty-eight tons of silver as tribute money from Ahaz of Israel?
72. The Persian king Xerxes is called by what name in the Bible?
73. What book of prophecy opens with the prophet standing by a river in Babylon?
74. What Old Testament historical book opens with a reading of a decree from the Persian king Cyrus?
75. What great river of the Middle East did Nineveh, the capital of Assyria, lie on?

Familiar Verse, Peculiar Order

☛ Placed in their proper order, the words are a familiar verse from Matthew.

burden and easy is my is light my yoke

59. Ezekiel
60. Chaldea, a name that occurs a few times in the Bible; Abraham was originally from "Ur of the Chaldees" (Genesis 11:28).
61. Persia (Esther 4:1-3, 15-16)
62. The sacred vessels from the temple of Jerusalem (Daniel 5:1-5)
63. From Persia; although Matthew's Gospel only refers to them as "wise men from the east" (Matthew 2:1), the original Greek Gospel has *magi*, which refers to a class of priest-magicians from Persia.
64. None are; the Persians worshiped several gods, including Ahura-Mazda and Mithra, but none are mentioned in the Bible.
65. Jonah, who convinced the people of Nineveh, the Assyrian capital, to repent
66. Darius (Daniel 5)
67. Persia (Nehemiah 1:1; Daniel 8:2)
68. Ezra (Ezra 7:12-20)
69. Parthia, which is mentioned only in Acts 2:9 (there were Parthians in Jerusalem on the Day of Pentecost); in spite of the Bible's relative silence about the Parthian Empire, it was an important political empire in New Testament days, a power that the Roman Empire feared.
70. Peter (1 Peter 5:13) (It is possible that "Babylon" may actually be a sort of code name for Rome and that Peter never actually visited Babylon itself.)
71. Tiglath-Pileser (2 Kings 16:7-8)
72. Ahasuerus (the book of Esther), which is his name in Hebrew. Some modern translations of the Bible name him as Xerxes, but the King James Version has Ahasuerus.
73. Ezekiel (1:1), where the prophet is standing by the river (or canal) Kebar
74. Ezra
75. The Tigris

Familiar Verse, Peculiar Order (answer)

My yoke is easy, and my burden is light. (Matthew 11:30)

J on the Bible Map

☞ All answers begin with the letter *J*.

1. What is the most-mentioned city in the Bible?
2. What was the largest of the twelve tribes of Israel?
3. What is the most-mentioned river in the Bible?
4. What very ancient city (mentioned often in the Bible) is also called the "city of palms"?
5. What Roman province included Jerusalem and the surrounding area?
6. In what seaside city did Peter receive his vision of a sheet holding a variety of unclean animals?
7. Where was wicked Queen Jezebel devoured by wild dogs?
8. In Jesus' parable of the Good Samaritan, where was the traveler headed when he was attacked by robbers?
9. What was the older name of the city of Jerusalem?
10. In what river was Jesus baptized by John?
11. What city's walls fell down while the Israelites marched around it?
12. From what port did Jonah depart when he was fleeing from the Lord?
13. Jacob wrestled with an angel by the side of what river?
14. David moved his capital from Hebron to what city?
15. In what city did Peter restore life to a woman named Tabitha?
16. What river's waters healed Naaman of his leprosy?
17. In the time of Elijah and Elisha, what town had a fraternity of prophets?
18. What city was besieged by Assyrian armies during Isaiah's time?
19. What area of Israel was Jesus born in?
20. What name is used in the Old Testament for the area we now call Greece?
21. Where was Naboth murdered because wicked King Ahab wanted to possess his vineyard?
22. What city of Israel is probably the oldest city in the world? (So the archaeologists say.)

J on the Bible Map (answers)

1. Jerusalem, of course, mentioned hundreds of times
2. Judah
3. The Jordan, mentioned hundreds of times
4. Jericho (Deuteronomy 34:3), so called because its tropical climate allows date palms and other tropical plants to flourish
5. Judea, which takes its name from the older tribe of Judah
6. Joppa, on the Palestinian coast (Acts 10)
7. Jezreel, where Jezebel and Ahab had a palace (2 Kings 9)
8. Jericho (Luke 10:30)
9. Jebus (Joshua 15:63; Judges 19:10), home of the Jebusites
10. The Jordan (Matthew 3)
11. Jericho (Joshua 6)
12. Joppa (Jonah 1:3)
13. The Jabbok (Genesis 32)
14. Jerusalem (2 Samuel 5:5)
15. Joppa (Acts 9:36-43)
16. The Jordan (2 Kings 5:10)
17. Jericho (2 Kings 2)
18. Jerusalem (Isaiah 36)
19. Judah, or Judea, which contains the town of Bethlehem
20. Javan, named for a son of Noah's son Japheth (Isaiah 66:19; Ezekiel 27:13); from Solomon's time onward, there was trading between Javan and Israel.
21. Jezreel (1 Kings 21)
22. Jericho, although you wouldn't necessarily know this from reading the Bible itself. (So if you missed this question, don't feel bad.)

Familiar Verse, Peculiar Order

☞ Placed in their proper order, the words are a familiar verse from Matthew.

bed take thy up walk arise and

Moabites, Edomites, and Other Ites: Israel's Neighbors

☞ Israel's occupation of the land of Canaan has never gone uncontested. From Genesis to the present day, other groups have vied with the chosen people for the Promised Land. Test your knowledge of Israel's neighbors in Bible times. (Note: We've devoted separate sections to Israel's *big* neighbors, Egypt, Babylon, Assyria, and the Roman Empire, so none of the questions here will deal with them.)

1. What people worshiped the grisly god Molech, sacrificing children to him?
2. What warlike people occupied the coastal plain near Israel and were always referred to as "the uncircumcised"?
3. What nation was so wealthy that their camels had gold chains around their necks?
4. What Old Testament people do today's Arabs trace their descent from?
5. What fierce tribe threatened to gouge out the eyes of all the inhabitants of Jabesh Gilead?
6. What woman was given as a wife after her future husband brought in two hundred Philistine foreskins as a gift to her father?
7. What tribe was noted for wearing gold earrings?
8. Uriah, the first husband of King David's wife Bathsheba, was from what tribe?
9. What tribe occupied the site of Jerusalem before the Israelites took over?
10. What tribe did Moses live among when he fled Egypt for the first time?
11. King Balak called upon his prophet Balaam to curse the Israelites, but Balaam ended up blessing them. What nation were Balak and Balaam from?

Familiar Verse, Peculiar Order (answer)

Arise, take up thy bed and walk. (from Matthew 9:6)

Moabites, Edomites, and Other Ites: Israel's Neighbors (answers)

1. The Ammonites (Leviticus 18:21; 1 Kings 11:7); apparently an idol of Molech was heated, and the bodies of the slain children were placed in its arms.
2. The Philistines (see Judges 14:3; 1 Samuel 14:6); Israel and most of its neighbors circumcised male children, but the Philistines were noted for *not* doing so.
3. The Midianites (Judges 8:26)
4. The Ishmaelites, descendants of Abraham's son Ishmael (Genesis 16; 21); the Arabs base their belief on a proclamation of Muhammad.
5. The Ammonites (1 Samuel 11:2)
6. Michal, daughter of King Saul (1 Samuel 18:27)
7. The Ishmaelites (Judges 8:24)
8. The Hittites (2 Samuel 11:3); apparently there were many Hittite soldiers in Israel's armies.
9. The Jebusites (2 Samuel 5:6-9); the original name of Jerusalem was Jebus.
10. The Midianites (Exodus 2:15)
11. Moab (Numbers 22–24)

12. The judge Jephthah led the Israelites against what nation?
13. Samson was captured and blinded by what pagan people?
14. When David was in trouble with King Saul, where did he take his father and mother to protect them?
15. What warlike tribe often attacked Israel and was notable because "they had no fear of God"?
16. The man who killed King Saul was from what tribe?
17. The book of Obadiah is directed against what violent neighbor nation?
18. What pagan nation had a fish-shaped god named Dagon?
19. What neighboring country of Israel was descended from Jacob's hairy twin brother, Esau?
20. What nation was Milcom the god of?
21. The god Chemosh had child sacrifice as part of his worship. Solomon erected an altar for him, but Josiah tore it down. What nation worshiped him?
22. What pagan people captured the ark of the covenant from Israel?
23. Abraham's son by his concubine Keturah was the founder of what nomadic people?
24. In what country did Moses die?
25. Joshua, with God's help, defeated five kings of what nation?
26. What people could overpower Israel because of their advanced knowledge of metalworking?
27. What people did Joseph's brothers sell Joseph to?
28. What king of Israel had Ammonite women in his large harem?
29. What king of the Amalekites was spared death by Saul, only to be executed later by Samuel?
30. What overweight king of Moab oppressed the Israelites for eighteen years?
31. Moses' wife, Zipporah, was from what tribe?
32. What tribe was descended from a wild ass of a man?
33. Who grieved his Hebrew parents by marrying two Hittite women?
34. What brutal method did Phinehas, Aaron's grandson, use to kill an Israelite man and his Midianite lover?
35. By what other name is the Mediterranean Sea known in the Old Testament?
36. What tribe was noted for riding camels into battle?

12. The Ammonites (Judges 11)
13. The Philistines (Judges 14–16)
14. Moab (1 Samuel 22:3-4)
15. The Amalekites (Deuteronomy 25:17-18)
16. The Amalekites (2 Samuel 1)
17. Edom; the country had invaded and plundered Israel many times, and Obadiah announced God's judgment against them.
18. The Philistines (1 Samuel 5:2)
19. Edom (Genesis 25:30; 36:1); Edom was another name for Esau, just as Jacob's other name was Israel.
20. Ammon (1 Kings 11:5)
21. The Moabites (Numbers 21:29; 1 Kings 11:7; 2 Kings 23:13)
22. The Philistines (1 Samuel 5)
23. The Midianites—the son was named Midian (Genesis 25).
24. Moab (Deuteronomy 34:5); he was not allowed to enter the Promised Land.
25. The Amorites (Joshua 10–11)
26. The Philistines (1 Samuel 13:19-22)
27. The Ishmaelites (Genesis 37:25-28)
28. Solomon (1 Kings 11)
29. Agag (1 Samuel 15)
30. Eglon (Judges 3), who was assassinated by the Israelite leader Ehud
31. The Midianites (Exodus 2:21)
32. The Ishmaelites (Genesis 16:12), the descendants of Abraham's son Ishmael
33. Esau, son of Isaac and Rebecca (Genesis 27:46)
34. He drove a spear through the two of them when he caught them in the act (Numbers 25). He did this because many of the Israelite men were being led into pagan worship by the Midianite and Moabite women.
35. The Sea of the Philistines (Exodus 23:31)
36. The Midianites

37. When Joshua and his armies conquered Canaan, what tribe did Jerusalem belong to?
38. The cities of Ashdod, Gaza, and Gath belonged to what pagan nation?
39. Nahash, a pagan friend of King David, was king of what country?
40. Ahimelech, a friend of David in his outlaw days, was from what country?
41. What group of people destroyed the Lord's shrine at Shiloh?
42. What people worshiped a fly god named Baalzebub?
43. What Old Testament patriarch was described as "a Syrian ready to perish"?
44. What group of people told Abraham that they would not refuse him burial in their tombs?
45. Who was Jerusalem's first ruler?
46. What wise king of Israel received gifts and money from "all the kings of Arabia"?
47. What country controlled the distribution of iron and prevented Israel from having any really useful weapons?
48. Mesha, the pagan king described as a "sheepmaster," gave a gift of a hundred thousand sheep to Israel. What country did he rule?
49. Caphtor, an island in the Mediterranean Sea, was the original home of what pagan people (a continual thorn in Israel's side)?

Familiar Verse, Peculiar Order

☛ Placed in their proper order, the words are a familiar verse from Matthew.

find for he his it life loses my sake who will

E on the Bible Map

☛ All the answers begin with *E*.

1. What famous river of the Middle East is mentioned in connection with the Garden of Eden?
2. What neighbor nation of Israel was supposed to be descended from Jacob's twin brother, Esau?

37. The Amorites (Joshua 10)
38. The Philistines (Joshua 13:2-3)
39. The Ammonites (2 Samuel 10)
40. The Hittites (1 Samuel 26:6)
41. The Philistines (1 Samuel 4)
42. The Philistine people of Ekron (2 Kings 1:2); the name Baalzebub means "lord of the flies."
43. Jacob (Deuteronomy 26:5)
44. The Hittites (Genesis 23:5-6)
45. Adonizedek, a Jebusite (Joshua 10:1)
46. Solomon (1 Kings 10:15)
47. Philistia, whose people apparently were skilled in metalworking (1 Samuel 13:19-22)
48. The Moabites (2 Kings 3:4)
49. The Philistines (Jeremiah 47:4; Amos 9:7); archaeologists believe that Caphtor may be the ancient name for the Greek island of Crete in the Mediterranean.

Familiar Verse, Peculiar Order (answer)

He who loses his life for my sake will find it. (Matthew 10:39)

E on the Bible Map (answers)

1. The Euphrates (1,780 miles long), which flows through present-day Turkey, Syria, and Iraq
2. Edom

3. What is the most-mentioned pagan nation in the Bible?
4. In what village did the risen Jesus reveal himself?
5. Where did the Philistines carry the ark of the covenant after they captured it from the Israelites?
6. What tribe (and region) of Israel included the worship centers of Shiloh and Bethel?
7. Where did David, weary from fleeing from Saul, camp out?
8. Where did Saul command a sorceress to call up the ghost of the dead Samuel?
9. What pagan city was the site of a riot by the followers of the goddess Artemis?
10. Where did Samuel set up a stone to commemorate God's help in a victory over the Philistines?
11. In what Persian capital did they find the decree permitting the Jews to return to Israel?

Familiar Verse, Peculiar Order

☞ Placed in their proper order, the words are a familiar verse from Matthew.

also be heart your is there treasure where will your

Jerusalem the Golden

☞ No city in the world has been spoken about, written about, sung about, and argued about so much as Jerusalem. No other place in the Bible is mentioned so often (more than seven hundred times) or with such emotion. Test your knowledge of the Holy City.

1. Who made Jerusalem the capital of Israel?
2. What was the original name of the city?
3. What other name is commonly used in the Bible for Jerusalem?
4. Who lamented, "O Jerusalem, Jerusalem, which killest the prophets, and stonest them that are sent unto thee"?
5. What is the first book of the Bible to mention Jerusalem? (No, it isn't Genesis.)
6. What feast did Jesus go to Jerusalem to celebrate?
7. At what feast were devout men from many nations of the world gathered in Jerusalem?

3. Egypt
4. Emmaus (Luke 24:13)
5. Ekron (1 Samuel 5:10)
6. Ephraim
7. En Gedi (1 Samuel 23:29)
8. Endor (1 Samuel 28) (Incidentally, this incident is the source of the name Endora, the spiteful mother-in-law on the TV series *Bewitched*.)
9. Ephesus (Acts 19)
10. Ebenezer (1 Samuel 7:12)
11. Ecbatana (Ezra 6:2)

Familiar Verse, Peculiar Order (answer)

Where your treasure is, there will your heart be also. (Matthew 6:21)

Jerusalem the Golden (answers)

1. David, who moved the capital there from Hebron (2 Samuel 5:9)
2. Jebus, home of the Jebusites, who were finally driven out by David (2 Samuel 5)
3. Zion, which is the name of one of the hills of Jerusalem; the name occurs many times in the Bible as a synonym for the whole city.
4. Jesus (Luke 13:34)
5. Joshua (10:1)
6. The Passover (John 2:13)
7. Pentecost (Acts 2)

8. Who was the first king of Jerusalem? (No, it wasn't David—much, much earlier, in fact.)

9. What Old Testament book tells of rebuilding Jerusalem after the Babylonian captivity?

10. Who had a dazzling vision of the New Jerusalem, the heavenly city?

11. What Egyptian pharaoh attacked Jerusalem and carried off the temple treasures?

12. What does the name *Jerusalem* mean? (Hint: a name very inappropriate for this strife-torn city)

13. Who, today, refer to Jerusalem as *Al-Kuds al-Sharif?*

14. What king bribed Ben-Hadad, the king of Syria, by giving him all the temple and palace treasures of Jerusalem?

15. Who claimed that no prophet could die outside Jerusalem?

16. What Assyrian king threatened Jerusalem but had his army destroyed by the Lord?

17. Who built the original walls of Jerusalem?

18. What female ruler came to Jerusalem with a camel caravan carrying luxurious gifts to Solomon?

19. The army of what well-known Babylonian king broke down the walls of Jerusalem?

20. What king's name is most closely associated with Jerusalem?

21. Which of the twelve tribes of Israel included the city of Jerusalem in its territory?

22. What king ruled in Jerusalem when Jesus was born?

23. Who went with his family to Jerusalem when he was twelve years old?

24. In Jesus' parable of the Good Samaritan, where was the unfortunate traveler from Jerusalem headed?

25. What woman did Jesus tell that, in times to come, God would not be worshiped at Jerusalem, but everywhere?

26. Why was the apostle Paul arrested in Jerusalem?

27. What king built an aqueduct to bring water into Jerusalem?

28. What was the subject of the apostles' council at Jerusalem?

29. What valley of Jerusalem was associated with gory child sacrifice?

30. Who started a riot in Jerusalem by pitting the Pharisees against the Sadducees?

31. Who was taken to the Jerusalem temple as an infant?

8. We don't know. The first one mentioned in the Bible is Adonizedek, who contended with the conquering Joshua (Joshua 10:1).
9. Nehemiah
10. John, author of Revelation
11. Shishak (1 Kings 14:25-26)
12. "Peace," in Hebrew
13. Muslims; in Arabic, the name means "the sanctuary."
14. Asa (1 Kings 15)
15. Jesus (Luke 13:33)
16. Sennacherib (2 Kings 18-19)
17. Solomon (1 Kings 3:1)
18. The queen of Sheba (1 Kings 10:2)
19. Nebuchadnezzar (2 Kings 25:1-4)
20. David; Jerusalem is referred to as "the city of David" dozens of times in the Old Testament.
21. Benjamin, originally, although the city's close association with David made Jerusalem the key city of the tribe of Judah (see Judges 1:21)
22. Herod (Matthew 2:1)
23. Jesus (Luke 2:42)
24. Jericho (Luke 10:30)
25. The woman at the well (John 4)
26. For bringing a Gentile (Trophimus the Ephesian) into the temple area, which was restricted only to Jews (Acts 21:27-29)
27. Hezekiah (2 Kings 20:20)
28. Whether Gentiles had to be circumcised before becoming Christians (Acts 15)
29. The valley of Hinnom (2 Kings 23:10); it had been the place where some Jews sacrificed their children to the heathen god Molech, a practice denounced by the Hebrew prophets.
30. Paul, at his trial before the Sanhedrin (Acts 23); Paul started the riot by mentioning the resurrection of the dead, which the Pharisees believed in and the Sadducees denied.
31. Jesus (Luke 2:22)

32. Which of the four Gospels refers to Jerusalem as "the Holy City" (a name commonly used in the Old Testament)?
33. Whose family went every year to Jerusalem to celebrate the Passover?
34. Who led the Jewish group from Babylon to rebuild the temple in Jerusalem?
35. What notable building is lacking in the New Jerusalem?
36. Who took Jesus to a pinnacle of the temple in Jerusalem?
37. What massive trees were used to make the beams and pillars in the Jerusalem temple?
38. Who prophesied judgment on the people of Jerusalem because they burned incense to idols on their roofs?
39. Who pitched a tent in Jerusalem to house the ark of the covenant?
40. What king set up golden bull idols at Dan and Bethel so that his people would not go to Jerusalem to worship?
41. What Babylonian king caused famine in Jerusalem?
42. Who held a long feast when the Jerusalem temple was dedicated?
43. Which apostles healed the crippled man at the Beautiful Gate in Jerusalem?
44. What criminal did the people of Jerusalem cry out to be released?
45. What tribe of Israel sacked Jerusalem and burned it?
46. What king fortified Jerusalem with catapults for throwing stones?
47. What Assyrian field commander tried to intimidate King Hezekiah by speaking anti-Israel propaganda to the people of Jerusalem?
48. What prophet went naked as a way of wailing over the fate of Jerusalem?
49. What church took up a large love offering for the needy believers in Jerusalem?
50. What evil queen was executed near Jerusalem's Horse Gate?
51. What kind of bird did Jesus compare to his love for Jerusalem?
52. Which prophet told the people of Jerusalem to cut off their hair as a sign the Lord had rejected them?
53. Where did Jesus weep over Jerusalem?
54. What pool in Jerusalem was the place where Jesus cured a man born blind?

32. Matthew (4:5; 27:53), which is appropriate, since Matthew's is the most Jewish of the four Gospels
33. Jesus' (Luke 2:41)
34. Zerubbabel (Ezra 5)
35. The temple (Revelation 21); there is no temple because God himself is in the city.
36. The devil (Matthew 4:5-7)
37. The cedars of Lebanon (1 Kings 5:6)
38. Jeremiah (19:13)
39. David (1 Chronicles 15:1)
40. King Jeroboam (1 Kings 12:26-31)
41. Nebuchadnezzar (2 Kings 25:1-3)
42. Solomon (1 Kings 8:65)
43. Peter and John (Acts 3:2)
44. Barabbas (Luke 23:18), who was imprisoned at the same time as Jesus
45. Judah (Judges 1:8); this occurred at the time when Jerusalem was considered to be within the territory of the tribe of Benjamin.
46. Uzziah (2 Chronicles 26:14-15)
47. Rabshakeh (2 Kings 18:17-37)
48. The prophet Micah (1:8)
49. Antioch (Acts 11:27-30)
50. Athaliah, Ahab's daughter (2 Chronicles 23:15)
51. A hen gathering her chicks (Matthew 23:37)
52. Jeremiah (7:29)
53. The Mount of Olives (Luke 19:41)
54. The pool of Siloam (John 9:7-11)

55. In John's vision of the New Jerusalem, how many gates does the city have, and what are they made of?
56. What kind of branches were thrown down in front of Jesus on his entry into Jerusalem?
57. Who brought costly stones for the foundation of the temple in Jerusalem?
58. What two apostles were put into prison in Jerusalem for preaching the gospel?
59. What world conqueror carried away furnishings from the Jerusalem temple and put them in the temple at Babylon?
60. What river flows through Jerusalem?
61. What book mentions people who had worn purple (or scarlet) now pawing through the garbage of Jerusalem?
62. How many angels will be at the gates of the New Jerusalem?
63. Which apostle referred to heaven as the "Jerusalem which is above"?
64. What Jerusalem tower collapsed, killing eighteen men?
65. What pool in Jerusalem was a healing place when an angel came by and stirred up its waters?
66. Who knelt toward Jerusalem and prayed looking out of his eastern window in Babylon?

Familiar Verse, Peculiar Order

☛ Placed in their proper order, the words are a familiar verse from Matthew.

am are gathered I in midst in my name of or the them there three together two where

A on the Bible Map

☛ All answers begin with the letter A.

1. In what city were believers first called Christians?
2. What large pagan empire was a constant thorn in the side of Israel?
3. What famous Greek city of culture was visited by Paul, who delivered a sermon to a crowd of skeptics?

55. Twelve, made of pearl (as in "pearly gates") (Revelation 21)
56. Palm branches (as in "Palm Sunday") (John 12:13)
57. Solomon (1 Kings 5:17)
58. Peter and John (Acts 4:3)
59. Nebuchadnezzar (2 Chronicles 36:7)
60. None does. Jerusalem is a rarity among world cities in that it does not lie on a river. Jerusalem's water supply has always presented problems.
61. Lamentations (4:5); the "purple" (or scarlet) refers to expensive clothing—meaning the rich were reduced to scavenging through garbage to find food.
62. Twelve (Revelation 21:12)
63. Paul (Galatians 4:26)
64. The tower of Siloam (Luke 13:4)
65. The pool of Bethesda (John 5)
66. Daniel (6:10)

Familiar Verse, Peculiar Order (answer)

Where two or three are gathered together in my name, there am I in the midst of them. (Matthew 18:20)

A on the Bible Map (answers)

1. Antioch (Acts 11)
2. Assyria, mentioned more than 150 times in the Bible
3. Athens (Acts 17)

4. What mountain did Noah's ark come to rest upon?
5. What is the site of the future (and final) showdown battle mentioned in the book of Revelation?
6. What town was the home of the wealthy friend of Jesus who buried Jesus in his own tomb?
7. What was the capital of the great kingdom of Assyria?
8. What town was the hometown of the prophet Jeremiah?
9. What Canaanite city, conquered by Joshua, has a two-letter name that means "ruined"?
10. What name is given in the New Testament to the area we now call Greece?
11. What European body of water was Paul shipwrecked in?
12. What name was given to the field Judas Iscariot bought with his "blood money"?
13. What cultured Egyptian city was hometown to Paul's brilliant friend Apollos?
14. What New Testament region has the same name as a dry city in Texas?
15. In what valley did the moon stand still while Joshua's troops defeated the Amorites?
16. What was the hometown of the Jews who opposed Stephen and brought about his death by stoning?
17. What city was the site of Paul's longest sermon?
18. What city, named for a Greek god, did Paul pass through on his way from Philippi to Thessalonica?
19. What is an alternate name for the Dead Sea?
20. What tribe (and region) of Israel was in western Galilee?
21. In the New Testament, what name is given to the region we now call Turkey?
22. What town in Egypt has the same name as a present-day dam in Egypt?
23. What city was Paul's "home base" for his several missionary journeys?
24. What name is given to the area northeast of Israel that we now call Syria?
25. What country, east of Israel, had the town of Rabbah as its capital?
26. What empire was ruled by the mighty emperor Sennacherib?
27. The first three chapters of Revelation are addressed to seven churches in what area?

4. Ararat (Genesis 8:4)
5. Armageddon (Revelation 16:16)
6. Arimathea—the friend being the famous Joseph of Arimathea, of course (Matthew 27:57)
7. Asshur (Ezekiel 27:23)
8. Anathoth
9. Ai (Joshua 7–12)
10. Achaia, which was the name the Roman Empire gave to this province
11. The Adriatic Sea (Acts 27:27)
12. Akeldama, which means "field of blood" (Acts 1:19)
13. Alexandria (Acts 18:24)
14. Abilene (Luke 3:1)
15. Aijalon (Joshua 10:12) (A very hard question! If you knew this, give yourself a pat on the back.)
16. Alexandria, in Egypt (Acts 6–7)
17. Antioch, in Pisida (Acts 13)
18. Apollonia, named for the god Apollo (Acts 17:1)
19. The Sea of the Arabah (Deuteronomy 3:17)
20. Asher
21. Asia
22. Aswan (Ezekiel 29:10)
23. Antioch, in Syria
24. Aram, mentioned almost seventy times in the Bible
25. Ammon, home of the Ammonites; the town of Rabbah is now the city of Amman, the capital of Jordan.
26. Assyria (2 Kings 19)
27. Asia

28. Where did Paul live after his conversion to Christianity?
29. What Philistine city was the site of the temple of the pagan god Dagon, which was destroyed by the presence of the ark of the covenant?
30. What was the name of the public forum in Athens where Paul delivered his sermon?
31. What country did the sons of Sennacherib flee to after they murdered their father? (Hint: it's the name of one of the former countries of the Soviet Union.)
32. What empire conquered Israel and killed or enslaved most of its inhabitants?

Familiar Verse, Peculiar Order

☞ Placed in their proper order, the words are a familiar verse from Matthew.

can two man masters no serve

Moabites, Edomites, and Other Ites: Israel's Neighbors (Part II)

1. In what land did Moses see a burning bush that was not consumed?
2. What did the Israelite leader Ehud use to kill fat King Eglon of Moab?
3. Whose ill-fated daughter came out dancing after his victory over the Ammonites?
4. What strongman was ordained before birth to deliver Israel from the Philistines?
5. What barley farmer married a Moabite woman and became an ancestor of David?
6. Whose daughters became the mothers of the Moabites and the Ammonites?
7. Who was commissioned by an angel to save Israel from the Midianites?
8. Who sold out Samson for the price of eleven hundred pieces of silver from each of the Philistine chieftains?

28. Arabia (Galatians 4:25)
29. Ashdod (1 Samuel 5)
30. The Areopagus (Acts 17)
31. Armenia (2 Kings 19:37); note that not all translations have "Armenia" here—some say "Ararat."
32. Assyria (2 Kings 17)

Familiar Verse, Peculiar Order (answer)

No man can serve two masters. (Matthew 6:24)

Moabites, Edomites, and Other Ites: Israel's Neighbors (Part II) (answers)

1. Midian (Exodus 3:1-2)
2. A two-edged dagger (Judges 3:16-21); Eglon was so obese that Ehud's dagger got completely lost in the fat.
3. The Israelite judge Jephthah's (Judges 11:34); Jephthah had made a vow to sacrifice her.
4. Samson (Judges 13:2-5)
5. Boaz, who married Ruth (Ruth 1:22–2:3)
6. Lot's (Genesis 19:30-38)
7. Gideon (Judges 6:11-23)
8. Delilah (Judges 16:5)

9. One of Gideon's soldiers dreamed of a Midianite tent being overturned by an unlikely object. What was it?
10. What warriors were so extravagant that even their camels wore necklaces?
11. What prophet claimed that Edom, Moab, Ammon, and Tyre all had sorcerers?
12. What prophet of Moab had a talking donkey?
13. What king sacrificed his son on the city wall when the Moabites were losing the battle to Israel?
14. During Saul's reign an earthquake occurred during the attack on the Philistines at Michmash. Who led the attack?
15. What wicked king of Judah built a Syrian style altar and offered up his son as a sacrifice?
16. In the time of the judges, what tribe did the Israelites hide from in caves?
17. What Israelite woman lived in Moab but returned to Israel after her husband's death?
18. What warrior people defeated by Gideon wore purple garments?
19. What judge from Gilead was called to be a commander against the Ammonites?
20. This goddess of Canaan was associated with depraved worship practices. After Saul's death, his armor was placed in her temple by the Philistines. What was her name?
21. In Saul's time, what marauding people drove the Israelites into caves?
22. What Israelite leader met his future wife at a well in Midian?
23. What boy (and future king) ran into the Philistine camp to confront their best warrior?
24. What judge of Israel had his Philistine wife given to his friend?
25. What Syrian king was getting drunk at a time when he was supposed to be making war on the Samaritans?
26. What judge and his men killed 120,000 Midianites?
27. What tribe was descended from the son of Lot named Ben-Ammi?
28. What strongman burned the Philistines' grain by tying torches to the tails of foxes?
29. What king was critically wounded by Philistine arrows?
30. What judge confused the Midianite army by having his men break the jars they were using to cover their torches?

9. A cake of barley bread (Judges 7:13)
10. The Midianites (Judges 8:24-26)
11. Jeremiah (27:3-10)
12. Balaam (Numbers 22:21-33)
13. Mesha, king of Moab (2 Kings 3:27)
14. Saul's son Jonathan (1 Samuel 14:15)
15. Ahaz (2 Chronicles 28:1-4, 23)
16. The Midianites (Judges 6:2)
17. Naomi, Ruth's mother-in-law (Ruth 1)
18. The Midianites (Judges 8:26)
19. Jephthah (Judges 11:6)
20. Ashtaroth, or Ashtoreth (1 Samuel 7:3; 31:10; 1 Kings 11:33)
21. The Philistines (1 Samuel 13:5-7)
22. Moses (Exodus 2:15-21)
23. David (1 Samuel 17:48-49)
24. Samson (Judges 14:20)
25. Ben-Hadad (1 Kings 20:12-19)
26. Gideon (Judges 8:10)
27. The Ammonites (Genesis 19:38)
28. Samson (Judges 15:4-5)
29. Saul (1 Samuel 31:3)
30. Gideon (Judges 7:16-21)

31. What two animals owned by the Philistines carried the ark of the covenant back to Israel?
32. What woman with a cumbersome name was the Hittite wife of Esau?
33. What Syrian king fled when 100,000 of his soldiers were killed by the people of Israel?
34. What beautiful woman of Israel was married to a Hittite warrior?
35. Who killed six hundred Philistines with an ox goad?
36. What oppressive nation did the judge Gideon deliver Israel from?
37. What king of Israel had an Ammonite mother?
38. What king of Israel headed up the slaying of forty-seven thousand Syrians?
39. What Israelite king's body was fastened to the wall of Beth Shan by the Philistines?
40. What happened to the Syrian soldiers when Elisha prayed?
41. Who asked his Midianite brother-in-law to be the Israelites' guide through the wilderness?
42. What man of Bethlehem migrated to Moab to escape a famine?
43. What camel-riding raiders did Saul and David fight against?
44. What godly king of Judah tore down the idols devoted to the gods of the Moabites and Ammonites?
45. Rabbah was the capital city of what enemy nation of Israel?
46. What neighbor nation was noted as having kings as rulers long before the Israelites had a king?
47. What tribe was descended from Abraham's son by his Egyptian maid?
48. What king of Judah watched while an invading army of Edomites, Ammonites, and Moabites all destroyed each other (instead of destroying Judah)?
49. What Syrian king besieged Samaria, causing great famine that led to cannibalism?
50. What nation south of Egypt invaded Israel but was fought off by King Asa's army?
51. Which Old Testament book describes the defeat of the Cellulites?

31. Two cows (1 Samuel 6:7-12)
32. Aholibamah (Genesis 36:2, 5)
33. Ben-Hadad (1 Kings 20:29)
34. Bathsheba, wife of Uriah and later wife of David (2 Samuel 11:3)
35. The Israelite judge Shamgar (Judges 3:31)
36. The Midianites (Judges 6–9)
37. Rehoboam, Solomon's son, whose mother was one of Solomon's many wives (1 Kings 14:21)
38. David (1 Chronicles 19:18)
39. Saul's (1 Samuel 31:10)
40. They were struck blind (2 Kings 6:18).
41. Moses, whose brother-in-law Hobab was asked to be the "eyes" in the desert (Numbers 10:29-32)
42. Elimelech, whose sons married the Moabite women Ruth and Orpah
43. The Amalekites (1 Samuel 15:3; 27:8-9; 30:1-17)
44. Josiah (2 Kings 23:13)
45. The Ammonites (2 Samuel 12:26)
46. The Edomites, the descendants of Jacob's brother, Esau (Genesis 36:31-39)
47. The Ishmaelites, descended from Ishmael, son of Abraham's concubine Hagar (Genesis 16)
48. Jehoshaphat (2 Chronicles 20)
49. Ben-Hadad (2 Kings 6:24-30)
50. Cush, which is called "Ethiopia" in some Bible translations; it roughly corresponds to the modern nation of Sudan. (2 Chronicles 14:9-12)
51. Cellulites—body fats—are not mentioned in the Bible, nor are they a tribe. (They are hard to defeat, however.)

Familiar Verse, Peculiar Order

☛ Placed in their proper order, the words are a familiar verse from the New Testament.

casts fear love out perfect

G on the Bible Map

☛ All answers begin with the letter G.

1. What region did Jesus grow up in and do much of his ministry in?
2. What "sea" is actually a large inland lake, mentioned many times in the New Testament?
3. What province in Asia (present-day Turkey) received an epistle from the apostle Paul?
4. What Philistine city was the prison for the blinded (and sheared) Samson?
5. In what famous Jerusalem garden did Jesus pray before he was arrested?
6. What mountain was the "sacred mount" for the Samaritans?
7. What land (mentioned in a folk hymn, as well as the Bible) is "there no balm in"?
8. On what hill was Jesus crucified?
9. What famous nation in Europe is also referred to as Achaia in the New Testament?
10. What was King Saul's capital city?
11. What tribe of Israel was named after a son of Jacob and the concubine Zilpah?
12. What Philistine city was home to the giant Goliath?
13. In what region did Jesus heal the man possessed by the demon(s) named Legion?
14. What Israelite city was captured by the Egyptian pharaoh and then later given as a wedding present when the pharaoh's daughter married Solomon?
15. What river (unknown today) is mentioned as one of the "four rivers" in the Garden of Eden?
16. On what mountain did Saul and his sons die fighting the Philistines?

Familiar Verse, Peculiar Order (answer)

Perfect love casts out fear. (1 John 4:18)

G on the Bible Map (answers)

1. Galilee, of course
2. The Sea of Galilee
3. Galatia
4. Gaza (Judges 16:21)
5. Gethsemane
6. Gerizim (John 4:20); the Samaritans, unlike the orthodox Jews who despised them, did not hold Mount Sinai in high esteem.
7. Gilead (Jeremiah 8:22)
8. Golgotha (Matthew 27:33)
9. Greece
10. Gibeah, one of several Gibeahs in the Old Testament; Saul's capital is often referred to as "Gibeah of Saul."
11. Gad
12. Gath (1 Samuel 17:4)
13. The region of the Gadarenes (Luke 8:26) or of the Gerasenes (Matthew 8:28); with either Gospel, the correct answer begins with G.
14. Gezer (1 Kings 9)
15. The Gihon (Genesis 2:13)
16. Gilboa (1 Samuel 31)

17. In what region of Egypt did the Hebrew slaves live?
18. What spring was the main water source for the city of Jerusalem?
19. What wicked city was destroyed along with Sodom?
20. What name does the Bible use for the Mediterranean?
21. At what place was Saul made the first king of Israel?
22. Where did Joshua fight a battle where the sun and moon "stood still"?
23. Where did Saul strip off his clothes and join in with a band of frenzied prophets?

Familiar Verse, Peculiar Order

☞ Placed in their proper order, the words are a familiar verse from Matthew.

and first the God his of kingdom righteousness seek

Doing As the Romans Do (Part II)

1. Who told Paul that he would bear witness to the Lord in Rome?
2. What Roman soldier admitted that he had used money to buy his Roman citizenship?
3. What Roman governor had a Jewish wife named Drusilla?
4. Who uttered the famous words "I appeal to Caesar"?
5. What Roman governor accused Paul of being insane?
6. Publius was the Roman ruler of what island in the Mediterranean (famous because Paul was shipwrecked there)?
7. Besides Rome, what three Italian cities are mentioned in the Bible?
8. When Acts ends, how many years had Paul been in Rome?
9. Did Paul write the Letter to the Romans before or after he came to Rome?
10. What Christian woman did Paul ask the Roman Christians to receive warmly?
11. What Greek city was known throughout the empire as a den of sin?

17. Goshen, mentioned many times in Exodus
18. Gihon, which is the Hebrew word for "spring" (2 Chronicles 32:30)
19. Gomorrah, of course (Genesis 19)
20. The Great Sea
21. Gilgal (1 Samuel 11:15)
22. Gibeon (Joshua 9–11)
23. Gibeah (1 Samuel 10:5)—one of several Gibeahs in the Old Testament; this particular Gibeah is called Gibeah of God.

Familiar Verse, Peculiar Order (answer)

Seek first the kingdom of God and his righteousness.
(Matthew 6:33)

Doing As the Romans Do (Part II) (answers)

1. The Lord (Acts 23:11)
2. Claudius Lysias (Acts 22:28)
3. Felix (Acts 24:24)
4. Paul (Acts 25:11); it was a Roman citizen's right to be tried before the emperor.
5. Festus (Acts 26:24)
6. Malta (Acts 28:7)
7. Syracuse, Rhegium, and Puteoli (Acts 28)
8. Two
9. Before
10. Phoebe (Romans 16:1)
11. Corinth

12. What New Testament book never mentions Rome but is very clearly anti-Roman?
13. Were there Romans in Jerusalem on the Day of Pentecost?
14. Which Roman governor planned to execute the apostle Peter?
15. What city (with a very Roman name) witnessed the conversion of the Roman soldier Cornelius?
16. What was the name of the Roman province in which Jesus lived?
17. What Roman province was the first European territory visited by Paul?
18. The area we now call Greece was known in the New Testament by its Roman name. What was it?
19. What Roman territory mentioned in the Bible was farthest from Palestine?
20. Cilicia was the home province of what New Testament leader?
21. The Roman province of Asia, mentioned often in the New Testament, lies in what modern country?
22. What epistle of Paul's was sent to a province instead of to a particular city or individual?
23. The book of Revelation is addressed to the "seven churches" in which Roman province?
24. What Roman province, mentioned often in the New Testament, has the same name as a nation in the Middle East today?
25. The Egyptian city of Alexandria was the great intellectual center of the Roman Empire. What Christian leader was a native of Alexandria?
26. What Roman official became a Christian under Paul's influence?
27. Who said to Pilate, "We have no king but Caesar"?
28. The Roman Empire's official language, Latin, is mentioned only once in the Bible, in connection with a famous sign. What did the sign say?
29. Who ordered a guard posted at Jesus' tomb?
30. Who bribed the Roman guards at Jesus' tomb, paying them to say that Jesus' body had been stolen?
31. At what Jewish feast did the Roman governor customarily release a prisoner?

12. The book of Revelation, which is probably written to encourage Christians who were being persecuted by the Romans
13. Yes (Acts 2:10)
14. Agrippa (Acts 12)
15. Caesarea (Acts 10)
16. Judea
17. Macedonia (Acts 16)
18. Achaia
19. Spain (Romans 15:24)
20. Paul; its chief city was Tarsus, Paul's hometown.
21. Turkey
22. Galatians
23. Asia
24. Syria
25. Apollos (Acts 18:24)
26. Sergius Paulus, governor of Cyprus (Acts 13)
27. The chief priests (John 19:15)
28. "Jesus of Nazareth, the King of the Jews" (John 19:19-20)
29. Pilate (Matthew 27:65)
30. The chief priests (Matthew 28:11-15)
31. Passover

32. What was the name of the governor's palace in Jerusalem?
33. Which Gospel mentions Pilate and Herod becoming friends after both had met Jesus?
34. What was the name of the imperial bodyguard?
35. What book of the New Testament bears the same name as a Roman emperor?
36. What Roman emperor ruled in the New Testament period but is not mentioned in the Bible at all?
37. What island has a St. Paul's Bay, commemorating Paul being shipwrecked there on his way to Rome?
38. What epistle is addressed to Christians in the Roman provinces of Pontus, Galatia, Cappadocia, Asia, and Bithynia?
39. When Paul "appealed to Caesar," which Caesar (emperor) was he appealing to?
40. Who was the first apostle to witness to a Roman official?
41. A famine during the reign of the emperor Claudius had been predicted by what Christian prophet?
42. In the Roman division of Jewish land, what territory lay between Judea and Galilee?
43. What famous body of water, called "our sea" by the Romans, is never mentioned in the Bible?
44. Cyrene, the homeland of the man who carried Jesus' cross, was a Roman province on what continent?
45. What type of Roman flunky was widely considered to be dishonest and corrupt?
46. What is the only Roman coin mentioned in the Bible?
47. When Paul was in Rome, could he possibly have seen the famous Colosseum?
48. Augustus, the Roman ruler who ordered the census at the time of Jesus' birth, was what relation to the famous Julius Caesar?
49. Quirinius, the Roman governor of Syria, is mentioned in which Gospel?
50. Luke's Gospel mentions something important happening "in the fifteenth year of the reign of Tiberius Caesar." What happened?

32. The Praetorium (Mark 15:16)
33. Luke (23:12)
34. The Praetorian guard; in the New Testament, the guards were not necessarily the emperor's private guard, but any guards associated with the empire's officials.
35. Titus
36. The mad emperor Caligula, who reigned after Tiberius and before Claudius
37. Malta
38. 1 Peter
39. Nero, who is not actually mentioned by name in the New Testament
40. Peter, who preached to the Roman centurion Cornelius (Acts 10)
41. Agabus (Acts 11:28)
42. Samaria
43. The Mediterranean; though mentioned often as "the sea," it is never called by any particular name.
44. Africa
45. Tax collector (also called publican)
46. The denarius, mentioned many times, although many translations use the word *penny*
47. No; it wasn't built until several years after his stay in Rome.
48. His nephew
49. Luke (2:2)
50. John the Baptist began preaching (Luke 3)

Familiar Verse, Peculiar Order

☛ Placed in their proper order, the words are a familiar verse from the New Testament.

are dead in die Lord the the who blessed

M and *N* on the Bible Map

☛ All answers begin with either *M* or *N*.

1. What river (the longest in the world) is mentioned often in the Bible, but never by its usual name (which begins with *N*)?
2. What was Jesus' hometown?
3. On what small Mediterranean island was Paul shipwrecked?
4. What was the capital of the ancient empire of Assyria?
5. What tribe of Israel was the largest in land area?
6. What neighboring nation of Israel worshiped a bloodthirsty god called Chemosh?
7. To what large pagan city did Jonah preach a message of repentance?
8. What Roman province included the cities of Thessalonica, Philippi, and Berea, all visited by the apostle Paul?
9. What empire was sometimes under Assyrian control, later under Persian control?
10. What cave was (and still is) the burial place of Abraham, Sarah, Isaac, Rebecca, and Jacob?
11. On what island was Paul bitten by a venomous snake that had no effect on him?
12. What great body of water is called "The Great Sea" in the Bible?
13. Which neighbor nation of Israel was famous for using camels as cavalry transportation?
14. What country was home to the good woman Ruth?
15. The prophecies of the book of Nahum are directed against which famous pagan city?
16. On what Jerusalem hill did Solomon build the Lord's temple?
17. Where did King Saul slaughter a band of priests because they had aided David?
18. What great city was founded by Asshur?

Familiar Verse, Peculiar Order (answer)

Blessed are the dead who die in the Lord. (Revelation 14:13)

M and *N* on the Bible Map (answers)

1. The Nile, which is often just referred to as "the river" or "the stream"
2. Nazareth (We hope you didn't say "Bethlehem," which was his *birthplace,* but not the town he grew up in.)
3. Malta (Acts 28)
4. Nineveh, which is mentioned many times in the Bible
5. Manasseh
6. Moab
7. Nineveh, the capital of Assyria
8. Macedonia
9. Media, land of the Medes (see Esther 1:3; Isaiah 13:17; Daniel 5:31); the Persian ruler Darius is called "Darius the Mede."
10. Machpelah (Genesis 23; 25:9; 49:30; 50:13)
11. Malta (Acts 28)
12. The Mediterranean
13. Midian (Judges 6)
14. Moab
15. Nineveh; the book begins with the words "The burden of Nineveh."
16. Moriah (2 Chronicles 3:1)
17. Nob (1 Samuel 21–22)
18. Nineveh, capital of the Assyrian empire, which is named after Asshur (Genesis 10:11)

19. What name do we still use for the dry, scrubby area in the south of Israel?
20. What Greek city was the first place the apostle Paul set foot in Europe?
21. In what town of Galilee did Jesus restore to life a widow's son?
22. From what mountain did Moses see the Promised Land?
23. On what mountain did Abraham almost sacrifice his son Isaac?
24. What was the prophet Micah's hometown?
25. In what town was Jesus almost killed after he taught in the synagogue?
26. Jesus said that a certain pagan city would rise up to judge his contemporaries for rejecting him. Which city?
27. What tribe of Israel was located north of the Sea of Galilee?
28. Where did Abraham entertain three mysterious messengers from the Lord?
29. Moses' wife was from what country?
30. What great Egyptian city is often called Noph in the Old Testament (and has a modern namesake in Tennessee)?
31. At what place did Samuel present Saul to the Israelites as their first king?
32. What neighbor nation of Israel was supposedly descended from the incestuous union of Lot and his daughter?
33. What other name is Egypt called in the Bible?
34. Jethro, Moses' father-in-law, was a priest of what nation?
35. At what place near the Red Sea did the pharaoh believe he had trapped the Israelites?
36. The area we now call Iraq was called what in the Bible?
37. In what country did Moses die?
38. Where did Moses anger the Lord by not following his instructions in bringing water from a rock?
39. Where was good king Josiah of Judah killed fighting the Egyptian pharaoh?
40. Where did Cain wander after he killed his brother Abel?
41. The prophet Balaam, whose donkey spoke to him, was a native of what country?
42. What was the hometown of Jesus' most famous woman follower?

19. The Negev
20. Neapolis (Acts 16:11)
21. Nain (Luke 7:11)
22. Nebo (Deuteronomy 34)
23. Moriah (Genesis 22:2)
24. Moresheth (Micah 1:1)
25. Nazareth, his hometown (Luke 4:16-30)
26. Nineveh, capital of Assyria (Luke 11:30)
27. Naphtali
28. Mamre (Genesis 18:1)
29. Midian (Exodus 2)
30. Memphis (see Isaiah 19:13; Jeremiah 2:16; Ezekiel 30:13); the King James Version has "Noph," but some newer translations have "Memphis."
31. Mizpah (1 Samuel 7; 10)
32. Moab (Genesis 19:30-38)
33. Mizraim (see Genesis 10:6); this is the usual Hebrew word for Egypt. Some translations use Mizraim; some use Egypt.
34. Midian
35. Migdol (Exodus 14:2)
36. Mesopotamia, an area that includes the great Tigris and Euphrates rivers (see Genesis 24:10; Judges 3:8; Acts 2:9)
37. Moab (Deuteronomy 34:5)
38. Meribah (Numbers 20)
39. Megiddo (2 Kings 23)
40. The land of Nod (Genesis 4:16)
41. Moab (Numbers 22–24)
42. Magdala, home of Mary Magdalene (Luke 8:2)

Familiar Verse, Peculiar Order

☛ Placed in their proper order, the words are a familiar verse from Matthew.

and be and knock find shall it opened
seek shall unto ye you

T on the Bible Map

☛ All answers begin with the letter *T.*

1. What was the apostle Paul's hometown?
2. Where was Jonah headed when he ignored the Lord's command to go to Nineveh?
3. What Greek city received two epistles from the apostle Paul?
4. King Hiram, a friend of King David, ruled over what pagan seacoast town?
5. Lydia, the Christian woman who was a "seller of purple," lived in what town?
6. The prophet Amos was a shepherd in what small village?
7. What river, flowing through present-day Iraq, is mentioned often in the Bible, particularly in connection with the kingdom of Babylon?
8. What town became capital of Israel after the reign of Solomon?
9. The fiery prophet Elijah was from what town?
10. In what Italian town did Paul stop on his way to Rome?
11. Where was Paul when a group of Christians knelt and prayed with him on the beach?
12. Where was Paul when he had his vision of a Macedonian man calling for him to help the Macedonians?
13. What Philistine town was the home of Samson's wife?
14. What important pagan coastal town was visited by Jesus?
15. What horrible place was used for sacrificing children?
16. What town on the Sea of Galilee shore was named for a Roman emperor?
17. What town was Job's friend Eliphaz from?
18. What river was the great city of Nineveh situated on?
19. In what town did Paul bring to life a young man who had fallen out of a window while Paul was preaching?

Familiar Verse, Peculiar Order (answer)

Seek, and ye shall find; knock, and it shall be opened unto you. (Matthew 7:7)

T on the Bible Map (answers)

1. Tarsus, the capital of the Roman province of Cilicia (Acts 21:39)
2. To Tarshish (Jonah 1:3), which may be an ancient name for Spain, though no one is sure
3. Thessalonica
4. Tyre (2 Samuel 5:11), one of the great cities of the ancient world
5. Thyatira (Acts 16:14); the "purple" was a dye used on cloth.
6. Tekoa (Amos 1:1)
7. The Tigris, which flows about 1,150 miles and into the Persian Gulf; sometimes in the Bible it is merely called "the river" instead of its usual name.
8. Tirzah (1 Kings 14:17); Jerusalem continued to be the capital of the southern kingdom (Judah), and later the northern kingdom of Israel moved the capital from Tirzah to Samaria.
9. Tishbe—a place that is mentioned only in connection with him, "Elijah the Tishbite" (1 Kings 17:1)
10. Three Taverns (Acts 28:15)
11. Tyre (Acts 21:3-6)
12. Troas (Acts 16:8-12)
13. Timnah (Judges 14)
14. Tyre (Luke 6:17)
15. Topheth (2 Kings 23:10); the place had such a bad reputation that sometimes the name is used as a synonym for hell.
16. Tiberias (John 6:23), named for the emperor Tiberius
17. Teman ("Eliphaz the Temanite," Job 2:11); the people of Teman had a reputation for wisdom.
18. The Tigris
19. Troas (Acts 20:5-12)

Familiar Verse, Peculiar Order

☞ Placed in their proper order, the words are a familiar verse from Matthew.

them fruits know shall by their ye

At Beth's House

☞ *Beth* is the Hebrew word for "house," and it occurs in several notable place names in the Bible. Every answer to the questions below contains a "beth" in it.

1. David and Jesus were both born in which town?
2. What town was the home of Jesus' friends Lazarus, Mary, and Martha—and the place where Jesus raised Lazarus from the dead?
3. What fishing village was home to the disciples Peter and Andrew?
4. What pool in Jerusalem became a healing place when an angel came down and stirred up the waters?
5. Where did Jacob, sleeping on a stone pillow, have his famous dream of a stairway reaching to heaven with angels going up and down it?
6. Where was Jesus when a woman anointed his feet with an expensive jar of perfume?
7. What town was used by rebel King Jeroboam as a religious center in place of Jerusalem?
8. The events in the book of Ruth take place near which famous town?
9. In what place was the body of the dead King Saul fastened to a city wall?
10. What town on the Sea of Galilee was the site of Jesus feeding the five thousand?
11. The prophet Hosea thought the city of Bethel was so wicked that he gave it a new name meaning "house of wickedness." What was the name?
12. At what site on the Jordan was John the Baptist active?
13. Micah the prophet predicted that Israel's Messiah would come from what town?

Familiar Verse, Peculiar Order (answer)

By their fruits ye shall know them. (Matthew 7:16)

At Beth's House (answers)

1. Bethlehem, of course; the name means "house of bread."
2. Bethany; the name means "house of unripe dates." (Who named those towns, anyway?)
3. Bethsaida, a name meaning (appropriately) "house of fishing"
4. The pool of Bethesda (meaning "house of grace") (John 5); the people believed that the waters would heal when they were "troubled" by the angelic visitor.
5. Bethel, which means "house of God" (Genesis 28:10-22)
6. Bethany, at the home of Simon the leper (Matthew 26:6-13)
7. Bethel (1 Kings 12); having broken off part of the kingdom of Israel, Jeroboam didn't want his people going south to Jerusalem to do their religious duties.
8. Bethlehem; Ruth, who married Boaz, was the great-grandmother of David, a famous Bethlehem man.
9. Beth Shan (1 Samuel 31); the body was fastened there by the victorious Philistines. Inappropriately, the town name means "house of quiet."
10. Bethsaida (Luke 9:10)
11. Beth Aven (Hosea 4:15)
12. Bethany—or Bethabara in some translations (John 1:28)
13. Bethlehem, of course (Micah 5:2)

Familiar Verse, Peculiar Order

☛ Placed in their proper order, the words are a familiar verse from Genesis.

God his in man own so image created

S on the Bible Map

☛ Answers to these questions all begin with S.

1. On what mountain did Moses receive the Ten Commandments?
2. What area was considered off-limits to devout Jews?
3. What is the common biblical name for the Dead Sea?
4. What country was home to the queen who paid Solomon a visit?
5. What was the southernmost of the twelve tribes of Israel?
6. At what place was the Lord's tabernacle set up?
7. What large Roman province, mentioned many times in the New Testament, is also the name of a present-day nation?
8. What wicked city was destroyed by fire from heaven?
9. What Persian city is the setting for the book of Esther?
10. What city in Sicily was visited by the apostle Paul?
11. In what town in Samaria did Jesus meet the woman at the well?
12. What famous mountain is also referred to by the name Horeb?
13. What city was established as a capital by Omri, the king of Israel?
14. At what place was John the Baptist baptizing?
15. What ancient city was the capital of the old kingdom of Lydia, and also one of the seven churches mentioned in Revelation?
16. What city in Cyprus was visited by Paul and Barnabas?
17. What town was home to Melchizedek, the priest-king who received offerings from Abraham?
18. What land, mentioned in the Old Testament, was probably the area we now call Ethiopia?

Familiar Verse, Peculiar Order (answer)

So God created man in his own image. (Genesis 1:27)

S on the Bible Map (answers)

1. Sinai (Exodus 19)
2. Samaria—which is why Jesus' parable of the Good Samaritan is so important; his listeners were shocked to think that anything good could come from this area.
3. Salt Sea; either name is appropriate, since it is both very salty and devoid of living things (except tourists).
4. Sheba (1 Kings 10), which is probably in what is now Arabia
5. Simeon
6. Shiloh (Joshua 18)
7. Syria
8. Sodom (Genesis 19)
9. Susa
10. Syracuse (Acts 28:12)
11. Sychar (John 4)
12. Sinai
13. Samaria (1 Kings 16:24)
14. Salim (John 3:23)
15. Sardis (Revelation 1:11; 3:4)
16. Salamis (Acts 13:5)
17. Salem (Genesis 14)
18. Seba—although the Bible scholars are still arguing about this

19. What Old Testament land was famous for its gold, incense, and other valuables?
20. What city was the original capital of the northern kingdom of Israel?
21. What pagan city was visited by Jesus, who claimed its people probably had more faith than those in some of the Jewish towns?
22. In what desert region did the Israelites receive manna and quail from the Lord?
23. What ancient city was probably the original capital of the kingdom of Babylon?
24. What city was the lodging place for the ark of the covenant?
25. What city was the site of one of the seven churches of Revelation (and also noted as a center of caesar worship)?
26. Where did Samson fall in love with Delilah?
27. Where was the arrogant King Herod struck down with a fatal disease?
28. What far western area of the Roman Empire was a place Paul wanted to visit—and is also the name of a present-day nation?
29. At what place did some of Jacob's sons trick the male inhabitants into getting circumcisions?
30. What Greek island, famous for its *Winged Victory* statue, was one of Paul's ports of call?
31. What name is often used as an alternate name for the country of Edom?
32. After Joseph's remains were brought by the Israelites out of Egypt, where were they buried?

Familiar Verse, Peculiar Order

☛ Placed in their proper order, the words are a familiar verse from Matthew.

for and the forever glory is kingdom power the and the thine

19. Sheba (Psalm 72:10; Isaiah 60:6)
20. Shechem; the capital was later moved to Samaria.
21. Sidon (Matthew 11:21)
22. The Wilderness (Desert) of Sin (Numbers 33)
23. Shinar (Genesis 11)
24. Shiloh (Psalm 78:60)
25. Smyrna (Revelation 2:8)
26. Sorek (Judges 16:4)
27. Sidon (Acts 12:23)
28. Spain (Romans 15:24); there is a possibility that he may actually have visited there.
29. Shechem (Genesis 34)
30. Samothrace (Acts 16:11); the famous headless statue is often referred to as the *Winged Victory of Samothrace.*
31. Seir, which is the name of an important mountain in the area
32. Shechem (Joshua 24:32)

Familiar Verse, Peculiar Order (answer)

For thine is the kingdom, and the power, and the glory, forever. (Matthew 6:13)

Do You Remember?

☞ Would you like to see how much Bible trivia you can remember? Answer the questions (which you should have answered already in this section), and then see how well you rate on the scale on page xii.

1. What famous peninsula lies between Egypt and Israel?
2. The Roman general Titus destroyed the Jerusalem temple in the year A.D. 70. Who predicted this?
3. The name Beer occurs in many place names in the Old Testament. What important feature of human life is a Beer (in Hebrew)?
4. After the death of the sinister Persian prime minister Haman, who received the Persian king's signet ring?
5. What was the older name of the city of Jerusalem?
6. What country controlled the distribution of iron and prevented Israel from having any really useful weapons?
7. In John's vision of the New Jerusalem, how many gates does the city have, and what are they made of?
8. What Canaanite city, conquered by Joshua, has a two-letter name that means "ruined"?
9. What Israelite leader met his future wife at a well in Midian?
10. The Roman Empire's official language, Latin, is mentioned only once in the Bible, in connection with a famous sign. What did the sign say?

Do You Remember? (answers)

1. The Sinai Peninsula
2. Jesus (Luke 21)
3. A well—very important, especially in a dry country like Israel
4. Mordecai, Esther's kinsman (Esther 8:2-13)
5. Jebus (Joshua 15:63; Judges 19:10), home of the Jebusites
6. Philistia, whose people apparently were skilled in metalworking (1 Samuel 13:19-22)
7. Twelve, made of pearl (as in "pearly gates") (Revelation 21)
8. Ai (Joshua 7–12)
9. Moses (Exodus 2:15-21)
10. "Jesus of Nazareth, the King of the Jews" (John 19:19-20)

PART 12

Everything Left Over

Test Your Bible IQ

☛ This quiz contains questions covering the topics in part 12, "Everything Left Over." Do your best, then turn the page to see how you did. If you are brave enough to see how your Bible IQ rates, turn to page xii for our scale.

1. Who walked in the Garden of Eden in "the cool of the day"?
2. What (formerly) proud king of Babylon praised God for humbling him?
3. What prophet was told to lie on his right side for forty days?
4. Who commanded the sun and moon to stand still while the Israelites defeated the Amorites in battle?
5. What lake is called the Salt Sea in Genesis 14:3?
6. Who bragged for forty days in front of the Israelite army?
7. What devoted woman went to Jesus' tomb on Easter morning and mistook the risen Jesus for the gardener?
8. What organ of the body is pride associated with?
9. What color did the moon become when the sixth seal (in Revelation) was broken open?
10. What did Moses receive after being with the Lord forty days?

Test Your Bible IQ (answers)

1. God (Genesis 3:8)
2. Nebuchadnezzar (Daniel 4:37)
3. Ezekiel (4:6)
4. Joshua (10:12-13)
5. The Dead Sea; the Dead Sea is dead because it has a high salt content; nothing can live in it.
6. Goliath (1 Samuel 17:16)
7. Mary Magdalene (John 20:15)
8. The heart
9. Blood red (Revelation 6:12)
10. The Ten Commandments (Exodus 34:28)

What's Wrong with This Question?

☞ You aren't expected to know the answers to these. There is no right or wrong *answer.* There *is* something slightly askew about the question itself. But what? You'll get the hang of it.

1. What kind of wood did Moses use to build the ark?
2. How old was Moses when he entered the Promised Land?
3. Which of Jesus' disciples contributed the most writings to the Old Testament?
4. Who first translated the Gospels from Hebrew into English?
5. What did God create on the seventh day—animals or the stars?
6. What happened to the disciple Thomas when he tried to walk on the water?
7. Which book of the Bible mentions being kind to cats?
8. Which apostle was cremated after dying in Jerusalem?
9. How many shepherds came to see the baby Jesus in Jerusalem?
10. Who succeeded Samson as king of Israel?
11. Who was the father of the ten tribes of Israel?
12. For how many years did David lead the Israelites through the wilderness?
13. What Old Testament book forbids eating veal?
14. Which Supreme Court decision prohibits the reading of the Bible in private schools?
15. Why did Moses send the plague of frogs upon Israel?
16. What led Julius Caesar to decree the Roman census mentioned in Luke 2?
17. For what crime was John the Baptist burned at the stake?
18. On what mountain did Peter deliver the Sermon on the Mount?
19. In which Gospel does Jesus condemn speaking in tongues?
20. How many times did Jesus tempt Satan?
21. Who drove Adam and Eve and their children out of Eden?
22. What books did Timothy write in addition to 1 Timothy and 2 Timothy?
23. How many Israelites did Samson kill with the jawbone of an ass?
24. How old was David when he dedicated the temple to the Lord?

What's Wrong with This Question? (answers)

1. Moses didn't build the ark. Noah did.
2. Moses didn't enter the Promised Land. He died in Moab.
3. None contributed to the Old Testament. Several contributed to the *New* Testament.
4. The Gospels were written in Greek, not Hebrew.
5. He created nothing on the seventh day. This was the day he rested from his work.
6. Thomas didn't try to walk on water. Peter did.
7. Cats are not mentioned in the Bible—not house cats, anyway.
8. Cremation is not mentioned in the Bible.
9. The newborn Jesus was in Bethlehem, not Jerusalem.
10. Samson was a judge of Israel, not a king.
11. There were twelve tribes of Israel, not ten.
12. David didn't lead them through the wilderness. Moses did.
13. None does. Veal was commonly eaten in Israel.
14. The Supreme Court decisions prohibit Bible reading in *public* schools, not private schools. (Happily, the Supreme Court doesn't yet have much influence on private schools.)
15. The plague was on Egypt, not Israel.
16. Julius Caesar didn't order the census. Augustus Caesar did.
17. He was beheaded, not burned.
18. Jesus, not Peter, delivered the Sermon on the Mount.
19. Jesus said nothing about speaking in tongues.
20. Satan tempted Jesus—not vice versa.
21. Adam and Eve had no children when they were driven from Eden.
22. Timothy didn't write either of those. They were written *to* him from Paul.
23. Samson killed *Philistines,* not his fellow Israelites, with the jawbone.
24. David didn't build or dedicate the temple; his son Solomon did.

25. Which New Testament book prohibits eating pork?
26. In the book of Esther, who does God speak to in a dream?
27. Who wrote 3 Chronicles?
28. Who deposed Nebuchadnezzar as king of Egypt?
29. In which Gospel does Jesus turn wine into water?
30. From what prison did Paul write the Epistle to the Hebrews?
31. Who led the Israelites across when God parted the Dead Sea?
32. What method was used to execute the apostle Paul?
33. Who was the mother of Abraham's twelve sons?
34. In what city of Israel does the book of Job take place?
35. What book of the Bible is quoted in the U.S. Constitution?
36. What woman preached the famous sermon on the Day of Pentecost?
37. In the Song of Solomon, who is God compared to?
38. What prophet condemned the wickedness of King Josiah?
39. How many days was Noah in the belly of the great fish?
40. How many years were the Hebrews slaves in Babylon?

Familiar Verse, Peculiar Order

☛ Placed in their proper order, the words are a familiar verse from the Old Testament.

that Lord they the renew shall their upon wait strength

Tending Our Gardens

1. What wicked king had a man murdered for the sake of an herb garden?
2. Who was buried in a tomb in a garden?
3. Who was the craftiest beast in the Garden of Eden?
4. Who walked in the Garden of Eden in "the cool of the day"?
5. What prophet protested against idol worshipers who made sacrifices in gardens?
6. What king, famous for his extravagant building projects, also planted vineyards, gardens, and orchards?
7. What sensuous book mentions the sweet voices of lovers in a garden?

25. None does. Leviticus, in the *Old* Testament, prohibits eating pork.
26. God is not mentioned at all in the book of Esther.
27. There is a 1 and a 2 Chronicles, but not a 3.
28. Nebuchadnezzar was king of Babylon, not Egypt.
29. Jesus turned water into wine—not wine into water.
30. The Epistle to the Hebrews is anonymous. Paul did not write it, though some older Bible versions say (or imply) that Paul wrote it.
31. God parted the Red Sea, not the Dead Sea.
32. Paul's death is not recorded in the Bible. (According to an old tradition, he was beheaded in Rome by order of Emperor Nero.)
33. Abraham didn't have twelve sons—his grandson Jacob did.
34. It does not take place in Israel, but in the faraway land of Uz, which may (or may not) refer to a part of Arabia.
35. The Bible is not quoted in the Constitution.
36. The Bible does not mention any woman preachers.
37. God is not mentioned in the Song of Solomon.
38. Josiah was one of the best and most devout kings in the Bible.
39. Noah wasn't in the fish—Jonah was.
40. They were slaves in Egypt, not Babylon.

Familiar Verse, Peculiar Order (answer)

They that wait upon the Lord shall renew their strength.
(Isaiah 40:31)

Tending Our Gardens (answers)

1. Ahab, who had Naboth slain so he could possess Naboth's vineyard and turn it into an herb garden (1 Kings 21)
2. Jesus (John 19:41)
3. The serpent, of course (Genesis 3:1)
4. God (Genesis 3:8)
5. Isaiah (65:3)
6. Solomon (Ecclesiastes 2:4-5)
7. Song of Solomon (2:14; 8:13)

8. What evil kings of Judah, father and son, were buried in the garden of Uzza?
9. What four rivers (two of which are in present-day Iraq) are connected with the Garden of Eden?
10. In what book does a woman call on the north wind and south wind to blow on her garden?
11. Who planted the first garden?
12. What mighty emperor held a marathon seven-day banquet in his garden courtyard?
13. What two trees grew in the Garden of Eden that grow nowhere else?
14. What devoted woman went to Jesus' tomb on Easter morning and mistook the risen Jesus for the gardener?
15. In what garden did Jesus agonize on the night of his arrest?
16. Which of Jesus' parables concerns something planted in the garden?
17. What Old Testament prophet refers several times to Eden as the "garden of God"?
18. What prophet told the Jews to plant gardens in Babylon as a sign that they would be there a long time?

Familiar Verse, Peculiar Order

☞ Placed in their proper order, the words are a familiar verse from Matthew.

world a and does gains he his if it loses
man profit soul the what whole

Pleased to Be Proud

1. What did Jesus say would happen to proud people?
2. Who tears down the proud man's house?
3. What prophet condemned people for being proud of their jewels?
4. According to James, what type of Christian should be proud of his high position?
5. According to Proverbs, what does pride breed?
6. What organ of the body is pride associated with?

8. Manasseh and Amon (2 Kings 21:18, 26)
9. Gihon, Pishon, Tigris, and Euphrates (Genesis 2:10-14)
10. Song of Solomon (4:16)
11. God (Genesis 2:8)
12. Ahasuerus, king of Persia and husband of Esther (Esther 1:5)
13. The tree of life and the tree of knowledge of good and evil (Genesis 2:9)
14. Mary Magdalene (John 20:15)
15. Gethsemane (Matthew 26:36)
16. The parable of the mustard seed (Luke 13:19)
17. Ezekiel
18. Jeremiah (29:5)

Familiar Verse, Peculiar Order (answer)

What does it profit a man if he gains the whole world and loses his soul? (Matthew 16:26)

Pleased to Be Proud (answers)

1. He said nothing—or at least the Gospels do not record any words he uttered about pride.
2. The Lord (Proverbs 15:25)
3. Ezekiel, who claimed that they made their jewelry into idols (Ezekiel 7:20)
4. The poor one (James 1:9)
5. Quarrels (Proverbs 13:10)
6. The heart

7. According to Ecclesiastes, what is better than pride?
8. In Revelation, who uttered proud words and blasphemies?
9. According to Jeremiah, what is the one thing a person should boast about?
10. Which king of Judah met his downfall after he became proud?
11. According to Moses, what great event would be forgotten because the Hebrews had become proud?
12. What sinful deed were the Christians of Corinth proud of?
13. What (formerly) proud king of Babylon praised God for humbling him?

Familiar Verse, Peculiar Order

☛ Placed in their proper order, the words are a familiar verse from Psalms.

a Lord new O song the unto sing

Brother Sun, Sister Moon, and Other Heavenly Bodies

1. What city has no need of the light of the sun?
2. On what day of creation did God make the sun and moon?
3. What event was going on when the sun was darkened and the curtain in the temple was torn in two?
4. What miraculous food melted in the heat of the sun?
5. Who warned Israel against worshiping the sun, moon, and stars?
6. Who commanded the sun and moon to stand still while the Israelites defeated the Amorites in battle?
7. What happened when an angel poured out the fourth bowl of wrath on the sun?
8. Who peeved his eleven jealous brothers by telling them of his dream of eleven stars bowing down to him?
9. What praise-filled book proclaims, "Praise ye him, sun and moon: praise him, all ye stars of light"?
10. What woman lamented the sun's darkening of her skin? (Remember, this was long before people were conscious of melanoma and premature aging.)

7. Patience (Ecclesiastes 7:8)
8. The Beast (Revelation 13:5)
9. That he knows the Lord (Jeremiah 9:24)
10. King Uzziah (2 Chronicles 26:16)
11. Their deliverance from slavery in Egypt (Deuteronomy 8:14)
12. One of them was living in sin with his stepmother, for which Paul chastised them (1 Corinthians 5:1-2).
13. Nebuchadnezzar (Daniel 4:37)

Familiar Verse, Peculiar Order (answer)

O sing unto the Lord a new song. (Psalm 96:1)

Brother Sun, Sister Moon, and Other Heavenly Bodies (answers)

1. The New Jerusalem, heaven (Revelation 22:5)
2. The fourth day (Genesis 1:14-19); interestingly, *light* was made on the second day, *before* the sun and moon.
3. Jesus had died on the cross (Luke 23:45).
4. The manna the Israelites ate in the wilderness (Exodus 16:21)
5. Moses (Deuteronomy 4:19); the warning was needed, since most of the ancient cultures did indeed worship the heavenly bodies.
6. Joshua (10:12-13)
7. The sun scorched people, who then cursed God (Revelation 16:8-9).
8. Joseph, Jacob's son (Genesis 37:9)
9. Psalms (148:3)
10. The bride in the Song of Solomon (1:6)

11. According to Genesis, why was the moon created?
12. What denoted the beginning of the month for the Israelites?
13. What is the name of the bizarre star that will cause the earth's waters to become undrinkable?
14. Which Old Testament book proclaims that God is a "Sun and shield"?
15. Which prophet predicted the coming of the "sun of righteousness," who has been identified with Christ?
16. What items in Jerusalem proved that some of the Israelites worshiped the sun?
17. What prophet stood in the temple court and saw people bowing to worship the sun?
18. What righteous king on his sickbed watched the sun miraculously go backward?
19. What prophet fainted from the heat of the sun, until God made a shady vine for him?
20. Whom were the wise men speaking to when they said, "We have seen his star in the east, and are come to worship him"?
21. Where was Jesus when his face shone like the sun?
22. What is the only book of the Bible to mention constellations by name?
23. Who was in such a violent storm at sea that for days he didn't see the sun or the stars?
24. What prophet condemned people for worshiping a god in the form of a star?
25. Who was told by God that his descendants would be as numerous as the stars?
26. Who predicted that at the end of time the stars would fall from the heavens?
27. What color did the moon become when the sixth seal (in Revelation) was broken open?
28. What wicked king of Judah built altars for the worship of Baal and of the stars?
29. What apostle claimed he had been struck down at midday by a light brighter than the sun?

11. To denote the passing of weeks and seasons (Genesis 1:14)
12. The new moon, which is often mentioned in the Old Testament as being a special day
13. Wormwood, a name denoting bitterness (Revelation 8:10-11)
14. Psalms (84:11); this is poetic and is not intended to literally identify God with the sun.
15. Malachi (4:2)
16. Horses (probably horse statues) and chariots dedicated to the sun (2 Kings 23:11)
17. Ezekiel (8:16)
18. Hezekiah (Isaiah 38:7-8)
19. Jonah (4:8)
20. Herod (Matthew 2:2)
21. On the Mount of Transfiguration, with Moses and Elijah (Matthew 17:2)
22. Job, which mentions Orion and the Pleiades (9:9; 38:31), the Bear (Arcturus, 9:9), and others
23. The apostle Paul (Acts 27:20)
24. Amos (5:26), who may have been referring to a star-shaped idol
25. Abraham (Genesis 22:17)
26. Jesus (Mark 13:25)
27. Blood red (Revelation 6:12)
28. Manasseh (2 Kings 21:3-5)
29. The apostle Paul (Acts 26:13)

Familiar Verse, Peculiar Order

☞ Placed in their proper order, the words are a familiar verse from Luke.

but call came righteous I not sinners the to

Salt of the Earth

☞ We take salt for granted these days—in fact, it is so easily available that many folks have to reduce their salt intake. This was not a problem in Bible times, when salt was a valuable commodity, as it was for most of human history.

1. Who was turned into a pillar of salt?
2. What kind of people were rubbed down with salt?
3. Who healed Jericho's water supply by throwing salt into it?
4. What lake is called the Salt Sea in Genesis 14:3?
5. By what other name is the Salt Sea (Dead Sea) known in the Old Testament?
6. Who told Christians to let their speech always be "seasoned with salt"?
7. Which book of the Old Testament commands salting the meat offered as sacrifices?
8. Who annihilated the city of Shechem and then sowed its soil with salt?
9. Who asked the question "Can that which is unsavory be eaten without salt?"
10. In which Gospel does Jesus say, "Everyone shall be salted with fire"?
11. "Ye are the salt of the earth" is from the Sermon on the Mount, in which Gospel?

Familiar Verse, Peculiar Order

☞ Placed in their proper order, the words are a familiar verse from Matthew.

blood covenant the is my new of this

Familiar Verse, Peculiar Order (answer)

I came not to call the righteous, but sinners. (Luke 5:32)

Salt of the Earth (answers)

1. Lot's wife (Genesis 19:26), who was punished for looking back on the destroyed city of Sodom
2. Newborn infants, apparently to purify them (Ezekiel 16:4)
3. Elisha (2 Kings 2:19-22)
4. The Dead Sea; the Dead Sea is dead because it has a high salt content; nothing can live in it.
5. The Sea of the Arabah
6. Paul (Colossians 4:6)
7. Leviticus (2:13)
8. Abimelech (Judges 9:45), who apparently wanted to make the land unfruitful forever
9. Job (6:6)
10. Mark (9:49)
11. Matthew (5:13)

Familiar Verse, Peculiar Order (answer)

This is my blood of the new covenant. (Matthew 26:28)

Forty, the Ultimate Biblical Number

☛ Why is the number forty so significant in the Bible? No one is sure. It is often used simply to express long duration. Whatever the significance was for the biblical authors, it is used often in Scripture—enough to supply us with the questions here.

1. Who was told by God that rain would fall for forty days and forty nights?
2. Who boasted that he had five times received the punishment of forty lashes minus one?
3. Who prophesied that the pagan city Nineveh would be destroyed in forty days?
4. What wise king reigned in Israel for forty years?
5. Who was forty years old when he married Rebekah?
6. What did Noah release from the ark after forty days?
7. With whom was God grieved for forty years?
8. Who was the target of an assassination plot by forty men?
9. Who was tempted by the devil for forty days?
10. Which prophet asked, "Have ye offered unto me sacrifices and offerings in the wilderness forty years, O house of Israel?"
11. Who pleaded with God not to destroy Sodom for the sake of forty righteous people?
12. What man-and-woman military leadership team gave Israel forty years of peace?
13. What food did the Israelites eat for forty years?
14. Who was in the midst of a cloud for forty days?
15. What did Moses receive after being with the Lord forty days?
16. Who explored the land of Canaan for forty days?
17. Why did God make Israel wander in the wilderness for forty years?
18. What leader did forty thousand Israelites muster under?
19. Who subdued the Midianites so that Israel had forty years of peace?
20. Who bragged for forty days in front of the Israelite army?
21. What king died at the age of seventy after reigning for forty years?
22. What prophet received a gift of forty camel loads of Syrian luxuries?
23. What king slaughtered forty thousand Syrian foot soldiers?

Forty, the Ultimate Biblical Number (answers)

1. Noah (Genesis 7:4)
2. Paul (2 Corinthians 11:24)
3. Jonah (3:4)
4. Solomon (2 Chronicles 9:30)
5. Isaac (Genesis 25:20)
6. A raven (Genesis 8)
7. The Israelites in the wilderness (Hebrews 3:17)
8. Paul (Acts 23:21)
9. Jesus, of course (Luke 4:2)
10. Amos (5:25)
11. Abraham (Genesis 18)
12. Deborah and Barak (Judges 5:31)
13. Manna (Exodus 16:35)
14. Moses (Exodus 24:18)
15. The Ten Commandments (Exodus 34:28)
16. The twelve Israelite spies (Numbers 13:25)
17. Because they had done evil (Numbers 32:13)
18. Joshua (Joshua 4:13)
19. Gideon (Judges 8:28)
20. Goliath (1 Samuel 17:16)
21. David (2 Samuel 5:4)
22. Elisha (2 Kings 8:7-9)
23. David (1 Chronicles 19:18)

24. Who reigned forty years after beginning his reign at age seven?
25. Who complained that the governors of Israel had taxed the people forty shekels of silver?
26. What prophet was told to lie on his right side for forty days?
27. Who fasted for forty days and forty nights?
28. Which apostles healed a man who had been crippled for forty years?
29. What hairy man was forty years old when he married a woman named Judith?
30. What leader died on Mount Hor after the Israelites had been out of Egypt for forty years?
31. Who was ministered to by angels after forty days in the wilderness?
32. What prophet predicted that Egypt would lie desolate for forty years?
33. Who went without food or drink for forty days because he was in the Lord's presence?
34. Who was forty years old when he became a spy for Moses?
35. Who gave Israel forty years of peace from the Arameans?
36. Which Old Testament book sets the maximum number of lashes at forty?
37. Who died from a broken neck after he had been Israel's judge for forty years?
38. What son of Saul became king at age forty?
39. What king had forty thousand stalls for his horses?
40. Which book mentions that Jesus was seen for forty days after his resurrection?
41. What judge of Israel had forty sons?
42. Who came to the rescue after Israel suffered under the Philistines for forty years?
43. What notable Jerusalem building was forty cubits long?

Familiar Verse, Peculiar Order

☞ Placed in their proper order, the words are a familiar verse from Matthew.

God not Lord shall tempt the you your

24. King Joash of Judah (2 Chronicles 24:1)
25. Nehemiah (5:15)
26. Ezekiel (4:6)
27. Jesus (Matthew 4:2)
28. Peter and John (Acts 4:22)
29. Esau, Jacob's brother (Genesis 26:34)
30. Aaron (Numbers 33:38)
31. Jesus (Mark 1:13)
32. Ezekiel (29:12)
33. Moses (Deuteronomy 9:9)
34. Joshua (14:7)
35. Othniel (Judges 3:11)
36. Deuteronomy (25:3)
37. Eli, Samuel's mentor (1 Samuel 4:18)
38. Ish-Bosheth (2 Samuel 2:10)
39. Solomon (1 Kings 4:26)
40. Acts (1:3)
41. Abdon (Judges 12:14)
42. Samson (Judges 13)
43. The temple (Ezekiel 41)

Familiar Verse, Peculiar Order (answer)

You shall not tempt the Lord your God. (Matthew 4:7)

What's Wrong with This Question? (Part II)

1. Which disciple betrayed Jesus in the Garden of Galilee?
2. What message did Herod order placed on Jesus' cross?
3. How many missionary journeys did Peter make in Acts?
4. How long was Moses on Mount Zion receiving the Law?
5. In which epistle does Paul refer to the virgin birth of Jesus?
6. Was Jesus descended from Moses on Mary's side or on Joseph's?
7. What prophet was carried into exile when the Persians conquered Jerusalem?
8. How long was Samson married to Delilah?
9. Which books of prophecy were written by Moses?
10. How many times did Paul deny Jesus?
11. Which book of the Bible was the basis for the movie *The Last Temptation of Christ?*
12. By what nation was Israel's ark of the covenant destroyed?
13. What historical figure is symbolized by the number 666 in the book of Daniel?
14. What happens in the book of Revelation when the angel Gabriel blows his trumpet?
15. Where was the prophet Elisha standing when a chariot of fire carried him to heaven?
16. Which prophet condemned Solomon for committing adultery with Bathsheba?
17. What did God do after he created Adam and Eve from the dust?
18. What happened to Job after he cursed God for all his suffering?
19. Which of Jesus' disciples became leader of the Christian community in Jerusalem?
20. Who predicted that the Messiah would be born in Nazareth?
21. Who wrote the Epistle to Jude?
22. Which Old Testament book contains the words "God helps those who help themselves"?
23. Of the ten Minor Prophets in the Old Testament, which book is longest?
24. In which Gospel does Jesus curse an olive tree for not bearing fruit?

What's Wrong with This Question? (Part II) (answers)

1. Jesus was betrayed in the Garden of Gethsemane, not Galilee.
2. A message was placed there by Pilate, not Herod.
3. Acts records several missionary journeys by Paul, not Peter.
4. Moses received the Law on Sinai, not Zion.
5. Paul does not mention the Virgin Birth.
6. Moses is not in Jesus' genealogy. Jesus was descended from the tribe of Judah (David's tribe), while Moses was of the tribe of Levi.
7. The Babylonians, not the Persians, conquered Jerusalem.
8. They were never married. It was (we might say today) an unfulfilling relationship.
9. Moses wrote the five Books of the Law, not prophecy.
10. Peter, not Paul, denied Jesus.
11. The movie was based not on the Bible, but on a book by modern Greek author Nikos Kazantzakis.
12. There is no mention in the Bible of its destruction. It was (probably) captured by some invader. As the movie *Raiders of the Lost Ark* indicated, the ark might still exist somewhere.
13. The number 666 (and whatever it symbolizes) occurs in Revelation, not Daniel.
14. Contrary to popular belief, Gabriel is not the angel who blows the trumpet. The trumpeting angels in Revelation are not named.
15. Elijah, not Elisha, was taken into heaven.
16. David, not Solomon, committed adultery with Bathsheba. (Solomon was their son.)
17. He created Adam from the dust, but not Eve. She was taken later from Adam's rib.
18. Job never did curse God, though Job's wife urged him to do so.
19. None did. In the book of Acts, the leader of the Jerusalem church appears to be James—not James the disciple, but James the brother of Jesus.
20. No one. There was a prediction that he would be born in Bethlehem, as indeed he was.
21. The book of Jude is actually an epistle *from* Jude, not *to* him.
22. Those words are not found in the Old Testament or the New.
23. There are twelve Minor Prophets, not ten.
24. It was a fig tree, not an olive tree, that Jesus cursed.

25. Who, besides Moses, contributed to the book of Proverbs?
26. In what land did the prophet Jeremiah have his vision of the valley of dry bones?
27. What is the only Old Testament book that does not mention hell?
28. To whom did Jesus say, "I am the salt of the earth"?
29. Which of Noah's four sons was first to leave the ark?
30. Which of the Gospels records Jesus' seven last words from the cross?
31. When Samson anointed Saul as king of Israel, who led the celebration?
32. Who ordered the sign on Jesus' cross that read, "I am the King of the Jews"?
33. What prophet predicted that Jesus would be crucified on the Sabbath day?
34. Where did Mary, Joseph, and baby Jesus flee when Herod ordered the killing of the infants of Jerusalem?
35. When King Nebuchadnezzar had his dream of seven fat cows and seven lean cows, what Israelite interpreted it for him?
36. Besides Paul, which of Jesus' disciples were married?
37. Why was Moses not allowed to offer a sacrifice in the temple?
38. Which of Paul's epistles predicts the destruction of the temple in Jerusalem?
39. How many of Paul's seven epistles were written to individuals?
40. Who was Israel's king when Moses received the Law on Mount Sinai?
41. Which Babylonian ruler allowed the Jews to return from their exile in Babylon?
42. Which book records the deep faith of King Manasseh?
43. What man was the first person to see that Jesus' tomb was empty?
44. Who wrote the song "Joy to the World" after being inspired by the Gospel accounts of Jesus' birth?
45. How many missionary journeys did Paul and John make together?
46. How did Abraham begin the practice of resting on the Sabbath?

25. The main author of Proverbs was King Solomon, not Moses.
26. Ezekiel, not Jeremiah, had the vision of the valley of dry bones.
27. *None* of the Old Testament books mention hell.
28. Jesus said "You are the salt of the earth"—referring to his disciples.
29. Noah had three sons, not four.
30. None of them records all seven. We get the "seven last words" by combining all four Gospel accounts of the Crucifixion.
31. Samuel, not Samson, anointed Saul as king.
32. The sign actually read, "Jesus of Nazareth, the King of the Jews" (John 19:19).
33. He was crucified on a Friday, the day *before* the Sabbath.
34. Herod ordered the killing of the infant boys of Bethlehem, not Jerusalem.
35. The Egyptian pharaoh, not Nebuchadnezzar, had the cow dream, which was interpreted by Joseph.
36. Paul was not one of Jesus' disciples.
37. The temple did not exist in Moses' lifetime.
38. Jesus, not Paul, predicted the fall of the temple.
39. Paul wrote thirteen epistles, not seven.
40. Israel had no king in Moses' day—not for another three hundred years, in fact.
41. It was Cyrus, the *Persian* king, who conquered the Babylonians and who allowed the Jews to return from exile.
42. Manasseh was in fact one of the most wicked kings on record, even sacrificing his own son in a heathen ritual.
43. It was two *women,* not men, who first saw the empty tomb.
44. The song, written by Isaac Watts in the 1700s, in fact is not about Christmas at all. Watts wrote it as a sung version of Psalm 98, which celebrates the rule of God as king. It says nothing about Jesus' birth in Bethlehem.
45. Paul and John did not travel together.
46. The Sabbath is not actually mentioned before the time of Moses.

Familiar Verse, Peculiar Order

☞ Placed in their proper order, the words are a familiar verse from the Old Testament.

wicked no there for is peace the

Familiar Verse, Peculiar Order (answer)

There is no peace . . . for the wicked. (Isaiah 48:22)

Do You Remember?

☛ Would you like to see how much Bible trivia you can remember? Answer the questions (which you should have answered already in this section), and then see how well you rate on the scale on page xii.

1. What two trees grew in the Garden of Eden that grow nowhere else?
2. According to Proverbs, what does pride breed?
3. What is the name of the bizarre star that will cause the earth's waters to become undrinkable?
4. Who was turned into a pillar of salt?
5. What man-and-woman military leadership team gave Israel forty years of peace?
6. What's wrong with this question: Where was the prophet Elisha standing when a chariot of fire carried him to heaven?
7. Who planted the first garden?
8. What righteous king on his sickbed watched the sun miraculously go backward?
9. What leader died on Mount Hor after the Israelites had been out of Egypt for forty years?
10. What apostle claimed he had been struck down at midday by a light brighter than the sun?

Do You Remember? (answers)

1. The tree of life and the tree of knowledge of good and evil (Genesis 2:9)
2. Quarrels (Proverbs 13:10)
3. Wormwood, a name denoting bitterness (Revelation 8:10-11)
4. Lot's wife (Genesis 19:26), who was punished for looking back on the destroyed city of Sodom
5. Deborah and Barak (Judges 5:31)
6. Elijah, not Elisha, was taken into heaven.
7. God (Genesis 2:8)
8. Hezekiah (Isaiah 38:7-8)
9. Aaron (Numbers 33:38)
10. The apostle Paul (Acts 26:13)

Don't Miss J. Stephen Lang's Other Fascinating Books of Bible Trivia

THE BEST OF BIBLE TRIVIA 1: KINGS, CRIMINALS, SAINTS, & SINNERS 0-8423-0464-9

THE BEST OF BIBLE TRIVIA 2: PALACES, POISONS, FEASTS, & BEASTS 0-8423-0465-7

THE BEST OF BIBLE TRIVIA 3: ANGELS, DEMONS, SCROLLS, & SCRIBES 0-8423-0466-5

THE COMPLETE BOOK OF BIBLE TRIVIA 0-8423-0421-5

THE ILLUSTRATED BOOK OF BIBLE TRIVIA 0-8423-1613-2